OCR
Economics

A2

Colin Bamford | Susan Grant | Stephen Walton

www.heinemann.co.uk

✓ Free online support
✓ Useful weblinks
✓ 24 hour online ordering

01865 888080

OCR
RECOGNISING ACHIEVEMENT

Heinemann

Official Publisher Partnership

Heinemann is an imprint of Pearson Education Limited, a company incorporated in England and Wales, having its registered office at Edinburgh Gate, Harlow, Essex, CM20 2JE. Registered company number: 872828

www.heinemann.co.uk

Heinemann is a registered trademark of Pearson Education Limited

Part 1 © Susan Grant 2008
Part 2 and Chapter 12 © Colin Bamford 2008
Chapters 9–11 © Stephen Walton 2008
Glossary © Colin Bamford and Susan Grant 2008

First published 2008

12 11 10 09 08
10 9 8 7 6 5 4 3 2 1

British Library Cataloguing in Publication Data is available from the British Library on request.

ISBN 978 0 435692 21 6

Edited by Bill MacKeith
Designed by Tek-Art
Typeset by Tek-Art
Original illustrations © Pearson Education Ltd 2008
Illustrated by Tek-Art
Picture research by Christine Martin
Cover photo/illustration © Getty Images/PhotoDisc
Printed and bound in the UK by Scotprint

Websites
There are links to relevant websites in this book. In order to ensure that the links are up-to-date, that the links work, and that the sites are not inadvertently linked to sites that could be considered offensive, we have made the links available on the Heinemann website at www.heinemann.co.uk/hotlinks. When you access the site, the express code is 2230P.

Contents

About the authors

Professor Colin Bamford is OCR's Chief Examiner in GCE Economics. He has over 30 years' experience of teaching economics and assessing and setting A Level examination papers. He is well known among students for the range of textbooks and articles he has produced on various aspects of the subject. He is Associate Dean and Head of the Department of Logistics and Hospitality Management at the University of Huddersfield, West Yorkshire, and the current President of the Economics and Business Education Association.

Susan Grant is a Principal Examiner for OCR and has years of experience in setting examination papers and assessing candidates' performance. Susan is currently teaching economics at Abingdon and Witney College and Wood Green School in Witney, Oxfordshire. She is the author of more than 15 economics books and is a regular contributor to the *British Economy Survey*.

Stephen Walton is a Principal Examiner for OCR's Global Economy A2 unit. For the past 12 years he has been responsible for setting examination papers and assessing candidates' scripts at A Level. Stephen is currently Head of Economics and Business at the King's School in Chester. He is a co-author of economics textbooks endorsed by OCR and Cambridge International Examinations (CIE).

Acknowledgements

The authors would like to thank their OCR colleague Mark Jackson for his helpful comments on the first draft of the manuscript. We should also like to thank Ray Horridge for the comments and suggestions he has made to the text on behalf of OCR. Thanks also go to Diane Bramley for word processing the Transport Economics unit. We should also like to thank our students at Witney College, Wood Green School, The King's School, Chester, and in the Department of Logistics and Hospitality Management at the University of Huddersfield for giving us ideas on how we can make our subject interesting as well as relevant. Finally, thanks to the staff at Heinemann for their advice and support.

Text extracts

p.3, Fig. 1.1; p.7, Table 1.3: *both* National Statistics website: www.statistics.gov.uk; p.7, Table 1.4: Eurostat website; p.11, Table 1.7: National Statistics website: www.statistics.gov.uk; p.12, Table 1.8: OECD website; p.21, Table 1.10; p.75, Table 4.3; p.86, Table 4.9: *all* National Statistics website: www.statistics.gov.uk; p.108, Table 5.1: Department for Transport; p.119, Table 6.1: Freight Transport Association; p.159, Table 7.2: Department for Transport; p.164, Table 7.4: Civil Aviation Authority; p.166, £5.5bn road-widening plan: *Financial Times*; p.166, Table 7.5: Transport for London; p.168, Table 7.6: *Transport Reviews*, p.169, Fig. 7.11; p.174, Table 8.1: *both* Department for Transport; p.180, Table 8.4; p.181, Table 8.5: *both* Cross London Rail Links (Crossrail) / Transport for London / Department for Transport; p.200, Fig. 9.3: National Statistics website: www.statistics.gov.uk; p.203, Table 9.1: United Nations; p.203, Fig. 9.6; p.204, Fig. 9.7; p.204, Fig. 9.8: *all* HM Treasury; p.206, Don't expect a rate cut: Spiegel Online International; p.208, Fig. 9.11: HM Treasury; p.216, Fig. 9.16: World Bank; p.218, Fig. 9.17; p.220, Fig. 9.18: *both* HM Treasury; p.223, Fig. 9.20; p.223, Fig. 9.21; p.225, Fig. 9.23: *all* European Central Bank website, Statistical Data Warehouse; p.231, Fig. 9.25; p.234, Fig. 9.26: *both* Bank of England; p.236, Fig. 9.28; p.237, Fig. 9.29; p.238, Fig. 9.30: *all* National Competitiveness Council; p.249, Fig. 10.5; p.250, Fig. 10.6: *both* International Monetary Fund; p.251, Fig. 10.7; p.252, Fig. 10.8: *both* UNCTAD; p.253, Fig. 10.9; p.254, Table 10.3: *both* World Trade Organization; p.262, Fig. 10.13; p.263, Fig. 10.14: *both* European Central Bank, Statistical Data Warehouse; p.265, Table 10.5: CIA World Factbook; p.266, Table 10.6: HM Treasury; p.266, Table 10.7: Czech National Bank; p.276, Fig. 10.17; p.279, Fig. 10.19: *both* European Commission; p.283: India: Growth or Development? *The Guardian*; p.281, Fig. 11.1; p.281, Fig. 11.2: *both* Gapminder, www.gapminder.org; p.286, Table 11.1: UNDP; p.287, Fig. 11.3; p.287, Fig. 11.4; p.288, Table 11.2; p.289, Table 11.3: *all* World Bank; p.298, Development Blooms in Ethiopia: Department for International Development; p.290, Table 11.4; p.294, Fig. 11.6: *both* World Bank; p.301, Fig. 11.7: Polyp/*New Internationalist*, www.newint.org; p.302, Table 11.6: Commission on Growth and Development; p.304, Millennium Ecosystem Assessment: Millennium Ecosystem Asssment; p.307, Table 11.8: New Economics Foundation.

Crown copyright material is reproduced with the permission of the Controller, Office of Public Sector Information (OPSI).

Photos

p.9 Corbis/Gideon Mendel; p.10 Shutterstock/iofoto; p.14 Shutterstock/Eugene Bochkarev; p.18 Getty Images/PhotoDisc; p.20 Alamy/David Preutz; p.35 Corbis/BBC; p.38 Corbis/Reuters; p.42 Alamy/Speedpix; p.43 Getty Images/PhotoDisc; p.57 Alamy/Mike Abrahams; p.58 Science Photo Library/BSTP/Astrek-Chw Lille; p.62 Corbis/Chen Xiaogen/Xinhua Press; p.67 PA Photos/PA Wire/Yol Mok; p.85 Shutterstock/Elena Elisseeva; p.89 Pearson Education Ltd/Martin Sookias; p.92 Alamy/Libby Welch; p.107 Shutterstock/Losevsky Pavel; p.115 Alamy/Photofusion Picture Library/Martin Bond; p.123 Airplane Pictures/Stuart Lawson; p.130 Alamy/Dave Porter; p.137 Shutterstock/Linux Patrol; p.140 Pearson Education Ltd/Jules Selmes; p.150 Corbis/Bettmann; p.155 Alamy/Justin Kase ztwoz; p.157 Getty Images/Steve Raymer/Asia Images; p.161 Getty Images; p.164 Getty Images; p.170 PA Photos/PA Archive; p.185 Corbis/ZEFA/Larry Williams; p.248 Alamy/brianafrica; p.251 Getty Images/PhotoDisc; p.314 Corbis/Antoine Serra/In Visu; p.320 Corbis/Bettmann.

Introduction

This book explicitly follows the OCR A2 Advanced GCE qualification. It is divided into three parts, each with four chapters. The first two parts provide a comprehensive set of teaching and learning material for each of OCR's optional units; Economics of work and leisure and Transport economics. The third part provides this for the compulsory The Global Economy unit.

The book builds upon the content of the OCR-endorsed *OCR AS Economics* (Heinemann, 2008). It follows the same format.

● Each chapter starts with a list of learning outcomes that are the same as in OCR's approved specification.

● The text of each chapter provides up-to-date subject content and a selection of features (Economics in context) to enable meaningful delivery in the classroom.

● This content is supported by a list of essential definitions and activities, which can be used in class or for homework (see 'Stretch and challenge' below). Learning tips provide advice on revision (marked 'Building on AS'), key elements of the A2 specification (marked 'Stepping up to A2'), and how to avoid common mistakes.

● At the end of each part, there is an Exam Café feature. This is designed to help your examination preparation and performance. It includes some student answers to questions, feedback from examiners and a full-length sample practice paper.

The structure of the A2 course and the pattern of assessment are shown below.

Skills to be developed at A2

There are two main skills you need to develop from AS if you wish to succeed at A2:

1. *Data response/interpretation.* Refer back to the 'Economist's tool kit' section in the AS book and make sure you are competent in the data-handling skills that are set out. At A2, though, you need to do more than just know how to handle data – you must be able to interpret data in terms of the economic concepts that underpin the data. In other words, there is more emphasis on the explanation of (say) a trend in a time series or variations around an average in a set of data. You may also be asked to make comparisons between two sets of information in a data set. This requires practice – the golden rule is 'Do not

Unit F583
Economics of Work and Leisure

or

Unit F584
Transport Economics

Data response question

One structured question from choice of three

Unit F585
The Global Economy

Pre-released stimulus material

Data interpretation

Essay-style questions

just regurgitate the data' as this will not gain any marks.

2. *Essay-style writing.* The need to write in a clear, logical, coherent way cannot be underestimated if you are serious about getting a good grade at A2. This can only come with practice. You can enhance your ability to write this way by reading appropriate features and articles in a quality newspaper or in periodicals such as *Economics Today*.

The general advice provided on page xi of the AS book is still applicable at A2. In addition, it is important to get into the habit of writing in an analytical rather than a descriptive way. This involves recognising the key points and concepts … but without too much description. As stated in the AS book, try to use the terminology of economics whenever you can and use meaningful diagrams where appropriate. These are the skills that are required for answers that meet the AO3 assessment objective.

To get beyond this level, if the question has command words such as 'discuss' or 'comment', you need to review what you have written and make meaningful conclusions. If the command word is 'discuss', then you need to consider both sides of any argument or issue. A good tip in trying to remember to do this is to say to yourself 'Think about the two-handed economist!' By this we mean that when asked about their opinion, economists often say 'on the one hand … but on the other hand'. Where the command word is 'comment', a similar style of answer is required, except that you may only need to make an assessment of one side of the argument. Your comment, though, should be based on the content of your answer. It will have no meaning if it is no more than an 'off-the-cuff' or highly opinionated remark.

The essay-style questions at A2 require you to write for rather longer than you will have had to write for the last question of the AS examinations. As a rule of thumb, you will need to spend around 2 minutes for each mark that is available. So, on the optional units, you need to spend around 30 minutes on your part a) and around 35–40 minutes on your part b)

answer. It is particularly important that you make the most of what you know by structuring your essay in an effective way.

One possible structure for an essay question that has 'explain' or 'analyse' as its command word is:

● *an introduction* which sets out the proposition of the question

● *a series of paragraphs*, possibly with a diagram, that explain and analyse the evidence, particularly from economic theory, as to why you believe the proposition to be true

● *a conclusion* that summarises how you have proved that the proposition is true.

Where the command word is 'discuss' or 'comment', the structure should explicitly make clear that you have made some evaluation of the issue involved. A possible structure for such an essay is:

● *set the context and outline the issue* that has to be evaluated

● *analyse the evidence, including the theory*; this should include alternative viewpoints and applications, drawing upon a range of sources

● *a concluding paragraph* that summarises both sides. If appropriate, make an overall judgement on the issue that you have evaluated. (See 'Stretch and challenge', below.)

So, how might you make it clear to the OCR examiner that you have evaluated an issue in your essay? Here are a few ways of doing this:

1. The issue you have been asked to discuss may be inaccurate or out of date. Data or evidence may not support it or not fully support it.

2. Alternative viewpoints may have been put forward. If so, say what these are and, ideally, who has made them.

3. The source or context of what you have been asked to evaluate could be biased. This could well be the case if a source is given.

4. First-hand evidence that you have researched could support an alternative viewpoint.

Above all, when making any evaluation, make sure that your claims are based on evidence. This is important. You will get few, if any, marks for highly opinionated remarks that lack any sort of underpinning evidence.

Synoptic assessment

All three A2 units are 'synoptic'. This is a technical term that is used to mean that some of the examination questions will require you to relate your previously acquired AS knowledge of economics to a different context. For example, what you learned about demand at AS level will be useful in helping you understand 'derived demand', a topic that is included in both of the optional units. Another example is in the case of the AD/AS model; your AS knowledge will be developed further when analysing policy issues in the Global Economy unit in Part 3.

Stretch and challenge

This is a feature of all new A levels. It is incorporated into each A2 unit and is contained in the style of essay questions where there is an AO4 assessment objective. Here you are required to evaluate economic arguments and evidence, making informed judgements in essay-style questions. As the term suggests, it is a way of OCR examiners rewarding

those students who clearly think and write as economists and who are able to demonstrate that they have the knowledge and skills to make informed judgements.

To help you understand what 'stretch and challenge' involves, some questions in the activities have been highlighted as requiring this skill. These questions will test your ability to really think about what you have learned and whether you have been able to weigh up the evidence available to make an informed judgement.

This general introduction has explained what you need to know about OCR's A2 Economics. The emphasis has been on the skills that you will need to develop as you move from AS level to A2. These skills will gradually be developed as you are guided through the A2 units. Keep referring back to what is required and see how you feel you are coping with what is needed to succeed at this second stage of your A level course.

As we said in the AS book, 'We hope you will find this book interesting, informative and useful.' The content of the A2 course is topical and relevant to a study of economics in the twenty-first century. We hope you enjoy your course and do well in the examinations.

Good luck!

Economics of work and leisure

This part builds on the work you did in AS Unit F581 to explore the economics of work and leisure. You will examine some of the key labour and leisure market issues.

Chapter 1 concentrates on the main features of the labour and leisure markets. You will examine some of the recent trends in UK employment and earnings, making some comparisons with other countries. You will also explore the difference between work and leisure and, by using examples, the meaning of market concentration ratios.

Chapter 2 continues with the theme of leisure. It focuses on how the type of market structure and degree of contestability influence the behaviour and performance of firms. You will consider the meaning of revenue and costs and analyse how costs are influenced by economies of scale. You will explore the market structure and contestability of a number of leisure industries and a number of possible objectives that firms can pursue.

Chapter 3 focuses on the factors determining wages and employment. Particular attention is paid to the demand for and supply of labour, although other factors are considered. You will also examine how wage rates differ between different groups. In this chapter, you will come across a number of new concepts including marginal revenue product and economic rent.

The final chapter of this part, Chapter 4, explores a range of causes of labour market failure and government responses to that failure, including the national minimum wage. You will explore the role of trade unions, the significance of labour market flexibility, the nature of inequality and poverty and some key challenges facing labour markets.

When you have completed this part you should be able to:

● describe the structure of, and changes in, earnings and employment in the UK

● distinguish between work and leisure and a range of leisure activities

● explain the influences on firms' costs and revenue

● apply models of market structures to firms in leisure markets

● explain how wages and employment are determined

● analyse the influences on the elasticities of demand for and supply of labour

● evaluate the causes and consequences of labour market failure

● explain the nature, measurement and causes of inequality.

1 Nature of work and leisure and trends in employment and earnings

On completion of this chapter, you should be able to:

- understand the structure of earnings and employment in the UK
- describe, in general terms, the recent trends in UK employment and earnings
- explain the above trends using the categories of age, gender, ethnicity, occupation, region and sector
- make broad comparisons in terms of employment and earnings structure between the UK and the rest of the EU, and between the UK and other selected non-EU economies
- explain what is meant by unit labour cost and productivity
- discuss the implications of variations in unit labour costs and productivity
- distinguish between work and leisure and the range of leisure activities
- understand how to categorise leisure time into its competing uses
- understand in broad terms the contribution of the leisure industries to an economy
- understand and apply concentration ratios within the leisure industry.

Work and leisure are closely connected. We can be working or enjoying leisure time. We spend some of the income we earn on leisure activities and leisure products and some of us are, or will be, employed in the leisure industry.

This chapter focuses on the nature of work and leisure, distinguishing between the two, and it examines a number of features of employment, earnings and leisure markets.

Earnings and employment

EARNINGS

One of the main reasons people work is to earn money. Workers, when wanting to impress their friends, may tell them how much they are earning. In arguing with an employer, however, that they are underpaid they are likely to quote their wage rate. The wage rate is the payment which an employer contracts to pay a worker. In addition to the wage rate, **earnings** include overtime pay, bonuses and commission.

> **DEFINITION**
>
> **Earnings:** wages plus overtime pay, bonuses and commission

Some time ago, a distinction used to be made between a salary and a wage. A salary was seen as a monthly payment while a wage was seen as a weekly payment. Nowadays, with most workers being paid monthly, no distinction is usually made between the two.

THE STRUCTURE OF EARNINGS

Earnings change as a result of a change in wage rates, bonuses or commission paid. Overtime pay, bonuses and commission payments are more volatile than wage rates.

When monthly changes in UK earnings are compared, the months from December to April show the largest increases, as these are the months in which bonus payments are highest. On an annual basis, earnings have risen relatively steadily in recent years, at an annual average of 3.9 per cent between 2002 and 2006. The earnings of public sector workers have increased slightly more rapidly than those of private sector workers. This contrasts with the period from 1993 to mid 2001 when private sector workers enjoyed higher increases.

Rises, levels and composition of earnings vary between industries and occupations. In 2006, the average annual earnings of full-time workers were £27,945.

Average earnings in a number of industries, including agriculture, forestry and fishing, wholesale and retail trade and transport, were less than this. Earnings in the hotels and restaurant industry were the lowest, at £17,337. Other industries enjoyed above-average earnings. These included education and public administration. It was, however, financial services that enjoyed the highest average earnings, at £37,450, and one of the most rapid increases in earnings.

THE STRUCTURE OF EMPLOYMENT

The structure or pattern of employment in the UK has changed in recent years, and continues to change. Figure 1.1 shows how, over the seventeen-year period from 1978 to 2005, there was a notable decline of nearly 4 million jobs in manufacturing. There was also a significant rise in finance and business services of approximately 2.6 million jobs.

THE ACTUAL AND POTENTIAL LABOUR FORCE

As noted in the *OCR AS Economics*, the labour force includes both the employed and the unemployed. People who are working or seeking work are said to be economically active.

Potentially the labour force could be greater if more of those who are **economically inactive** were to join it. Governments seek to raise the economic activity

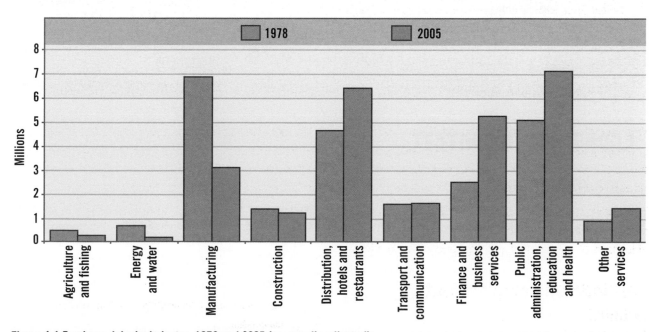

Figure 1.1 Employee jobs by industry, 1978 and 2005 (seasonally adjusted).
Source: *Labour Market Review 2006*

rate, which is also often referred to as the **labour force participation rate**, in order to increase aggregate supply. In recent years, an increase in the economic activity rate of women has contributed to economic growth in a number of countries.

In the UK, while the economic activity of women has risen, that of men has fallen. In 2006, the total number of people of working age who were economically inactive was 7.9 million. Figure 1.2 shows the main categories of those who were economically inactive.

Discouraged workers are people who would like a job but who are not seeking one, as they believe they would be unable to find one. In 2006, the number of discouraged workers was very low but their number tends to rise during economic downturns.

The UK's economic activity rate compares favourably with that of both the USA and the average for the EU – see Table 1.1.

DEFINITIONS

Economically inactive: working age people who are neither in employment, nor unemployed, and so are not part of the labour force

Labour force participation rate: the proportion of working age people who are economically active

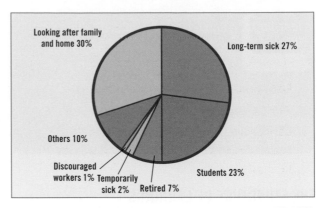

Figure 1.2 Composition of the economically inactive in the UK, 2006

	All of working age	Male	Female
UK	78	83	73
EU	70	78	63
USA	66	73	59

Table 1.1 Economic activity rates (%), 2005

As well as seeking to raise the economic activity rate, the UK government is also trying to increase the **employment rate**, setting itself the target of 80 per cent of working age people being in work. The UK's employment rate is above that of the EU average, and in recent years it has been the highest of the **G8** countries. In 2005, the UK had an employment rate of 74.7 per cent (males 79.1 per cent, females 70 per cent), compared with an EU employment rate of 64 per cent (males 71.5 per cent, females 56.6 per cent).

ECONOMICS IN CONTEXT

JOB SEPARATIONS

Job separations occur when workers and jobs separate. The term is useful, as it emphasises that there is a variety of reasons why a worker may no longer be employed in the same job. A worker may voluntarily leave a job to enter higher education or to be a homemaker. In some cases, the separation of the worker from the job may not be voluntary. A worker may be made redundant or, in the case of temporary employment, his/her contract may come to an end.

There are some interesting features of job separations in the UK. One is that younger workers experience more job separations than older ones. Another is that women's job separations tend to be voluntary, whereas men's job separations are more likely to be involuntary. As might be expected, those leaving jobs voluntarily are more likely to get back into employment than those who leave involuntarily.

The UK industry that in 2006 had the highest rate of job separation, most of it voluntary, was hotels and restaurants. The one with the lowest rate was education.

rapidly than private sector employment. Public sector workers now account for 20 per cent of the labour force, with the three largest areas being the National Health Service, education and public administration. In 2006, the region with the highest percentage of its labour force in the public sector was Northern Ireland, with 29.1 per cent, and the East Midlands was the lowest, with 18.5 per cent.

Workers in the public sector differ from those in the private sector in a number of ways. There is a higher proportion of female workers, 65 per cent against 41 per cent, and a higher proportion have a degree, 48 per cent in comparison to 27 per cent. In addition, more public sector workers are members of trade unions than are private sector workers.

Part-time employment has also grown in absolute terms. In 1996 there were 6.5 million **part-time workers**. This had grown to 7.3 million in 2006. As a percentage of the labour force, this was still 25 per cent. Women form the largest proportion of part-time workers – 77 per cent in 2006. It is interesting to note, however, that while the proportion of female workers working part-time has been relatively constant, at approximately 44 per cent, the proportion of male workers working part-time has been increasing, from 8 per cent in 1996 to 10 per cent in 2006. More than 75 per cent of part-time workers have chosen to work part-time. The unavailability of a full-time job as a reason for working part-time has become less important in the last decade.

DEFINITIONS

Employment rate: the proportion of working-age people who are in work

G8: the group of major economies consisting of Canada, France, Germany, Italy, Japan, Russia, the UK and USA

ACTIVITY ····

	All of working age	Male	Female
Economic activity rate	79.0	83.7	74.0
Employment rate	74.6	78.7	70.1

Table 1.2 The UK labour market (%), 2006

Explain why the employment rate is lower than the economic activity rate.

learning tip

STEPPING UP TO A2

Your understanding and awareness of changes in the UK labour market have to be more sophisticated and in more depth at A2 than at AS.

DEFINITION

Part-time workers: people working less than 30 hours a week

Recent trends in employment

The total number of people in employment in the UK has grown in recent years, increasing by 2.9 million between 1996 and 2006 to 29 million. Since 1998, public sector employment has grown more

The number of self-employed workers is increasing. In 2006 there were 3.7 million self-employed people in the UK, accounting for 13 per cent of all those in employment. More men are self-employed than women and the self-employed work longer hours than employees. A third of self-employed men run construction businesses while nearly a quarter of self-employed women run service businesses, including dry cleaning, hairdressing and beauty treatments.

The number of temporary workers has fallen from 1.7 million in 1996 to 1.4 million in 2005. The reasons for undertaking **temporary work** have changed, with a smaller proportion saying they are undertaking this type of work because they are unable to find a permanent job.

Other recent changes in employment have been the growth in the number of people undertaking **homeworking**, and the nature of homeworking itself. Between 1997 and 2005, the number of homeworkers increased from 2.3 million to 3.1 million. In the past, homeworkers tended to be low paid and low skilled, carrying out jobs such as typing and filling envelopes. Now a number of homeworkers are managers and professionals. Most are men, most are self-employed and most are teleworkers – see below. While men tend to be working in different places, using home as their base, women are more likely to be working at home. Among the industries in which homeworking is an important feature are construction, banking, finance and insurance.

DEFINITIONS

Temporary work: casual work, seasonal work, working for employment agencies, fixed-period contract work

Homeworking: working either at home or in different places away from the central office, production or distribution facilities, using the home as a base

Homeworking provides advantages for workers, employers and the economy. Workers have more control over when they work, which helps with family commitments and may reduce stress. Employers benefit from lower office costs, access to a greater pool of workers (including those with disabilities and family commitments), lower rates of sickness and higher productivity. Reducing the need to commute lowers congestion and pollution. There are, however, some possible disadvantages. Workers may feel more isolated and may receive less training.

An increasingly important form of homeworking is **teleworking**. This involves using a telephone and a computer to carry out work. This may be done, for instance, at home, in an Internet café or a train or plane.

DEFINITION

Teleworking: working using a telephone and a computer at home, in an Internet café, or a train or plane

learning tip

Keep up to date with changes in the UK labour market by reading quality newspapers and by visiting the Office for National Statistics website. Go to www.heinemann.co.uk/hotlinks, insert the express code 2230P, and click on 'Office for National Statistics'.

Recent trends in earnings

The earnings workers receive are influenced by a number of factors, including their educational qualifications, skills, which area they work in, the industry they work in, their age, gender and occupation. Table 1.3 shows how earnings have changed in different industrial categories in recent years.

Table 1.4 compares average gross earnings in the 25 countries that were members of the EU in 2005, showing that the UK was in second position.

AGE

UK workers are getting older. In 1991, the average age of people in the UK labour force was 37. By 2001 this had risen to 39 years and by 2006 it had risen to 40 years. The proportion of workers in

Agriculture, forestry and fishing	32.7
Mining and quarrying	34.9
Food products, beverages and tobacco	23.2
Textiles, leather and clothing	24.9
Chemicals and man-made fibres	19.7
Basic metals and metal products	32.5
Engineering and allied industries	29.0
Other manufactures	23.3
Electricity, gas and water supply	17.6
Construction	25.5
Wholesale trade	24.0
Retail trade and repairs	19.4
Hotel and restaurants	37.1
Transport, storage and communication	27.5
Financial intermediation	23.9
Real estate, renting and business activities	23.8
Public administration	29.1
Education	28.4
Health and education	37.5
Other services	23.2

Table 1.3 Rise in average earnings (including bonuses) (%), 2000–06

Source: *Annual Abstract of Statistics 2007*, Office of National Statistics (ONS)

Denmark	47,529
UK	42,866
Luxembourg	42,135
Germany	41,694
Ireland	40,462
Netherlands	37,900
Belgium	36,672
Austria	36,032
Sweden	34,049
Finland	33,290
France	30,521
Italy	24,803
Cyprus	20,586
Spain	20,439
Portugal	14,715
Malta	11,180
Hungary	7,798
Czech Republic	7,406
Slovakia	6,374
Poland	6,270
Estonia	6,240
Lithuania	4,688
Latvia	4,247

Table 1.4 Average gross earnings in EU countries (euros), 2005

Source: Eurostat website

employment aged over 50 years rose from 24 per cent in 1991 to 26 per cent in 2006.

Other EU countries are also experiencing an ageing population. Italy's is ageing most rapidly, followed by Germany. Ireland's is ageing the least rapidly, followed by Slovakia.

Older workers tend to change their jobs less frequently and to be less geographically and occupationally mobile than young workers. They are less likely to lose their jobs, but if they do become unemployed, they take longer to return to work.

There is some debate as to the effects older workers have on firms' wage costs. As older workers change their jobs less frequently, they reduce firms' turnover costs, including recruitment and initial training costs. Their experience may also have positive effects on productivity. This downward pressure on wage costs is, however, usually more than offset by the tendency for pay to rise with age.

ACTIVITY ⋯⋰

Average full-time earnings in Norway rose by 4.8 per cent between 2005 and 2006. Male workers are, on average, paid more than female workers. There are more female workers than male workers in the Norwegian public sector and a higher proportion of part-time workers in the country are female. Just under half of all female workers work part-time.

Norway and the other Nordic countries at the start of 2008 were facing not a shortage of jobs but a shortage of workers. Table 1.5 shows the unemployment rate for the four Nordic countries, in comparison with the average for the EU27 (27 member states of the EU).

The Nordic countries were seeking to recruit workers from abroad to fill skill shortages to reduce inflation and promote international competitiveness.

a) Using the information provided, compare the Norwegian and UK labour markets.

Denmark	2.0
Finland	6.1
Norway	2.0
Sweden	6.0
EU27	6.7

Table 1.5 Unemployment rates (%), February 2008

b) Explain what the passage indicates was happening to wage rates in the Nordic countries at the start of 2008.

STRETCH AND CHALLENGE

c) To what extent does Table 1.5 support the view that the Nordic countries 'were facing not a shortage of jobs but a shortage of workers'?

ACTIVITY ⋯⋰

The Netherlands is placed twelfth in terms of the proportion of workers in the 55 to 64 age range in the EU in 2005. The proportion of older workers varies across Dutch industries. In 2005, the three Dutch industries with the highest proportion of older workers were education, agriculture and fishing, and public administration. The two industries with the lowest proportions were hotels and restaurants, and financial services.

Wage rates usually rise automatically with age in the Netherlands. In the case of male workers, the average income doubles between 25 and 50.

a) Identify one reason why the average age structure of the labour force of different industries may vary.

STRETCH AND CHALLENGE

b) Discuss whether an ageing labour force will reduce the international competitiveness of a country's firms.

GENDER

Women continue to form an increasing proportion of the UK's labour force. In 1971, women formed 38.5 per cent of the labour force, but this had risen to 44.7 per cent by 2002 and to 45.9 per cent by 2006. This rise reflects an increase in the economic activity rate of women and a decline in the economic activity rate of men, as already mentioned.

The major rise in the economic activity rate of women has come in the 25 to 44 age range. There is a variety of reasons why women are participating in the labour force more. These include increased job opportunities for women, increased pay, changing social attitudes and increased expectations of higher living standards. Women are also tending to have children later and returning to work more quickly.

The pattern of employment of women and men is different. The highest-paid occupations are still currently dominated by men. For instance, 90 per cent of the chief executives of major companies are men and 96 per cent of aircraft pilots are men. In contrast, the lowest-paid occupations are dominated by women, with 81 per cent of checkout operators, 79 per cent of cleaners, 74 per cent of waiting staff and 71 per cent of sales assistants being female. The difference in the pattern of employment is sometimes referred to as **occupational segregation**.

Most checkout operators are women

Women, on average, are less well paid than men. Table 1.6 shows how the gender pay gap varies between different regions of the world.

DEFINITION

Occupational segregation: the dominance of an occupation by one gender

Region	%
Africa	15.6
Asia	23.2
Americas	23.0
Europe	14.5
Oceania	12.8
World	15.6

Table 1.6 Regional gender pay gap

ETHNICITY

People from ethnic minorities are, on average, less well paid than the general population. They are also

ACTIVITY ⋯⋮

A significant proportion of women managers in the UK are having to move down the career ladder when they have children because part-time opportunities in higher-level jobs are restricted.

In order to find jobs that allow them to spend time with their children, one third of all corporate managers have to switch to lower-skill jobs, including clerical work. Women managers of shops, salons and restaurants are more seriously affected by occupational downgrading. Almost half give up their managerial responsibilities and become, for example, sales assistants and hairdressers.

One disadvantage faced by those who have downgraded is a loss of income. Women working part-time have hourly earnings that are, on average, 26 per cent lower than women working full-time.

a) What is meant by 'occupational downgrading'?

STRETCH AND CHALLENGE

b) Discuss the impact that giving up managerial responsibilities for a period of time may have on women's long-term career prospects and earnings.

disadvantaged by having lower employment rates than white people, as shown in Figure 1.3. The lower wages and higher unemployment arise in part from discrimination. If employers believe, through

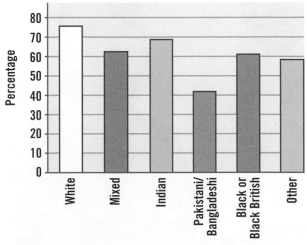

Figure 1.3 Employment rate by ethnic group, winter 2004 to autumn 2005 (UK)

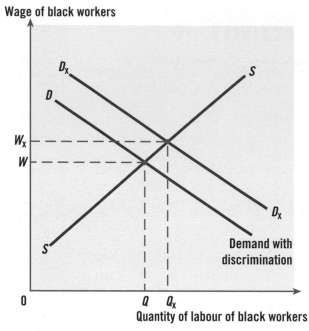

Figure 1.4 The effect of negative discrimination

prejudice, that the productivity of black workers is lower than it actually is, the wage rate paid to those workers will be below the allocatively efficient level as shown in Figure 1.4.

Asian and Asian British women are the least economically active members of the population.

Professionals of Chinese and Indian origin

Bangladeshi women are least likely to be members of the labour force. This low rate reflects, in part, language difficulties as well as cultural differences.

People from ethnic minorities, particularly Chinese, Pakistani and Bangladeshi people, are more likely to be self-employed than the population as a whole. A number work in the distribution, hotel and restaurant sectors.

There is a higher than average proportion of people of Chinese, Indian and white Irish origin working in managerial and professional occupations while there is a lower than average proportion of black Caribbeans, black Africans and Bangladeshis.

OCCUPATION

Over the last two decades the largest increase in UK jobs has been in banking, finance and insurance. The number of jobs in these areas rose from 2.7 million to 5.4 million between 1981 and 2006. As Figure 1.1 showed, there have also been increases in the numbers employed in public administration, education and health care. On the other hand, jobs have been lost in agriculture and fishing, energy and water, manufacturing and construction.

There has been a rise in the proportion of workers in managerial and professional posts. In 2006, 28 per cent of workers were in such an occupational category.

REGIONS

In recent years, total employment has been increasing in most regions. The largest rise has been in London, the West Midlands and the South East. Employment has fallen, however, in the Yorkshire and Humberside region, the East Midlands and the East region.

In 2005, the average gross annual pay for full-time workers was £26,884. London had by far the highest average earnings and the North East and Northern Ireland the lowest. High earnings in London reflect the high quality of jobs there. The relatively low employment rate, however, means there is a significant gap between the rich and poor in the capital city.

Table 1.7 shows how earnings and employment rates vary between the different regions of the UK.

Region	Average weekly earnings (£)	Employment rate (%)
North East	452	71
North West	480	73
Yorkshire & Humberside	467	74
East Midlands	469	76
West Midlands	476	73
East	512	78
London	698	69
South East	539	79
South West	473	78
England	526	75
Wales	454	71
Scotland	480	75
Northern Ireland	452	69

Table 1.7 Regional average weekly earnings and employment rates, 2005
Source: *Annual Survey of Hours and Earnings*, Office for National Statistics, 2007

SECTORS

There continues to be a decline in the numbers employed in the **secondary sector** in the UK.

Manufacturing lost more than a million jobs between 1997 and 2007. In contrast, employment in the **tertiary sector** continues to account for a higher proportion of

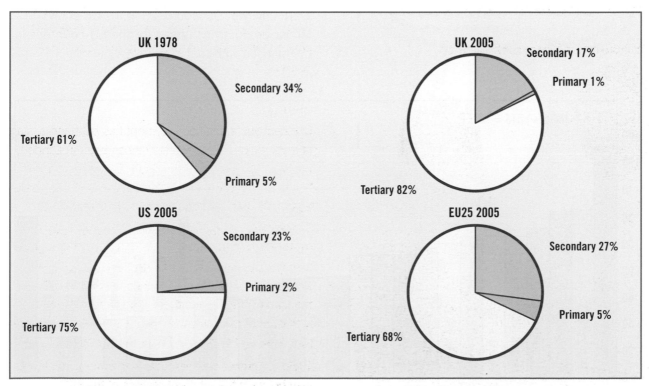

Figure 1.5 Composition of employee jobs by sectors

employment. A shift in employment from the **primary** and secondary sectors to the tertiary sector is the common pattern that occurs as an economy grows. Figure 1.5 compares jobs by sectors over time in the UK and between the UK, USA and EU25.

> ### DEFINITIONS
>
> **Primary sector:** the first stage of production, including industries such as agriculture, fishing, forestry and mining, involved in the extraction and collection of raw materials
>
> **Secondary sector:** the second stage of production, which involves the processing of raw materials into semi-finished and finished goods. It includes manufacturing and construction
>
> **Tertiary sector:** the third stage of production, which covers industries producing services including education, financial services, health care and tourism

Of EU countries in 2005, Luxembourg had the highest proportion of jobs in the tertiary sector, 83 per cent, and Romania had the lowest, 37 per cent. Romania also had the highest proportion of jobs in the primary sector, 32.3 per cent, while the UK had the lowest rate. The secondary sector was most significant in the Czech Republic, 39.5 per cent, and least significant in Luxembourg, at 16 per cent.

Unit labour costs and productivity

Unit labour costs are the labour costs per unit of output. Labour costs include the complete range of costs employers incur when they employ workers. They include not only wages but also the cost of recruiting and training workers, national insurance contributions, redundancy payments and benefits in kind. Wages do, however, constitute over 80 per cent of total labour costs. So they, together with productivity, are the two key influences on unit labour costs. If productivity increases at a faster rate than the wages paid, unit labour costs are likely to fall. It is interesting to note that while wage rates are high in the USA, unit labour cost is lower than in most EU countries. This is because of the higher productivity of US workers. Figure 1.6 shows labour productivity figures for the EU countries in comparison with that of the USA.

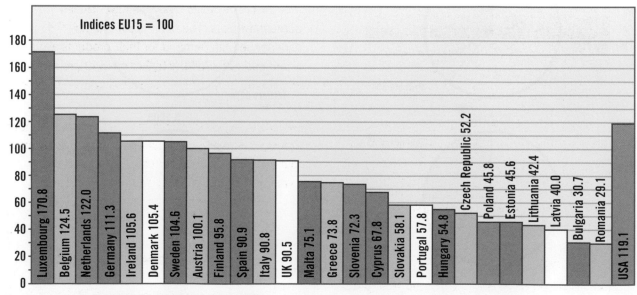

Figure 1.6 Labour productivity per hour worked, 2005

The relatively poor performance of the UK against the USA and some EU countries has been attributed to low levels of capital per worker, educational shortcomings, insufficient innovation and an inefficient transport system.

ECONOMICS IN CONTEXT

THE TAX WEDGE

The **tax wedge** is the gap between what employers pay for labour and what workers receive in disposable income. It consists of income tax and the social security contributions of employers and workers. A large tax wedge tends to discourage job creation.

Tax wedges are higher in the EU than in the USA. Table 1.8 shows the gap between labour costs and take-home pay as a percentage of total labour costs in a number of countries.

Country	%
Belgium	55.5
Hungary	54.5
Germany	52.2
France	49.2
Italy	45.9
Netherlands	44.0
Turkey	42.7
Spain	38.9
UK	34.1
Canada	31.3
USA	30.0
Switzerland	29.6
Japan	29.3
South Korea	19.6

Table 1.8 The tax wedge in selected countries, 2007

Source: OECD (Organisation for Economic Co-operation and Development) website

learning tip

STEPPING UP TO A2

Offshoring and outsourcing are topics new at A2. These are developments that are influencing the UK labour market.

Variations in unit labour costs

If a country's firms have higher unit labour costs than firms in rival countries, this may make their products less price competitive. The impact will be influenced by whether the proportion of labour costs in total costs and capital costs differ between countries. It is possible that firms in a country may have higher unit labour costs but still have lower average total cost, if production in the country is more capital intensive and/or it uses capital more efficiently.

Even if higher unit labour costs reduce price competitiveness, they may not lower quality competitiveness. The country's firms may still experience high demand for their products at home and abroad if the higher costs of production are matched by higher quality and consumers are prepared to pay for this.

Nevertheless, concern over the competitive pressure coming from countries such as China and India due to their lower unit labour costs has caused some EU and US firms to engage in **outsourcing** and in some cases **offshoring**. Initially, India was the main destination of the export of jobs from the UK with, for instance, a number of airlines, banks and insurance companies moving their call centres and back-office administrative jobs there. These moves were assisted by improved communications and an increase in the number of English-speaking IT graduates in India. By 2003, India accounted for more than 80 per cent of global outsourcing. In more recent years, however, a number of other countries have started to attract jobs from the UK. These include the Czech Republic, Hungary, Malaysia, Mexico and Vietnam.

DEFINITION

Offshoring: transferring part of the process to another country. The production may be outsourced or may be undertaken by the firm but in another country

ACTIVITY ··· ⫶

In March 2008, British Gas announced a fivefold increase in profits. This was the same year in which it also made redundancies in the UK, while moving more of its customer service business overseas. Energywatch revealed that, between December and February, the company had received more complaints per 100,000 customers than any other energy supplier. The company, however, argued that it was necessary to use offshoring to cut back on costs in order to remain competitive.

a) Identify three groups who may have benefited from British Gas's decision to move work abroad.

STRETCH AND CHALLENGE

b) Discuss whether offshoring will always increase a company's profits.

Leisure

Leisure is an experience that occurs outside working hours within the time when people are free to select what they do. People's time can be divided into three main categories:

- work/education

- maintenance time, for example, time spent looking after children, sleeping, bathing, eating and undertaking domestic work – the activities necessary for existence

- leisure.

So leisure time is the time that people have left to spend in ways they wish after they have completed their work/educational and maintenance commitments.

Leisure can also be regarded as a product – something we consume. We demand leisure products. Some we pay for, such as a ticket to a football match, and some we are not charged directly for, such as jogging.

Of course it is not always clear cut as to what constitutes leisure. Someone may regard time spent gardening as maintenance time while another person may regard it as leisure time. Similarly, one person studying an A level subject may be doing so for 'leisure reasons' while another might be doing it with the intention of using the qualification to gain access to higher education. In addition, while some people, for example, play football for fun, others are paid to play.

Leisure time is not evenly distributed between people. Retired people have the most free time, while women working full-time have the least.

Gardening is both leisure and maintenance

CHOICE BETWEEN WORK AND LEISURE

A key determinant of how much leisure time many adults have is how long they spend working. This is affected by the income and substitution effects that will be discussed in Chapter 3. The trade-off between work and leisure also explains why overtime rates are usually above the standard pay rates. If employers ask their workers to work longer hours, they are also asking them to have less leisure time. The fewer the hours of leisure that people have, the more valuable those hours become to them and the more they have to be compensated to give them up.

FORMS OF LEISURE

Leisure activities can be divided into categories in a number of ways. One category is home-based activities, such as reading, accessing Facebook and gardening; another is out-of-home activities, such as eating out, visiting a club and going to the cinema. In the UK, the most popular home-based leisure activity is watching television. The number of hours people watch tends to increase with age. For instance, while 25–44 year olds watched 125 minutes a day in 2005, those aged over 65 watched 227 minutes. In every age group, men watch more television than women. The most common leisure activity outside the home in the UK is visiting the pub.

Another form of categorisation is into broad categories such as educational and cultural, sporting, social and caring, and nature and environmental. The most detailed form of categorisation is into particular activities such as music, film, tourism and theatre.

learning tip

BUILDING ON AS

Before reading the next two sections, check the information on the factors influencing demand and supply in *OCR AS Economics*, pages 28–31 and 35–37.

STEPPING UP TO A2

In answering exam questions about leisure, remember the importance of applying economics. An answer that contains detailed knowledge of Manchester United's recent performances might be interesting, but it is not an economics answer.

The supply of leisure

Leisure activities are supplied by:

● *the private sector.* Private sector firms supply a range of leisure activities through, for example, health clubs, travel agents, cinemas, theme parks and professional football clubs. The most common aim of these firms is to maximise profits, so a rise in price will usually result in them supplying more.

● *the public sector.* Local authorities and agencies acting on behalf of the government, such as the Arts Council, also directly supply a range of leisure activities, including libraries, public playing fields, sports centres, museums and art galleries. They charge either no price or a low price for these activities. The state also subsidises some leisure activities by giving grants, including grants from National Lottery funds to private sector companies supplying leisure services. The motive behind the state's intervention is linked to the merit good nature of many leisure activities and the question of equity.

● *the voluntary sector.* A number of voluntary organisations supply leisure services; for example, tennis clubs, angling clubs and craft societies. These are usually self-financed through subscriptions and charges.

FACTORS INFLUENCING DEMAND FOR A PARTICULAR LEISURE ACTIVITY

These include:

● *the price of the activity.* Some leisure activities are provided free to the consumer such as walking, watching hockey on local playing fields and making use of public libraries. Other activities involve costs.

For example, someone who plays tennis may pay to belong to a tennis club and will buy tennis-related equipment.

● *the price of complementary goods and services.* Someone who enjoys visiting the theatre may also have to pay to travel to the theatre, in which case a taxi or bus service is a complementary good.

● *the price of substitutes*, including not only other leisure activities but also work.

● *tastes.* Tastes in leisure activities change over time. For example, in recent years the popularity of quizzing has increased, while the popularity of tenpin bowling has declined.

● *age composition.* The increase in the average age of the population has led to a rise in the demand for holidays specially designed for the over-50s and an increase in spending at garden centres.

● *gender composition.* For example, a higher percentage of men than women engage in DIY and a higher percentage of women read than men.

● *advertising.* Advertising can be a potent force. Advertisements for films and concerts can help to raise attendances.

● *major events.* A major event can generate demand for related activities. For example, attendances at football matches usually rise after a World Cup competition and a concert can help sell a group's music.

● *exchange rate.* A fall in the exchange rate makes the country's or area's products more price competitive in terms of other countries' currencies. This can result in a rise in the number of tourists visiting the country or region.

Changes in the leisure market

In recent years there have been a number of changes in the market.

● There has been a rise in the proportion of home-based leisure activities. For example, the number of households owning a home computer has increased from 26 per cent in 1996/97 to 64 per cent in 2005/06.

● There has been a rise in gambling. This is largely accounted for by the introduction of the National Lottery in 1994 and the growth of online gambling.

● There has been a rise in expenditure on leisure activities. This has been the result of rising income and more leisure time. Some of this rise in expenditure has gone on merchandise associated with leisure activities. For example, anglers buy magazines on angling and football supporters buy football shirts sold by their clubs.

● There has been an increase in the influence of the USA. For example, theme parks and private health clubs spread from the USA to Europe.

Holidays and leisure travel

Leisure travel can be referred to as tourism. It involves people moving from their usual place of residence to a destination in which they make use of facilities and undertake activities. People can spend their holidays as tourists in their own countries or visiting other countries.

In the UK and most other countries, tourism has grown significantly in the last two decades and tourism is now the largest industry in the world.

In 2007, more than 1.6 million people in the UK were employed in the tourism industry. Different kinds of

ACTIVITY ···⟩

The London Eye has been a great success and has regularly been in the top ten of tourist destinations in the UK. Since its opening in March 2000, it has been copied on a smaller scale in a number of UK cities, including Birmingham and York. Now, more countries are planning to open their own versions, this time with most being larger than the London Eye. For example, Singapore opened the Singapore Flyer in 2008 and in 2009 Beijing, Berlin and Dublin are opening their own versions.

a) Identify two ways in which the success of a tourist attraction can be judged.

STRETCH AND CHALLENGE

b) Discuss whether the opening of other wheels will reduce the revenue received by the London Eye.

firm are involved in providing holidays and leisure travel. These include tour operators, travel agents, airlines and ferry operators.

THE GROWTH OF TOURISM

The tourist industry has increased because of:

- an increase in disposable income
- a reduction in working hours
- a fall in the real cost of travel
- early retirement
- people living longer
- a reduction in time spent on domestic tasks
- improved transport
- increased advertising
- increased awareness of the benefits.

THE EFFECTS OF TOURISM
Income and employment

The growth of the tourist industry has increased income and employment in a number of countries. This effect can be greater than it first appears. Obviously, tourists create income and employment directly for hotels, restaurants and attractions that cater for tourists. However, they also create income and employment in a wide range of other industries. Some of these supply goods and services to the tourist industry. For example, insurance firms, farms and taxi firms. Others benefit from the spending by local people and firms arising from the income brought in by the tourists. So an initial rise in income of, for example, £30m in an area and the creation of 2,000 extra jobs may eventually lead to a rise in income of £90m and 5,000 more jobs. This knock-on effect on income and employment is referred to as the **tourism income multiplier**.

DEFINITION

Tourism income multiplier: the extent to which a change in income from tourism causes GDP to change

The initial jobs created in the tourist industry, however, may not be of a very high quality, as many are unskilled. Workers in the tourist industry also tend not to be very well paid. In addition, the effect on income and employment will not be very great if a significant proportion of the goods and services used in the tourism industry is bought in from abroad. For example, a hotel in Petra in Jordan run by a UK company may buy some of its furniture and linen from the UK. Some of the senior staff it employs may also come from the UK.

The balance of payments

The effects on the country's balance of payments position will also be influenced by where the firms in the tourist industry obtain their materials and foods from and on the national origin of the firms. The UK firm running the hotel in Petra will send profits back to the UK.

Countries not only have tourists visiting them but also their own citizens are tourists in other countries. When foreigners visit the UK, their expenditure is counted as an export – we are selling them a service. In contrast, when UK citizens holiday abroad they are buying tourist services from other countries and so their spending counts as an import. Exports of tourism appear as a credit item and imports as a debit item under 'personal trade' in the services section of the balance of payments. In recent years, the UK has had a personal travel deficit. Americans are the main visitors to the UK, while Spain is the main destination for UK tourists.

Culture

Where there are notable differences in the income levels and culture of the tourists and local inhabitants, social tensions can arise. Tourists may act in such a way, for example, getting drunk and gambling, which upsets the sensibility of the locals. Tourists' greater spending power may result in resources being switched from meeting the needs of locals to meeting the needs of the tourists. For instance, houses for locals may be demolished in order to build hotels.

Local culture may be threatened by the presence of tourists in a number of ways. One is referred to as the demonstration effect. This is where the locals, particularly the younger locals, copy the culture of tourists, especially in terms of clothes, films, music, food, drink and social attitudes. The presence of tourists, especially wealthy tourists, changes the type of goods and services demanded and thereby changes the skills and working patterns of the locals. The process whereby contact with tourists actually changes the culture of a country is called acculturation.

Environment

Tourism may damage the environment in a number of ways including:

● visual pollution. The building of hotels, funfairs, etc. can reduce the visual attractiveness of an area

● noise and air pollution caused by the planes and coaches transporting the tourists

● waste generated by tourists

● congestion arising from the influx of tourists and people catering for the needs of tourists

● destruction of the natural environment, for example, to build golf courses for tourists

● heavy use of water supplies often in areas where the locals are short of water.

The ability of an area to cope with tourists in such a way that it does not damage the features that attract the tourists in the first place is referred to as its carrying capacity.

A fully developed tourist resort

Spectator sports

People watch a range of activities, including athletics, cricket and tennis. One sport that has become more popular to watch in recent years is football. League football clubs raise revenue in a variety of ways:

● *merchandise sales*. Clubs have sold items such as shirts and scarves for some time, but now most have branched out into a whole range of items including duvet covers and watches.

● *sponsorship*. League football clubs are sponsored by firms and their players wear the sponsor's name on their shirts. The competitions they play in are also sponsored.

● *selling television coverage*. In recent years the amount of money received by the top clubs from television companies paying for the right to screen their games has increased dramatically. This has enabled the clubs to raise their players' wages to unprecedented levels.

● *ticket sales*. Clubs are faced with the problem of a fixed supply of seats. In recent years, a number of the top clubs have built new stadia, but demand for tickets to the matches of some of the major clubs still often exceeds the supply. To increase their profits, clubs charge different prices according to:

○ the age of the spectators

○ where people sit in the stadium

○ the quality of the seating; for example, charging more to hire a box

○ the expected quality of the game – for example, charging fans more for watching their team play Chelsea than for watching them play Wigan.

The national economy and leisure

As well as leisure having an impact on the national economy, changes in the national economy also have an impact on leisure and leisure industries. When the economy is expanding, and personal incomes rising, demand for most leisure products rises.

Expansionary monetary and fiscal policies benefit most leisure industries. For example, a lower rate of interest will reduce firms' costs and increase aggregate demand. Lower income tax will also increase aggregate demand by raising disposable income. Leisure products tend to be disproportionately affected by changes in disposable income as many are superior goods having positive income elasticity of demand greater than 1.

A fall in the exchange rate particularly benefits the home tourist industry as it makes the cost of holidays in the domestic country relatively cheaper, in terms of foreign currency, while making foreign holidays, in terms of domestic currency, relatively more expensive.

Broadcasting

Watching television is a major leisure activity for many people. Television broadcasting in the UK is an industry in a period of rapid change in a number of respects. These include: the switch-off of the analogue signal that started in 2008 and is due to be completed by the end of 2012; the ever-increasing

number of channels, which is fragmenting the audience; financial pressures particularly on ITV and Channel 4; the rise of independent production companies; and the continuing debate about the role of public service broadcasting. People now watch programmes not just on televisions but increasingly on broadband-enabled computers and mobile devices.

The BBC began regular television broadcasting in 1932 and had a monopoly of broadcasting until 1955, when ITV was launched. In 1966, the number of channels increased to three with the launch of BBC2. Channel 4 started in 1982, analogue satellite channels in 1989 and Channel 5 in 1997.

DEFINITION

Monopoly: a single seller

ECONOMICS IN CONTEXT

PRIVATE AND PUBLIC EXPENDITURE ON LEISURE

UK and US households spend more on leisure than households in most other countries. This contrasts with spending on leisure by the UK and US governments, which is relatively low. This is surprising as, generally, the richer a country, the higher both private and public spending on leisure tends to be.

Another country that has an unusual pattern of spending on leisure is Ireland. In this case, what is surprising is the relatively low household spending on leisure for what is now an affluent country. Table 1.9 compares household and government spending on leisure in a number of countries.

Country	Household spending % of GDP	Government spending % of GDP
UK	7.9	0.6
USA	6.4	0.3
Sweden	5.7	1.1
Spain	5.6	1.3
France	5.2	0.8
Netherlands	5.1	1.1
Italy	4.4	0.9
Ireland	2.8	0.5

Table 1.9 Household and government spending on leisure as a percentage of GDP, 2006

TELEVISION COMPANIES

The BBC is a state corporation and runs a number of channels in addition to BBC1 and BBC2. These include BBC3, BBC4, CCBC, Cbeebies and BBC News 24. ITV PLC is, as its name suggests, a public limited company operating in the private sector. It owns 11 of the 15 regional franchises, among them ITV Central and ITV Yorkshire. Other companies run the franchises in Scotland, Northern Ireland and the Channel Islands.

Channel 5 is an interesting organisation as, in effect, it is semi publicly owned. It has to support itself by advertising but is alone among the commercial broadcasters in not having to pay anything to the government for its spectrum use. In return for this privileged position, it has to meet the needs for specialist and minority audiences. Channel 5 is owned by RTL, which is a subsidiary of Bertelsman. BSkyB is the main satellite broadcaster and is part of the Murdoch empire.

The BBC is financed mainly by the licence fee but also by the sale of its programmes abroad and by the sale of merchandise, including magazines. ITV, Channel 4 and Channel 5 are financed mainly by advertising revenue.

INDEPENDENT PRODUCTION COMPANIES

Television companies produce some of their own programmes but also buy in programmes from independent production companies. Among these companies are Endemol (responsible for *Big Brother*), Celador (which produces *Who Wants to Be a Millionaire?*) and Hat Trick (*Have I Got News for You*).

RADIO

The BBC began broadcasting radio programmes in 1922. The first licensed commercial radio station, LBC, was started in 1973. There are now more than 200 local commercial radio stations and four national ones: Virgin, Classic FM, Atlantic 252 and Talksport. The BBC dominates the national market but there is more competition in terms of local radio, particularly in the London regional market.

learning tip

STEPPING UP TO A2

To keep up with developments in television and radio broadcasting, it is useful to visit the Guardian's media website. Go to www.heinemann.co.uk/hotlinks, insert the express code 2230P, and click on 'Media Guardian'.

The cinema industry

Cinema operators receive most of their revenue from box office takings. This source accounts for approximately 72 per cent of their revenue. The other 28 per cent comes from merchandise sales, including popcorn, and advertising.

Recent years have witnessed the growth of the multiplex. The first one in the UK was opened in 1985 in Milton Keynes. By 2005 there were 2,449 multiple screens. It is thought that the rise of the multiplex, providing greater choice and often combined with improved facilities such as restaurants and ample car parking spaces, has contributed to the doubling of cinema admissions over the period 1987 to 2007.

Cinema operators that are not operating in the multiplex sector average two screens per site and

Cinema attendance has increased with multiplexes

Year	Sites	Screens	Total number of admissions (millions)	Gross box takings (£ millions)	Revenue per admission (£)	Revenue per screen (£ thousand)
1998	761	2,638	135.2	504.9	3.73	191.4
1999	751	2,825	139.1	549.7	3.95	194.6
2000	754	3,017	142.5	572.8	4.02	189.9
2001	766	3,248	155.9	645.0	4.14	198.6
2002	775	3,402	175.9	755.3	4.29	222.0
2003	776	3,433	167.3	742.0	4.44	216.1
2004	773	3,475	171.3	769.6	4.49	221.4
2005	771	3,486	164.7	770.3	4.68	221.0
2006	783	3,569	156.6	762.1	4.87	213.5

Table 1.10 Cinema statistics
Source: *Annual Abstract of Statistics 2007*, ONS

often seek to attract visitors by specialising in particular types of films.

In 1995/96, 51 per cent of people went to the cinema. This increased to 60 per cent in 2005/06. Attendance varies with age. For example, while 90 per cent of 15–19-year-olds visited the cinema in 2006, only 33 per cent of over-65-year-olds had. Table 1.10 shows details about the UK cinema industry in recent years.

learning tip

STEPPING UP TO A2

Market concentration ratios are a key tool in market structure analysis. You need to get used to calculating and interpreting these. These are relatively straightforward and important tasks. You will gain more practice in Chapter 2.

ACTIVITY ····❖

In 2007, the UK cinema industry had a bumper year for box office takings. The top grossing film was *Harry Potter and the Order of the Phoenix*, which took £49.4m. The Film Distributors' Association (FDA) attributed the industry's success to a strong line of films and one of the wettest summers on record.

Cinema-going has trebled since the 1980s. However, while box office takings rose from 2002 to 2007, cinema going fell by 7.4 per cent.

The UK cinema industry is facing increasing competition from, for instance, HDTV, computer games and online social sites. Although it is worried about the increased level of competition in the leisure market, it seems to be unconcerned about the prospect of an economic recession. A spokesperson for the industry said in 2008: 'If there is any kind of economic downturn, cinema is well placed because of the escapist nature of it.'

a) What evidence is there in the above text that the price of cinema tickets rose from 2002 to 2007?

b) What does the passage suggest about the income elasticity of demand for cinema going?

STRETCH AND CHALLENGE

c) Discuss how the cross elasticity of demand between cinema going and the price of pay-TV may change in the future.

Market concentration ratio in leisure industries

In assessing the level of competition in an industry it is useful to examine a **market concentration ratio**. This shows the share of the largest firms in the industry in terms of sales, employment or some other measure.

The higher the market concentration ratio, the less competitive pressure there is in an industry and the more market power the largest firms have.

Figure 1.7 shows two different measures of market concentration in the cinema operators industry. This shows that the four firms' concentration ratio in terms of sites is 32 per cent while in terms of screens it is higher, at 62.9 per cent.

Figure 1.8 shows how the market concentration ratio of the four largest tour operators decreased between 2002 and 2006 but the share of the largest firm increased. There was also a change in the ranking of My Travel Group.

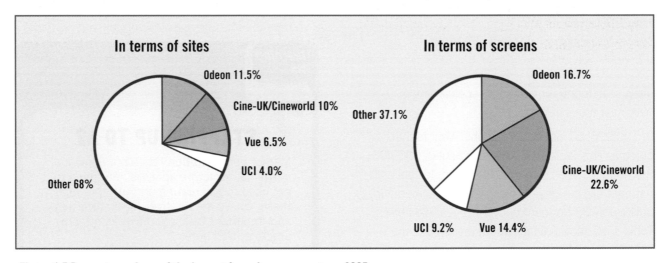

Figure 1.7 Percentage share of the largest four cinema operators, 2005

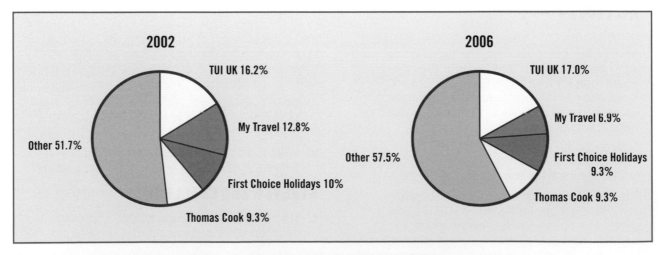

Figure 1.8 Percentage share of the largest travel firms in terms of passengers carried

One of the complicating factors in assessing the degree of market power in both the cinema and travel industries is that the firms are often changing hands.

For instance, in 2007 TUI UK merged with First Choice Holidays to form TUI Travel.

ACTIVITY ⋯⋮

Channel	2000	2008
BBC 1	27	21
BBC 2	11	7
ITV	29	17
Channel 4	11	7
Channel 5	6	5
Other	16	43

Table 1.11 UK television audience share (%)

a) Which television channel experienced the greatest proportionate fall in its market share?

b) Why was the BBC's viewing share actually higher than 28 per cent in April 2008?

c) Comment on the change in market concentration in terms of channel share of viewing figures between 2000 and 2008.

2 Market structures and competitive behaviour in leisure markets

On completion of this chapter, you should be able to:

- understand the nature of costs in the short run and long run
- understand the nature of and influences on firms' revenues
- explain what is meant by economies and diseconomies of scale and how firms might be affected by them
- explain the models of market structure:
  - O monopoly
  - O oligopoly
  - O monopolistic competition
- evaluate the implications of different market structures for resource allocation in theory and practice
- explain the characteristics of a contestable market
- apply the outcomes of the models of market structures to the actual behaviour of firms in the leisure markets
- discuss the relationship between efficiency and market structures in leisure markets
- analyse and comment upon the structure of leisure markets including those for holidays and leisure travel, spectator sports, broadcasting and cinema admissions
- Explain what is meant by regulation
- Evaluate the impact of regulation and ownership in selected leisure markets
- Discuss the objectives and behaviour of firms in leisure markets.

Chapter 1 finished with a discussion of market concentration ratios in leisure markets. This chapter explores the structure and behaviour of firms operating under different market conditions. It starts by examining costs and revenues, which are crucial factors in the decisions firms make. It then examines the effects of different levels of actual and potential competition and the objectives of firms. Particular attention is paid to market structures and competitive behaviour in leisure markets.

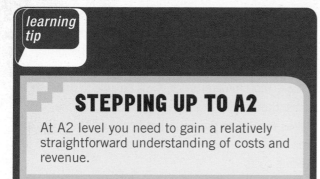

STEPPING UP TO A2

At A2 level you need to gain a relatively straightforward understanding of costs and revenue.

DEFINITIONS

Short run: the time period when at least one factor of production, usually capital, is in fixed supply

Fixed costs: costs that do not change in the short run with changes in output

Variable costs: costs that change with changes in output

Short-run costs of production

Firms face a variety of costs. Economists and business people often distinguish between short-run and long-run costs of production. The **short run** is defined as the time period when at least one factor of production, usually capital, is in fixed supply. This means, for instance, that a cinema operator does not have the time to sell off its existing building or end a renting contract agreement or to extend an existing building or acquire a new one.

In this time period, some of the firm's costs will be fixed and some will be variable. A business person is likely to refer to **fixed costs** as overheads or indirect costs. Such costs do not change with output in the short run. If a cinema operator cannot alter the size or number of its buildings, its business rates will remain the same even if it shows more films. Among the other fixed costs it may face are insurance and pensions paid to former employees.

In contrast to fixed costs, **variable costs** alter as output changes. These costs will include, in the case of a cinema operator, the cost of hiring films, ice cream and pop corn bought to sell to cinema goers and the cost of employing temporary staff to, for instance, sell programmes.

Sometimes it can be difficult to decide whether labour costs are fixed or variable. As indicated, the deciding factor is whether the costs will vary with output in the short run. Overtime and bonus payments as well as payment to temporary staff will clearly vary with output while the wage rate paid to what are regarded as permanent staff will not.

The difference between fixed and variable costs can be seen when a premier league football club

is relegated to the championship. The club will be likely to provide less of a service in the sense of selling fewer tickets and merchandise. It will cut accommodation costs for away games by staying at cheaper hotels and may make some stewards and temporary staff redundant. It may, however, have difficulty renegotiating interest payments on loans and altering the pay of some of its star players.

ACTIVITY ⋯⋮

In 2007, TUI Travel, a major tour operator, cut bonuses to staff, as its sales of holidays were not as high as anticipated. In 2008, it announced that it was planning to take the more radical measure of closing 100 shops in a bid to reduce a range of both fixed and variable costs.

a) Explain why staff bonuses are a variable cost.

b) Identify two fixed costs that TUI Travel could reduce by closing some of its shops.

TOTAL, AVERAGE AND MARGINAL COSTS IN THE SHORT RUN

Total cost (TC), as its name suggests, is the total cost of producing a given output. It is made up of fixed and variable costs in the short run. As output rises, total cost increases.

Average cost (AC), also often called unit cost, is total cost divided by output. For instance, a television production company's total cost may amount to £300,000 a week. If it produces 20 hours of television programmes, the average cost per hour made is £20,000. Average cost, in turn, can be divided into **average fixed cost** (AFC) and **average variable cost** (AVC) in the short run. If a television production company makes more hours of programming, it can spread its fixed costs more thinly. Average variable cost tends to fall at first, as output rises, and then tends to increase. This pattern occurs because at first, as a firm increases its output, it usually employs its resources more efficiently. Then,

when a certain output is reached, the fixed supply of at least one factor of production becomes more of a problem and the combination of resources becomes less efficient. As a television production company starts to make more programmes, it will be able to make more efficient use of, for example, cameras and studios. As it makes even more programmes, however, its studios are likely to become overcrowded which is likely to push up average costs.

Marginal cost (MC) is the change in total cost arising from changing output by one unit. It is a key cost as firms are constantly considering whether to reduce or increase output. Marginal cost influences average cost. It is falls in marginal cost that reduce average cost and rises in marginal cost that push up average cost.

DEFINITIONS

Average cost: total cost divided by output; also called unit cost

Average fixed cost: total fixed cost divided by output

Average variable cost: total variable cost divided by output

DEFINITION

Marginal cost: the change in total cost resulting from changing output by one unit

Output	Total cost	Marginal cost	Fixed cost	Variable cost	Average cost	Average fixed cost	Average variable cost
0	100	–	100	–	–	–	–
		80					
1	180		100	80	180	100	80
		70					
2	250		100	150	125	50	75
		50					
3	300		100	200	100	33.33	66.67
		60					
4	360		100	260	90	25	65
		80					
5	440		100	340	88	20	68
		100					
6	540		100	440	90	16.67	73.33

Table 2.1 Costs of production (£)

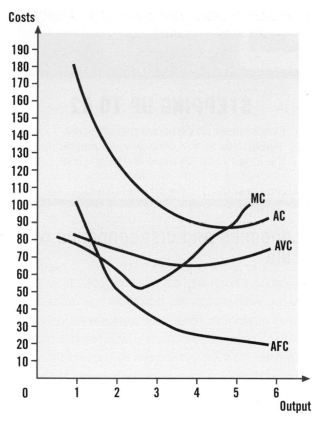

Figure 2.1 Cost curves

Figure 2.1 shows how the marginal cost curve cuts average cost and average variable cost at their lowest points.

Long-run costs

The **long run** is the period of time when it is possible to alter all factors of production. Firms can build more offices, factories, install new machinery and train more skilled labour. As the quantity of all resources can be altered, all costs are variable. For instance, a football club could build a new stadium, replace underground heating and bring through apprentice players to the first team.

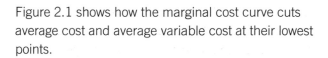

DEFINITION

Long run: the period of time when it is possible to alter all factors of production

Table 2.1 shows how the different types of costs change, or in one case stay constant, as output changes.

Total costs again rise with output in this time period. There are thought to be a number of possible shapes of a firm's long-run average cost curve. Figure 2.2 shows three possibilities: a) shows a

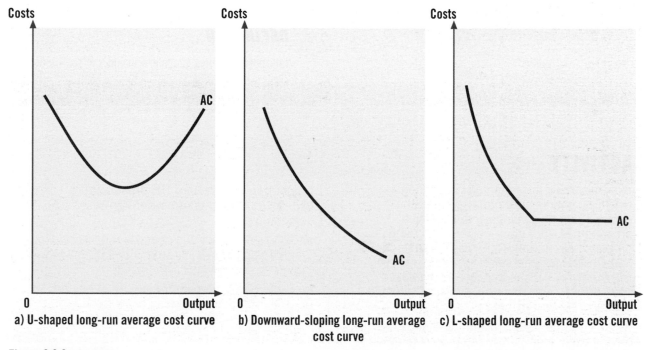

a) U-shaped long-run average cost curve

b) Downward-sloping long-run average cost curve

c) L-shaped long-run average cost curve

Figure 2.2 Cost curves

firm experiencing **economies of scale** and then **diseconomies of scale**; b) illustrates a firm enjoying economies of scale over a high range of output; while c) shows a firm reaching the **minimum efficient scale** of production and then experiencing **constant returns to scale**.

DEFINITIONS

Economy of scale: a reduction in long-run average costs resulting from an increase in the scale of production

Diseconomy of scale: an increase in long-run average costs caused by an increase in the scale of production

Minimum efficient scale: the lowest level of output at which full advantage can be taken of economies of scale

Constant returns to scale: long-run average cost remaining unchanged when the scale of production increases

STEPPING UP TO A2

Economies and diseconomies of scale explain how firms' costs are influenced in the long run by changes in the scale of production of firms and industries.

Economies and diseconomies of scale

Economies of scale are benefits in the form of lower long-run average costs that result from an increase in the scale of production. These benefits may arise from the growth of the firm or the industry. Diseconomies of scale, in contrast, are the disadvantages that occur if the scale of production of the firm or industry becomes too large.

INTERNAL ECONOMIES OF SCALE

Internal economies of scale are the cost benefits a firm gains when it grows in size. For example, a cinema operator may achieve a number of benefits from growing in size:

DEFINITION

Internal economies of scale: economies of scale that occur within the firm as a result of its growth

ACTIVITY ···›

With advances in technology, including smaller cameras and digital editing, the average cost of making some television programmes, including quizzes and reality programmes, is falling. In contrast, the cost of making dramas and some other programmes is increasing. This is because of increased competition from more channels for talented actors, stars and writers.

As well as making programmes themselves or buying them from UK independent television production companies, UK broadcasters can buy programmes from foreign television companies.

a) What impact are the changes in the costs of producing television programmes likely to be having on television schedules?

b) Explain what impact the ability to buy foreign television programmes is likely to have on the cost of producing UK programmes.

● *Purchasing economies of scale*. When firms buy in bulk they often pay less per unit purchased. A large cinema operator may be able to negotiate more favourable terms with a film distributor to hire films than a small operator and may receive a discount on purchases of large quantities of popcorn, sweets and soft drinks.

● *Selling economies*. A larger firm can make fuller use of sales and distribution facilities than a small one. It does not cost twice as much to use an HGV that is twice the size of a lorry. They can also advertise in a more cost efficient way. A large cinema operator that takes out a half-page advertisement in a local newspaper pays less than twice what a smaller operator for a quarter-page advertisement will do.

● *Technical economies of scale*. Large firms can afford to use expensive, high tech equipment and use it efficiently. A small cinema operator is unlikely to find it financially viable to operate a multiplex.

● *Managerial economies of scale*. As a firm grows in size, it becomes possible and beneficial to employ specialists. Accountants are among the specialist workers employed by large cinema operators. In contrast, a small-scale cinema operator with just one screen may only have the owner and one or two other employees. In such a case, the three people will have to perform a range of tasks.

● *Financial economies of scale*. Large firms usually find it easier and cheaper to raise finance than small firms. Banks are more willing to lend to large, well-known firms such as Vue and often charge a lower rate of interest per pound lent than that charged to small cinema operators. Large firms are also more likely to find willing buyers of their shares as their names may be well known.

● *Risk-bearing economies*. As a firm's output rises, it can produce a greater range of products. Diversifying the product range reduces the chance of experiencing a loss, should one of the products prove to be unpopular. A cinema operator running a number of multiplexes is unlikely to be seriously affected if one of the films it is showing fails to attract a large audience. In contrast, a one-screen operator may go out of business if a film it has scheduled to show for a number of weeks does not attract viewers.

EXTERNAL ECONOMIES OF SCALE

External economies of scale are savings in costs available to firms arising from the growth of the industry as a whole. The rise in UK tourism has resulted in a number of benefits that are open to any firms in the industry, irrespective of their size. The large size of the UK tourism industry has led to colleges and universities running courses in travel and tourism. Such courses help in the training of the staff of tour operators and travel agents.

A travel agent or tour operator may be able to take advantage of a pool of skilled and trained labour if it moves close to other firms in the same industry. Another external economy is the development of ancillary industries. For instance, some firms specialise in travel insurance.

A large industry can also allow firms to specialise in particular sectors of the market. For instance, a tour operator may specialise in holidays to South America.

Two other examples of external economies of scale are the development of a good reputation and improved infrastructure. If a country or an area builds up a reputation for producing a good quality product, all the firms in the industry can benefit from this. The growth of an industry can also encourage a government, and in some cases the private sector, to improve infrastructure that services the industry. For instance, one of the reasons for the expansion of UK airports has been the growth of the tourism industry.

INTERNAL DISECONOMIES OF SCALE

Internal diseconomies of scale can occur if a firm grows too large in size. One of the main challenges

DEFINITIONS

External economies of scale: economies of scale that result from the growth of an industry and benefit firms within the industry

Internal diseconomies of scale: diseconomies of scale experienced by a firm caused by its growth

that can arise when a firm becomes large is management control. It can be difficult to run a large firm, keeping a check on everything that is happening and co-ordinating production. Large size, with a number of tiers of management, can increase the time it takes senior managers to take decisions and so can make the firm slower to respond to changes in market conditions. Industrial relations can also worsen as a firm grows. This is because there are more people between whom there can be disputes and because it may take longer to resolve any concerns workers have as they may have to go through a number of channels.

EXTERNAL DISECONOMIES OF SCALE

If an industry grows too large, it may result in higher average costs for its constituent firms. This upward pressure is most likely to occur if the firms are concentrated in the same area. Among the causes

DEFINITION

External diseconomies of scale: diseconomies of scale resulting from the growth of the industry, affecting firms within the industry

of **external diseconomies of scale** are increased competition for resources, which drives up their price, and higher levels of pollution and traffic congestion.

In Figure 2.3 external diseconomies of scale would shift the average cost curve up from AC to AC_1. In contrast, external economies of scale would shift the AC curves down from AC_1 to AC. Average cost curve AC_1 also indicates the ranges of output over which economies of scale and diseconomies of scale are experienced.

learning tip In explaining economies of scale, it is useful to give examples relating to particular industries.

The nature of firms' revenues

Firms sell goods and services in return for revenue. The total payment a firm receives is not surprisingly called total revenue (TR). While total cost is expected to rise with output, total revenue may not always move in the same direction as sales.

A cinema operator, for instance, may increase the ticket prices but may earn more revenue if demand is inelastic. Similarly, a premiership football club may lower the price of tickets to a match against an

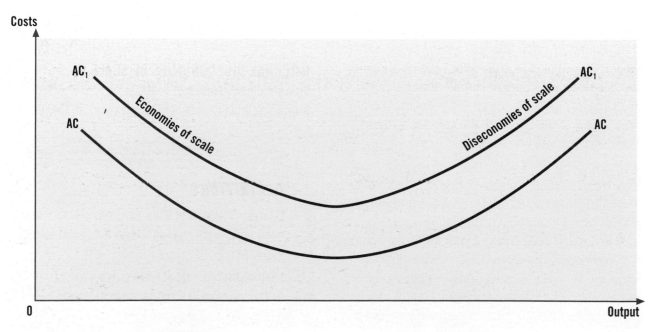

Figure 2.3 Economies and diseconomies of scale

unfashionable club. It may sell more tickets but its total revenue will fall if demand is inelastic.

In deciding whether to sell more or less of a product, firms take into account **marginal revenue** (MR). This is the change in total revenue resulting from selling one more or one less of a product. **Average revenue** (AR) is total revenue divided by output sold and is the same as price. Table 2.2 shows the average, total and marginal revenues for a firm.

such a case, the firm is said to be a **price taker**. Its output and sales are not affecting price. Such a firm would be operating in a very competitive market with many rival firms selling identical products. Under conditions of so-called '**perfect competition**', a firm cannot raise the price it charges, since consumers will just switch to its rivals, and it cannot lower price as price will have been driven down to the lowest possible viable level.

In practice, however, the vast majority of firms, including those in the leisure industry, do not operate

DEFINITIONS

Average revenue: total revenue divided by the output sold

Marginal revenue: the change in total revenue resulting from the sale of one more unit

DEFINITIONS

Perfect competition: a market structure with many buyers and sellers, free entry and exit and an identical product

Price taker: a firm that has no influence on price

Table 2.2 shows what is actually an unusual case as the price does not fall with the quantity sold. In

Output sold (units)	Average revenue	Total revenue	Marginal revenue
0	0	0	0
			10
1	10	10	
			10
2	10	20	
			10
3	10	30	
			10
4	10	40	
			10
5	10	50	
			10
6	10	60	
			10
7	10	70	

Table 2.2 A firm's average, total and marginal revenues (£)

under conditions of perfect competition. They have some degree of market power. Their output and sales influence price. They are **price makers** and in order to sell more, they have to lower price. Table 2.3 shows the revenues for such a firm.

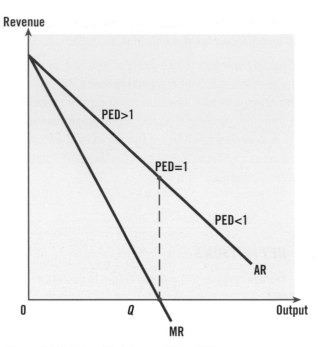

Figure 2.4 Relationship between AR and MR

> **DEFINITION**
>
> **Price maker:** a firm that influences price when it changes its output

This table shows that total revenue is maximised where marginal revenue is zero. Average revenue and marginal revenue start at the same point, but then marginal revenue is below average revenue. It is marginal revenue that reduces average revenue. Figure 2.4 shows this relationship in diagrammatic form.

The table also shows that at first, when MR is positive, demand is elastic – reductions in price are leading to higher total revenue. When total revenue does not change and MR is zero, there is **unit elasticity of demand**. Demand becomes inelastic

Output sold (units)	Average revenue	Total revenue	Marginal revenue	PED
0	0	0	0	
			20	elastic
1	20	20		
			16	elastic
2	18	36		
			12	elastic
3	16	48		
			8	elastic
4	14	56		
			4	elastic
5	12	60		
			0	unit elasticity
6	10	60		
			– 4	inelastic
7	8	56		

Table 2.3 Average, total and marginal revenues of a firm with market power (£ and price elasticity of demand, PED)

when MR is negative. Figure 2.4 also shows this relationship in diagrammatic form.

> **DEFINITION**
>
> **Unit elasticity of demand:** when a given percentage change in price causes an equal percentage change in demand, leaving total revenue unchanged

> **learning tip**
>
> ## STEPPING UP TO A2
>
> The marginal concept is very important in economics. This is because many economic decisions are based on whether to increase or decrease something.

INFLUENCES ON REVENUE

The more market power a firm has, the more any change in its output will influence price. Whether such a change in price results in a rise in total revenue will, as we have seen, be determined by price elasticity of demand.

Average and total revenue will increase if, for any reason, demand increases. A successful advertising campaign, for example, which attracts more customers, will raise revenue.

A firm operating under conditions of monopoly or oligopoly may seek to raise its revenue in the longer term by driving a competitor or competitors out of business through **predatory pricing**. A tour operator, for instance, may lower price to drive out its rivals if it believes it has lower costs or thinks it can sustain losses for a longer period of time.

Changes in income can affect revenue. Most leisure products have income elastic demand. A 2005 Spanish study found that the cultural services of cinema, theatre and other shows were very sensitive to changes in income. It estimated an income

elasticity of demand of 1.75, meaning that this group of cultural products is both a normal and a **superior good**. Demand for holiday travel also has a positive income elasticity of demand with demand for luxury, foreign holidays being particularly income elastic.

Changes in the price of related products also affect a firm's revenue. A rise in the price of car and public transport, for instance, may reduce demand for cinema tickets and tickets to county cricket matches. In these cases, transport is a complement to a leisure product. A new car may be a substitute for a foreign holiday and a film on subscription television may be a substitute for seeing the film at the cinema.

Among the other factors that may influence demand, and hence revenue, are weather and special events. A period of bad weather in the UK, for example, may increase television viewing and the number of foreign holidays bought but may reduce attendance at some sports events. A good performance of the Scottish football team at the World Cup would be expected to raise attendance at Scottish league games.

> **DEFINITIONS**
>
> **Predatory pricing:** setting price low with the aim of forcing rivals out of the market
>
> **Superior good:** a good with positive income elasticity of demand greater than one

> **learning tip**
>
> ## STEPPING UP TO A2
>
> Understanding the characteristics, behaviour and performance of different market structures is a key part of the A level course and it is an area you will need to spend some time on.

Market structures

The structure of a market describes the level of competition in a market. Economists make predictions about the behaviour and performance of firms according to which market structure they are thought to fit into.

The three market structures that describe the level of competition that applies in the vast majority of markets are monopoly, oligopoly and monopolistic competition.

Care, however, has to be taken in terms of how a market is defined. The more broadly a market is defined in terms of products or geographical coverage, the greater the level of competition there is likely to be. There is, for instance, more competition in the leisure industry as a whole than in the cinema industry. There is also more competition in the global holiday market than in the national holiday market.

In deciding in which market structure firms operate, economists examine a number of key indicators. One is, as noted at the end of the previous chapter, the market concentration ratio. Economists also look at whether there are barriers to entry and exit, the type of profits earned in the long run and the behaviour and performance of firms.

BARRIERS TO ENTRY AND EXIT

A **barrier to entry** is an obstacle that makes it difficult for a firm that is currently not producing the product to start making it. The barrier that stopped other firms broadcasting during the period of the BBC's monopoly was a legal one – the law stopped them. A patent also uses the force of law, keeping an invention the property of the inventor for a number of years.

Other barriers that prevent new firms entering a market include high start-up costs, brand names, economies of scale and **limit pricing**. If expensive capital equipment is needed to operate in the industry, potential entrants may have difficulty raising the finance and may be concerned about the risks involved. Brand names may have helped to build up brand loyalty with consumers being reluctant to try new brands. Economies of scale, as we have seen, can allow large firms to enjoy low costs of production.

This will mean that new entrants operating on a smaller scale will find it hard to compete. The entry of new firms may also be actively discouraged by a monopolist or oligopolists. They may deliberately lower their prices to make it difficult for any entrants to cover their costs, which are likely to be relatively high.

As well as barriers to entry, there may also be **barriers to exit.** Three main barriers to exit are:

● *sunk costs*. These are costs involved in building or buying assets, such as a Formula 1 racetrack, that cannot be recovered by selling or using in another market should the firm leave the industry.

● *advertising expenditure*. Spending on a large, long-term advertising plan would be wasted should a firm exit the market.

● *contracts*. A firm may be legally obliged to supply a product for a period of time.

Awareness of barriers to exit act as a barrier to entry, since firms will be discouraged from entering a market if they know there are costs in leaving it.

DEFINITIONS

Barriers to entry: obstacles to new firms entering a market

Barriers to exit: obstacles to firms leaving a market

Sunk costs: costs incurred by a firm that it cannot recover should it leave the market

Limit pricing: setting a price low to discourage the entry of new firms into the market

MONOPOLY

As noted in Chapter 1, the BBC had a monopoly of television broadcasting in the UK from 1932 to 1955. This was what was known as a pure monopoly. In such a market there are significant barriers to entry

The BBC kept its monopoly until 1955

financial sense, as it would add more to total cost than total revenue.

Figure 2.6 includes not only the marginal cost and marginal revenue curves of a monopolist but also its average revenue and average cost curves. The figure shows that the firm makes **supernormal profit**. Such a profit arises when the revenue a firm receives is greater than the costs it incurs. **Normal profit** is the price of enterprise and is included in the costs of production. It is the minimum necessary to keep the firm in the industry in the long run. The existence of barriers to entry and exit enable a

and exit. In the case of a pure monopoly, the firm *is* the industry, the product is unique and the firm is a price maker.

A private sector monopolist is likely to want to make as much profit as possible. Economists refer to this objective as **profit maximisation**. Profits are maximised where marginal revenue equals marginal cost. In Figure 2.5 this would be an output of Q_1.

A firm's profit will continue to rise when the addition to total revenue is greater than the addition to total cost. Output Q_1 would give more profit than output Q. Up to Q_1, raising output is adding more to revenue than cost. Producing more than Q_1 would not make

DEFINITIONS

Profit maximisation: achieving the highest possible profit where marginal cost equals marginal revenue

Supernormal profit: profit earned where average revenue exceeds average cost

Normal profit: the level of profit needed to keep a firm in the market in the long run

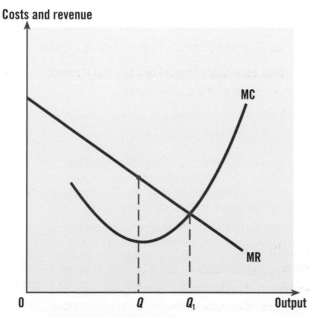

Figure 2.5 Profit-maximising output

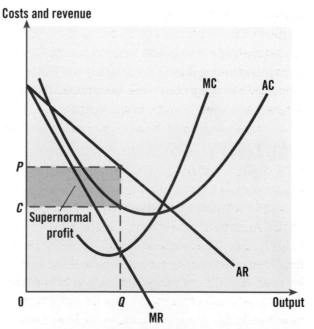

Figure 2.6 Output of a profit-maximising monopolist

monopolist to protect any supernormal profits in the long run.

In some markets, it can be more efficient to have just one firm. This occurs when there is what is called a **natural monopoly**. This is a situation where one firm can supply the market at a lower cost than two or more firms due to the existence of economies of scale and the avoidance of wasteful duplication.

> **DEFINITIONS**
>
> **Natural monopoly:** a market where long-run average costs are lowest when output is produced by one firm
>
> **Legal monopoly:** a market where a firm has a share of 25 per cent or more
>
> **Dominant monopoly:** a market where a firm has a 40 per cent or more share

As well as a pure monopoly, economists and regulators also refer to a **legal monopoly** and a **dominant monopoly**. The former refers to a firm that has a market share of 25 per cent or more and the latter to a firm with a 40 per cent or more share.

OLIGOPOLY

An **oligopoly** is a market with a high three- to five-firm market concentration ratio, as such a market structure is dominated by a few large firms. There

> **DEFINITION**
>
> **Oligopoly:** a market structure dominated by a few large firms

are high barriers to entry and exit that allow firms to earn supernormal profits in the long run. The product is usually differentiated – that is, made to seem different from products made by competitors – and firms are price makers. Two other key features of this market structure are that firms are interdependent and that there is a high level of non-price competition. In making its decisions on price, launching an advertising campaign and other matters, a firm considers the reaction of its rivals and constantly watches what its rivals are doing. Firms often seek to attract customers by ways other than charging a lower price.

Analysing the behaviour of firms operating under conditions of oligopoly is a relatively complex process. This is because the firms may adopt a variety of strategies. One is to cut price in a bid to gain a larger share of the market. Such a move is likely to provoke a price war, with rival firms matching each other's price reductions. Price wars have broken out in the holiday travel market and other markets on a number of occasions.

Price cutting, though, is not a popular strategy as it is high risk and often does not bring long-term benefits. The disadvantages of altering price are emphasised

ACTIVITY ···:

On 18 April 2008, a Twenty20 cricket competition started. Called the Indian Premier League (IPL), it was created by the Board of Control of Cricket in India (BCCI). A consortium consisting of India's Sony Entertainment Television network and Singapore-based World Sport group secured the global broadcasting rights of the IPL. The deal will pay the BCCI a record US$1bn over ten years. This is enabling the BCCI to pay cricket stars in excess of £50,000 per season.

To counter the IPL, Sir Allan Stamford, a billionaire banker from Texas, has offered to put up £5m for England to play five Twenty20 games against his West Indies all-star side.

a) If another Indian cricket organisation wants to start up a professional Twenty20 cricket competition, identify two barriers to entry it would face.

b) Explain three factors that could cause an increase in attendance at cricket matches.

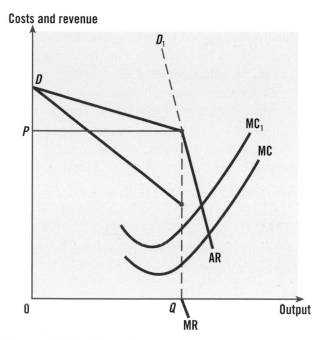

Figure 2.7 Kinked demand curve

in the **kinked demand curve** diagram as illustrated in Figure 2.7.

Above the current price of P, the firm expects its demand curve to be relatively elastic. This is because it is likely to think that its rivals will not follow any price rise it initiates, and so choosing to raise price will lose it a significant number of sales. Below the current price, demand is relatively inelastic, as the firm anticipates that its rivals will match any price cuts so that a lower price will not result in many more sales.

The kinked demand curve suggests that price rigidity is likely to exist in an oligopoly and that firms are likely to put more reliance on non-price competition than on price competition. This non-price competition takes a variety of forms including large-scale advertising, competitions, free gifts and brand names.

The kink in the demand (AR) curve also means that the MR curve has a discontinuity at an output of Q.

This is because one demand (AR) curve takes over from another and so the MR curve changes. In turn, this means that a small change in marginal cost does not alter the profit maximising output. In this case a rise in marginal cost from MC to MC_1 leaves output unchanged at Q.

Firms may also seek to reduce the risks of a price war by colluding with rivals. Formal collusion involves firms forming a **cartel**. In such a situation the firms produce separately but sell at one agreed price. They are, in effect, acting as a monopoly. Cartels are illegal in most countries, including the UK, but nevertheless some firms take the risk. Such collusion is more likely to be successful if the firms have similar costs and if the cartel includes all the major firms in the industry. In practice, as members of a cartel have an incentive to cheat, such formal collusion tends to break down over time. Tacit collusion is more common than formal collusion. Tacit collusion usually takes the form of price leadership. This involves firms following the price strategy of one firm. This firm may be the dominant firm in the market, the firm with the most experience in setting price or a barometric firm – the firm most sensitive to changes in market conditions.

One theory that is used to examine the behaviour of oligopolists is **game theory**. This is a theory that was developed by John von Neumann in 1937 and later refined by a number of economists and mathematicians including John Nash (the subject of the movie *A Beautiful Mind*). It seeks to analyse the behaviour of competitors that lack full information and also take into account the actions and reactions of rivals. It can be used to identify a range of decisions facing oligopolists and their possible outcomes. For example, an oligopolist deciding whether to cut the price of a product or launch a

DEFINITION

Kinked demand curve: a demand curve made up of two parts; it suggests oligopolists follow each others' price reductions, but not price rises

DEFINITIONS

Cartel: a group of firms that produce separately but sell at one agreed price

Game theory: a theory of how decision makers are influenced by the actions and reactions of others

John Nash – economist and mathematician

new product will consider what will happen if all of its major rivals do the same, if they do not do the same and if only one or two rivals follow suit.

> **learning tip**
> Remember that there can be any number of firms in an oligopolistic market. What determines whether the market is oligopolistic or not is the degree of dominance of the largest firms.

MONOPOLISTIC COMPETITION

This market structure has a relatively high degree of competition between firms each of which produces a product that is similar but slightly different from that of its rivals. It is characterised by a large number of small firms, easy entry and exit, product differentiation and non-price competition. As each product is slightly different, each firm faces a downward-sloping demand curve and is a price maker.

The lack of barriers to entry and exit means that normal profit is earned in the long run as shown in Figure 2.8. In the short run, if market demand increases, the **incumbent firms** will earn supernormal profit. Firms outside the market will be attracted by these high profits to enter the market. Their entry will cause the market supply curve to shift to the right, driving down price until normal profit is earned again.

Monopolistically competitive firms seek to increase consumer loyalty by making their products as distinctive as possible. This may be through small-scale advertising, after-sales service, better location of outlets and improved quality.

> **DEFINITIONS**
>
> **Monopolistic competition:** a market structure in which there is a large number of small firms selling a similar product
>
> **Incumbent firms:** firms already in the market

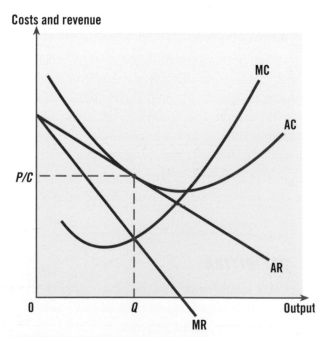

Figure 2.8 Long-run output of a firm producing under conditions of monopolistic competition

Resource allocation and efficiency in different market structures

There is some debate about how the level of competition and the nature of that competition influence resource allocation and efficiency. Traditionally, a monopoly has been seen as inefficient. Check back to Figure 2.6. It shows price being set above the marginal cost – output is below and price is above the allocatively efficient levels. The diagram shows that the firm is not productively efficient as average cost is not minimised. A monopolist may also fail to provide the quality of product consumers desire. In addition, a monopoly may not achieve **dynamic efficiency**, as the lack of competition may mean that it does not spend much on research and development and does not innovate.

> **DEFINITION**
>
> **Dynamic efficiency:** efficiency in terms of developing and introducing new production techniques and new products

Where economies of scale are significant, however, prices may be lower under conditions of both monopoly and oligopoly than under a more competitive market structure. In addition, monopolies and oligopolies may innovate. This is because, due to the ability to earn supernormal profits in the long run, they are likely to have significant funds to undertake research and development, and to develop new products and methods. They may also consider that the existence of barriers to entry and exit will enable them to protect any supernormal profit they make from introducing new products and methods. The theory of creative destruction also suggests that the existence of barriers will encourage firms outside the market to develop superior products and methods, since doing so may enable them to overcome the barriers.

A lack of competitive pressure, however, may mean that even when economies of scale are significant, they may be outweighed by **X inefficiency**. Figure 2.9 shows X inefficiency with actual average cost being greater than attainable average cost.

> **DEFINITION**
>
> **X inefficiency:** the difference between actual costs and attainable costs

Figure 2.9 X inefficiency

When there is not the pressure to keep average costs low, there may be what is sometimes called organisational slack. This can take a number of forms, including over-manning, managers taking long lunches and awarding themselves high pay rises, and not constantly reviewing the most cost effective sources of supplies.

ACTIVITY ⋯⋮➤

There continues to be a debate about whether it is justifiable that the BBC is funded by a licence fee. Some commercial broadcasters have complained that this gives the BBC an unfair advantage and creates a market distortion and allocative inefficiency. They argue that they have to make their programmes even more attractive than the BBC's in order to offset the disutility they may experience from viewers having to watch adverts and/or the payment viewers have to make.

There is also the argument that the licence fee system is becoming out of date. It is essentially a tax on television owners, but an increasing number of people are downloading programmes on their laptops using BBC iPlayer and in the future more people may decide not to own a television.

a) Explain one argument in favour of the BBC being financed by the licence fee.

b) Do viewers necessarily experience disutility from watching adverts?

STRETCH AND CHALLENGE

c) Discuss whether the licence fee creates allocative inefficiency.

ECONOMICS IN CONTEXT

THE FUTURE OF PUBLIC SERVICE BROADCASTING

Public service broadcasting is high-quality programming designed to cater for all groups, develop a well-informed citizenship, promote cultural interests and make people aware of and tolerant of other communities. Examples of public service programmes include news programmes, regional programmes, high-class documentaries, children's programmes and programmes catering for ethnic minorities.

In 2008, Ofcom (Office of Communications, the industry regulator) published proposals on the future of public service broadcasting. This report was stimulated largely by two factors. One was concern that declining viewer numbers and advertising and consequently declining revenue might mean that ITV, Channel 4 and Channel 5 might not be able to provide public service content. The other factor was a desire to increase competition in the public service area. It proposed four ways in which public service broadcasting may develop:

● let the current trend continue, resulting in declining commercial public service content
● remove all public service obligations from ITV, Channel 4 and Channel 5
● only the BBC and Channel 4 to retain a public service remit

● make additional funding available to any commercial company that wants to make public service programming.

The last two proposals would involve the need for more money. Ofcom identified four possible sources for this:

● provide direct public funding
● use some of the BBC's licence fee to fund public service broadcasting on Channel 4
● allow commercial companies to charge more for adverts
● impose a tax on the industry.

As well as by Ofcom's proposals, the future of public service broadcasting and, indeed, broadcasting in general, will be influenced by whether the UK adopts the EU's audiovisual media service Directive. The Directive emphasises that audiovisual media services are important for society, democracy, education and cultural diversity. It seeks to create a level playing field between traditional television-based broadcasts and online broadcasts, by applying the same regulations to both. In addition, it sets a target for all channels to invest in and broadcast more than 50 per cent of home-grown drama, documentary and film.

Look back to Figure 2.8. It shows that a firm producing under conditions of monopolistic competition fails to achieve allocative efficiency. It restricts output in order to maximise profit and so under-produces the product. The diagram also shows that the firm is not productively efficient and is operating with excess capacity. Indeed, monopolistic competition is criticised on the grounds that there are too many firms producing too low an output at relatively high prices and wasting resources. A greater output could be produced at a lower cost by fewer firms.

It is thought, however, that consumers gain from the existence of choice of sellers and product differentiation. Many consumers like differences in products. In a bid to differentiate their products and gain a competitive edge, firms may also innovate and so raise the quality of their products and possibly reduce their prices.

STEPPING UP TO A2

Contestability is a relatively sophisticated concept that provides an insight into firms' behaviour.

A contestable market

As well as classifying markets according to the level of actual competition, it is also possible to classify them according to the level of potential competition. In 1982, William Baumol developed the theory of **contestable markets**. This theory stresses that what determines how firms behave and their efficiency

DEFINITION

Contestable market: a market in which there are no barriers to entry and exit and the costs facing incumbent and new firms are equal

is not actual but potential competition. A market may have a high concentration ratio but still face competitive pressure.

A perfectly contestable market is one which has no barriers to entry and exit, in which new firms into the industry have the same costs as, and have access to the same type of technology as that available to, incumbent firms, and in which there is no brand loyalty.

Not only are there no actual barriers to entry in a perfectly contestable market, there are no potential barriers. The existing firm or firms would not engage in limit pricing to discourage the entry of new firms.

There may be only one firm in the industry, but if the market is contestable, the threat of competition should ensure that the firm is efficient and earns only normal profit in the long run. With the absence of barriers to either entry or exit, firms will enter the market if supernormal profits are made. They may come in, reap the benefits and then leave the industry. This is referred to as **hit-and-run competition**. Such a tendency means that the market is very responsive to changes in consumer demand.

DEFINITION

Hit-and-run competition: firms quickly entering a market when there are supernormal profits and leaving it when the profits disappear

A contestable market should benefit consumers by being both productively and allocatively efficient. The incumbent firm or firms will seek to keep costs as low as possible and will not raise price above marginal cost, for fear of attracting new firms into the industry. In practice, a market is unlikely to be perfectly contestable. The degree of contestability can vary and a market can become more or less contestable over time.

The importance of barriers to entry and exit

Barriers to entry and exit determine the level of competition and contestability in a market. The lower the barriers, the more contestable and potentially competitive a market is. If it is easy for firms to enter and leave a market, supply will adjust quickly and smoothly in line with changes in consumer demand. There will be pressure on the incumbent firms to keep their costs low and profit will stay at the normal level in the long run.

Over time barriers can change, and with them the nature of the market. With the rise in start-up costs for Formula 1 teams, it could be argued that the market is becoming less contestable. In constructing and maintaining barriers, resources may be wasted. There may be excessive advertising expenditure, the taking out of patents just to prevent rivals being able to produce the products or use the methods, and there may be excess capacity. High expenditure on advertising would mean that any potential entrants may be put off by the need to match such spending. Patents may also discourage new firms from entering a market, since they will know that they cannot produce products to the same design for some time. In addition, they may be dissuaded by the awareness of the incumbent firm's or firms' excess capacity, since such capacity would enable the incumbent firms to raise output and lower price should they enter the market.

Behaviour of firms in leisure markets

The behaviour of firms in leisure markets is influenced by both their structure and contestability.

High costs make Formula 1 less contestable

Figure 1.7 at the end of Chapter 1 showed that the market share enjoyed by the four largest cinema operators is relatively high, particularly in terms of ownership of screens. There is a relatively high number of small cinema operators, but as well as being dominated by a few large firms, the market has a number of other characteristics of an oligopoly. There are barriers to entry. One is the relationship that incumbent cinema operators have with film distributors. This may make it difficult for entrants to get 'first run' films. There may also be some degree of brand loyalty.

Cinema operators do engage in non-price competition. They compete for the best sites, advertise the films they are showing, offer a different range of films and provide a different range of additional facilities, such as car parking in the case of multiplexes. Cinema operators can also earn high profits in the long run.

Figure 1.8 at the end of Chapter 1 indicates that tour operators are also in an oligopolistic market. Mergers between tour operators have made the market more concentrated and increased the power of the largest companies. The travel agent market may still be regarded as exhibiting many of the features of monopolistic competition. It is not very difficult to set up a travel agency. There is a relatively high number of high street travel agents which tend to work below full capacity, offer slightly different holiday packages and engage in small-scale advertising.

As previously mentioned, television broadcasting started off as a monopoly. It then moved to oligopoly with BBC1, BBC2, ITV and Channel 4 dominating the market and engaging in non-price competition. There were also at this time occasions on which the television companies colluded over scheduling. Now, with the reduction in barriers to entry and developments in technology, there is an increasing number of channels and ways of delivering programmes. This is moving the market towards monopolistic competition and making it more contestable. These trends are increasing competitive pressure in the industry with, for instance, television companies bidding fiercely for the rights to major sports events and reducing the profits of the commercial channels.

The market for independent television production is moving in the opposite direction. In 1990, quotas were introduced requiring at least 25 per cent of BBC and ITV programmes to be made by outside, independent television production companies. When Channel 4 was launched in 1982, it was given a mandate to commission everything from independents. Both these measures made the television production market more contestable. A relatively high number of new independent television production companies were set up. In more recent years, however, the larger independent television companies have bought up smaller ones. In 2008, the top five independent television production companies, including All3Media, accounted for 43 per cent of the output of the sector. The profits of these dominant companies have been increased both by the growth in their market share and by the 2003 Communications Act, which gave the independents the rights to the programmes they make. Before this Act, the rights had belonged to the broadcasters. To increase profits in the light of moves by the television broadcasting companies to increase their in-house production, the large independent television production companies are currently trying to increase their exports sales.

It is not always straightforward to assess the market structure in the case of spectator sports. For instance, Manchester United might be regarded as a monopoly, in the sense that its product may be seen as unique. It might, however, be regarded as an oligopolist. There are four major premiership clubs that dominate the Premier League. These are the ones that qualify for Europe and gain a high share of advertising sponsorship and television revenue. There are a number of barriers to entry into the top rank of the premiership. An owner or owners starting a football club from scratch would have to spend a considerable amount of money building a stadium to the necessary standard, buying and paying good-quality players and recruiting a strong manager. There would also be a time delay before the club entered the leagues and progressed to the premiership, if indeed it was successful. Other barriers to entry include brand loyalty and the need to obtain planning permission to build a stadium.

Athletics has fewer barriers to entry

In terms of becoming a professional sports person, it is easier to enter some sports than others in the UK. For instance, most children can build up their skills in football and athletics at school and it is usually possible to join a club for free where further training can be received. Given sufficient skill and dedication, a person from almost any type of background has a chance of becoming a professional athlete and a professional football player. It is more difficult to become a professional golfer or tennis player in England and Wales. This is because not many state schools provide the opportunity for their students to play these sports. There is a limited number of municipal golf courses or tennis courts. Membership of private clubs is relatively expensive, as is private tuition.

learning tip

If you are asked whether a market is a monopoly, oligopoly or monopolistically competitive, remember that in practice not all the characteristics of that market may fit one market structure. Decide on the basis of which market structure most of its characteristics fit, paying particular attention to the market concentration ratio, if available. Acknowledge any features that do not fit and explain any other information it would be useful to have to make your decision.

Try to keep up to date with developments in leisure markets, as the level of competition and contestability can vary over time.

ACTIVITY ⋯⋙

In Australia there are three major cinema operators, Greater Union, Hoyts and Village, which account for more than half of all the screens in the country and 70 per cent of national box office takings. There are a few medium-sized operators and many small operators. There are a higher number of film distributors in the country, some domestically owned and some foreign owned. They usually charge cinema operators a percentage of ticket sales revenue that varies over time. For instance, a distributor may charge 60 per cent of takings in the first week when the crowds are likely to be highest, 50 per cent the next week and perhaps 20 per cent five weeks later.

a) From the information in the passage, explain what type of market structure best describes the Australian cinema industry.

b) Identify two other pieces of information it would be useful to have in deciding on the type of market structure.

c) Explain one reason why film distributors may vary their charges over time.

STRETCH AND CHALLENGE

d) There has recently been some merger activity among Australian distributors. Discuss the impact this may have on the amount film distributors charge cinema operators.

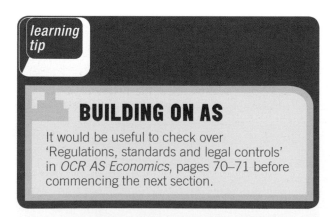

learning tip

BUILDING ON AS

It would be useful to check over 'Regulations, standards and legal controls' in *OCR AS Economics*, pages 70–71 before commencing the next section.

Regulation

Regulation involves rules, administered by a government agency or another body. These rules are designed to influence barriers to entry and exit, the prices charged, product standards and how the product is sold. In the case of government regulations, the regulations are backed up by law and operated by a government agency. These regulations are designed to correct market failure arising from the abuse of market power, lack of information, under-consumption of merit goods and other causes.

The British Board of Film Classification, for instance, is the UK's independent regulator of the film and video industry. In the past, its main role was to censor films – in effect, treating parts of films as demerit goods. Now its main function is to classify films into various categories. These include U (universal, suitable for all but children under three) and 18 (suitable for those aged 18 and over). In this role, it is seeking to overcome information failure.

Ofcom is the independent regulator for the UK communications industry, including television and radio broadcasting. It has been given a statutory duty to further the interests of consumers by promoting competition and protecting them from harmful or offensive material, both in terms of programmes and advertising. One of its tasks is to examine specific complaints by viewers of television programmes and listeners to radio programmes.

UK travel agents and tour operators are regulated by the trade organisation, ABTA (the Association of British Travel Agents). This covers firms responsible for the sale of over 80 per cent of package holidays and nearly half of independent travel arrangements. Members have to adhere to ABTA's own code of conduct. One of its main aims is 'to ensure that the public receive the best possible service from members'. ABTA sets out specific guidelines in its code on a range of activities, including advertising, sale and provision of services. If a member is found to have breached the code, it can be fined and/or expelled from ABTA. The association increases consumers' confidence in its members and seeks to protect their interests.

Spectator sports are regulated by governing bodies. For instance, UK Athletics oversees the sport and is responsible for developing and implementing the rules and regulations of the sport. It randomly tests for performance-enhancing and other illegal drugs.

This is both for health reasons and to ensure fair competition. Cricket is governed by the England and Wales Cricket Board (ECB), which is responsible for the direction of cricket in the country. The Football Association (FA) is the governing body of football in England and is responsible for changes in the rules of the game. All professional football clubs are members of the FA.

A number of sports are governed by both national and international bodies. The International Amateur Athletics Federation (IAAF) is the world athletics governing body and the International Cricket Council (ICC) runs world cricket. The Fédération Internationale de Football Association (FIFA) is the body responsible for the organisation and governance of football's major international tournaments.

The Royal and Ancient Golf Club of Saint Andrews is responsible for the administration of the rules of golf and the development of the game both in the UK and Europe, Africa, Asia Pacific and the Americas (outside the USA and Mexico).

The leisure industry, as with other UK industries, is also influenced by the work of the Office of Fair Trading (OFT). The OFT is a government body that enforces consumer protection and competition law. It seeks to ensure that markets work in a competitive way. This involves checking that firms do not abuse any market power they have and do not engage in anti-competitive practices. If the OFT is concerned about the behaviour of a firm or firms in an industry, it can ask the Competition Commission to carry out an investigation. In April 2008, for instance, a Competition Commission report argued that British Airports Authority (BAA) was not being responsive to airline customers. It also found that 'BAA's common ownership of seven airports in the UK may not be serving well the interests of either airlines or passengers'.

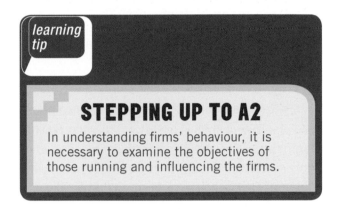

learning tip

STEPPING UP TO A2

In understanding firms' behaviour, it is necessary to examine the objectives of those running and influencing the firms.

The objectives of firms

The objective or objectives that a firm follows are influenced by a number of factors, including the type of organisation it is, and the priorities of the managers and/or owners.

ACTIVITY ⋯⋯

In 2007, Ofcom fined three television companies over rigged phone-ins and viewer quizzes. The BBC was fined £50,000 after it was found that a *Blue Peter* production assistant had posed as a member of the public. Channel 4's *Richard and Judy* show received a £150,000 fine for making shortlists of potential winners before phone lines closed, preventing subsequent entrants from having a chance of winning. The breakfast television company GMTV received an even heavier fine, indeed, the biggest fine Ofcom had ever imposed, of £2.7m, for the same offence, one which cost viewers even more in wasted phone calls.

These fines and the adverse publicity surrounding them led to a significant decline in the number of premium rate phone-ins and quizzes.

In 2008, Ofcom proposed new broadcasting rules to ensure that programmes that invite viewers and listeners to ring or text in are not simply designed to raise revenue. Under the Ofcom proposals, channels will have to ensure that the main aim of the programme is not to generate call revenues.

a) Identify two reasons why television programmes run phone-ins and quizzes.

b) Explain two reasons why television programmes reduced the number of phone-ins and viewer quizzes.

c) Analyse why regulation of television phone-ins and quizzes is necessary.

The long-standing mission of the BBC is 'to inform, educate and entertain'. Recently, a more detailed mission statement has been developed, which emphasises the duty of providing a public service. The BBC's charter breaks down this overriding duty into six parts:

● to sustain citizenship and civil society

● to promote education and learning

● to stimulate creativity and cultural excellence

● to represent the UK, its nations, regions and communities

● to bring the UK to the world and the world to the UK

● to take a leading role in the digital switchover.

In contrast to the BBC, it is often assumed that the main objective of firms in the private sector is profit maximisation. The idea of profit maximisation as a prime objective, however, has come in for two main criticisms. One is that, in practice, it can be difficult to calculate marginal cost and marginal revenue and that firms often use a more straightforward approach to pricing, such as adding a given percentage to costs. The other main criticism is that in public limited companies, often found in oligopolistic markets, there is a separation of ownership and control. The owners, that is, the shareholders, are likely to want as high a profit as possible. The managers, however, may have other objectives.

One alternative objective is **sales revenue maximisation**. This is because managers' salaries are more often linked to the growth of sales than to profit performance. High and expanding sales can also help to attract external finance and may result in greater economies of scale. To maximise sales revenue, a firm would continue to produce more as long as extra output would increase revenue. In theory, therefore, it would produce where MR is zero.

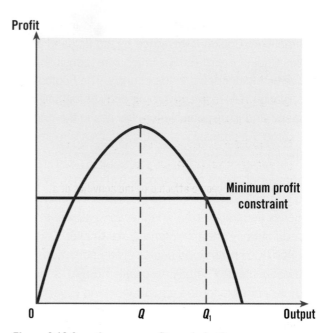

Figure 2.10 Growth versus profit maximisation

In practice, however, this objective is usually subject to a minimum profit constraint, based on the level needed to keep shareholders content.

A linked objective to sales revenue maximisation is growth. Managers may want the size of their firms, in terms of resources, to increase. This is because the manager of a growing company employing 20,000 workers is likely to earn more, have higher status and increased career prospects than a manager of a company employing 2,000 workers. A manager, content in the job, may also feel more secure as the company grows. This is because once a firm reaches a certain size it becomes difficult for another firm to take it over. As with the sales revenue objective, it is thought that the growth objective is also subject to a minimum profit constraint. Figure 2.10 shows that the profit maximising output would be Q, while the **growth maximisation** output would be Q_1.

With imperfect information and conflicting objectives, it may be more realistic to aim for a satisfactory level of profit than a maximum level. **Profit satisficing** can also allow a firm to pursue a number of objectives. A firm consists of groups of **stakeholders**, including owners, managers, workers and creditors. While owners may want high profits, accountants may want the firm to cut costs, managers of the marketing department may want to run an advertising campaign

DEFINITION

Sales revenue maximisation: the objective of achieving as high a total revenue as possible

DEFINITIONS

Growth maximisation: the objective of increasing the size of the firm as much as possible

Profit satisficing: aiming for a satisfactory level of profit rather than the highest level of profit possible

Stakeholders: people affected by the activities of a firm

and workers may want an improvement in staff facilities. While cutting costs may raise profits, the other two objectives may conflict with profit maximisation in the short term. Being prepared to sacrifice some profit, however, may enable a firm to achieve a satisfactory performance in more areas.

At times, a firm's main objective may just be survival. When a firm enters a new market or, for instance, a football club joins a higher league, it is likely to face a challenging environment. It will have to adjust quickly to the new situation and seek to ensure that it can continue to operate. A firm may also experience difficulties due to a rise in costs of production or a fall in demand. If a firm believes that the situation will improve, it may strive to continue in the industry.

Although some of the alternative objectives may appear to conflict with profit maximisation, this may only be a short-term conflict. In the long run, they may be compatible with profit maximisation. For instance, high profits provide finance for growth.

One objective that may conflict in the longer term with profit maximisation is **utility maximisation**. Someone owning a firm, even in the private sector,

DEFINITION

Utility maximisation: the aim of trying to achieve as much satisfaction as possible

may be doing so because of the satisfaction they gain rather than the profit they can earn. This motive is thought to apply in the case of a number of sports clubs. For instance, the owner or owners of a football club in Football League Division 2 may get pleasure

ECONOMICS IN CONTEXT

THE DIFFERING MOTIVES OF UK AND US SPORTS TEAMS

A number of UK cricket, football and rugby clubs make losses and are supported by donations from wealthy owners and from supporters clubs. In contrast, most US baseball, basket and American football teams make a profit.

It is thought that most owners of US professional teams are profit maximisers. In most cases, US teams are local monopolies with permanent league status and with the knowledge that US leagues will not permit another league member to locate within the team's area. This market power increases US teams' ability to earn supernormal profits. The willingness of owners to relocate their teams to cities that do not have a team, if they believe greater profit can be earned there, supports the view that they are motivated mainly by profit.

In contrast, it is thought that the owners of a number of UK sports clubs see their clubs not as businesses but as a consumption activity from which they derive satisfaction. For instance, the owner of a football club may identify his or her priority to be winning games, even if this means paying very high wages to attract the top players. The manager may also think that his salary, and future job prospects, will be more closely linked to the performance of the team than to the profitability of the club.

There are some signs, however, that the owners of UK football clubs in particular are changing from utility maximisers to profit maximisers. One reason for this is that clubs such as Manchester United, Real Madrid and Barcelona have shown that there is the potential to earn high profits in what is becoming a global sports market. Another reason is that more football clubs are becoming public limited companies. Shareholders have yet to receive high dividends but they may put more pressure on the club to aim for maximum profit.

from being involved in the club but is unlikely to expect to make a profit. The owners of some golf clubs and tennis clubs, however, appear to be more profit orientated. Even in these cases, it could be argued that they do not seek to make as high a profit as possible. The evidence for this is the long waiting lists to join a number of clubs. This suggests that the clubs could earn more profit by charging higher fees.

3 Labour demand, supply and wage determination

On completion of this chapter, you should be able to:

- explain what is meant by the derived demand for labour in terms of marginal revenue product
- explain the derivation of the supply curve of labour, both in the short and long run
- discuss the usefulness of supply-side concepts, including net advantages and pecuniary and non-pecuniary benefits
- understand what is meant by elasticities of demand for, and supply of, labour and explain the factors that determine both
- analyse how wage rates are determined in theory in a competitive labour market
- evaluate the usefulness and relevance of the above model of wage determinants with reference to contemporary, real-world labour markets
- define the terms transfer earnings and economic rent and explain their application to labour market situations.

The previous chapter examined the influences on firms' behaviour and performance in different market conditions and in different leisure markets. This chapter focuses on labour markets and what determines wages and employment in these markets.

Derived demand

As with the demand for all the factors of production, demand for labour is a **derived demand**. Factors of production are not wanted for their own sake but for

DEFINITION

Derived demand: demand for one item depending on the demand for another item

ACTIVITY ····⋗

In the first quarter of 2008, the UK housing market experienced a downturn. House prices fell and house-building firms started to slow down their rate of construction on existing sites and delay the start of new schemes, particularly in parts of the Midlands and the North of England.

a) Explain what you think is most likely to have happened to the employment of plasterers and bricklayers in this period.

STRETCH AND CHALLENGE

b) Discuss why the employment of plasterers and bricklayers might not have changed in the way expected in a).

what they can produce and what that output can be sold for. So, the number of workers a firm wishes to employ depends principally on the revenue that can be earned from what is produced. If demand rises or the price of the products made increases, a firm will usually seek to employ more workers.

THE AGGREGATE DEMAND FOR LABOUR

The aggregate demand for labour is also a derived demand. It depends crucially on the level of economic activity. If the economy is growing and firms are optimistic that it will continue to grow in the future, employment is likely to be rising. In contrast, if output is declining and firms are pessimistic about the future, employment is likely to be falling. Employment may also decrease even if the economy is growing, if it is growing at a slower rate than the trend growth rate. With advances in technology and improvements in education and training, firms may be able to match higher aggregate demand with the existing number of workers or possibly even fewer workers.

A FIRM'S DEMAND FOR LABOUR

How many workers, or working hours, a firm seeks to employ is influenced by a number of factors. These include:

● *demand* and expected future demand for the products produced and the revenue that can be earned from the output. As just mentioned, this is the key influence.

● *productivity*. The higher the output per worker hour, the more attractive labour is as a resource.

● *wage rate*. A rise in the wage rate above any rise in labour productivity will raise unit labour costs and is likely to result in a contraction in demand.

● *complementary labour costs*. As already noted, as well as wages, firms incur other costs when they employ labour. So, for example, if national insurance contributions rise, demand for labour is likely to fall.

● *the price of other factors of production* that can be substitutes for or complements to labour. If, for instance, capital becomes cheaper and is a substitute to labour, firms may seek to replace some of the workers by machines.

learning tip

STEPPING UP TO A2

Marginal revenue product is a new concept at the A2 level. It will help you to explore the key determinant of demand for labour in more depth.

MARGINAL REVENUE PRODUCT

Marginal productivity theory suggests that the demand for any factor of production depends on its marginal revenue productivity. According to this theory, the quantity of any factor of production employed will be determined where the marginal cost of employing one more unit equals the **marginal revenue product** (MRP) of that factor.

The MRP of labour is the change in a firm's revenue resulting from employing one more worker. It is found by multiplying marginal product (MP) by marginal revenue (MR). The **marginal product of labour** (MPL) is the change in total output that results from employing one more worker. As more workers are employed, so MPL may increase. Once a certain level of employment is reached, however, MPL may fall as diminishing returns set in.

DEFINITIONS

Marginal revenue product (MRP): the change in a firm's revenue resulting from employing one more worker

Marginal product of labour (MPL): the change in output that results from employing one more worker

In a perfectly competitive market, MR will equal price and will be constant, whereas under conditions of monopolistic competition, oligopoly and monopoly,

Number of workers	Total output	Marginal product	Marginal revenue (£)	Marginal revenue product (£)	Total revenue (£)
1	20	20	× 20	= 400	400
2	80	60	× 20	= 1,200	1,600
3	160	80	× 20	= 1,600	3,200
4	220	60	× 20	= 1,200	4,400
5	260	40	× 20	= 800	5,200
6	280	20	× 20	= 400	5,600

Table 3.1 Marginal revenue product

MR falls with output. Table 3.1 shows how MRP is calculated in a perfectly competitive market.

If the wage rate is constant at £800, the firm will employ five workers, since this is where the marginal cost of labour (MCL) equals MRP. At this level of employment, the total cost of workers will be 5 x £800 = £4,000. This level of employment is the one where the gap between total revenue and the total cost of labour is greatest, i.e. £5,200 less £4,000 = £1,200.

Figure 3.1 shows the MRP curve and a MCL curve based on a constant wage rate.

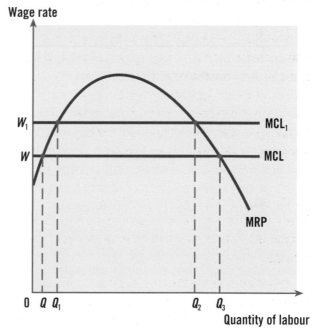

Figure 3.2 Level of employment

The MRP curve is shown as a downward-sloping curve or line. This is because if MRP equals MCL at two points, the higher output is chosen.

In the case of Figure 3.2, a firm will employ Q_3 amount of labour at a wage rate of W (not Q) and Q_2 quantity at a wage rate of W_1 (not Q_1). The MRP and demand curve for labour will shift out to the right if the MPL and/or MR increase. For example, the demand for electricians will increase if the productivity of electricians rises, perhaps due to increased training, and/or if the price of their services rises due to, for example, a switch from gas to electrical appliances. This increase in MRP is illustrated in Figure 3.3.

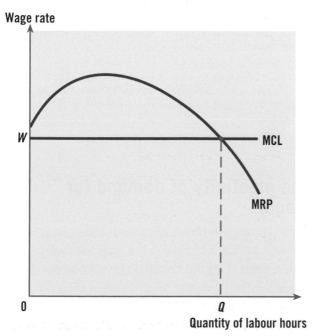

Figure 3.1 Interaction of marginal revenue product and marginal cost of labour

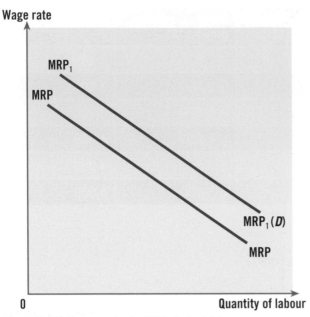

Figure 3.3 An increase in the MRP of electricians

In practice, it can be difficult to measure MRP. This is because it is often difficult to isolate the contribution one worker makes to changes in output. Workers often work in teams, employment frequently changes by more than one worker and it can be difficult to separate out the contribution made by labour and capital.

In addition, it is difficult to measure the MP of some workers in the tertiary sector. For example, is a doctor who operates on 20 people in a day with varicose veins more productive than another doctor who carries out one multiple organ transplant? Do you think a teacher who teaches five high-ability students who all gain an A grade at A level economics is more productive than one who teaches 20 mixed-ability students, only two of whom gain an A grade?

learning tip

STEPPING UP TO A2

The important point to remember about MRP theory is that it emphasises that demand for labour depends on what that labour can produce and what it can be sold for.

ACTIVITY ···•

A firm sells its product for £15 and this price does not alter with the quantity sold. It pays a wage rate of £300 a week that does not alter with the level of employment. Table 3.2 shows the total output produced with a differing number of workers.

No. of workers	Total output
1	8
2	20
3	40
4	55
5	65
6	72

Table 3.2 Total output

a) Calculate the number of workers the firm should employ according to MRP theory.

b) If the wage was to halve, how many more workers would the firm employ?

BUILDING ON AS

Before considering the section on the elasticity of demand for labour, it would be useful to re-familiarise yourself with the concept of price elasticity of demand – see pages 42–44 of *OCR AS Economics*. Here you have to apply the concept to the labour market in some detail.

The elasticity of demand for labour

While a change in MP or MR will shift the demand curve for labour, a change in the wage rate will cause a movement along the demand curve for labour. The extent to which demand will contract or extend as a result of a change in the wage rate is measured by the elasticity of demand for labour. This elasticity is also sometimes referred to as the wage elasticity of demand. The formula is:

$$\text{Elasticity of demand for labour} = \frac{\% \text{ change in the quantity of labour demanded}}{\% \text{ change in wage rate}}$$

If employers are relatively sensitive to a change in the wage rate, demand will be elastic. This means that a change in the wage rate will cause a larger percentage change in the quantity of labour demanded.

There are a number of factors that influence the elasticity of demand for labour. These include:

● *the price elasticity of demand for the product produced.* If demand for the product is inelastic, the demand for the labour that produces it is also likely to be inelastic. This is because the rise in the price of the product that will result from the rise in the wage rate will cause a smaller percentage fall in demand for the product. So, as output will not change by much, employment will not fall significantly.

● *the proportion of wage costs in the total costs.* If wages account for a significant proportion of total costs (as in labour-intensive industries), demand will be elastic. The reason is because a change in the wage rate will have a large impact on total costs. If the wage rate falls, total costs will fall by a noticeable amount and demand for labour will rise by a greater percentage.

● *the ease with which labour can be substituted by other factors.* If it is easy to substitute capital for labour, demand for labour will be elastic. A rise in the wage rate will cause workers to be replaced by machines. Demand for labour will fall by a greater percentage than the rise in the wage rate.

● *the elasticity of supply of complementary factors.* If wages fall and it is easy to obtain more of the factors that are used alongside labour, demand for labour will be elastic.

● *the time period.* Demand for labour is more elastic in the long run when there is more time for firms to reorganise their production methods.

Figure 3.4 shows elastic demand for labour. The rise in the wage rate from W to W_1 causes a greater percentage fall in demand for labour.

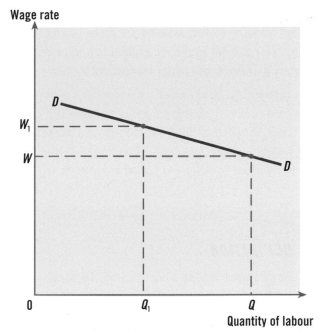

Figure 3.4 Elastic demand for labour

DEGREES OF ELASTICITY OF DEMAND FOR LABOUR

The more **flexible** a country's **labour market** is, the more elastic demand for labour will be. Recent estimates have put the USA's elasticity of demand for labour at −1.0, meaning that a 5 per cent rise in the wage rate would reduce employment by 5 per cent. It has been found that two-thirds of the change in employment is due to firms changing their output and one-third due to the substitution of capital and labour.

Demand for labour in capital-intensive industries, for example the chemical industry, tends to be inelastic. This is because labour forms a small percentage of the industries' total costs. In contrast, demand for labour in labour-intensive industries, such as building, is usually elastic. In such industries a rise in the wage rate would be likely to have a significant impact on the demand for labour, due to its effect on costs of production, price and demand for the product.

The elasticity of demand for labour tends to be higher for young than adult workers and for unskilled than for skilled workers. A fall in the wage rate may persuade a firm to take on young, inexperienced workers. A rise in the wage rate is more likely to

53

encourage firms to get rid of unskilled rather than skilled workers. Skilled workers are more productive, more likely to have long-term contracts and more difficult to replace by capital equipment.

The demand for all unskilled workers is not always, however, elastic. This is because not all low-skill jobs can be automated or filled by unemployed workers. For instance, even demand for catering staff may be relatively inelastic if there is full employment.

> **DEFINITION**
>
> **Flexible labour market:** a labour market that adjusts quickly and smoothly to changes in the demand for and supply of labour

THE SIGNIFICANCE OF ELASTICITY OF DEMAND FOR LABOUR

Elasticity of demand for labour influences a union's bargaining strength. A union has more bargaining strength when it is representing labour that is in inelastic demand. It will know that it can push for higher wages without endangering the employment of its members to any great extent.

A government, in considering the effects of raising a minimum wage or providing employment subsidies,

> **learning tip**
>
> ## STEPPING UP TO A2
>
> The backward-sloping labour supply curve and the income and substitution effects that it is based on are concepts that are likely to be new to you. Take care to learn the difference between the two effects and consider how these work when the wage rate falls.

will take account of the elasticity of demand. Altering a minimum wage will affect mainly unskilled workers. If demand for such workers is elastic, there is a risk that an increase in the minimum wage will have a noticeable effect on employment. Employment subsidies may be used to encourage firms to take on unskilled workers. This time, the wage elastic demand for such labour would be likely to have a beneficial effect on employment.

The short-run supply curve of labour

In the short run, there may be insufficient time for individuals to change occupation. In this time period, a key influence on the supply of labour is changes in the wage rate on offer. It is thought that, at low wages, a rise in the wage rate will cause an extension in the supply of labour, with a worker being encouraged to work more hours. After a certain wage is reached, however, the offer of a higher wage rate may cause a worker to choose to work fewer hours. S/he may decide a given income level is sufficient to meet her/his financial requirements and may be keen to have more leisure time in which to enjoy her/his earnings. For example, a worker may currently work 40 hours at £30 per hour. This gives a gross income of £1,200 per week. A rise in the wage rate to £40 would enable the worker to earn the same amount by working 30 hours, giving 10 hours more leisure time. This change in response to an increase in the wage rate gives rise to a **backward-sloping labour supply curve**, as illustrated in Figure 3.5. Up to the wage rate of £30, the supply of labour extends, but any rise above £30 causes supply to contract.

> **DEFINITION**
>
> **Backward-sloping labour supply curve:** A labour supply curve showing the *substitution effect* dominating at low wages and the *income effect* dominating at high wages

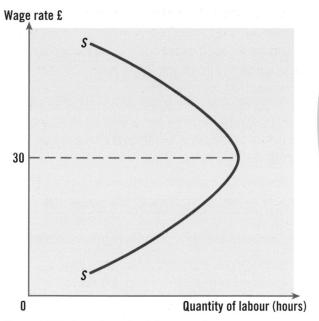

Figure 3.5 Backward-sloping labour supply curve

The behaviour of the worker can be explained by the income and substitution effects. The **income effect of a wage rise** is to reduce the number of hours people work. This is because, as the wage rate rises, the worker buys more of most goods and services, including leisure. In contrast, the **substitution effect of a wage rise** is to increase the number of hours worked. A higher wage rate increases the return from working and increases the opportunity cost of leisure, so the worker selects to work more hours.

At a low wage rate, it is thought that the substitution effect is likely to outweigh the income effect. The workers will work more hours in order to raise their material living standard. However, once the wage rate has reached a certain level, in this case £30 an hour, the income effect may outweigh the substitution effect. The worker is now able to buy more leisure time.

The income and substitution effects emphasise that the number of hours the worker decides to work is influenced by the number of hours on offer and the relative importance that the worker attaches to income and leisure.

Of course, many workers are unable to alter the number of hours they work in their main jobs. They are contracted to work, for instance, 35 hours a week and are not offered the opportunity to vary these hours. With increasing flexibility in labour markets, however, more workers are now being provided with a choice as to how many hours they work.

ACTIVITY ····⋮►

Workaholics Anonymous, which was set up in 1983 in New York, now has a number of branches in the UK. Its members meet to talk about why they feel the need to overwork, the problems that this causes them and the strategies that can be used to achieve a better work/leisure balance. They are encouraged, for instance, to consider responding to an offer of higher pay by working fewer and not more hours.

Studies have shown that working long hours on a regular basis leads people to neglect their families, relationships and health. This neglect and stress, in turn, leads to marriage break-ups, heart attacks and mental health problems. Overworking can also reduce productivity – sometimes to such an extent that a worker produces less in, for example, a 45-hour week than in a 35-hour week.

a) From the passage, identify:

  i) two private costs of overworking

  ii) one external cost of overworking.

b) Explain whether Workaholics Anonymous seeks to promote the income effect or the substitution effect of a wage rise.

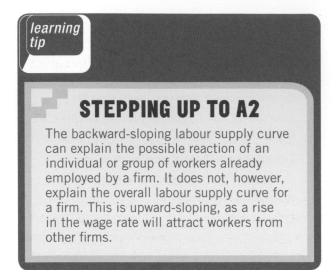

The long-run supply curve of labour

In the long run, there is time for people to change their occupations. In this time period, the supply of labour to a given firm or occupation is influenced by the net advantages of the job. These include both the pecuniary (financial) and non-pecuniary features of the job.

PECUNIARY FACTORS

The pecuniary factors include the wage rate, the opportunity to work overtime and the possibility of bonuses. The higher the wage rate, the more people are likely to want to do the job. For example, a relatively high number of people seek to become accountants because of the high wages on offer. People who are keen to raise their incomes by working extra hours at higher rates or by being highly productive will be attracted to firms and occupations offering overtime work and bonuses.

NON-PECUNIARY FACTORS

There is a wide range of non-pecuniary advantages and disadvantages of jobs that impact on the supply of labour. These include:

- *the convenience and flexibility of hours.* Long and unsociable working hours are likely to discourage potential workers. Nursing homes find it difficult to recruit night-time nursing staff. In contrast, flexibility of hours persuades some people to work as supply teachers.

- *status.* The high status achieved by pilots, for example, makes it an attractive job.

- *promotion chances.* Some people are prepared to work initially for relatively low wages, for example in the media, in the hope that they will progress on to high-paid jobs.

- *flexibility of location.* It is becoming increasingly possible in certain occupations, such as architects and designers, to work at least some days from home. This increases the attractiveness of the occupations.

- *qualifications and skills.* The higher the qualifications and skills required, the fewer the number of people who are able to undertake the occupation. While the supply of sales assistants, for example, is relatively high, the supply of barristers is relatively low.

- *job security.* The more secure a job is, the more attractive it is likely to be. For example, university professors enjoy a relatively high degree of job security.

- *pleasantness of the job.* Everything else being equal, more workers will be attracted to more pleasant jobs. It might be expected that the supply of sewage workers, for example, would be relatively low as it is not a particularly pleasant job. However, the unpleasantness is more than offset by the low level of qualifications required. Some of the sewage workers may not be particularly keen to work in the occupation but they may not have the qualifications to switch to alternative jobs.

- *holidays.* Long holidays are likely to attract workers. Some people may be encouraged to become teachers because of the relatively long holidays on offer.

- *perks and fringe benefits.* Company cars, paid trips abroad, profit-sharing schemes, free private health care, and good company pension schemes are likely to make a given occupation more attractive. For example, pilots receive a number of benefits, including very cheap flights for their families, generous pension schemes and the opportunity to retire early.

- *the quantity and quality of training on offer.* Workers are likely to be attracted to firms that provide good training.

- *location.* Some people like to work close to home. This cuts down on the cost of and time taken travelling.

- *the recent performance of the firm/occupation.* Workers are likely to want to work for firms that are doing well and expanding and in occupations that are in increasing demand. This factor is linked to the previous influences, as an expanding firm and an occupation growing in demand may be expected to offer higher wages, more training, greater promotion chances and more job security than static or declining firms and occupations.

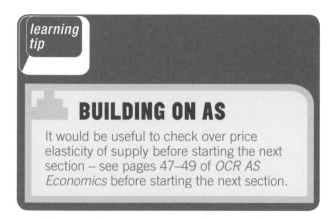

learning tip

BUILDING ON AS

It would be useful to check over price elasticity of supply before starting the next section – see pages 47–49 of *OCR AS Economics* before starting the next section.

The elasticity of supply of labour

As already noted, the wage rate on offer is a key influence on the supply of labour. The extent to which the supply of labour changes as a result of a change in the wage rate is measured by the **elasticity of supply of labour**. The formula is:

Elasticity of supply of labour =
% change in the quantity of labour supplied
—————————————————————
% change in wage rate

DEFINITION

Elasticity of supply of labour: the responsiveness of the supply of labour to a change in the wage rate

The factors that influence the elasticity of supply of labour are:

- *the qualifications and skills required.* The supply of skilled workers is more inelastic than the supply of unskilled workers, as there are fewer skilled than unskilled workers. For example, the supply of vets is more inelastic than the supply of pet shop assistants.

- *the length of training.* A long period of training may discourage some people from undertaking the occupation. It will also mean that it will take some time before people are qualified to do the job even if the wage rate rises. In addition, should the wage rate fall, people who are a long way into their training may not leave the job.

- *the immobility of labour.* The easier workers find it to switch jobs (occupational mobility) and the easier they find it to move from one area to another (geographical mobility), the more elastic the supply will be.

- *the time period.* As with demand, supply will be more elastic the longer the time period involved. A rise in the wage rate of barristers, for example, may not have much effect on the supply of barristers in the short run. In the long run, however, it will adjust, as more students will be encouraged to study law and undertake the necessary training.

Barristers require a long period of training

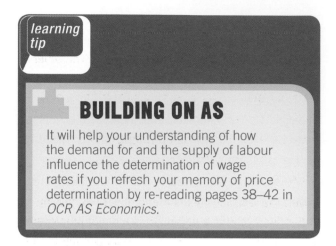

BUILDING ON AS

It will help your understanding of how the demand for and the supply of labour influence the determination of wage rates if you refresh your memory of price determination by re-reading pages 38–42 in *OCR AS Economics*.

Wage determination

In a competitive labour market, the demand for and the supply of labour play the key roles in determining wage rates.

Wages are likely to be high when demand is high and inelastic and supply is low and inelastic. In contrast,

Demand for brain surgeons is inelastic

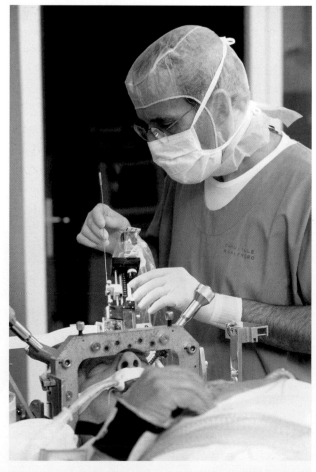

wages are likely to be low where supply is high relative to demand and both demand and supply are elastic.

For example, brain surgeons are paid considerably more than waiters and waitresses. The supply of brain surgeons is low relative to demand. It is limited by the long period of training involved and the high qualifications required to start that training. These features also make supply inelastic. A rise in the wage rate will not attract many new brain surgeons in the short run. Demand is also inelastic as brain surgeons are a vital part of an operating team and there is no viable substitute. The MRP of brain surgeons is high. Private sector medicine shows that the services of brain surgeons can be sold for a high price. Figure 3.6 shows the market for brain surgeons.

In contrast, the supply of waiters and waitresses is high and elastic. The job requires no qualifications and the minimum of training. So there is a large number of people capable of doing the job and a rise in the wage rate may attract an extension in supply. The marginal revenue productivity of waiters and waitresses is also low and so demand is low. Figure 3.7 shows the market for the labour of waiters and waitresses.

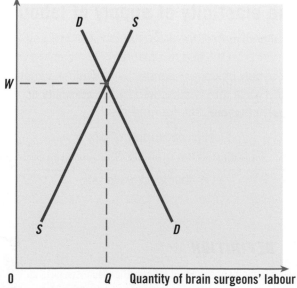

Figure 3.6 Market for brain surgeons

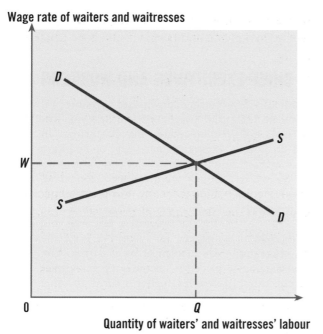

Wage rate of waiters and waitresses

Quantity of waiters' and waitresses' labour

Figure 3.7 Market for waiters and waitresses

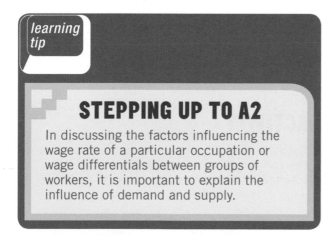

learning tip

STEPPING UP TO A2

In discussing the factors influencing the wage rate of a particular occupation or wage differentials between groups of workers, it is important to explain the influence of demand and supply.

OTHER INFLUENCES ON WAGE DETERMINATION

In practice, demand and supply are not the only influences on the wage of many workers. The other influences include the relative bargaining power of employers and workers, government policy and public opinion.

Wages are likely to be higher when workers have strong bargaining power relative to their employers.

Government policy affects wage rates both directly and indirectly. The government is a major employer, it passes legislation that affects the bargaining power of workers and employers (trade union reform) and directly affects wage rates (the National Minimum Wage).

Attitudes towards 'what people deserve to be paid' influence wages via the amounts that workers ask for and employers offer. Public opinion tends to value sacrifice in the form of being prepared to undergo long periods of training and study. It also tends to value more highly certain groups over other groups. In many societies, work dominated by white, middle-class males is held in higher esteem than work undertaken mainly by lower class females and people from ethnic minorities.

OTHER INFLUENCES ON THE MARKETS FOR BRAIN SURGEONS AND WAITERS/WAITRESSES

As well as the market forces of demand and supply discussed under 'Wage determination' above, other

ACTIVITY ·····

The expansion of university education has reduced the value of some degrees, according to a 2008 study from the Institute of Education. The average university leaver in 2008 could expect to earn £160,000 more over the course of their lifetime than those who enter the job market with just A levels. Those with an arts degree, however, were earning the same as those who had only A level qualifications. The graduates in medicine could expect the highest earning premium at £340,315 compared with only £51,549 for those taking degrees in geography.

a) Explain why 'the expansion of university education has reduced the value of some degrees.'

b) Why do students undertake geography degrees even though the return is relatively low?

STRETCH AND CHALLENGE

c) Should universities set tuition fees according to how much a degree subject is valued by employers?

ECONOMICS IN CONTEXT

THE WIDENING PAY DIFFERENTIAL BETWEEN CHIEF EXECUTIVES AND WORKERS

In both the USA and the UK, the pay gap between company chief executives and workers is widening. In 2006, the USA's highest earner was Terry Semel, the chairman and chief executive of Yahoo at the time, who received $71.1m in pay. In the UK, the highest earner was Sir Martin Sorrell of WPP, who received £17m.

The pay gap between chief executives and their employees is growing at a more rapid rate in the USA. In 2006, the average

US chief executive earned 179 times more than the average US worker. In the same year, UK chief executives earned 98 times as much as the average worker. This contrasts with 1986 when UK chief executives earned only 25 times as much as the average worker.

Two main factors are thought to be contributing to this widening pay gap. One is globalisation. The increased competition from low-wage economies is

putting downward pressure on the wages of workers in low value-added manufacturing. In contrast, increased competition for the services of chief executives from multinational companies throughout the world is pushing up their pay. It is also considered that the growth in takeovers and mergers, by increasing both the size of companies and their share prices, is encouraging companies to offer higher returns to chief executives.

---

influences affect the pay of brain surgeons and waiters and waitresses:

● *relative bargaining strength*. Most brain surgeons are members of the British Medical Association (BMA), a strong professional organisation. The Association has large funds and has built up a close relationship with government health ministers. Any industrial action it may take would have significant consequences and brain surgeons cannot be replaced by capital equipment or other types of doctors. By contrast, waiters and waitresses have low bargaining power. Very few belong to a trade union and they can usually be replaced by unemployed workers.

● *government policy*. An ageing population, advances in technology and increasing expectations of the quality of life have increased public spending on health care and increased demand for brain surgeons. The government pays a high salary to brain surgeons who work for the NHS. Government policy also influences the pay of a number of waiters and waitresses who receive the National Minimum Wage.

● *public opinion*. Surgeons are held in high public esteem. They are perceived as providing a vital service, of having undergone a long period of training and of being well qualified and highly skilled. Most of the top surgeons are still male and middle class,

whereas a high proportion of the people who serve at tables are female, a significant proportion are also from ethnic minorities and recently from eastern Europe.

ACTIVITY ····⋮·▸

Teachers in Turkey earn considerably more than the average wage in the country. In contrast, teachers in Norway earn less than the average wage in their country.

a) Explain two possible reasons why Turkish teachers are relatively well paid.

STRETCH AND CHALLENGE

b) Discuss whether Norwegian teachers will migrate to Turkey.

Wage differentials

Wage differentials are differences in wages such as that between brain surgeons and waiters and waitresses. Wage differentials occur between occupations, industries, firms, regions and within these categories.

As we have seen, differences in wages can be explained by differences in demand and supply, bargaining power, the impact of government policy and public opinion.

Over time, wage differentials between groups can widen or narrow. For example, the differential between the pay of Premier League football players and that of League Division 2 players has widened in the last two decades. This is largely because of the increased revenue that the top clubs have been able to earn from television coverage contracts and merchandise sales.

ACTIVITY ····⦂

Occupation	£
Chief executives	148,998
Consultants	82,246
Lawyers	55,157
Bank managers	49,508
Accountants	49,240
IT professionals	41,833
Police officers	37,001
Teachers	34,597
Nurses	26,753
Librarians	25,556
Clergy	21,895
Hairdressers	17,821
All occupations	30,504

Table 3.3 Gross average earnings per annum, 2007

a) What was the earning differential between lawyers and hairdressers in 2007?

b) Explain two factors that occupations receiving above-average earnings have in common.

STRETCH AND CHALLENGE

c) Discuss why lawyers are paid more than hairdressers.

WAGE DIFFERENTIALS BETWEEN PARTICULAR GROUPS

Skilled and unskilled workers

Skilled workers are paid more than unskilled workers principally because the demand for skilled workers is higher and their supply is often less. The MRP of skilled labour is high because the skills possessed by the workers will lead to high output per worker. It is also often more difficult to substitute skilled labour with machines and unemployed workers than is the case with unskilled workers.

Skilled workers usually have a high level of **human capital**. Investing in human capital by providing education and training raises the productivity of labour and so increases workers' earnings potential. A 2004 study by the University of Ottawa found that a 1 per cent rise in literacy scores relative to the international average is associated with an eventual 2.5 per cent relative rise in labour productivity and a 1.5 per cent rise in GDP per head. It also found that reducing the number of people with very low skills had more of an impact on average productivity than increasing the number with the highest skills.

DEFINITION

Human capital: the skills, knowledge and experience that workers possess

Male and female workers

Despite equal pay legislation, men are still paid more than women. When comparing weekly pay, part of the explanation lies in the fact that more women work part-time than men. However, even when hourly pay rates are compared, men still earn more than women, although the gap is narrowing. In 1976, when the Equal Pay Act was introduced, the gender pay gap was 29 per cent. Between 1997 and 2006, the pay gap fell further from 17.4 to 12.6 per cent.

There are a number of reasons why women still earn less than men. One is that, on average, the MRP of women is lower than that of men. In the past, a

ECONOMICS IN CONTEXT

POSITIVE DISCRIMINATION

Not all discrimination is negative and not all starts with employers. Most customers of Chinese restaurants like to think the restaurants are serving 'genuine' Chinese food. This preference leads them to be attracted to restaurants with waiters and waitresses of Chinese ethnicity. They will be under the impression that the restaurants have Chinese owners and chefs.

In practice, some Chinese restaurants are owned by people from other ethnic origins and the chefs are not necessarily Chinese. Knowing people's desire for authentic Chinese food leads owners of Chinese restaurants to favour workers of Chinese origin in those jobs visible to the customers. They may be prepared to hire a Portuguese-born chef and a UK-

Positive discrimination in restaurants

born accountant, for example, but are likely to discriminate in favour of Chinese serving staff.

---

relatively important reason was that men were better qualified than women. This is now changing, with more women than men studying at UK universities. However, the MRP of women remains below that of men because women are disproportionately concentrated in low-paid occupations that generate low marginal revenue. These occupations include care work, catering and cleaning.

Some women lose out on promotion chances because of leaving the labour market at crucial times in order to bear and raise children. Another factor that still exists is discrimination, with some employers undervaluing the services of female workers.

Part-time and full-time workers

Part-time workers, on average, receive lower hourly earnings than full-time employees. Again, there are a number of reasons that explain this differential. One is that the supply of people wanting to work part-time is high relative to the demand. Part-time work is convenient for people bringing up children, pursuing university studies and other interests and careers.

Part-time workers are also less likely to receive training, both on and off the job, than full-time workers, so their productivity tends to be lower. In addition, a smaller proportion of part-time workers belong to trade unions and a higher proportion are women.

Ethnic minorities

As noted in Chapter 1, people from ethnic minorities tend to be lower paid than white workers. One particular group that receives low pay is workers of Bangladeshi origin. This is due, in part, to a high proportion of Bangladeshis working in the catering industry. Another reason is that the qualifications of Bangladeshis, particularly Bangladeshi women, are currently below those of the rest of the population. A third reason is discrimination.

learning tip

STEPPING UP TO A2

Economic rent and transfer earnings are important but relatively straightforward concepts.

Economic rent and transfer earnings

As well as receiving different wages, the nature of the wages that different groups of workers receive varies.

Transfer earnings are what a worker could earn in her/his best paid alternative employment – the opportunity cost of performing the current job. They are equivalent to the minimum amount that has to be paid to ensure that the worker stays in her/his present job.

Economic rent is the surplus over transfer earnings and so is total earnings minus transfer earnings. For example, a woman may earn £800 a week as an optician. If the best paid alternative job she is willing and able to do is as an advertising executive earning £620 a week, her economic rent is £180 and her transfer earnings are £620.

DEFINITIONS

Economic rent: a surplus paid to a factor of production above what is needed to keep it in its current occupation

Transfer earnings: the amount a factor of production could earn in its best alternative occupation; the minimum amount that has to be paid to ensure that a worker stays in her/his present job: if her/his wage falls below this level, s/he will transfer to the alternative employment

Figure 3.8 shows that the total wage received by the workers is *OWXQ*. Of this *YWX* is economic rent and *OYXQ* is transfer earnings. This figure shows that economic rent is the area above the supply curve and below the wage rate. The amount of economic rent earned by the workers will vary. The first worker employed would have been prepared to work for considerably less than the wage rate actually paid. So a relatively high proportion of her/his wage will be economic rent. Whereas the last worker employed would have been prepared to work only for the going wage rate and so earns no economic rent.

The proportion of earnings that constitute economic rent depends on the elasticity of supply of labour.

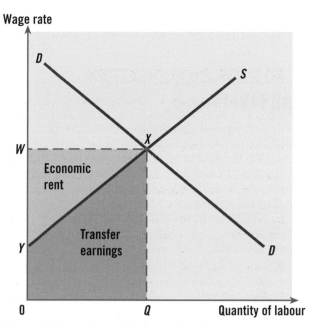

Figure 3.8 Economic rent and transfer earnings

Economic rent will form a large proportion when supply is inelastic. For example, many of the footballers playing in the Premier League are thought to earn a large amount of economic rent. Supply is inelastic as most footballers enjoy playing football and would continue to play even if their pay was cut. Most would earn considerably less in their next best paid jobs. These footballers are also highly paid.

In contrast, the more elastic the supply of labour is, the greater the proportion of earnings is accounted for by transfer earnings. For instance, a relatively high number of bar staff may only just be prepared to work for the going wage rate. If the wage rate were to fall, a relatively high number may switch to other unskilled work.

It has to be noted, however, that, as people take into account not just pecuniary but also non-pecuniary

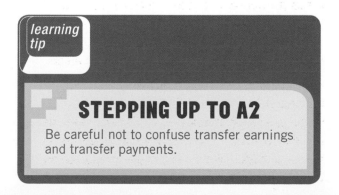

learning tip

STEPPING UP TO A2

Be careful not to confuse transfer earnings and transfer payments.

factors when deciding what job to do, some people are earning less than they could earn in another occupation. They are, in effect, receiving negative economic rent.

ACTIVITY ····⦂>

A 2008 report by the National Audit Office found that the 22,000 general medical practitioners who in 2006 ran their own practices had received a large pay rise but were working fewer hours, with many no longer being on call at night. The average pay of GP partners in 2006 was approximately £114,000, up from £72,000 in 2003. In contrast, the 11,000 salaried GPs were earning only about £47,000, up from £45,500 in 2003.

The rise in pay to GP partners was seen as having been successful in attracting people to the post. Between 2003 and 2006, the number of GP partners rose by 4,000.

a) What happened to the wage differential between GP partners and salaried GPs between 2003 and 2006?

b) Using the information in the passage, calculate the probable economic rent and transfer earnings received by the average GP partner in 2006.

c) i) Again using the information provided in the passage, calculate the elasticity of supply of the labour of GP partners.

ii) Comment on your findings.

iii) Discuss whether the change in the number of workers or the change in the number of hours worked is the more reliable source of information for calculating the elasticity of supply of labour.

4 Market failure and the role of the government and unions in the labour market

On completion of this chapter, you should be able to:

- understand the causes of market failure in the labour market
- analyse the nature of the various causes of labour market failure and explain the consequences for wage rates, labour supply and demand, and levels of employment
- discuss the wider economic effects of labour market failures
- describe, in general terms, the trends in trade union membership in the UK
- understand the forms of bargaining in the UK and use them to evaluate theories of wage determination
- identify different types of labour market flexibility
- discuss the consequences of flexibility for the operation of labour markets in the UK
- analyse why government intervenes in the labour market
- evaluate the consequences of such intervention
- understand the nature and causes of inequality and evaluate measures to reduce inequality in the UK
- discuss the implications of an ageing population and government responses to this issue of growing importance
- discuss how the UK labour market is affected by EU directives and evaluate their effects on UK firms and workers
- discuss the impact of immigration on labour markets.

Labour market failure and government labour market policies affect our lives directly, by influencing our chances of finding employment and the wage rate we receive. They also have an indirect impact on our lives by impacting on the availability of the products we buy and the price we pay for them.

This chapter explores a number of reasons why labour markets may be inefficient and explores some of the ways governments seek to correct market failure.

Labour market failure

Labour market failure occurs when the market forces of demand and supply do not result in an efficient allocation of labour resources. Evidence of labour market failure occurs in a number of forms. The most obvious is a surplus of some forms of labour and a shortage of others. Other examples include workers being in jobs that they are not best suited for, a lack of training, and wage rates being above or below their equilibrium rate.

Among the causes of labour market failure are abuse of labour market power, imperfect information, skill shortages, economic inactivity, unemployment, discrimination, segmented labour markets and geographical and occupational immobility of labour.

> **learning tip**
>
> ## BUILDING ON AS
>
> You may wish to check your understanding of market failure before reading the next few pages (see *OCR AS Economics*, pages 55–64).
>
> ## STEPPING UP TO A2
>
> At A2 level you have to consider the significance of market power from both the selling and the buying side.

ABUSE OF MARKET POWER

Trade unions may have different degrees of market power in the sale of labour services. They may push the wage rate above the equilibrium level and thereby cause unemployment. It is unlikely, however, that a trade union would push up the wage rate indefinitely, since such a policy would result in one very highly paid member! Trade unions may also engage in restrictive practices, such as job demarcation, when workers will only undertake tasks outlined in their job descriptions. Such action will influence the flexibility of the labour force.

Market power is also found on the demand side. Monopsonists and oligopsonists are buyers of labour who have the power to determine the wage rate that is likely to be lower than in a perfectly competitive labour market.

MONOPSONY AND OLIGOPSONY

A **monopsonist** is a firm that is the only buyer (i.e. employer) and an **oligopsonist** is one of a few dominant firms buying a certain type of labour. Examples of monopsonist employers are the Ordnance Survey, which is the main employer of mapmakers in the UK, and the NHS, which employs a very high proportion of nurses in the country.

There are a number of publishing firms in the UK. Some of these are small, but the main purchasers of the labour of editors, proofreaders and related occupations are large publishers such as Pearson. These large publishing companies are oligopsonists.

> **DEFINITIONS**
>
> **Monopsonist:** a single buyer
>
> **Oligopsonist:** one of a few dominant buyers

> **learning tip**
>
> ## STEPPING UP TO A2
>
> Be careful not to confuse monopoly with monopsony and oligopoly with oligopsony. Remember in this case '-poly' is connected with sellers whereas '-sony' is connected with buyers.

ACTIVITY ⋯⋯⋮⋗

When the BBC was the only television station in the UK, it was a monopsonist buyer of the labour of television presenters. The picture is now very different.

In December 2007, the corporation announced record pay deals for some of its top presenters. Jonathan Ross became the highest-paid presenter in British broadcasting history with a three-year £18m pay deal, Graham Norton received a three-year £5m deal and Jeremy Paxman a £940,000-a-year deal.

Jonathan Ross

The announcement was made at the same time that the BBC was considering cutting 2,500 jobs in the news section. A BBC spokesperson, however, said that the corporation had to 'face commercial realities in the increasingly competitive world of multi-channel television'.

a) What has happened to the BBC's purchasing power in the market for the labour of television presenters?

STRETCH AND CHALLENGE

b) Discuss whether the BBC was overpaying Jonathan Ross.

The determination of wages and employment

Monopsonists and oligopsonists are price makers. They influence the wage rate. To employ more workers, they have to raise the wage rate. So the marginal cost of labour (MCL) will exceed the average cost of labour (ACL), which is equivalent to the wage rate.

Table 4.1 shows how the marginal cost of labour exceeds the average cost of labour. For example, to attract a fourth worker costs the employer an extra £25 since s/he not only pays the worker £16 but also pays an extra £3 to each of the first three workers employed. In this circumstance, a union can raise the wage rate without causing unemployment.

Figure 4.1 shows that, in the absence of union action, the number of workers employed will be Q

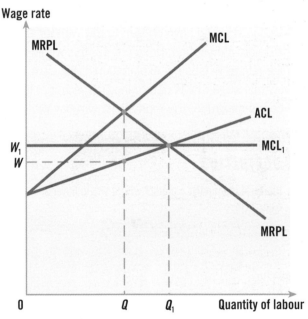

Figure 4.1 Possible effect of union action in a monopsonistic labour market

Number of workers	Average cost of labour (wage rate) per hour (£)	Total cost of labour per hour (£)	Marginal cost of labour per hour (£)
1	10	10	10
2	11	22	12
3	13	39	17
4	16	64	25
5	20	100	36
6	25	150	50

Table 4.1 Average and marginal cost of labour

(where MRPL equals MCL) and the wage rate will be W (found from the ACL curve). A union may then raise the wage rate to W_1. This then becomes the new marginal cost of labour (MCL$_1$), as there will be one wage rate for all union members. Employment now rises to Q_1. It also means, however, that once the wage rate has been settled by negotiation, the monopsonist will not have to increase the wage rate to attract labour.

BILATERAL MONOPOLY

When a trade union negotiates with a monopsonist employer, the situation is referred to as a **bilateral monopoly**. In this case, the wage rate will be determined by the relative bargaining strength of the two sides. If the monopsonist is very powerful, the outcome will be a wage rate close to that which the monopsonist would have chosen to pay without any trade union intervention. In Figure 4.2 this would be a wage rate of W (see the explanation of Figure 4.1 as to how this wage rate is determined). The upper limit will be the maximum the monopolist can pay without threatening the existence of the firm, for example W_1. The stronger the trade union is, the closer the wage rate is likely to be to this upper limit. A trade union does, however, have to take into account the possible adverse effect that pushing up the wage rate may have on the number of workers employed.

DEFINITION

Bilateral monopoly: a market with a single buyer and seller

Factors influencing an employer's bargaining strength

An employer will be stronger, the:

● greater the financial reserves it has with which it can last out any dispute

● lower the proportion of its workers who are in a union or professional body

● greater the degree of substitution between capital and labour

● higher the rate of unemployment, since this will mean it can substitute existing workers with unemployed workers

● lower the support workers have from the public

● lower the disruption any industrial action would cause to the productive process

● more branches the firm has which employ non-union labour or labour in different unions – so that production can be moved in the case of a dispute

● more legislation favours employers.

Trade unions

Trade unions are labour organisations that seek to promote the interests of their members. Probably their best known function is to negotiate the pay and conditions of employment of their members with employers. For example, the University and College Union (UCU) negotiates lecturers' pay at a national level with the Higher Education Funding Council and will negotiate with individual universities over possible redundancies. Unions lobby the government through the Trades Union Congress (TUC), the national body of the trade union movement.

In addition to their negotiating role, trade unions also carry out a number of other functions. They provide a channel for communication between workers and employers. The presence of a trade union may reduce labour turnover and raise the level of training.

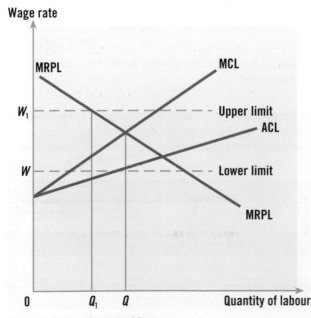

Wage rate

Figure 4.2 Bargaining positions

They tend to reduce income inequality. Pay scales in unionised firms tend to be flatter than in non-unionised ones.

A number of unions provide benefits and services for their members including financial services and legal advice. Some are also involved in lobbying national government on behalf of their members and setting minimum qualifications standards.

THE EFFECT OF TRADE UNIONS ON WAGES AND EMPLOYMENT

If all the workers in a labour market are members of a trade union, the body will act as a monopoly seller. This will alter the supply curve of labour. Figure 4.3 shows the effect of a trade union forcing the wage rate up from W to W_1. The union members will now be prepared to work for W_1 or above, and so the supply curve becomes W_1XS. The diagram also shows employment falling from Q to Q_1.

A union may also seek to raise the wage rate by pressing for employers to raise the qualifications or skills required to do the job. Such an approach, if successful, would shift the supply curve of labour to the left, which would be expected to raise the wage rate.

The effect that trade union action has on employment will be influenced, in part, by the type of market structure in which the employers sell their products. Pushing up the wage rate in firms that operate under conditions of perfect competition or monopolistic competition may have an adverse effect on employment. In these two market structures, firms can only earn normal profit in the long run. So a rise in their costs will cause marginal firms to leave the industry, causing output and employment to fall.

In any type of market structure, a trade union may seek to raise the employment of its members while raising the wage rate by supporting measures to increase labour productivity (for example, participating in training initiatives) or measures to increase demand for the product (for example, participating in an advertising campaign). In both cases, if the measures are successful, the marginal revenue product, and hence the demand curve, will shift to the right.

Factors influencing a trade union's bargaining power

A trade union will be stronger, the:

● greater the financial reserves of the organisation

● higher the proportion of workers in the organisation

● more inelastic the demand for the firm's product

● lower the degree of substitution between capital and labour

● lower the proportion of labour costs in total costs

● lower the rate of unemployment

● greater the support the workers have from the general public

● more legislation favours the rights of workers

● more disruption any industrial action would cause.

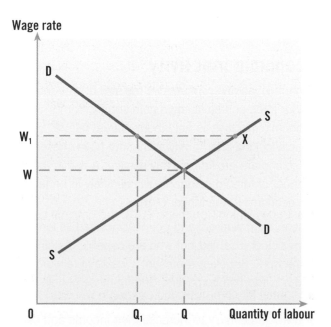

Wage rate

Figure 4.3 Effect of a trade union pushing up the wage rate

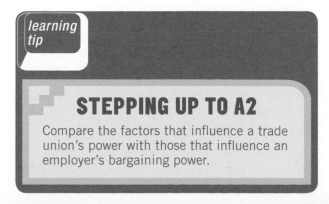

learning tip

STEPPING UP TO A2

Compare the factors that influence a trade union's power with those that influence an employer's bargaining power.

ACTIVITY ···⁞⟩

Nurses' pay has risen in recent years, but not by as much as that of Formula 1 mechanics.

a) Assess the relative bargaining power of nurses and the NHS.

b) Explain why the marginal productivity of Formula 1 mechanics has risen in recent years.

IMPERFECT INFORMATION

Workers may be in jobs that are less well paid and that they enjoy less than other jobs they are capable of doing, or they may be unemployed because they are unaware of suitable vacancies. Similarly, employers may not appoint the most productive workers because they are not in touch with all the potential workers. Obtaining information on job vacancies and potential workers, applying for jobs and interviewing applicants involves a variety of costs. For workers, it takes time, effort and money to look for a new job, fill out application forms and attend interviews. Employers incur costs in advertising jobs, assessing applications, interviewing people and inducting new staff. So both groups have to consider the benefits of searching for a better employment situation against the costs of searching.

SKILL SHORTAGES

Skill shortages occur when firms have difficulties recruiting people with the required skills. They usually result in an increase in firms' costs of production. This is because some firms, competing for the scarce labour, may bid up the wage rate of such staff, while others may try to fill the vacancies with less efficient, unskilled workers.

It has been estimated that one-tenth of UK adults have no qualifications and between 2 million and 3 million workers lack adequate numeracy and literacy skills. Such low skill levels have an adverse effect on productivity and result in some job vacancies remaining unfilled.

One cause of skill shortages is a lack of training. Training is a merit good. It has greater private benefits than consumers realise and has positive externalities.

If left to market forces, it would be under-consumed and too few resources would be devoted to it. This is because some workers and some firms take a short-term view and underestimate the benefits of training. In addition, some firms are afraid that other firms may reap the benefits of their expenditure by poaching their staff. Approximately 40 per cent of UK employers offer no training to their workers.

ACTIVITY ···⁞⟩

China is experiencing skill shortages in a number of areas. Its lack of lawyers and judges is causing a backlog of cases. Many firms are finding difficulty in recruiting accountants. It is predicted that the situation will get worse. For instance, it has been estimated that the country will need more than 400,000 extra pilots by 2025, a number far exceeding those expected to be trained by all the world's airlines.

a) What is causing China's demand for skilled labour to increase?

b) Explain two possible macroeconomic disadvantages that may arise from China's skill shortages.

STRETCH AND CHALLENGE

c) Discuss whether China will necessarily experience skill shortages in the future.

Economic inactivity

Economic inactivity influences the size of a country's labour force and so its aggregate supply. Some economic inactivity is not labour market failure. Most people looking after family and home have chosen to do so and are providing a key service. A rise in the number of full-time students will be likely to benefit the economy in the longer term.

Discouraged workers and people classified as long-term sick or disabled but who are capable of doing some work, however, represent a waste of resources and a burden on taxpayers. Getting these people into the labour force would increase aggregate supply and would be likely to increase their income and self esteem.

Unemployment

Unemployment means that labour markets are not clearing. Some of those willing and able to work cannot obtain a job. The existence of unemployment means that a country is not producing all that it is capable of. It will not be producing on its production possibility curve and so will not be achieving productive efficiency.

The extent to which unemployment causes labour market failure is obviously influenced by the number of people who are out of work. It is also influenced by how long people are out of work. The longer someone is unemployed, the more they get out of touch with the skills required and the greater the risk that they may give up hope of gaining a job.

Unemployment can arise as a result of a lack of aggregate demand. Such cyclical unemployment can also be referred to as **disequilibrium unemployment**, as it occurs when the aggregate demand for labour (ADL) is not equal to the aggregate supply of labour (ASL) at the going real wage rate.

Figure 4.4 shows ASL exceeding ADL, leading to unemployment of $Qb–Qa$. It might appear that the solution to this type of unemployment would be to cut the wage rate. However, not only might this be difficult, with workers resisting cuts in wage rates, but

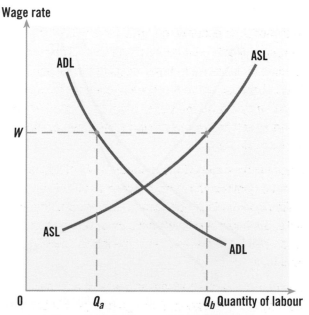

Figure 4.4 Disequilibrium (cyclical) unemployment

there is also a significant chance that it would lead to a downward, deflationary spiral. The cut in wages would reduce aggregate demand, which in turn would lower ADL, leading to a further cut in wages, and so on.

Unemployment can also arise due to problems with the supply of labour. Some people may be unemployed because they are unaware of vacancies, unsuited to take up vacancies or are unwilling to take up the vacancies. In other words, they are experiencing voluntary, frictional and structural unemployment. Some economists argue that people experiencing these types are all voluntarily unemployed because they could put more effort into finding out about job vacancies, could be more prepared to find employment and be more prepared to accept, for a period of time at least, a lower-paid job than ideally they would like.

In such a situation, there will be a gap between the aggregate labour force (ALF) and those prepared to work at the going wage rate, the aggregate supply of labour (ASL). Figure 4.5 shows this difference and unemployment of Q_c–Q. The gap between ASL and ALF narrows as the wage rate rises, as more of the labour force is prepared to work the higher the wage rate.

The unemployment that exists when the ADL equals the ASL at the going wage rate is sometimes referred to as **equilibrium unemployment** or the **non-accelerating inflation rate of unemployment (NAIRU)**. As the name NAIRU suggests, it is consistent with the level of unemployment at which there is no upward pressure on the wage rate and inflation. If unemployment falls below the level, perhaps because a government raises aggregate demand in a bid to reduce unemployment, the rate of inflation increases. In contrast, if unemployment rises above NAIRU, this time perhaps because the government is seeking to reduce inflation, the wage rate and inflation will fall.

DEFINITIONS

Disequilibrium unemployment: unemployment caused by the aggregate supply of labour exceeding the aggregate demand for labour

Equilibrium unemployment: unemployment that exists when the labour market is in equilibrium

Non-accelerating inflation rate of unemployment (NAIRU): the level of unemployment that exists when the labour market is in equilibrium; also called *equilibrium unemployment*

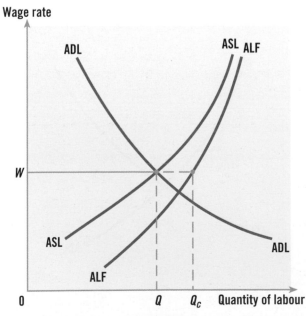

Figure 4.5 Equilibrium unemployment

In the 1980s, it was estimated that the UK's NAIRU was 8 per cent, whereas in 2008, the figure was put at 5 per cent. The fall has been attributed largely to government supply-side policies. While in the 1980s 50 per cent of the unemployed were long-term unemployed, this figure is now 21 per cent (see Table 4.2). It is thought that the higher the proportion of long-term unemployed in the jobless total, the higher the NAIRU. This is because those out of work for a long time exert less influence on wage bargaining – they are, in effect, not competing with those in work for the jobs.

Country	% of total unemployment
Germany	52
Italy	50
Netherlands	43
France	42
Japan	32
Spain	30
UK	21
Sweden	16
USA	10

Table 4.2 Unemployment of 12 months and over in selected countries, 2006

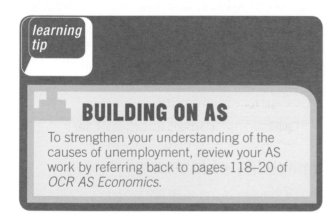

learning tip

BUILDING ON AS

To strengthen your understanding of the causes of unemployment, review your AS work by referring back to pages 118–20 of *OCR AS Economics*.

Discrimination

Discrimination results in an inefficient allocation of resources and inequitable wage differentials.

● The group discriminated against clearly suffers. They are likely to be paid less than other workers doing the same job and find it harder to gain employment. In addition, some may have to settle for less demanding jobs than they are capable of undertaking, may be overlooked for promotion and may not be selected to go on training courses. The existence of discrimination may also discourage members from the discriminated group from applying for well-paid jobs and from seeking to gain higher qualifications.

● Producers who discriminate have a smaller pool of labour to select from. They may also not make the best use of, for example, any black workers they do employ. They will raise the costs of production and make them less competitive against rival firms at home and abroad.

● Consumers will experience higher prices if producers discriminate. They will also experience higher prices and less choice if they themselves discriminate against firms that employ workers from a particular group.

● The government may have to pay out more welfare benefits to groups that are discriminated

ACTIVITY ⋯⋮

At the end of 2007, Germany had achieved an employment rate of 70 per cent. This was in line with the 2010 employment goal agreed by the EU as part of the 'Lisbon strategy' aimed at boosting the bloc's competitiveness.

Unemployment fell throughout the year, with the long-term unemployed finding employment faster than any other group, bringing their share of the total down to 40 per cent.

Some economists attributed the fall to the previous government's reforms, collectively known as the Hartz laws, which cut welfare benefits for many jobseekers. Others claimed it was the result of economic growth. Joachim Wolff, economist at the Federal Labour Agency's research centre said 'It is not difficult to isolate the structural and cyclical factors behind falling unemployment'.

The reduction in long-term unemployment has led some German economists and politicians to raise questions about the existence of *Sockelarbeitslosigkeit* – hard-core unemployment that cannot be reduced even in the best of economic circumstances.

a) What is meant by an employment rate of 70 per cent?

b) Explain the structural and cyclical factors that could cause unemployment to fall.

c) What is the concept of Sockelarbeitslosigkeit equivalent to?

against and may have to spend time and money introducing and monitoring anti-discrimination legislation.

● The economy will lose out as a result of the misallocation of resources. Output will be below the potential output that could be achieved if the groups were not discriminated against in terms of employment, pay, promotion and training.

THEORIES OF DISCRIMINATION

A number of theories have been put forward to explain negative discrimination. Two of these are:

● *Becker's theory.* Gary Becker, professor of economics at Chicago University, argues that some people may be prepared to experience higher costs rather than come into contact with members of a particular group. In effect, people pay in the form of lower profits to avoid employing, for example, women workers and in the form of higher prices to avoid buying from firms employing female workers.

● *statistical discrimination.* This arises because of imperfect information. Some economists argue that employers discriminate as a result of seeking to reduce their costs. They do not know, in advance, the productivity of workers. So when deciding whom to employ, how much to pay and whom to promote and train, they make decisions on generalisations about groups of workers. For example, an employer may assume that workers aged 50 and over are less productive than younger workers. As a result, the firm may use age as a screening device when deciding on job applicants, may not promote older workers or send them on training courses, and if deciding on redundancies may select older workers first.

> **learning tip**
> Try to be objective in your analysis of labour. For instance, avoid comments such as 'women only work for pin money' or 'all male employers exploit female workers'.

Segmented labour markets

There are a number of barriers that exist to the free movement of workers between different sections of

the labour market. Indeed, in practice, there are a number of different labour markets.

If there were no barriers to the entry into or exit from labour markets, it would be expected that workers would move from low-wage to high-wage jobs, equalising wages. Some barriers increase the efficiency of labour markets. For instance, I would not want to be operated on by a surgeon who lacks the appropriate qualifications and skills or to be driven by a taxi driver who does not have a driving licence. Some barriers, however, may not be necessary and may have been introduced to push up workers' wages and in some cases to keep particular groups out.

> **learning tip**

> ## STEPPING UP TO A2
> As with product markets, labour markets can be considered on a local, national and international level.

Immobility of labour

Labour immobility comes in two main forms. One is **geographical immobility**, which relates to obstacles that workers experience in moving from jobs in one area to jobs in another. When this occurs, shortages of workers in one area and surpluses in others are not corrected and regional unemployment and geographical wage differentials continue to exist. Geographical immobility arises for a number of reasons. These include differences in the availability and price of housing in different areas and family ties.

> **DEFINITION:**
> **Geographical immobility of labour:** barriers to the movement of workers between different areas

The other type of immobility is **occupational immobility**. This is concerned with the barriers that workers experience in changing occupations. These obstacles come in the form of the need for qualifications and skills to perform particular jobs and sometimes even include social barriers. The barriers contribute to occupational wage differentials and structural unemployment.

> **DEFINITION:**
>
> **Occupational immobility of labour:** barriers to workers changing occupations

At a time of considerable technological change and globalisation, it is increasingly important for workers to be able to move smoothly from one job to another and from one area to another.

Other causes of labour market failure

These include:

● *attachment between workers and employers*. Some workers may stay in less well paid jobs because they like working for their employers and have a good working relationship with them. Employers may also feel a sense of loyalty to their existing labour force. This attachment reduces the mobility of labour and makes supply more inelastic. It may, however, increase productivity.

● *inertia*. Workers may not move to higher-paid jobs and employers may not seek to replace less productive workers by more productive workers due to laziness.

The economic effects of labour market failures

Labour market failures lead to a range of effects. As previously mentioned, they can result in unemployment and skill shortages, and to workers being in the wrong jobs. Such misallocation of resources increases firms' costs of production and reduces consumer surplus. On a macro scale, it reduces firms' international competitiveness and has an adverse effect on the country's trade position.

Inefficient labour markets also raise government costs in terms of state benefits, labour market legislation and spending on education, training and regional policy.

The trends in trade union membership in the UK

The trend in UK trade union membership, as in many other countries, is downwards. Table 4.3 shows that membership has fallen by nearly half a million between 1999 and 2004. There was a rise between 1997 and 1999 but, to date, this proved short lived. Union membership as a proportion of the labour force has also fallen from 58 per cent in 1984 to 34 per cent in 2002 and 29 per cent in 2004.

Year	Number of members (millions)	Number of trade unions
1999	7.89	237
2000	7.77	226
2001	7.75	216
2002	7.73	210
2003	7.55	206
2004	7.47	193

Table 4.3 UK trade union membership and the number of trade unions
Source: Table 7.26, *2007 Annual Abstract*, ONS, 2007

One key reason why trade union membership has been declining is thought to be the decline in union power. Unions lost some of their power as a result of legislation passed in the 1980s and 1990s and a rise in the number of companies deciding not to recognise unions. (When a company does not recognise a union it means that the union does not have the right to negotiate on behalf of its members.)

Membership of trade unions and professional organisations is stronger within professional occupations, including, for instance, accountants and teachers. It is also interesting to note that now a higher proportion of women workers are members of trade unions than men – 30 per cent compared to 28 per cent.

LABOUR DISPUTES

The last four decades have seen a noticeable decline in labour disputes. In the 1970s the average number of working days lost per year was 12.9 million, in the 1980s it was 7.2 million and by the 1990s it had fallen to 660,000. In 2005 only 157,400 working days were lost. This is low both in historical terms and in international terms – see Table 4.4. As well as working days lost, there are two other measures of labour disputes. These are the number of stoppages and the number of workers involved in the stoppages.

Country	Working days lost
Iceland	400
Canada	210
Spain	180
Denmark	160
Italy	100
Ireland	50
France	45
USA	30
Sweden	20
UK	20
Germany	1
Japan	1

Table 4.4 Working days lost per 1,000 employees, annual average, 1996–2005

learning tip

STEPPING UP TO A2

Keep up to date with changes in trade union membership, the number of unions and the number of working days lost. The *Annual Abstract of Statistics* is a useful source of information for this.

ACTIVITY ⋯⋮

The number of trade unions is declining. This is due, in part, to the fall in membership, but it is also the result of the trend for trade unions to merge. Unite is now the UK's largest union, with 2 million members. It was formed from a merger of Amicus and the Transport and General Workers' Union. It represents workers in a wide range of industries, including engineering, agriculture, food and drink, chemicals, pharmaceuticals and from the public sector.

Some UK unions are now considering international mergers to increase their influence and cope more effectively with the impact of globalisation. Unite, for instance, has been having talks on a possible merger with the US United Steelworkers Union. This union also has members from the pharmaceutical industry and from the public sector, as well as other industries such as mining and metals.

a) Why might the number of trade unions decline in the future?

b) Explain the benefits members may gain from the merger of Unite and the United Steelworkers Union.

Forms of bargaining

Unions favour national collective bargaining. This gives them greater power and may enable them to take advantage of economies of scale in negotiation. It is expensive for a union to have to negotiate separate agreements with a large number of employers.

In large parts of the EU, collective bargaining is undertaken on the basis of multi-employer bargaining, with unions negotiating with associations of employers on industry-wide agreements. In contrast, in the USA, Japan and increasingly in the UK, local agreements are more common, especially in the private sector. In this case there is single-employer bargaining, with agreements being made at the company level or lower.

There is also an increasing trend towards performance-related pay agreements in the UK. These are agreements that relate a pay award to

ECONOMICS IN CONTEXT

FALLING TRADE UNION MEMBERSHIP IN THE USA

Trade union membership has been on a downward trend in the USA since the 1960s. It was, for instance, 20 per cent in 1980, 16 per cent in 1990 and 12 per cent in 2006. Half of US union members are now government employees.

There are thought to be four main reasons for the decline, although economists disagree about their relative importance. One reason is rising legal obstacles. In the USA, supervisors do not have a legal right to collective bargaining and this tends to discourage workers in this category from joining unions. The US National Labour Relations Board (NLRB), the politically appointed body that interprets US labour law, is currently considering whether to broaden the range of jobs considered to be supervisory.

A connected reason is employer opposition. Managers may use a variety of tactics to discourage workers from joining unions. These include the suggestion to workers that their prospects and job security will be harmed by joining a union.

Another reason is a structural change in the economy. Fewer US workers are now employed in the heavy industries and large firms, where unions have traditionally been strong. It has been noted, however, that in the USA membership has been declining not only in the manufacturing sector but also in the tertiary sector, including retailing and finance.

The fourth reason is that membership of a union is becoming less attractive to workers. With rising competition due to globalisation, unions have less power to protect members against job losses. Employers, through their human resource departments, are now providing some of the services that traditionally have been supplied by trade unions, including dealing with workers' grievances. The government also provides some services, such as unemployment insurance and workers' compensation and health and safety protection that were once important functions of trade unions. The view that employers and governments have taken over the role of trade unions is sometimes referred to as the substitution hypothesis.

performance. For example, an employer may offer a 3 per cent pay rise tied to a 2 per cent rise in productivity.

learning tip

STEPPING UP TO A2

Labour market flexibility is a topical issue and one new at A2.

Types of labour market flexibility

A flexible labour market is one that adjusts quickly and smoothly to changes in demand and supply conditions. It means that if more or fewer products are demanded, if the pattern of demand alters, if new technology is introduced or other changes occur, the labour market can adjust.

There are a variety of types of flexibility. These include:

● *numerical flexibility* – the ability to change the number of workers, or ease of hiring and firing

● *temporal flexibility* – the ability to change the hours people work

● *locational flexibility* – the ability to change where people work – at home, somewhere else or at the main place of work

● *functional flexibility* – the ability to change the tasks workers perform

● *wage flexibility* – the ability to change the amount paid to workers.

THE CONSEQUENCES OF FLEXIBILITY

A flexible labour market allows firms to match their production closely to demand. This should keep their average costs low, as they will not be overstaffed during periods of falling demand and should be able to raise output when demand increases by hiring extra workers. Low labour costs are a factor in keeping firms' products internationally competitive.

The impact of labour flexibility on workers is somewhat uncertain. Some workers enjoy working from home, some want to work part-time and some may want to be casual workers for a period of time. Supporters of flexible labour markets also argue that they create more employment. This is because firms are more likely to be willing to recruit workers during periods of rising demand if they know they can dismiss them equally quickly and with little cost, including in terms of severance pay, should demand fall. This may be particularly the case with young, untrained workers. A flexible labour market can also attract foreign direct investment that is also likely to boost employment.

However, while the chance of being in employment may be greater in a flexible labour market, so is the chance of being out of work, albeit for a short period. There is less job security and a greater need to be occupationally and geographically mobile. This can put stress on workers. Greater wage flexibility also tends to result in a greater wage inequality.

THE FLEXIBILITY OF THE UK'S LABOUR MARKET

The UK has a more flexible labour market than most of its fellow EU member countries. The last four decades have seen an increase in temporary employment, part-time employment, flexible hours, job sharing, career breaks and homeworking.

In the 1980s, the government undertook a series of labour market reforms with the result that there are now fewer restrictions on the hiring and firing of workers in the UK than in most other countries. Indeed, the USA is one of the few countries that has a lower level of employment protection than the UK.

Table 4.5 contrasts three types of labour markets found in the EU. The continental model is the least flexible. It has a relatively high degree of state

Features	Continental model (e.g. Austria, France, Germany)	Nordic model (e.g. Denmark, Finland, Sweden)	Anglo-Saxon model (e.g. Ireland, UK)
Level of government intervention	high	high	low
Power of trade unions	high	high	low
Regulations on dismissals	high	average	low
Minimum wage	high	high	high
Unemployment benefits	generous	generous but short term	not very generous
Employment rate	relatively low	high	high
Duration of unemployment	tends to be long term	short term	short term
Average no. of hours worked	low and flexible	relatively high	low
Sense of job security	high	relatively high	low
Labour market efficiency	low	high	high
Income equality	high	high	low
Priority	social cohesion	social cohesion, efficiency	efficiency, social cohesion

Table 4.5 European labour market models
Source: Susan Grant and Colin Bamford, *The European Union*, 5th edition (2006), Heinemann

intervention and job protection. The Anglo-Saxon model is the most flexible. In between comes the Nordic model, which has a relatively high degree of state intervention but one that seeks to persuade the unemployed back into work quickly and places more emphasis on raising labour productivity and labour market participation by means of education, training and special programmes.

GOVERNMENT MEASURES TO ACHIEVE LABOUR MARKET FLEXIBILITY

There is a number of measures a government can employ to increase the flexibility of the labour force. Increased labour market information, training and education should all make labour more mobile and therefore raise the responsiveness of labour to changes in the pattern of demand. A government may also elect to cut the marginal income tax rates and unemployment benefit, and link unemployment benefit more closely to the search for employment.

Firms will find it easier to adjust to changes in demand if the supply of labour becomes more responsive to changes in wage rates. Reducing marginal income tax rates will enable workers to keep more of their wages. This may increase the incentive for existing workers to increase the number of hours they work, for the unemployed to look for work more actively and for

those considering retiring to stay in the labour force for longer. These effects may occur if the substitution effect of any rise in net pay resulting from tax cuts exceeds the income effect. Studies have shown, however, that many workers do not alter the hours they work in response to tax changes and that, of those who do, as many work fewer hours as work more hours. However, cuts in marginal tax rates do seem to have some influence on people's decision as to when they will retire, if they have choice in the matter.

Cutting job seeker's allowance makes unemployment a less attractive prospect and so may reduce the time that the unemployed spend searching for a job. Of course, such a measure would only work if there are jobs available.

Removing employment protection legislation can make labour markets more efficient in responding to changing market conditions. For example, a law that requires employers to give workers a long period of maternity/paternity leave increases the cost of employing workers. Similarly, a law that gives workers the right to appeal against dismissal makes it more expensive to make workers redundant. Employment protection benefits those who have got jobs but can make it more difficult for the unemployed to gain work.

The UK government operates a welfare-to-work strategy. This provides benefits to people not to

ACTIVITY ····⫶›

In the period 1993 to 2007, there was a notable rise in employment in Spain. As much as half of this, however, was accounted for by what the Spanish call 'garbage' jobs. These are jobs based on short-term, temporary contracts with few benefits.

The widespread use of temporary contracts did help to halve Spanish unemployment in that period. Some economists, however, claim that temporary contracts have contributed to Spain's poor productivity relative to the rest of the EU. Temporary contracts often offer little training, and job insecurity can reduce motivation and enterprise.

Spanish employers, in contrast, argue that the Spanish labour market would be improved by more flexibility. In particular, they argue in

favour of reducing the costs of hiring and firing in Spain. Employers' share of social security as a percentage of wages was among the highest in the EU in 2007. Employees dismissed or made redundant were entitled to 45 days' pay for every year worked as opposed to eight days' pay in the UK.

a) Identify two benefits that low-quality jobs may lack.

b) Explain why temporary work may reduce productivity.

STRETCH AND CHALLENGE

c) Discuss whether reducing the number of days' pay a dismissed or redundant worker is entitled to would increase employment.

remain unemployed but to support them while they are actively seeking employment. This particularly targets those most prone to long-term unemployment, including lone parents with dependent children, people with disabilities and those living in disadvantaged areas. The idea is to require the unemployed to improve their employment opportunities in a number of ways, including undertaking training and work experience.

Government intervention in labour markets

A government may intervene in labour markets to correct labour market failure and so raise efficiency, and also to promote equity and social cohesion.

Government intervention affects wages and employment in a number of ways. These include the government's employment of public sector workers, the provision of information, regional policy, training, education, a national minimum wage (NMW), anti-discrimination legislation and trade union legislation.

THE GOVERNMENT AS AN EMPLOYER

Despite the major privatisation programmes of the 1980s and 1990s, the UK government remains a major employer. Indeed, the NHS is the third largest employer in the world behind the Chinese army and the Indian railways. Government decisions on the number of workers it employs and the wages it pays them has both a direct and an indirect effect on labour markets. For example, if the government decides to raise the pay of state school teachers, this will increase the average pay of teachers and will put upward pressure on the pay of teachers in the private sector.

LABOUR MARKET INFORMATION

To offset the level of labour market information the government provides information in a variety of forms. There is a state-funded careers service that provides details about requirements, working conditions and pay of a variety of occupations. Careers education is also part of the curriculum of state schools. Government job centres provide information about job vacancies and welfare benefit officials discuss with the unemployed what jobs are on offer and how to apply for them.

REGIONAL POLICY

Regional policy seeks to influence the distribution of firms and people. To reduce the problem of geographical immobility of labour and regional unemployment, governments employ a variety of measures. Financial assistance may be given to workers to relocate to areas where there are vacancies requiring their particular skills. More commonly, however, 'work is taken to the workers' by providing financial assistance for firms to locate and relocate in areas of high unemployment.

TRAINING

A government can seek to raise the level of training to the allocatively efficient level in a variety of ways.

● It can provide training directly to its own employees and to the unemployed and those changing jobs.

● It can subsidise individuals to engage in training and/or firms to provide training.

● It can pass legislation requiring firms to engage in a certain level of training.

ACTIVITY ····⋮

The UK government has set itself the target of boosting the proportion of the potential labour force with basic literacy and numeracy to 95 per cent by 2020 compared with 79 per cent and 85 per cent respectively in 2005.

One way the government is seeking to achieve its target is by the introduction of diplomas. These new qualifications launched in September 2008 are a cross between a fully academic and a fully vocational qualification. They are designed, in part, to attract teenagers who have traditionally dropped out of school at 16 or earlier because they do not like traditional academic work, leaving school with few or no qualifications.

a) How does literacy and numeracy influence productivity?

b) Discuss the impact that the diploma may have on the quantity and quality of the UK labour force.

EDUCATION

Increases and improvements in state educational provision should raise the qualifications and skill levels of workers. This should increase the occupational mobility of the labour force, reduce the shortage of skilled labour and raise the productivity of labour.

Measures to raise the qualifications and skills of workers are referred to as investment in human capital. If there is investment in developing the ability of a wide range of people, the problem of social exclusion (people not feeling a part of society) should also be reduced.

MINIMUM WAGE LEGISLATION

Minimum wage legislation is introduced to help raise the pay of low paid workers. To have any effect, the minimum wage has to be set above the market equilibrium wage rate.

Some economists argue that such intervention in the operation of free market forces raises firms' costs of production and results in higher unemployment. Figure 4.6 shows that the setting of a minimum wage of W_x above the equilibrium wage rate of W causes an extension in the supply of labour but also a contraction in the demand for labour causing

a shortfall of employment of $QS–QD$. Compared with the situation before the intervention of the government, employment falls from Q to QD.

There is a risk that the introduction of a NMW may encourage firms to seek to lower the cost of employing low skilled workers by cutting fringe benefits. It may also encourage workers who previously earned near the minimum wage level to press for a wage rise. If it does reduce wage differentials, it may also adversely affect labour mobility.

Other economists argue that the introduction of a NMW may not result in higher unemployment. Low-paid workers often have low bargaining power relative to their employers, some of which are monopsonists and oligopsonists. In these cases, the introduction of a NMW would raise both the wage rate and employment. Figure 4.7 shows that a NMW of W_x becomes the new marginal cost of labour and raises employment from Q to Q_1.

There are other reasons why a NMW may not cause unemployment. One is that the first effect of its introduction is to raise wages. This, in turn, raises demand for goods and services that, in turn, may increase demand for labour. The higher wages may also raise morale and cut sickness and so increase

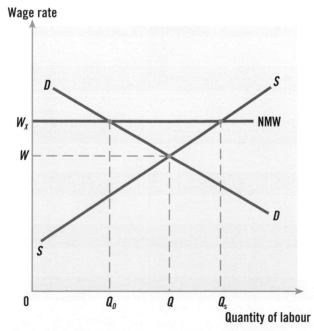

Figure 4.6 National minimum wage reducing employment

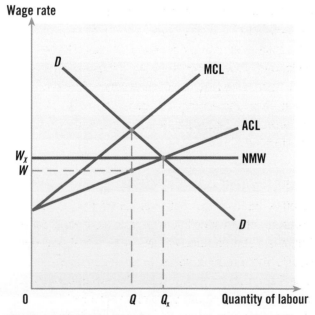

Figure 4.7 Effect of a NMW in a monopsonistic or oligonistic labour market

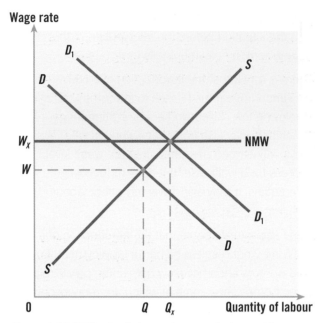

Figure 4.8 A NMW stimulating an increase in demand for labour

the productivity of those affected. Productivity will also increase if employers seek to gain a higher return from the now higher-paid workers by providing more training.

Rises in demand for products will shift the demand curve to the right and increase employment as illustrated in Figure 4.8. As most low wage earners are women who work part-time, an NMW may reduce the gender gap in pay. It may, however, not have much impact on income inequality if a relatively high proportion of those earning the NMW live in middle or high income households.

An NMW, affecting the pay of 1.8m workers, was introduced in the UK in April 1999. Initially sixteen and seventeen-year-olds were exempt. Table 4.6 shows how the rate has changed over time and Table 4.7 compares the proportion of employees receiving the NMW in a number of countries.

Country	% of employees receiving
Bulgaria	16.8
Latvia	12.0
Luxembourg	11.0
Lithuania	10.3
Slovenia	2.8
UK	2.2
Ireland	1.8
Malta	1.5
Spain	0.8

Table 4.7 Percentage of employees receiving the NMW in selected EU countries, January 2007

Time period	Aged 16–17	Aged 18–21	Aged 22 and over
April 1999 – May 2000		3.00	3.60
June 2000 – Sept 2000		3.20	3.60
Oct 2000 – Sept 2001		3.20	3.70
Oct 2001 – Sept 2002		3.50	4.10
Oct 2002 – Sept 2003		3.60	4.20
Oct 2003 – Sept 2004		3.80	4.50
Oct 2004 – Sept 2005	3.00	4.10	4.80
Oct 2005 – Sept 2006	3.00	4.25	5.05
Oct 2006 – Sept 2007	3.30	4.45	5.35
Oct 2007 – Sept 2008	3.40	4.60	5.52
Oct 2008 – Sept 2009	3.53	4.77	5.73

Table 4.6 National minimum wage rates per hour (£), April 1999–September 2009

learning tip

STEPPING UP TO A2

In assessing the impact of a NMW, it is useful to include demand and supply diagrams.

DISCRIMINATION LEGISLATION

In the UK legislation has made it illegal to discriminate on the grounds of gender, marital status, race and colour, since the 1970s. In 1995 the Disability Discrimination Act came into force which has made discrimination on the grounds of disability unlawful and in October 2006 the Employment Equality (Age Discrimination) Act outlawed discrimination on the grounds of age.

Such legislation may change attitudes over time. Employers may find that a group which they had previously discriminated against is more productive than they first thought. Some employers, however, may seek to get round such legislation and, in practice, it can be difficult to prove that discrimination has occurred.

TRADE UNION LEGISLATION

If it is thought that the power of trade unions has been weakened by previous legislation and that their bargaining power has been reduced too much in relation to that of employers, a government may repeal some of the legislation. If, however, it thinks that unions are abusing their labour market power, it may pass legislation that further reduces the industrial action they can take.

Income distribution

Both income and wealth are distributed unevenly in the UK. Wealth is the more unevenly distributed. While a person can survive without owning any assets by, for example, renting a house, it is not possible to survive without any income.

Within a country, the distribution of income can be considered in terms of how income is shared out between the factors of production (the functional distribution of income), between households (size distribution) and between different regions (geographical distribution of income).

THE FUNCTIONAL DISTRIBUTION OF INCOME

Income is flow of money over a period of time. Income can be earned by labour in the form of wages, by capital in the form of interest, by land in the form of rent and by entrepreneurs in the form of

ACTIVITY ⋯⋗

In March 2008, 19-year-old Leanne Wilkinson was awarded £16,000 in compensation in a ground breaking case against her former employer. It was the first time since age discrimination came into force in October 2006 that the law had been properly tested in a case involving a young worker.

Leanne was 18 when she was dismissed from her job as an administrative assistant at Springwell Engineering in Newcastle upon Tyne. She claimed that the company told her that she was too young for the post and that they needed an older person with more experience.

An employment tribunal ruled in her favour, stating that the company had relied on a

'stereotypical assumption that capability equals older age … age was the predominant reason for the decision to dismiss'.

a) On what grounds was Leanne Wilkinson dismissed?

b) Identify two benefits of employing young workers.

STRETCH AND CHALLENGE

c) Discuss the effect that anti-discrimination legislation may have on the flexibility of labour markets.

profits. Wages still account for the largest percentage of total income, but in both the UK and in world terms, the share of profits has been increasing at the expense of wages.

In addition to earned income and investment income, people can receive income in the form of state benefits. The relative shares of earned income, investment income and transfer payments depend on a variety of factors, but principally on the level of employment and the relative power of labour and capital.

THE SIZE DISTRIBUTION OF INCOME

Figure 4.9 shows how income became more unevenly distributed between 1981 and 2004/05. (The wider the gap between the 90th and 10th percentile, the greater the inequality within the distribution.)

Over the same period, the percentage share of national income earned by the highest paid 0.1 per cent rose from 1.2 per cent in 1980 to 3.5 per cent.

THE GEOGRAPHICAL DISTRIBUTION OF INCOME

As you saw in Chapter 1, income is unevenly distributed between the regions of the UK.

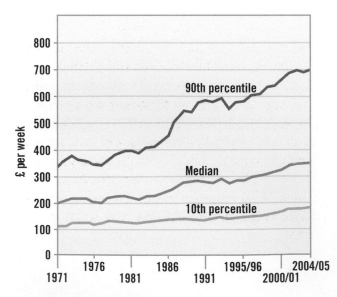

Figure 4.9 Distribution of UK real disposable household income (2004/05 prices)

Causes of differences in the geographical distribution of income include variation in:

● unemployment rates

● the proportion of the population claiming benefits

● the qualifications and the skills of the labour force

● industrial structure

● occupational structure

● living costs that give rise to differences in pay.

Of course, there are variations within regions. Even though London as a whole has a high income per head, it has some of the most deprived districts in the UK.

CAUSES OF INCOME INEQUALITY BETWEEN HOUSEHOLDS

These include:

● *unequal holdings of wealth.* As wealth generates income in the form of profit, interest and dividends, differentials in wealth cause differences in income.

● *differences in the composition of households.* Some households have, for example, three adults working, whereas others may contain no one in employment. Indeed, low income is closely associated with a dependency on benefits.

● *differences in skills and qualifications.* As we have seen, those with high skills and qualifications are likely to be in high demand and hence be likely to be able to earn high incomes.

● *differences in educational opportunities.* Those who have the opportunity to stay in education for longer are likely to gain more qualifications and develop more skills and so are likely to increase their earning potential.

● *discrimination.* The income of some groups is adversely affected by discrimination in terms of employment opportunities, pay and promotion chances.

● *differences in hours worked.* Most full-time workers earn more than part-time workers and those who work overtime earn more than those who work the standard hours.

ACTIVITY ⋯⋮⟩

The gap between the richest and the poorest has widened more rapidly in the USA than in most other countries in recent years. Table 4.8 shows how the top US earners have increased their share of income since 1960.

Whereas, in the past, Americans with the greatest incomes were living off the income generated by their accumulated fortunes, today's rich are mostly earning their money.

Globalisation and advances in technology have pushed up the earnings of top managers, entertainers and sports people, while pushing down the pay of the unskilled. In 2007, the average American executive earned 300 times the average wage.

a) How did the income share of 99 per cent of income recipients change between 1980 and 2004?

b) Explain how an increase in income inequality can result from:

  i) globalisation

  ii) advances in technology.

	1960	1980	2004
Top 0.01%	0.5	1.0	3.0
Top 0.1%	2.0	2.0	7.0
Top 1%	7.0	8.0	16.0

Table 4.8 Income share in the USA

Wealth

Wealth is a stock of assets that have a financial value. Economists distinguish between marketable and non-marketable wealth. Marketable wealth is wealth that can be transferred to another person, such as homes and shares, whereas non-marketable wealth is specific to a person and cannot be transferred; for example, pension rights.

Wealth distribution is uneven

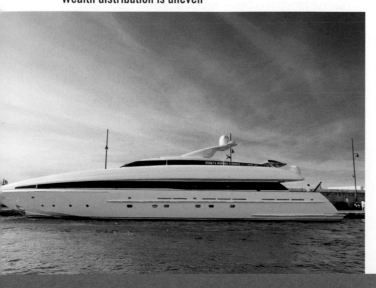

The distribution of wealth can be considered in terms of how it is distributed among the population (size distribution), the forms in which it is held and according to the characteristics of those holding wealth.

THE SIZE DISTRIBUTION OF WEALTH

Wealth is very unevenly distributed among the UK's population. Table 4.9 shows the size distribution of marketable wealth in the UK in four selected years. The table shows that wealth became slightly more unevenly distributed between 1996 and 1999 and then became slightly more evenly distributed. It is interesting to note that a fifth of the country's wealth is owned by only 1 per cent of the population and that the least wealthy 50 per cent of the population owned only 7 percent of the country's wealth in 2003.

	Percentage of marketable wealth owned			
	1996	1999	2001	2003
Most wealthy 1%	20	23	22	21
Most wealthy 5%	40	44	42	40
Most wealthy 25%	74	74	72	72
Most wealthy 50%	93	94	94	93
Total marketable wealth (£ billion)	2,092	2,752	3,744	3,783

Table 4.9 The distribution of wealth in the UK

Sources: *Social Trends* 37, ONS, 2007 and *Social Trends* 35, ONS, 2005

WEALTH DISTRIBUTION BETWEEN ASSETS

Wealth can be held in a variety of forms, including life insurance and pension funds, securities and shares and banking and building society deposits.

Some forms of wealth such as life insurance, housing and pension funds are more evenly distributed than other forms, such as shares and land.

WEALTH DISTRIBUTION BETWEEN DIFFERENT GROUPS

People can become wealthy through inheritance, through saving, the use of their entrepreneurial skills, work and chance.

As would be expected, wealth is unevenly distributed between age categories. For example, people in their 40s and 50s have had more time to accumulate savings than people in their 20s and 30s and they do indeed have greater wealth.

The amount of wealth held also varies between ethnic groups and gender. The group that currently has the lowest holding of wealth per head is people of a Bangladeshi background. Men have more wealth than women, although this may change in the future.

CAUSES OF WEALTH INEQUALITY

Among the causes of wealth inequality are:

● *inequality of income.* Work overtook inheritance as a source of wealth in the UK in the mid-1990s. Having a high income makes it easier for people to save and to gain higher interest rates on their savings.

● *differences in entrepreneurial skills.* Some people are self-made millionaires as a result of building up a business.

● *the pattern of inheritance.* In the UK, significant holdings of wealth have traditionally been passed on to the eldest son. This has kept wealth in the form of large estates concentrated in a few hands. In contrast, in many other countries where property and other assets are distributed among the children on the death of the parents, wealth becomes more evenly distributed over time.

● *marriage patterns of the wealthy.* The wealthy tend to marry other wealthy people. This further concentrates wealth in the hands of the few.

ACTIVITY ···⋮

There were 92 women in the 2007 *Sunday Times* Rich List, an annual report on the UK's 1,000 wealthiest people. This was an increase of 28 on ten years previously. It is predicted that the proportion of women in the list will increase dramatically in the next two decades. Indeed, it has been estimated that female millionaires will outnumber male millionaires by 2020 and that five years later, women will own 60 per cent of the country's wealth.

In the past, much of women's wealth came from marriage, inheritance and divorce. Now most of it comes from business ownership, investments and employment.

a) What is predicted will be the percentage point rise in the proportion of females in the UK's wealthiest 1,000?

b) Explain what factors will determine the proportion of wealth owned by women in the future.

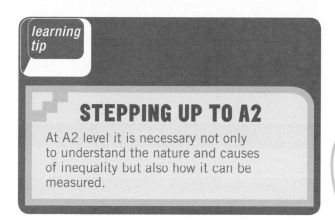

STEPPING UP TO A2

At A2 level it is necessary not only to understand the nature and causes of inequality but also how it can be measured.

Measuring inequality

Wealth and income inequality can be measured in a number of ways. As indicated above, the distribution of wealth owned or income earned by a given percentage can be compared. Decile or quintile groups (tenths and fifths) can also be compared. The bottom quintile group, for example, shows the share of income of the poorest 20 per cent of households, individuals or adults. The bottom decile group is the poorest 10 per cent.

Another measure is percentiles. These show the income or wealth level above or below which a certain proportion of people fall. For instance, the 90th percentile is the income level above which only 10 per cent of people fall. The 90:10 ratio is the incomes of the people 10 per cent from the top compared with the 10th percentile, those 10 per cent from the bottom. The advantage of this measure is that it excludes those at the very top and bottom of the income distribution from comparisons. This ratio was 4:1 in 2006, which was the same as in 1996.

A further measure is the **Gini coefficient**. This is often used to make international comparisons of income inequality. It is found by using a Lorenz curve.

DEFINITION

Gini coefficient: used to make international comparisons of income inequality. It is found by using a *Lorenz curve.*

LORENZ CURVE

A common method of illustrating income or wealth distribution is by using a **Lorenz curve.** This diagram is named after the American statistician, Max Otto Lorenz.

DEFINITION

Lorenz curve: a diagram commonly used to illustrate income or wealth distribution, named after the American statistician, Max Otto Lorenz.

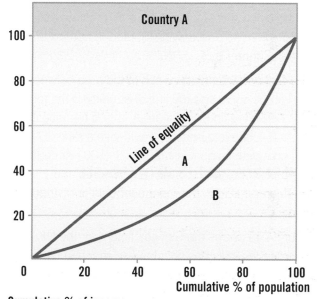

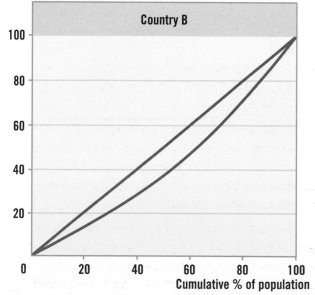

Figure 4.10 Lorenz curves

The horizontal axis on the diagram measures the cumulative percentage of the population starting with the poorest. In the case of income distribution, the vertical axis measures the cumulative percentage of income earned. A 45° line is included. This is called the line of equality, as it shows a situation in which, for example, 40 per cent of the population earn 40 per cent of the income. The actual cumulative percentage income shares are then included on the diagram. In practice, this will form a curve which starts at the origin and ends with 100 per cent of the population earning 100 per cent of income but lies below the 45° line. The greater the degree of inequality, the greater the extent to which the curve will be below the 45° line. Figure 4.10 shows that income is more unevenly distributed in country A than in country B.

The Gini coefficient is the ratio of the area between the Lorenz curve and the line of equality to the total area below the line. On Figure A, this is the ratio of A/A + B. Complete equality would give a ratio of 0 and complete inequality a ratio of 1 (100 per cent). So, in practice, the ratio will lie between 0 and 1 and the nearer it is to 1, the more unequal the distribution of income.

Figure 4.11 shows the Gini coefficient for the UK. Income inequality has not changed much in recent years. This contrasts with what happened during the period of Conservative governments from 1979 to 1997. In 1979 the Gini coefficient was 0.25, it was 0.27 in 1985 and by 1997 had risen to 0.33. Table 4.10 compares the UK's Gini coefficient with that of some other economies in 2006.

Brazil	0.57
China	0.47
USA	0.45
India	0.36
UK	0.35
Japan	0.31
Germany	0.28

Table 4.10 Gini coefficient of selected economies, 2006

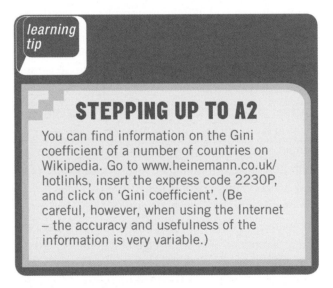

learning tip

STEPPING UP TO A2

You can find information on the Gini coefficient of a number of countries on Wikipedia. Go to www.heinemann.co.uk/hotlinks, insert the express code 2230P, and click on 'Gini coefficient'. (Be careful, however, when using the Internet – the accuracy and usefulness of the information is very variable.)

Government intervention to affect distribution of income and wealth

The extent to which a government intervenes to affect the distribution of income and wealth depends on the extent to which it believes that the free market distribution would be inequitable, the effects that such inequality will have on society and the effects it believes any intervention will have on incentives and efficiency.

Economists who believe in the efficiency of markets do not favour significant intervention. This is because

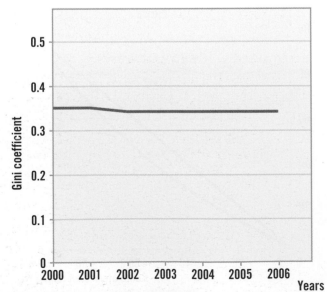

Figure 4.11 UK Gini coefficient 2000–06

they believe that differences in income act as signals encouraging workers to change jobs and differences in wealth promote saving and investment. They also think that the provision of benefits above a minimum level can encourage voluntary unemployment.

In contrast, other economists believe that intervention is justified, as market forces will not ensure an efficient allocation of income and wealth, and that low levels of income and wealth can cause considerable problems for the households involved, including having a detrimental effect on the educational performance of the children. They also think that significant differences in income and wealth can cause social division, with the poor feeling socially excluded.

WAYS IN WHICH GOVERNMENTS AFFECT THE DISTRIBUTION OF INCOME AND WEALTH

Governments influence the distribution in a number of ways, including:

● *taxation.* To assess the effects of taxation on the distribution of income and wealth, pre- and post-taxation distribution can be compared. In the UK, the overall effect of the tax system is to reduce inequality. However, while progressive taxes, such as income tax, make distribution more equal, regressive taxes, such as VAT, make the distribution more unequal.

● *provision of state benefits.* There are two types of cash benefits – means tested and universal. Means-tested benefits, such as working tax credit, are available to those who claim them and who can prove their income is below a certain level. Universal benefits are available to everyone in a particular group, irrespective of income. For example, all pensioners are currently entitled to a winter fuel allowance. Means-tested benefits reduce inequality and universal benefits form a larger percentage of the income of the poor.

● *provision of benefits in kind.* These include the provision of, for example, health care, education and school meals. The take-up of these benefits depends on the age composition of the household (for example, the elderly make the most use of the NHS) and attitudes and opportunities to access the provision (with, for example, more children from

affluent backgrounds going on to university).

● *labour market policy.* NMW, anti-discrimination acts of parliament and government subsidising of training tend to reduce income inequality.

● *macroeconomic policy.* This influences the distribution of income and wealth in a number of ways. For example, measures to reduce unemployment may benefit low-income households and regional policy may reduce geographical inequalities of income and wealth.

Poverty
ABSOLUTE POVERTY

Economists distinguish between absolute and relative poverty. People are said to be in **absolute poverty** when their income is insufficient for them to be able to afford adequate shelter, food and clothing. Even in rich countries, there are some people who still do not have any housing. In June 2007, the UK government recorded 498 people sleeping rough in England. This was a decline of 1,120 on the figure for 2000. Of course, the problem of absolute poverty is more extensive in poor countries. For instance, in 2008, 70 per cent of Nigeria's population was living on less than $1 a day.

> **DEFINITION**
>
> **Absolute poverty:** the inability to purchase the basic necessities of life

Sleeping rough is a sign of absolute poverty

RELATIVE POVERTY

While someone in the UK may consider themselves to be poor if they are living in poor accommodation and can only afford to go out once a week, someone in Mali, for example, might regard themselves as rich if they had the same standard of living. This reflects the difference between absolute and **relative poverty**.

> **DEFINITION**
>
> **Relative poverty:** a situation of being poor relative to others

People are relatively poor when they are poor in comparison to other people. They are those who are unable to afford a certain standard of living at a particular time. As a result, they are unable to participate in the usual activities of the society they live in.

The concept of human poverty, introduced in the UN's *Human Development Report* of 1997, sees poverty as a situation where people lack not only material goods but also access to items needed to enjoy a long, healthy and creative life, including self-esteem and the respect of others.

RELATIONSHIP BETWEEN RELATIVE AND ABSOLUTE POVERTY

Relative poverty varies between countries and over time. Someone who is regarded as poor in the USA might be regarded as relatively rich in some parts of the world. Twenty years ago in the UK, a personal computer might have been regarded as something of a luxury for a household, but now to participate in the activities of society it might be viewed as a necessity. If a country experiences a rise in income, absolute poverty may fall. However, if those on high incomes benefit more than those on low incomes, relative poverty may rise.

MEASURING POVERTY

To assess the extent to which poverty is a problem, it has to be measured. Economists often define as poor those people living in households with income below that of 60 per cent of average disposable income (adjusted for family size). The Labour government has set itself the target of reducing the numbers of children living in households in (relative) poverty by 50 per cent by 2010/11.

Particular groups are more prone to poverty than others. These include the unemployed, the old, the sick, lone parents and those from ethnic minorities. For example, in 2004/5 62 per cent of households with one adult unemployed, 33 per cent of Asian or Asian British households, 29 per cent of lone parent households, and 28 per cent of households with one or more disabled people had incomes below 60 per cent of median disposable income.

CAUSES OF POVERTY

Essentially, the amount of poverty experienced depends on the level of income achieved and how it is distributed. The reasons why particular people are poor include:

- *unemployment*. This is a major cause of poverty, with some households having no one in employment.

- *low wages*. Some workers in unskilled, casual employment earn very low wages. For example, a significant proportion of workers in Northern Ireland and the North East are on low wages. However, just because someone earns low wages does not necessarily mean they are poor. It is possible that they could live in a household with a high income-earning partner or parents.

- *sickness and disability*. Most of the long-term sick and disabled are dependent on benefits and this takes them into the low-income category.

- *old age*. For pensioners, state benefits are the largest source of income. Occupational pensions and investment income, however, are forming an increasing proportion of the income of some retired people.

- *the poverty trap*. This arises when the poor find it difficult to raise their disposable income because any rise in gross income results in them having to pay more in tax and receive less in benefits.

● *being a lone parent*. Not having a partner to cope with the raising of a child may make it difficult for someone to obtain full-time employment.

● *reluctance to claim benefits*. A number of people, either because they are unaware of their entitlements or because of fear of social stigma, do not claim benefits that could help to supplement their incomes.

THE EFFECTS OF POVERTY

Poverty, especially absolute poverty, has a number of serious adverse effects on those who experience it. The poor tend to suffer worse physical and mental health and have a lower life expectancy. The children of the poor suffer in terms of receiving less education, are less likely to have a computer at home and to travel abroad. All these factors tend to result in the children gaining fewer qualifications and a vicious circle of poverty developing. The poor can feel cut off and even alienated from society, unable to live the life that the majority can experience. Poverty also has damaging effects on the wider economy. It imposes a burden on government spending and reduces productivity.

GOVERNMENT POLICY MEASURES TO REDUCE POVERTY

Governments may seek to reduce absolute poverty by introducing measures that raise the income of the poorest groups. Governments may also try to reduce relative poverty by introducing measures that narrow the gap between the rich and the poor. Among the measures they might use are:

● *operating a NMW*. If set above the equilibrium level, this will help the low paid who stay in employment. As mentioned above, however, not all the low paid are in poor households. Indeed a relatively high number of minimum wage earners are secondary earners from middle-income and high-income families. In addition, not all the poor are in employment, such as the old and disabled.

● *cutting the bottom rate of income tax*. This may reduce the extent of the poverty trap and provide a greater incentive for people to work. In addition to the incentive, however, there also have to be the jobs available.

● *increasing employment opportunities*. This is thought to be significant, as a major cause of poverty is unemployment. Economists, however, disagree about the best methods of increasing the number of jobs on offer.

● *improving the quantity and quality of training and education*. This is a long-term measure but, again, an important one, as it will increase the productivity and potential productivity of those affected and thereby improve their job prospects and earning potential.

● *making use of the trickle-down effect*. This is a more controversial policy favoured by some economists. The idea is to cut the rate of corporation tax and the top rate of income tax with the intention of encouraging entrepreneurs to expand and thereby create employment for the poor. It is also thought

ACTIVITY ⋯⟩

There were concerns in 2007 that the government would not meet its target to halve child poverty by 2010 and end it by 2020. A report by the Joseph Rowntree Foundation claimed that poverty had worsened, with the working poor family being particularly badly hit.

The research found schools, hospitals and local government are among the biggest employers of low-paid workers aged over 25. Half of all poor children live in working households. Figures also showed that the number of children living below the poverty line rose by 100,000 in 2006.

a) Identify two costs to an economy of child poverty.

b) What is the 'poverty line'?

c) Explain one possible government policy measure to reduce the poverty suggested in the passage.

STRETCH AND CHALLENGE

d) Discuss whether it will ever be possible to eliminate poverty.

that higher spending by the rich may also stimulate the economy. However, it is difficult to forecast how the rich will behave and whether the poor will benefit from any expansion that does occur. For example, will they have the skills for any new jobs created and what about the poor who are unable to work?

● *increasing benefits*. Economists have differing views about the effects of raising benefits for the unemployed. Some think that it can raise aggregate demand and thereby create jobs, while others believe it will increase voluntary unemployment. There is more agreement on increasing benefits for those unable to work or retired. Those dependent solely on benefits fall into the lowest quintile of income and many of them would be unable to take out private insurance or invest in order to raise their income.

● *increasing the provision of affordable childcare*. This would enable more lone parents to undertake full-time employment and raise them out of poverty.

learning tip

STEPPING UP TO A2

You need to explore current issues in labour markets, including the challenges and opportunities posed by an ageing population, what to do about pensions and the effects of migration.

An ageing population

The UK, USA, Japan and most European countries have ageing populations. This simply means that the average age of their population is increasing. This demographic change is the result of a fall in both the birth rate and the death rate – women are having fewer children and people are living longer. It is having consequences for both the nature and the size of the countries' labour forces.

Older workers have experience, tend to stay with existing employers and lose few days through short-term illness. They are also often thought to be more

conscientious and interact well with customers. On the other hand, their skills may need to be updated, they tend to be less geographically and occupationally mobile, may be less adaptable and may be more at risk from serious illness.

A number of UK companies, including DIY companies and supermarkets, actively seek to recruit the over-50s. Their strategy is based on the belief that older workers have a lot to offer and that taking a positive attitude to their recruitment increases the pool of workers they can draw on.

Increased longevity is also increasing the dependency ratio in many developed countries. This means that there are more pensioners relative to workers. In the UK's case, there are currently approximately three workers for every one pensioner. It is predicted that by 2050 this will have changed to two workers for every one pensioner.

This change in the **dependency ratio** is putting upward pressure on government spending on health care, community care and pensions, it is stretching company pension funds and placing a greater

DEFINITION

Dependency ratio: proportion of the population who are too young, too old or too sick to work and so who are reliant on the output of those who are working

Some UK companies recruit over-50s

burden on the labour force. The extra cost involved in the ageing population is sometimes referred to as the demographic time bomb.

PENSIONS

UK state pensions are financed on a 'pay as you go' basis. This means that the pension payments received by current pensioners are paid for by the taxes paid by current workers. This has led to concern that the tax burden on workers might have to rise to finance the increased costs of pensions.

The UK government is considering a number of ways of trying to maintain pensioners' living standards while reducing the fiscal pressure of an ageing population. These include:

● *raising the retirement age*. It has already been announced that the state retirement age for women will be raised to 65 in phased transition from 2010 to 2020. The 2006 report entitled *A New Pension Settlement for the 21st Century*, produced by a Pension Commission led by Lord Turner, has recommended raising the state retirement age to 66 by 2030, 67 by 2040 and 68 by 2050. Increasing the working lifetime reduces the number of pensioners and increases the number of workers and so reduces the dependency ratio.

● *discouraging early retirement*. The government can set an example in terms of its own public sector workers, although this may prove to be unpopular. It can discourage early retirement in the private sector by giving favourable tax treatment to pension schemes that penalise early retirement. It is interesting to note that, while in 2006, 62 per cent of Americans aged between 55 and 64 were economically active, only 45 per cent of those in the EU were.

● *increasing the labour force by other means*. This approach may include seeking to increase the economic activity rate of lone parents and the disabled and permitting more immigration.

● *promoting occupational and personal pension schemes*. Relying more on private sector pension schemes may enable the government to reduce the real value of the state pension. Of course, the value of private pension schemes will be dependent

on whether sufficient contributions are made by both workers and employers, and how the financial investments made by the schemes perform.

● *encouraging a change in salary structures*. Studies have shown that productivity tends to peak when workers are in their 30s and 40s, whereas earnings tend to peak for workers when they are in their 50s. This may suggest that older workers are overpaid relative to their productivity, which may price some of them out of the labour market. Some Japanese employers are changing pay structures in which pay rises with seniority to more flexible systems.

ACTIVITY ⋯⋮⋗

Italy has one of the EU's fastest-ageing populations and one of the highest levels of spending on pensions. By 2030, Italy will have only two workers for every retired person. By 2050 this will become three workers for every two retired people.

The minimum retirement age in the country was raised from 57 to 58 in January 2008. It will be raised to 61 by 2012. Workers in jobs defined as 'arduous' will, however, enjoy indefinitely the right to retire at 57. This group of workers includes miners, shift workers, including bus drivers, and factory workers who do repetitive tasks – approximately 6 per cent of the labour force.

The Italian government has, so far, resisted cutting state pensions, largely due to the growing power of trade unions in the country. Some Italian politicians are worried that the government's reluctance to tackle the rising cost of an ageing population will lead to higher and higher taxes.

a) Identify two possible reasons why Italy's population is ageing.

b) Explain one factor that could increase the power of a country's trade unions.

c) Analyse the impact that the change in the retirement age in Italy may have on government spending on the elderly.

STRETCH AND CHALLENGE

d) Discuss one measure, not mentioned in the passage, that the Italian government could take to reduce the costs of an ageing population.

EU directives

EU directives are instructions to member countries to achieve particular outcomes. They usually allow the member countries some flexibility in terms of the laws they draw up to achieve the desired result.

Examples that have had an impact on the UK labour market are the Working Time Directive (1993), the Parental Leave Directive (1999) and the Equal Treatment Framework Directive (2000). The Working Time Directive sets a maximum 48-hour working week. The UK has implemented this but has negotiated an opt-out that allows workers to work for longer if they wish. The Parental Leave Directive increased paid maternity leave from 14 to 18 weeks and gave both men and women the right to three months' unpaid leave after the birth of a child. More recently, the UK's anti-ageism discrimination legislation was introduced on 1st October 2006 largely to meet the EU's directive to outlaw discrimination on the grounds of age.

Labour market directives protect workers' rights and may correct some forms of labour market failure, including discrimination. There is a risk, however, that excessive protection for those in work may depress economic growth and job creation.

Migration

The supply of labour in a country is influenced by the emigration and immigration of economically active people. Net immigration, with more people coming into the country to live than leaving the country, will add to the labour force. This increase in the number of workers can have a number of advantages. It can help overcome skill shortages, can reduce the dependency ratio, increase government tax revenue and help the economy to expand without encountering inflationary pressure.

Immigration can, however, bring a number of disadvantages. The countries from which the immigrants come may suffer skills shortages as a result of net emigration of some of their key workers. Ghana, for example, loses three-quarters of its trained doctors to emigration.

Immigration may disadvantage low-paid workers if some of the immigrants are prepared to work for lower wages. This may reduce their employment

ECONOMICS IN CONTEXT

TEMPORARY WORKERS

In early 2008, the UK government was still debating an EU agency workers' directive. This would give temporary workers, including those employed through agencies, the same rights as permanent workers after six weeks with an employer. These rights would cover, for example, holiday pay, sick pay and pensions.

UK unions support the directive, arguing that more workers are losing rights with the shift towards temporary and contract work. They argue that a two-tier labour force is being created in which some workers have very few rights. They also believe that some temporary workers are being exploited by their employers. They cite cases of rogue employment agencies that charge workers, particularly immigrants, excessive amounts for finding them work, for accommodation and transport.

Employers, however, are opposing the directive. They claim that it will increase the costs of production, reduce flexibility and increase employment. The Confederation of British Industry (CBI) has claimed that the measure could cost 250,000 temporary jobs, with companies switching from temporary workers to asking their employees to work overtime during busy periods. If they are right, an attempt to remove the discrimination between the 'insiders' with permanent jobs and the 'outsiders' with temporary jobs would result in an increase in the discrimination between the employed and the unemployed.

In 2008, an agreement was reached between the CBI, the Trades Union Congress (TUC) and the government that will give temporary workers the right to equal treatment after 12 weeks in the job. The government is seeking to get other EU members to agree to the longer qualifying period.

chances and put downward pressure on wages. It may, for instance, keep some neets out of jobs. (See *OCR AS* Economics, page 123, on neets.) Given the choice between a well motivated and hard-working immigrant worker and a reluctant, inexperienced and unskilled young person, an employer might be expected to select the former. In addition, immigration may place pressure on services such as health care and education if the immigrants bring their families with them and if they are concentrated in particular areas.

The UK has had net immigration since 1994. There was a surge in immigration from central and eastern Europe, particularly Poland, in 2004 to 2006 after EU membership expanded.

Many of the immigrants to the UK are attracted by the relatively low unemployment and high wages found in the country. Recent migrants are filling jobs at all skill levels. A notable proportion of those working in low-skilled jobs in, for example, hotel and catering, are thought to be over-skilled for their current jobs and may move into more demanding occupations in the future. Some of the immigrants are also expected to return to the countries they came from as economic prospects in those countries improve.

learning tip

Remember, in discussing the effects of immigration or indeed emigration on employment, that there is not a fixed number of jobs. Having more people in the country adds not just to aggregate supply but also to aggregate demand.

ACTIVITY ····∴‣

It was reported in early 2008 that the number of central and eastern European (CEE) immigrants coming to the UK was falling and that some were returning home. Indeed, more Poles were leaving the UK than entering it. Those leaving were attracted by rising pay and employment in CEE. The Polish economy experienced an upturn at the start of 2008 and the Polish currency, the zloty, was rising in value, in contrast to the pound sterling, which was falling in value.

a) Using an aggregate demand and aggregate supply diagram, analyse the effects of net immigration on an economy.

b) Explain why changes in the value of the zloty and the pound sterling may have influenced some Poles to return home.

c) Discuss why wage rates may converge between EU countries, while there may be significant differences between wage rates in the EU and in other parts of the world.

ECONOMICS IN CONTEXT

TWO VIEWS ON IMMIGRATION

In October 2007, two reports were published that gave different pictures of the effects of immigration on the UK. One, by the Institute of Directors, found that employers are recruiting immigrant workers because they are outperforming the existing labour force in terms of productivity, education and skills, work ethic, reliability, time they take off sick and flexibility, including willingness to work overtime. They said migrant workers are crucial to the hotel and catering industry and to agriculture, as they are prepared to do the jobs that the natives will not do.

In contrast, a Home Office report published in the same month highlighted some of the problems resulting from the recent immigration from CEE. Low-level crime, such as driving offences, have increased in some areas and this is increasing translation costs in courts. There is also pressure on affordable housing and rent levels, and on NHS services and support staff in state schools.

ExamCafé
Relax, refresh, result!

Relax and prepare

Avis

When I started A2, the AS seemed easy. I found MP theory hard but it made more sense when my teacher got us to work out the MRP of having one more person in our business studies project making chocolate biscuits for sale in our school. Finding examples made things clearer for me.

At first, I also found market structures difficult. Two weeks before the exam I drew a diagram for each one and wrote down beneath them the main characteristics. I showed them to my teacher. He checked and corrected them – I had confused monopoly and monopolistic competition. I put the corrected sheets on my bedroom wall and looked at them for a few minutes each day – it really helped.

Shaun

Labour and leisure was my favourite part of economics. I work in a local supermarket and much of what we covered I could relate to. I found that I was being paid just above the minimum wage for my age. I pointed this out to my boss who did nothing about it so I then asked my friends who work in other supermarkets in the town how much they were getting paid. When I found out, I applied for a job at —. I got it and I am now enjoying some economic rent! My work helped my understanding of this paper and this paper helped my work!

Kirsty

I was determined to get an A*. After each lesson, I read over my class work, did any exercise in the book we had not done in class and added some notes from my reading. I made myself a real pest by asking my teacher to explain anything I did not understand and by asking how I could improve my answers. Fortunately she was very understanding. She also made me realise that I needed to give examples where possible, to keep up to date with developments in labour and leisure markets and to explore topics in depth.

Refresh your memory

1. Which groups of people are economically inactive?
2. What is the difference between work and leisure?
3. What effect is the absence of barriers to entry and exit likely to have on the profits earned in a market?
4. How does monopoly differ from monopolistic competition?
5. What factors influence the demand for television production crew?
6. What would make the supply of teachers more elastic?
7. How does the immobility of labour lead to market failure?
8. What does it mean if a country's Gini coefficient increases?

Get the result !

EXAM QUESTION

Discuss whether the gap between the pay of male and female solicitors is likely to narrow in the future.

Jo's answer

Female solicitors may earn more in the future. They may work more hours, especially if it becomes easier to get childcare. Working more hours will increase their annual pay.

More female solicitors may join trade unions. This will increase their bargaining strength and push up their wage rates. Trade unions bargain for their members. They can back up their wage claims by threatening to take industrial action.

If discrimination is reduced, the pay of female solicitors may increase. Discrimination has kept down the pay of women. Without discrimination, demand for female solicitors may be higher.

An increase in demand raises the wage rate. Firms may be prepared to employ more women. They may also be prepared to promote more women. In lots of careers, the top jobs go to men. With less discrimination, there may be more women at the top of solicitors' firms. This will raise average pay.

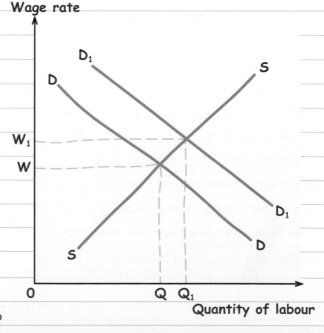

On the other hand, women solicitors' pay may stay low. Women are more concerned with non-pecuniary advantages of jobs. They may be prepared to work for low pay if working conditions and working hours are good. A lot of women want to have long holidays so they can look after their children and they may want to work close to home.

Comment

This is quite a tricky and demanding question. A major problem with Jo's answer is that she is not directly answering the question. She is writing about whether the pay of women solicitors will increase rather than whether the gender pay gap will narrow. Her answer is also rather descriptive. There is not much analysis. She does include a demand and supply diagram but she could have made more use of demand and supply analysis.

In the last paragraph, Jo seeks to evaluate by considering another possible outcome. She, however, does not achieve this, as she does not substantiate her comments. Are women more concerned than men about the non-pecuniary advantages of jobs? If they are, why does this result in their pay being low? The reference to women's pay being low also needed to be clearer – low in relation to what?

Juan's answer

The gap between the pay of male and female solicitors' pay is likely to narrow in the future, but the extent to which it does so will depend on a number of factors.

More women than men are now going to university and the qualifications that women are gaining are increasing. This should increase the productivity of female solicitors relative to male solicitors. This will increase the marginal revenue productivity of female solicitors. Higher MRP is likely to encourage employers to hire more female solicitors. This will shift the demand curve for female solicitors to the right, raising their relative pay.

The longer the period of training female solicitors undertake and the more qualifications they gain, the greater their chance of being promoted. It will also make their supply more inelastic, which again would tend to push up their relative pay. Of course, if there are more qualified people seeking to be solicitors, this would increase their supply. This increase may suppress wage rises. Indeed, there are more graduates coming on to the market each year, including law graduates.

Marginal revenue productivity can also be increased by increases in marginal revenue. Some areas of the law are better paid than others. For example, corporate law is very profitable and if more women solicitors move into more profitable areas of the law, their average pay will rise relative to that of male solicitors. Of course it can be difficult to measure labour productivity, particularly in terms of workers in service industries.

The gender gap between solicitors may be reduced by a reduction in negative discrimination. If some employers think that women solicitors are not as good as male solicitors they will undervalue their MRP. The diagram shows that the demand for female solicitors is lower than their MRP.

Wage rate of female solicitors

MRP

S

D

W_x

W

MRP

D = demand with discrimination

S

0   Q Q_x **Quantity of labour of female solicitors**

This results in the pay and the employment of female solicitors being below the efficient level. There is anti-discrimination legislation but it needs to be enforced. Some high-profile cases where legal firms are fined for discriminating against female staff may put pressure on any firms that are discriminating to stop the practice.

Over time, the gap between male and female pay in most jobs has narrowed as social attitudes to women working and the skills of women have altered. As more women work as solicitors and move up the career path, any discrimination may be reduced.

The Law Society, which represents solicitors, may also take up the case of female solicitors if it believes they are being discriminated against. Professional organisations often have relatively strong bargaining power. Now a greater percentage of women than men belong to trade unions and membership of professional organisations is strong among professional groups.

The gap between the pay of male and female solicitors may not be as great as the figures seem to imply. Female solicitors may be receiving lower pay because they are working fewer hours. Pay per hour may be closer between the two genders. If this is the case, whether the gap between the annual salaries of male and female solicitors will narrow will depend on how many hours the two groups work in the future. The number of hours people choose to work is influenced by the wage rate, their family circumstances and the number of hours on offer. As well as some women possibly working more hours in the future, some men may choose to reduce the number of hours they work in order to spend more time with their families.

The long working hours culture in the legal profession and the lack of flexibility of hours, particularly in terms of senior posts, may be making it difficult for women with young children to undertake these posts. If in the future, working hours shorten and become more flexible, this may make it possible for more women to accept promotion, which will raise their average pay.

If there is a gap between the hourly pay of male and female solicitors, the extent to which the gap may narrow will be influenced by how the skills and qualifications of the two groups change, what branch of law they enter and whether any discrimination continues.

Comment

Juan's answer starts in a direct and focused way. Juan then makes good use of demand and supply theory and applies MRP. He then considers discrimination in an objective way. His reference to the Law Society shows good general awareness. He makes pertinent comments about the possibility that the gender gap in hourly pay may be lower than in terms of annual pay.

Juan is evaluating throughout his answer, considering the extent to which possible changes may occur and their impact.

Hot tips

The economics of work and leisure exam is in two sections. The first section consists of a data response question with approximately six parts. The second section has three structured essay questions from which you have to select one.

1. The paper lasts for two hours and is marked out of 60, 25 for the data response and 35 for the essay. This obviously makes two minutes per mark. On this basis you should spend approximately fifty minutes on the data response question and one hour and ten minutes on the essay question.

2. On the data response question, there are two question parts that require you to evaluate. Most candidates remember to do this with the last question part, which starts with the word 'Discuss'. A number, however, forget to do this with the question part commencing with the words 'Comment on'.

3. In selecting which essay question to answer, take care that you can answer both parts well. It is better to produce good answers to parts a) and b) than a brilliant answer to one part and a poor answer to the other part.

4. Remember to base your answers on pertinent concepts drawn from both your AS and A2 studies. It

is, for instance, surprising how many candidates, when answering questions about wage determination and wage differentials, forget about demand and supply analysis.

5. The economics of work and leisure is concerned with people and as such involves some interesting but also some controversial subjects. These include the gender pay gap and the effects of immigration. Try to be objective when dealing with these areas and base your answers on economic analysis.

6. Labour and leisure markets are changing all the time with, for instance, new legislation being passed and market structures altering. This means that it is very important for you to keep up to date with developments in the subject. You can do this by reading economics magazines and checking on the news via a range of media.

7. Do not jump stages in your analysis. For instance, in analysing why supernormal profits may be earned in the long run in an oligopolistic market, it is not sufficient to just write 'because there are high barriers to entry into and exit from such a market'. You would need to explain what barriers to entry and exit are and how their presence influences market power.

Exam practice paper

Section A

Answer this question.

BBC radio stays ahead of commercial radio

BBC radio stations top the tables for national listening (see Table 1) and they are still the preferred employers for radio journalists.

	June 2005			June 2007	
	% share of radio listeners	Reach (million)*	% share of radio listeners	Reach (million)*
BBC Radio 2	16.0	13.3	15.6	13.1
BBC Radio 4	11.2	9.6	11.2	9.5
BBC Radio 1	9.2	10.2	10.3	10.9
BBC Radio 5 Live	4.4	5.7	4.5	6.1
Classic FM	4.3	6.3	4.0	5.7
Heart	2.2	3.1	2.3	3.3
Magic	2.0	2.9	2.4	3.4
Talksport	1.8	2.2	1.8	2.4
Galaxy	1.6	2.5	1.8	2.6
Virgin	1.5	2.4	1.5	2.5

*Based on the number of people listening to a station for at least five minutes a week.

Table 1 National listening figures

Radio broadcasting is going through a number of changes. New commercial stations are being set up and some people are suggesting the market will move towards monopolistic competition in the future.

2005 saw online advertising revenue overtaking radio advertising revenue for the first time. As well as facing this threat to their revenue, commercial radio stations are experiencing some problems retaining their staff. There is a significant gap in the pay for radio journalists between commercial radio and BBC radio. In 2008 a junior journalist at the BBC earned, on average, £22,000 a year compared to £14,000 in commercial radio. Some attribute this difference to the greater role of trade unions in the BBC. Most commercial radio staff do not belong to trade unions.

A significant proportion of those starting on commercial radio seeks to move to the BBC. This is not only because of the pay but also because of the more stable environment where a journalist can develop a long-term career path. In commercial radio there are few senior management posts. Despite these factors, commercial radio does not have problems attracting graduates. Many editors and programme managers say there is more demand for jobs than there are positions available.

1 a) i) Has the four-firm market concentration ratio increased or decreased in 2007 compared with 2005? Justify your answer. (2)

    ii) Which radio station experienced the greatest percentage increase in reach between 2005 and 2007? (1)

  b) i) State three characteristics of monopolistic competition. (3)

    ii Comment on the benefits to consumers of a market moving from oligopoly towards monopolistic competition. (5)

  c) Explain three reasons why a journalist may prefer to work for the BBC rather than for a commercial radio station. (6)

  d) Discuss whether an increase in trade union membership among commercial radio journalists would increase their pay. (8)

Section B

Answer one question.

2 A 2008 research study by the Law Society found that the average pay for male solicitors was £60,000, while it was only £41,000 for female solicitors.

  a) Explain why male solicitors are paid more than female solicitors. (15)

  b) Discuss whether the gap between the pay of male and female solicitors is likely to narrow in the future. (20)

3 French workers have, on average, 37 days holiday a year in comparison to 26 for workers in the UK. They also work fewer hours per day than UK workers.

  a) Explain what factors influence the number of hours a day an individual works. (15)

  b) Discuss whether more UK people will seek to work in France in the future. (20)

4 In the UK the national minimum wage (NMW) paid to 16–17-year-olds and 18–21-year-olds is set at approximately 62 per cent and 85 per cent of the adult rate. In contrast, in Spain the full rate is paid at 16.

  a) Explain the arguments for the UK maintaining the NMW. (15)

  b) Discuss whether the UK should pay the same NMW rate to all ages. (20)

PART 2

Transport economics

Transport economics has been a recognised branch of applied economics for the last 40 years or so. It started as a specialist field of study, but as interest in transport issues has grown and transport problems have increasingly affected our lives, it is now central to any study of economics in the twenty-first century.

Transport, by definition, is used by all of us. The function it performs is vital to the smooth operation of the economy and for business, both of which mean that it is a relevant and interesting subject for economists to study. Moreover, transport problems and issues are not confined to economies like our own. The demand for transport is soaring in countries such as China, India and Russia. The result is that they are now experiencing the sort of problems that the UK was facing a generation ago.

Many of the topics that you will study in this part ought to be already familiar to you as they regularly feature in newspapers and on television. For example:

● What can be done about the problems of congestion on our motorways, city centre roads, principal airports and on the rail network?

● Will road pricing ever happen on a wide scale?

● What will be the effect of rising oil prices and how might transport be more efficient in using oil?

● Should we really be flying? In particular, should there be restraint on the growth of low-cost airlines or is this just a consequence of market forces?

● Why is public transport an inferior alternative for many people?

● Why are rail fares so high and, yet, punctuality often lacking?

These are just a few of the topics you will come across in this part. One thing they have in common is that all have some form of economics that underpins them. Economists therefore have a pivotal role in putting forward alternative viewpoints and in advising governments about how to deal with them through transport policies.

In studying transport economics, you will have an opportunity to extend your knowledge of some of the concepts you studied at AS Level. This particularly applies to the content of Chapters 6 and 7, where you will be able to learn how the workings of the market system and examples of market failure apply to particular transport problems and issues. You will also learn how aspects of macroeconomics, particularly relating to taxation, government spending and managing the economy, have transport significance.

5 Transport, transport trends and the economy

On completion of this chapter, you should be able to:

- define 'transport' in terms of transport operations and infrastructure
- understand the advantages and disadvantages of the main modes of transport, for passenger and freight transport
- apply an understanding of these characteristics to appreciate why transport is a derived demand
- understand the structure of transport operations in the UK, in terms of private and public sector ownership and responsibilities
- interpret and understand the reasons for recent trends in the demand for transport in the UK and the rest of the EU
- apply economic principles to understand how and why transport forecasts are made and used by economists
- discuss the problems and implications of forecasting transport trends
- handle and interpret data on the economic importance of transport in the UK economy.

Transport issues regularly make headline news. This is hardly surprising, since transport is an essential part of our lives. Globally, the demand for transport continues to increase and, with it, an increase in interest in transport issues and policies.

As you will see, most of these issues can be traced back to the basic principles of economics studied at AS. Many are associated with market failure. Others have their foundation in the 'economic problem'. The role of the economist is to analyse these issues and make relevant policy recommendations.

Transport economics is a recognised branch of applied economics. The four chapters in this part of the book provide an introduction to some of the topics that make transport a fascinating part of modern economics.

A definition of 'transport'

Let us start with a basic definition of **transport**:

'Transport is the movement of people and goods for personal and business reasons.'

> **DEFINITION**
>
> **Transport:** the movement of people and goods for personal and business reasons

It covers three important aspects:

● *movement* – transport by definition involves the physical carriage of people and goods over a particular distance

● *purpose* – the reasons why people and businesses find it necessary to use some means of transport

● *carriage* – what is actually being moved, for example, people or goods, how many or how much. In the case of goods, the type of product moved is particularly relevant.

Two further aspects must be included. These are:

● the **mode of transport** used – at a basic level, this covers road, rail, air and sea transport, although within each, there are various alternatives available to users and potential users

● the **infrastructure** on which transport demand is taking place. This includes roads, motorways, sea channels, flight paths and rail tracks.

DEFINITIONS

Mode of transport: means of transport, basically road, rail, air and sea transport

Infrastructure: anything that provides for the operation of transport

It is particularly important to distinguish between passenger and freight transport. Some passenger transport modes – railways, ferries and many scheduled aircraft – are able to carry goods as well as people, although their main business is that of passenger transport. In the main, though, there are a set of modes that meet the needs for person transport and other modes that are exclusively for the carriage of freight.

The function of transport, therefore, is to meet the needs of people and firms for efficient movement.

The demand for transport

The demand for transport is a **derived demand**. For example, the demand that a company has for freight transport is derived from its needs to move goods from, say, a factory to customers. Without transport, these needs would not be met. It is the same for person transport – our demand for transport is derived from the needs we have in carrying out our daily lives. These needs are many, such as travelling to college, going to the supermarket and visiting friends. So, transport is demanded not just for what it is, but for what it does to enhance personal and business well-being. It is a type of input into the production process of firms and the lifestyles of people.

DEFINITION

Derived demand: demand that depends upon the final output that is produced

We can get a good indication of the derived demand nature of person transport from the National Travel Survey, a periodic survey of the travel patterns of households. Table 5.1 gives a summary of the main findings of the 2005 survey.

Table 5.1 shows that:

● excluding walking, 84 per cent of trips made by households are by car

● the greatest intensity of travel by car is for commuting and business trips

● relatively, the most important reason for using rail is for commuting and business travel

Family transport is a derived demand

Trip purpose	Walk	Car driver	Car passenger	Local bus	Rail/ Underground	Other	All modes
Commuting/business	20	122	19	14	12	11	198
Education	48	23	25	11	2	5	114
Shopping	51	87	44	17	2	5	206
Personal business	26	46	26	7	1	3	109
Leisure	49	99	94	13	6	16	277
Other	51	58	27	2	–		139
All purposes	245	435	236	63	23	42	1,044

Table 5.1 Trips per person per year by main mode and purpose, 2005
Source: *National Travel Survey*, 2005

● just 8 per cent of trips made are by bus, and these are spread across all journey purposes.

If you look elsewhere in the National Travel Survey, you will also find that:

● around a half of all car trips made are for journeys of less than five miles

● over the past ten years, the overall number of trips made by households has decreased by 4 per cent, with an 8 per cent fall in the number of commuting trips. The average length of trip for most purposes has, though, increased by 6 to 8 per cent.

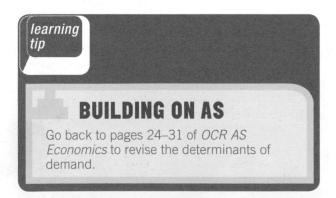

learning tip

BUILDING ON AS

Go back to pages 24–31 of *OCR AS Economics* to revise the determinants of demand.

So, what are the determinants of a household's demand for transport by any given mode? We can use your understanding of the determinants of demand to show that for private car transport these include:

● the cost of running a car

● the relative prices of other modes of transport

● household income

● car availability/ownership

● size of household

● taste and fashion

● quality factors relating to convenience, journey times and level of congestion.

As you can see, it is not particularly simple. Studies have shown that car availability, having a car available for the trip that has to be made, is invariably the most important determinant of demand. Once households acquire a car, it makes sense to use it for most of their travel needs.

ACTIVITY ····

a) See what statistical information you can find in *Transport Statistics, Great Britain*, and *Transport Trends* on the determinants of demand for private car transport and how these have changed over the past ten years.

b) Write down what you believe to be the main determinants of demand for transport by local bus. How do these differ from the determinants of demand for private car transport?

For freight transport, as stated earlier, demand is derived from the needs of firms for moving goods in the course of their day-to-day activities. The reasons for this demand and the mode of transport used are invariably a function of a firm's business. Let us take some examples:

● *a large supermarket chain.* Its demand for transport is for the delivery of goods from hundreds of suppliers to a regional distribution centre where loads are then put together for onward transport to their retail stores.

● *a food processing firm.* Very similar to the supermarket, involving the assembly of raw materials and the distribution of the final products to customers, either direct to the customers' premises or to their warehouse or distribution centre.

● *an electricity generating plant.* A relatively simple demand that involves moving coal or oil to the power station.

Unlike person transport, there are no particular statistics that show the breakdown of demand by journey purpose.

At the level of a firm, the demand for a particular mode of freight transport is determined by:

● the cost

● the convenience in terms of ease of collection and delivery

● the type of goods carried

● the level of service provided.

For most firms, as we shall see below, there is little or no modal choice. For most inland transport, firms have no choice but to move goods by road. The choice they have to make is whether to transport their products in their own vehicles or contract out to a third party. Rail freight is used by a growing number of companies, although most such traffic tends to be of heavy products over relatively short distances. The main exception is where companies use rail to move containers and bulk liquids to and from ports.

Advantages and disadvantages of the main modes of transport

It is clear from what has been stated above, that the choice of mode of transport by individuals and firms is heavily dependent upon non-price factors as well as the relative cost of transport between competing modes. These non-price factors are the fashion and taste determinants of demand.

Table 5.2 summarises these characteristics. For passengers and for freight, road transport has

Passenger transport	
Private car	most flexible and convenient mode; only one that can give door-to-door service; widely used for all types of journey purpose; can be used to carry shopping, luggage; least environmentally acceptable of main modes
Bus	users are limited by the service provided; most effective on main corridors in large towns and cities; more attractive to users when frequency involves only short waiting times
Rail	speedy carrier of large volumes of passengers over middle to long distances and for access into cities and large towns
Air	clearly has advantage of moving passengers over longer distances at speed; limited use for internal transport in the UK but widely used elsewhere

Freight transport	
Road	advantages in terms of convenience, flexibility and connectivity; suitable for carriage of most goods
Rail	best suited to moving bulk loads over varying distances; containers provide an efficient and speedy means of moving goods to ports and to rest of the EU; problems of interchange can reduce its efficiency
Air	appropriate for moving time-sensitive and expensive cargo, mainly over long distances
Sea	slow but cheap when moving bulk cargoes or containers, particularly over long distances

Table 5.2 Modal characteristics

ECONOMICS IN CONTEXT

BUS TRAVEL HITS 11-YEAR HIGH WITH A MILLION MORE JOURNEYS

A new report published by the Confederation of Passenger Transport (CPT) showed that a boom in bus use is helping to lift some of the gloom on the high street. In 2007, almost 1 billion bus journeys were made in the UK for shopping.

According to their On the Move report, the CPT believes that more shoppers are using the bus in response to increasing congestion, rising parking costs and soaring fuel prices. All of these make the bus more competitive than the car … leaving smart shoppers more cash in their pockets to spend in the shops.

The report was released just days after the first reading of the government's Transport Bill in the House of Commons. It gives various examples of local authorities and bus companies working together in quality partnerships to entice more people back onto buses. Significantly, it heralds the bus as a sustainable form of public transport and estimates that those people who travelled by bus last year saved 8.1 million tonnes of CO_2 emissions compared to if those journeys had been made by car. Bus operators are also trialling new low-carbon fuels to make their fleets greener, and investing in more low-floor vehicles to make their fleets more attractive.

substantial advantages over all other modes of transport for most types of demands. This is why in the UK, road has a dominant market share for inland transport. Rail's role is rather more specific and related to the characteristics shown in the table. Environmentally, however, it is more acceptable than road transport, excluding the bus, for transporting both people and goods.

DEFINITION

Privatisation: sale of state-owned business activity to the private sector

ACTIVITY ⋯⋮

Make a record of the number of journeys made each week by each member of your family by purpose and mode of transport used.

a) Summarise your findings

b) Explain how your findings

  i) support your understanding of derived demand

  ii) reflect the modal characteristics that are shown in Table 5.2.

Organisation of transport in the UK

As a consequence of extensive **privatisation**, the organisation of transport in the UK is now predominantly with the private sector. This is particularly so with respect to the operation of transport services, which is a fully private sector responsibility. The position for infrastructure is rather more complicated, although the private sector has had an increasingly important role in recent years. (A discussion of the arguments for privatisation follows in Chapter 6.)

Figure 5.1 shows the scale of private sector ownership of passenger and freight transport operations. A few typical companies are also shown. Many of these companies have business interests across more than one mode. First Group, for example, is the largest bus company in the UK, a major passenger train operating company and a small provider of rail freight services. Others, such as Stagecoach, National Express, Arriva and Go-Ahead, are substantial providers of bus and rail passenger services. A further interesting feature has been the way in which the largest providers of freight services have been taken over by non-UK companies.

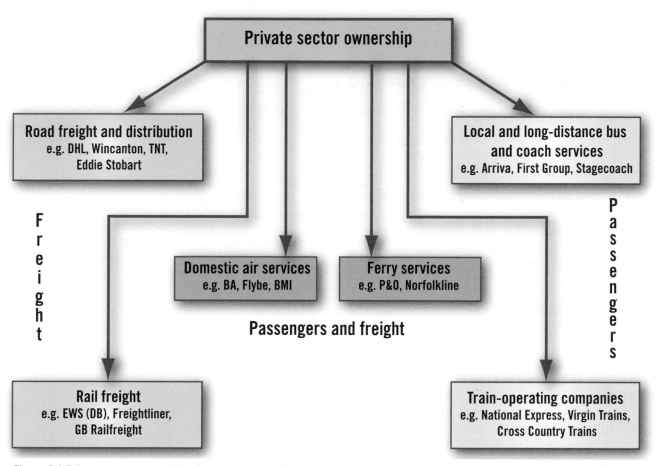

Figure 5.1 Private sector ownership of transport operations

Figure 5.1 excludes private vehicle ownership. This is because the nature of this type of ownership is that decisions on whether to use a car or motorcycle have always been taken freely by the individual, since these modes of transport are exclusively for private use. Use of the modes shown in Figure 5.1 is different, since it is collective.

The government has no direct part to play in providing transport services. Indirectly, though, through its policies with respect to revenue support (subsidy), it can have an influence on whether services actually operate. This form of support is necessary to provide for the retention of a range of loss-making local bus and rail services. If support is withdrawn, the services would also have to be withdrawn.

The provision of infrastructure can be in four forms. These are:

● *private goods.* This is the case with our principal airports owned by the British Airports Authority, and most other regional airports. The UK's main container ports are privately owned, along with some estuary crossings.

● *Public Private Partnership (PPP).* Metronet and Tube Lines, which are responsible for maintaining and upgrading London's underground, are this type of company.

● *a publicly owned plc.* One example is Network Rail, which describes itself as 'a not for dividend company'. Although it operates like a plc on a commercial basis, all profits that are made go back into the railway.

● *direct provision by government.* The best and most obvious example of this is in the case of new roads and motorways, which are quasi-public goods, funded directly by central and local government from tax revenue. (See *OCR AS Economics*, pages 64–66.)

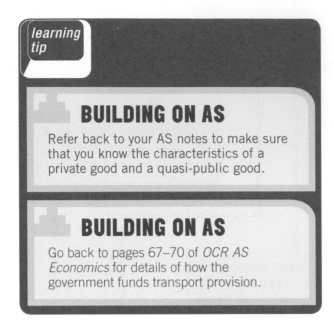

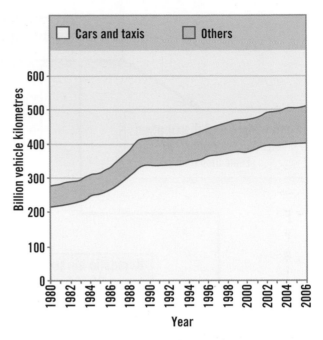

Recent trends in transport demand

Government statistics measure transport demand in two main ways, both of which involve the use of compound measures. These measures are:

● vehicle kilometres (road traffic)

● passenger kilometres and tonne kilometres (all modes).

Each measure takes into account the quantity demanded (vehicles, passengers, tonnes) and the distance travelled (kilometres). The measures are normally expressed in billions.

Figure 5.2 takes the first of these measures and looks at trends since 1980. Over this long period:

● total road traffic has increased by 84 per cent from 277 to 511 billion vehicle kilometres

● most of the growth, particularly for car traffic, occurred during the 1980s

● the distance travelled by heavy goods vehicles increased by 48 per cent.

We shall use this information later in Chapter 7 when analysing the growth of traffic congestion.

Rather more accurate measures of demand, taking into account all modes, are shown in Figures 5.3 and 5.4. Although still a crude indicator, the statistics

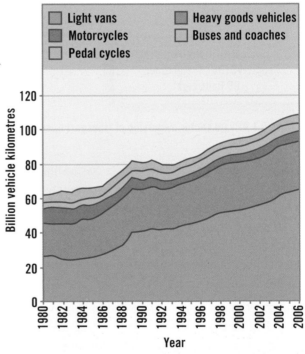

Figure 5.2 Road traffic growth, 1980–2006

used in these figures use more accurate measures of the volume of demand.

Figure 5.3 shows the trend in the total distance travelled by passengers in the UK since 1980. The following points can be made.

● Total demand for domestic travel increased by 65 per cent over the period 1980 to 2006.

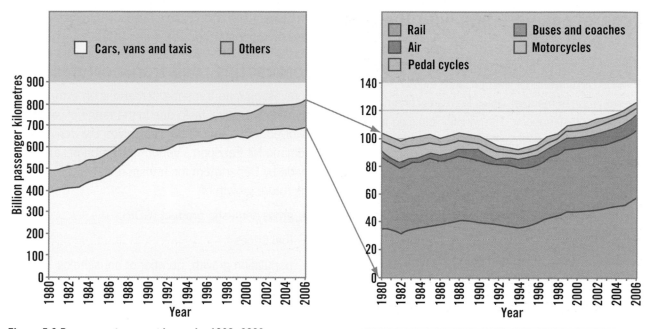

Figure 5.3 Passenger transport by mode, 1980–2006

Source: Department for Transport, Office of Rail Regulation and Civil Aviation Authority

● The majority of this growth has been due to increased travel by car. Over the period shown, the distance travelled by cars increased 77 per cent to 686 billion km in 2006.

● Travel by rail showed the largest absolute increase for the other modes of transport. Over the period shown, rail transport demand increased by 58 per cent, an additional 20 billion passenger kilometres. This growth, though, has only been since privatisation in 1994/95.

● Travel by bus and coach fell in the early part of the period, but nationally has increased slightly since 2000.

The trend in goods moved is shown in Figure 5.4. The following points can be made:

● The overall trend was upwards for most of the period, but with falls in demand broadly in line with the state of the economy.

● The majority of the increase is due to goods moved by road, which increased 79 per cent over the period.

● Road freight now accounts for 66 per cent of all goods moved, compared with 53 per cent in 1980.

● Goods moved by rail have increased by 70 per cent since privatisation and now account for around 9 per cent of all goods moved.

● Coastal shipping continues to be an important provider of domestic freight transport.

ACTIVITY ⋯⋮

a) Go back to Figures 5.3 and 5.4. Show how the determinants of demand can be used to explain the main trends from 1980 to 2006.

STRETCH AND CHALLENGE

b) Discuss the extent to which behavioural factors determine the demand for passenger transport.

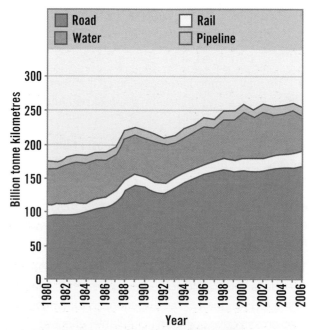

Figure 5.4 Goods transport by mode, 1980–2006

General comparisons with the rest of the EU

Any general comparison between the UK and the rest of the EU is difficult, not least because the EU is a very diverse group of member states from an economic and transport standpoint. The variations in road traffic and in modal shares of passenger and freight transport are substantial. These are a function of variations in living standards, car ownership levels, size of country, infrastructure, quality of public transport, fuel prices and the relative prices of transport modes, to name just a few of the variables involved.

Let us take just a few broad comparisons. For passenger transport from 1993 to 2003:

● Car ownership levels are highest in Germany, which, in turn, has by far the greatest volume of road traffic of any member state.

● Spain has experienced the greatest relative growth in road traffic by private car.

● France has recorded the greatest growth in the kilometres travelled by goods vehicles over the above period and has by far the largest volume of goods traffic of any member state.

● Of the new member states, transport by car has increased at the fastest rate of growth in the Czech Republic and Poland.

● The demand for rail transport increased most substantially in the UK and fell most in Poland.

For freight transport, from 1994 to 2004:

● The total demand increased in all member states, except Cyprus and Malta; the greatest percentage increase was in Ireland.

● Rail freight demand increased most in the UK; the greatest percentage increase in demand was in the Netherlands.

● Inland waterways provide substantial freight transport in Germany and the Netherlands; elsewhere they are virtually irrelevant.

This diversity of demand is one of the main reasons why, despite the inclusion of transport in the Treaty of Rome (1957), the EU has experienced fundamental problems in developing an acceptable, effective transport policy for the union as a whole. These

problems have been exaggerated by the accession of new member states in 2004 and 2007.

Forecasting road transport demand

Forecasting road transport demand is an extremely complex statistical task, due to the range of variables involved. (This should be clear, given the derived demand for transport.) Various assumptions are made by Department for Transport statisticians as to the future growth of:

● gross domestic product (GDP)

● fuel prices

● population growth, number of households

● car ownership/licence holders

● industrial output

● import of goods.

All impact on the future demand for passenger and for freight transport. Other assumptions that are made are that there are no significant changes in transport policies or travel behaviour.

Figure 5.5 shows the most recent estimates of forecast road traffic for the UK to 2025. Three

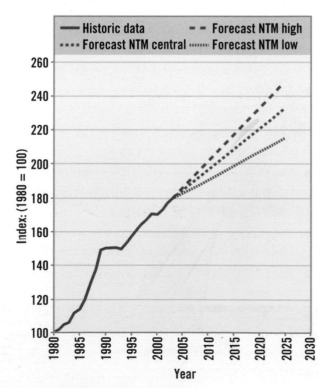

Figure 5.5 Traffic forecasts to 2025

forecasts are made. Depending upon key assumptions, there is a forecast range of 20 to 39 per cent growth in vehicle kilometres compared to the base of 2003. The central **forecast** lies slightly more towards the higher forecast, at 30.5 per cent.

Traffic forecasts have several important uses. These are:

● to determine future network needs at a national and at a local level. This is sometimes called the 'predict and provide' approach

● to estimate where the greatest traffic bottlenecks are likely to occur

● to be able to forecast the likely effects of particular transport policies, for example, road pricing (see Table 5.3).

Table 5.3 assumes an average charge of 3.6 pence per km. In the absence of road pricing, by 2025, the central forecast is for an increase in traffic of 30.5 per cent, in congestion of 28 per cent, in journey times of 4 per cent and a reduction in CO_2 emissions of 5 per cent due to the use of more environmentally acceptable vehicles.

Traffic congestion is forecast to increase

The importance of transport in the UK economy

Transport is an essential part of the UK economy. Its efficient functioning is essential for competitiveness, business and personal well-being. As the economy has grown, so too has the demand for transport. This is broadly shown in Figure 5.6.

> **DEFINITION**
>
> **Forecast:** a future estimate usually based on past information

ACTIVITY ⋯⋮⟩

a) Briefly describe why forecasting road traffic demand is difficult.

b) Use the information above to give the benefits arising from the introduction of road pricing by 2025.

STRETCH AND CHALLENGE

c) Discuss the extent to which road traffic forecasts alone should be used to determine whether new roads should be constructed.

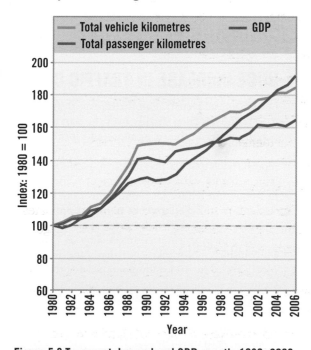

Figure 5.6 Transport demand and GDP growth, 1980–2006

Traffic	−7%	Journey times	−12%
Congestion	−52%	Traffic in congested conditions	−75%
CO_2	−7%		

Table 5.3 Effects of road pricing on forecast traffic in 2025

In general, there is a positive correlation between the annual change in GDP and the change in transport demand. This is to be expected, given the derived demand for transport. From the early 1990s onwards, though, the so-called intensity of the relationship has progressively 'decoupled'. What this means is that GDP has increased at a faster rate than the increases in demand for both passenger transport and for road traffic. For example, from 1992 to 2006, GDP increased by 49 per cent, compared with rises in road traffic and overall travel of 23 and 18 per cent respectively. This is broad evidence of transport demand becoming more sustainable (see Chapter 8).

There are other ways in which the economic importance of transport can be evidenced. Table 5.4 shows that in 2006, over 1 million people, around 6 per cent of the working population, were directly employed in the transport industry. In addition, around 850,000 were employed in transport-related

industries, such as retail distribution and vehicle manufacturing. The multiplier effects of both types of employment are substantial.

Transport	'000
Railways	54
Road haulage, bus and coach, other land	463
Coastal shipping, ferries	20
Air	91
Cargo handling and storage	325
Travel agencies, tour operators	117
Total	**1,070**

Table 5.4 Numbers employed in UK transport, 2006

Another way of assessing the importance of transport is to consider investment in transport. This is shown in Table 5.5.

ECONOMICS IN CONTEXT

HUGE INCREASE IN TRAFFIC OVER THE PAST 10 YEARS

Data from the Department for Transport shows that road traffic has risen sharply over the past decade as people are using their cars more and more, despite record fuel prices, higher taxes on vehicles and repeated calls to make greater use of public transport. This is hardly what the government is looking for in its quest to reduce CO_2 emissions from transport through its so-called greener transport policy.

As Figure 5.7 shows, the greatest rises in vehicle use have been in rural counties such as Cornwall, Lincolnshire, Norfolk, Northamptonshire and North Yorkshire. In London and parts of the Home Counties, the increases have been more modest.

So, why is this? To economists, it would appear to confirm that the demand for private transport is price inelastic. Motorists seem prepared to 'pay up' to continue to use their cars. There is some evidence of a shift towards more efficient cars and less being spent on vehicle servicing and maintenance, but all in all, people do not seem to want to adapt their lifestyles to drive less. It is not the response that the government wants to see ... an unwanted conclusion is that its transport policies have failed.

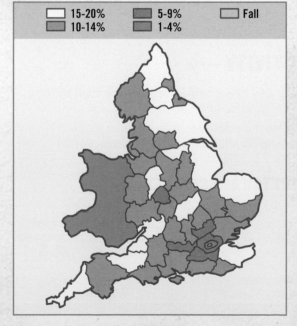

Figure 5.7 Traffic growth 1997–2007

Element	£ m
Road infrastructure	4,729
Road vehicles, incl. cars	49,900
Rail infrastructure	4,272
Rail rolling stock	2,088
Ports	202
Airports	1,495

Table 5.5 Investment in transport, 2004/05

An important feature of transport investment is that, over the last few years, the private sector has played an increasingly important role in providing new investment. This has been particularly the case for airport development and for new railway rolling stock.

In 2007/08, around 3.5 per cent of government spending was on transport. At around £20 billion, this expenditure was more or less equally allocated by central and local government on capital and current forms of expenditure (see Chapter 8). The largest sum is spent on the road network – around 50 per cent of the total.

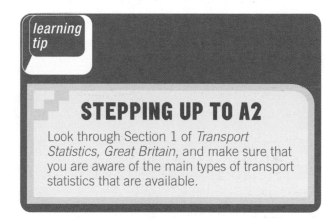

learning tip

STEPPING UP TO A2

Look through Section 1 of *Transport Statistics, Great Britain,* and make sure that you are aware of the main types of transport statistics that are available.

6 Market structures and competitive behaviour in transport markets

On completion of this chapter, you should be able to:

- understand the nature of costs in the short and long run
- understand the nature of, and influences on, firms' revenues
- explain what is meant by economies and diseconomies of scale, and how firms might be affected by these
- explain the models of market structure:
  - ○ monopoly   ○ oligopoly   ○ monopolistic competition
- evaluate the relative efficiency of these market structures in theory and practice
- analyse the natural monopoly argument applied to transport
- explain what is meant by contestability and the characteristics of a perfectly contestable market
- discuss the extent to which particular transport markets are contestable
- explain what is meant by deregulation and franchising
- evaluate the impact of deregulation in selected transport markets
- discuss the arguments for and against the privatisation of transport services
- evaluate the impact of privatisation on rail passenger and freight services
- discuss the objectives and behaviour of firms in transport markets.

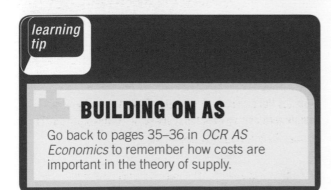

learning tip

BUILDING ON AS

Go back to pages 35–36 in *OCR AS Economics* to remember how costs are important in the theory of supply.

Costs in the short run and long run

Costs were briefly introduced at AS when considering the theory of supply. They are the monetary value of the inputs that are needed to produce a particular good or service. Two different types of costs can be recognised.

- **Fixed costs**. These are costs that have to be paid for by a business even if no output is being produced. For a service sector activity such as transport, these costs have to be paid irrespective of whether vehicles are being used. Typical examples are the rent that has to be paid on business premises or the interest paid on loans that have been taken out. It follows that as more output is produced, or as vehicles are used more, then total fixed costs can be spread out across a business.

● **Variable costs**. These costs vary directly with the level of output. For transport firms, these costs increase as vehicles are used more intensively. The most common examples are labour and fuel; for a manufacturing business, raw material costs tend to be an important variable cost item.

The **total costs** of a firm refer to the overall cost of producing a particular output or level of service.

As we have seen above,

Total cost = Fixed cost + Variable cost

The nature of costs in most types of transport operation is that fixed costs are a relatively high proportion of total costs. This is particularly true of air and rail transport, but for rather different reasons.

In air transport, a substantial fixed cost item is the annual sum that has to be paid to lease aircraft. Where aircraft are owned by the airline, this is the cost of any loaned finance and also depreciation. As a consequence, it is essential that aircraft are used as much as possible, therefore spreading out fixed costs. This is the main reason why low-cost carriers

such as Ryanair and easyJet have short turn-around times at airports and operate services 24/7.

For railways, Network Rail, the track authority, has a rather different problem. The fixed costs of maintaining some parts of the rail network are high in relation to total costs. The problem here is that in order to recoup these costs, relative charges to train operators are invariably higher on those parts of the network with low usage, compared with those parts where there are higher volumes of services.

Table 6.1 shows the typical costs of operating a 44-tonne articulated vehicle with six axles. Various assumptions about the working life of the vehicle, fuel prices and replacement costs have been made.

	£, per annum	Pence per mile
Standing costs		
Vehicle excise duty	1,200	1.71
Insurance	3,877	5.54
Depreciation	13,691	19.56
	18,768	**26.81**
Running costs		
Fuel	33,448	47.78
Tyres	3,353	4.79
Maintenance	10,672	15.25
	47,473	**67.82**
Total vehicle cost	66,241	94.63
Cost of driver	30,338	43.34
Cost of vehicle and driver	**96,579**	**137.97**
Business overhead costs	14,260	20.38
Total cost	**110,839**	**158.35**

Table 6.1 Vehicle operating costs of 44-tonne articulated vehicle with average annual mileage of 70,000 (April 2007)
Source : Freight Transport Association

DEFINITIONS

Costs: the value of inputs

Fixed costs: costs that are independent of output produced

Variable costs: costs that are directly related to the level of output produced

Total cost: the total cost of production or provision of a service

Here fixed costs, for the vehicle and business, are only 30 per cent of total costs. The two main variable cost items, fuel and the cost of the driver, are

58 per cent of total costs. Road hauliers have become increasingly concerned about the escalating price of diesel fuel and the wider effect this has on business costs and the rate of inflation.

Two further costs can be distinguished. These are average cost and marginal cost.

Average cost is the cost per unit. It is calculated by dividing total cost by the number of units produced or, in the case of transport services, by dividing total cost by the number of passengers or volume of freight carried. So,

$$\text{Average cost} = \frac{\text{Total cost}}{\text{Quantity}}$$

In turn, average cost can be split into average fixed and average variable elements.

Marginal cost is the change in total cost that occurs when output is changed by one unit. For a manufacturing firm, it is quite easy to understand what this means. In transport, it relates to the change in total cost that comes about when, say, one further passenger is carried or an additional tonne of goods is transported. So,

$$\text{Marginal cost} = \frac{\text{Change in total cost}}{\text{Change in quantity}}$$

For any firm, irrespective of the type of business, the most important cost is average cost, showing the cost per unit. This is essential information that is needed when firms determine prices.

Figure 6.1 shows the expected theoretical relationship between average fixed cost (AFC), average variable cost (AVC), average cost (AC) and marginal cost (MC). Points to note are:

● The AFC curve falls consistently, which is indicative of how total fixed costs are spread out as output increases.

DEFINITIONS

Average cost: the unit cost of production

Marginal cost: the change in total cost when one more unit of output is produced

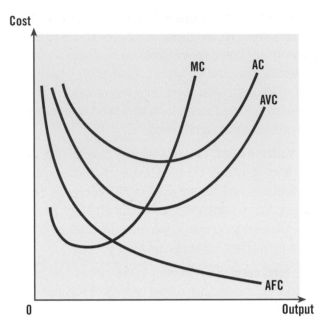

Figure 6.1 Typical short-run cost curves

● As output increases, average variable costs will initially decline before rising again, hence the U-shape.

ACTIVITY ⋯⋮▸

No. of planes	Fixed cost	Variable cost
0	1,000	-
1	1,000	400
2	1,000	550
3	1,000	650
4	1,000	700
5	1,000	1,000
6	1,000	1,600
7	1,000	2,400

Table 6.2 Daily fixed and variable costs of operating a landing slot at an airport

a) Calculate the average fixed cost, average variable cost, average cost and marginal cost for each of the levels of use.

b) Sketch each of the above cost curves on a graph.

c) Comment upon any differences you see between your sketch and Figure 6.1.

● Average variable costs will eventually outweigh the effect of the falling average fixed cost curve, causing the average cost curve to rise.

● The marginal cost curve always crosses the average variable cost and average cost curves at their lowest points.

BUILDING ON AS

Go back to page 28 of *OCR AS Economics* for more details on total revenue.

Revenue

Revenue is the receipts from sales. **Total revenue** is the quantity of a product sold multiplied by its price. In a competitive market, firms are **price takers** – they have to accept the ruling market price. In all other types of market, firms face a downward-sloping demand curve. Here, firms are **price makers** and their behaviour with respect to the price they charge will determine their total revenue. For example, in a market with elastic demand, an increase in price will lead to a fall in the quantity demanded and a larger fall in total revenue. So,

Total revenue (TR) = Quantity × price.

DEFINITIONS

Revenue: receipts from sales

Total revenue: quantity × price

Price taker: a firm in a competitive market that has to accept the market price

Price maker: a firm that has control over the market price

The **average revenue** (AR) is the total revenue divided by quantity. The firm's demand is its average revenue line.

The **marginal revenue** (MR) is the addition to total revenue resulting from the sales of one extra unit. Where firms face a downward-sloping demand curve, it follows that, since a firm can only sell more by reducing the price of all units, marginal revenue will always be lower than average revenue. This is shown in Figure 6.2. The figure also shows the total

DEFINITIONS

Average revenue: total revenue ÷ quantity

Marginal revenue: addition to total revenue from one additional sale

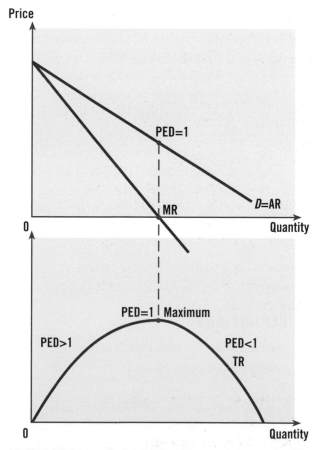

Figure 6.2 Relationship between average, marginal and total revenue

revenue curve. The shape of this is indicative of how consumers react to price changes at different prices due to variations in price elasticity of demand. Total revenue is maximised where the price elasticity of demand equals 1.

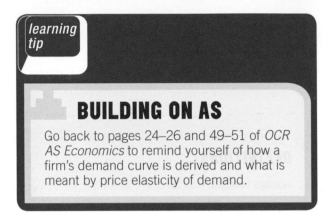

learning tip

BUILDING ON AS

Go back to pages 24–26 and 49–51 of *OCR AS Economics* to remind yourself of how a firm's demand curve is derived and what is meant by price elasticity of demand.

From short run to long run

Referring back to Figure 6.1, the optimum point of production for a firm is where the average cost (AC) is at its minimum point. This AC curve is sometimes referred to as a **short-run** average cost curve. By this, we mean that the firm is restricted in what inputs it can change in order to produce more output. At best, it can only buy more materials or hire more labour if the demand for its products increases. If a firm experiences a large increase in demand for its products (or indeed a large fall), then it will have to alter its scale of production. When this occurs, we move to the **long-run** period – this is when the firm can alter all of its inputs and the products it

DEFINITIONS

Short run: time period when a firm is unable to change factors of production except for one, usually labour

Long run: time period when all factor inputs can be changed

produces. So, all factors of production become variable in the long run.

learning tip

It should be stressed that neither the short run or the long run for any type of firm can be expressed in terms of days, weeks or months. The terms refer simply to the firm's ability or inability to alter factor inputs.

In the long run, therefore, since all inputs can be varied, it follows that firms can operate at different levels of capacity. One way in which this can be done is to increase the amount of capital or quality of technology used in relation to labour. In both cases, the expectation is that average costs will fall.

Figure 6.3 shows the long-run average cost (LRAC) curve of a firm. It is derived from a series of short-run curves as the firm expands its scale of production. The LRAC curve is sometimes referred to as an 'envelope', since it envelops a series of short-run average cost (SRAC) curves.

The shape of the LRAC in Figure 6.3 is downward-sloping in the first instance. For a manufacturing firm, as more efficient production methods are used, long-run average costs will fall as the scale of the business increases. At output Q, LRAC is minimised. This level of output is known as the **minimum efficient scale**.

DEFINITION

Minimum efficient scale: the lowest level of output where long-run average cost (LRAC) is minimised

In transport, long-run average costs fall due to an increase in the size of vehicles. Over time, aircraft such as the Boeing 747s and the A380, the new generation of ferries and large goods vehicles such as 44-tonne artics or draw-bar units, are on a much larger scale than their predecessors. Consequently, their so-called payload, the revenue-producing load,

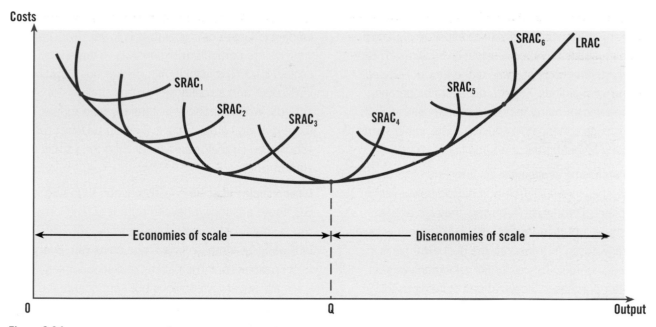

Figure 6.3 Long-run average costs

increases. For customers, the benefit can be one of falling real prices.

Economies of scale

There are various reasons why large-scale firms are able to move onto lower short-run average cost curves. An example of this would be a firm moving from $SRAC_2$ to $SRAC_3$ on Figure 6.3. The benefits that are gained through this expansion are called **economies of scale**.

Many economies of scale are internal to the business. Internal economies of scale come about because a firm decides to produce on a larger scale – the firm's

Bulk buying Boeing 737s is cheaper

> **DEFINITION**
>
> **Economies of scale:** the benefits gained through producing on a larger scale

output rises proportionately more than its inputs. The possible source of economies of scale depends to some extent on the nature of the firm. The following general sources can be applied to transport.

● **Technical economies**. These occur when the physical capacity increases, with a resultant fall in unit costs. As referred to earlier, these benefits can apply in most forms of passenger and freight transport through larger vehicles that carry more passengers or freight at reduced average cost. In short, output rises faster than total costs, so unit/ average costs fall.

> **DEFINITION**
>
> **Technical economies:** increased capacity or a technological development that results in lower long-run average costs

Another relevant transport application is where passenger transport companies especially cut costs through online advance reservation systems. This is a particular characteristic of the product offered by low-cost airlines. Other airlines, train operating companies and ferry service providers all use such systems as a means of reducing costs. Other forms of booking invariably incur an additional charge.

● **Purchasing economies**. As firms increase in scale, they increase their purchasing power with suppliers. Through bulk buying, they are able to purchase inputs more cheaply. Bulk discounts lower average costs. In transport, the best example is in the case of fuel. This essential yet expensive item is often purchased weeks ahead of being used. By purchasing huge quantities in advance, the large transport operations are able to buy fuel from suppliers at favourable prices. Another example is in the case of vehicles. Firms that run a standard fleet from one supplier often do so because of the bulk discounts available from manufacturers. easyJet, for instance, has a fleet of new Boeing 737s purchased in a bulk deal with the American manufacturer.

● **Managerial economies**. In large firms, these come about as a result of specialisation. In such firms, specialists are employed to act as operational, marketing, financial, human resource and other specialist types of manager. Smaller firms have invariably to rely on multi-task managers. Such cost savings are applicable in any type of business.

● **Financial economies**. Large firms usually have better and cheaper access to borrowed funds than smaller firms. This is because the perceived risk of lending to large-scale operators is lower. Transport vehicles are particularly expensive – a large lorry can cost £100,000, a new double decker bus £150,000–£180,000, and a passenger aircraft, millions of pounds. Where financial institutions lend money, there is always a risk. This is likely to be lower for an established large-scale operator than for a small new-start business.

Diseconomies of scale can also occur. In Figure 6.3, these are shown beyond output *Q*. The long-run average cost curve begins to slope upwards, indicating an increase in average costs with every further expansion. The causes of diseconomies of scale are not always obvious but can include the following:

● *Problems of communication.* In large firms, extra costs may be incurred in making managers aware of what is going on.

● *Problems of co-ordination.* Large firms invariably have layers of management and several tiers of decision making, which can sometimes hinder change.

● *Problems of industrial relations.* As firms increase in scale, workers may feel alienated and relationships with the employer may become more strained.

> **DEFINITION**
>
> **Diseconomies of scale:** causes of an increase in long-run average costs beyond the point of minimum efficient scale

> **DEFINITIONS**
>
> **Purchasing economies:** reduced unit costs due to bulk buying of inputs into a business
>
> **Managerial economies:** savings in long-run average costs due to the specialisation of management
>
> **Financial economies:** the cost savings that large firms may receive when borrowing money

In theory, factors such as those above will increase long-run average costs as a firm grows in its scale. These problems affect all firms. The extent to which any specifically apply to transport is not easy to determine. The nature of transport operations is that, even in large companies, the actual business units may be quite small. This is unlike manufacturing, where large numbers of workers may be employed on one site. Industrial relations problems, though, are not uncommon.

ECONOMICS IN CONTEXT

ECONOMIES OF SCALE IN EUROPEAN CAR MANUFACTURING

In February 2008, the French car manufacturer Renault announced that it had acquired a 25 per cent stake in Autovaz, Russia's largest car producer. Under this agreement, Autovaz, with its Lada marque of cars, hopes to double its sales to 1.5 million vehicles by 2015. The deal elevates the Renault-Nissan-Autovaz alliance to the largest European car producer, third globally behind General Motors and Toyota.

Unlike VW's takeover of the Czech manufacturer Skoda, the Renault-Nissan deal will accelerate the rejuvenation of the brand – it is not a means for the new partners to launch their own products in the Russian market through a 'local' producer. Recent and projected growth in the Russian car market is phenomenal and far outpaces that of both China and India. The Renault deal is hardly a surprise and follows substantial market growth experienced by Asian car makers. By 2010, Russia will have overtaken Germany as the biggest new car market in Europe.

Empirical research has shown that there are considerable economies of scale to be gained by car manufacturers. As output increases, the average cost per car falls. The minimum efficient scale is around 2 million cars per year. The most efficient European car manufacturers, such as VW-Audi, PSA and Renault-Nissan, need to produce this level to remain globally competitive. One way in which firms try to get maximum benefit from economies of scale is by using common components across a range of models produced throughout the same organisation. While Renault-Nissan plan to retain the Lada product, what is certain is that the new breed of Russian–made cars will contain components that are used elsewhere in the company's global manufacturing and assembly plants.

External economies of scale exist when the growth of an entire industry leads to falling long-run average costs for all firms in that industry. The effect in theory is shown in Figure 6.4.

An example is in the case of a major airport, where many different types of business cluster together in its vicinity, leading to lower average costs for each firm. Such businesses include those providing catering services, freight forwarders, courier services, express parcel operators and aeronautical engineering and servicing.

Firms and their objectives

So far, the term 'firm' has been used on various occasions, but it has never been defined. Essentially, a firm is the term used by economists as a unit of decision making that has various objectives that include:

- profit maximisation
- the avoidance of risk
- long-term growth.

At its lowest level, the firm may be a sole trader. Examples in transport include owner drivers with

> ### DEFINITION
>
> **External economies of scale:** falling long-run average costs that benefit all firms in an industry

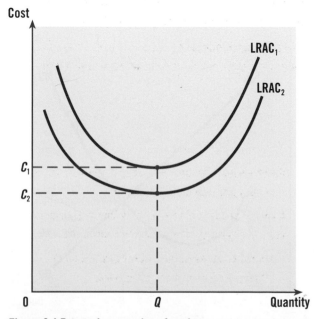

Figure 6.4 External economies of scale

a truck, a taxi or a private hire coach. The term is also used for national and multinational corporations such as DHL, First Group, Stagecoach Holding, P&O, British Airways and so on. In theory, all firms are headed by an entrepreneur (see *OCR AS Economics*, pages 6–7).

In the theory of the firm, a fundamental assumption is that a firm will seek to make as high a level of profit as possible. In other words, profit maximisation. This occurs when marginal cost is equal to marginal revenue. What this means is that the cost of producing the last unit of output is exactly equal to the revenue the firm receives from the customer. If the firm produces below this level of output, marginal revenue is greater than marginal cost. More profit can be made by expanding output. If the firm produces above the profit maximisation level of output, then marginal cost will be greater than marginal revenue. By producing more, the firm's profit is below its maximum. This important rule is shown in Figure 6.5.

There are several reasons in practice why firms may not operate exactly at the profit maximisation level of output.

● It is difficult to identify the profit maximisation position, since firms are unlikely to know their marginal cost and marginal revenue. What is more

likely is that they know their long-run average cost and will use this to determine prices by adding on a profit margin.

● Large profits might attract the attention of government watchdogs, damage employee relations and attract new entrants into a market to alienate consumers.

In transport, a particular complication is that, in some markets, firms make a loss and rely upon external subsidies from central and local government in order to provide services. This is true for most of the train-operating companies, which rely on an annual handout from the government in order to meet their franchise obligations. In local bus operation, certain routes or part routes are subsidised to ensure their continuation. If firms were working only towards profit maximisation, these services would not operate.

Network Rail, the track authority, provides an interesting example. Although it is a plc and is expected to operate as a private firm, any profits it generates go directly back into the organisation for use in future improvement projects. This is a direct consequence of the bankruptcy of its predecessor, Railtrack, a privatised company.

A second objective of firms is **profit satisficing**. As the term indicates, it refers to circumstances whereby a firm makes a reasonable level of profit that is sufficient to satisfy its shareholders or its owners while not maximising profits. One reason for this objective is that the firm's managers may be unwilling to take unnecessary risks that are likely to occur with a profit maximisation objective. A second reason is that it may be consistent with keeping stakeholders (employees, customers, the local community as well as shareholders and owners) satisfied. For example,

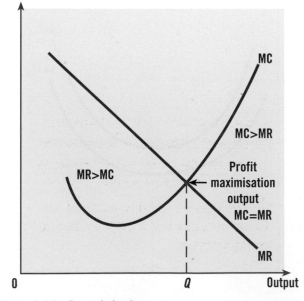

Figure 6.5 Profit maximisation

employees want higher wages, customers want lower prices, and the local community may want an environmentally sustainable operation. These and other objectives are likely to be in conflict, especially in the short run. A third reason for satisficing is if a firm has close business rivals. This makes its owner or managers cautious, as there is a risk of failure if an aggressive 'go for growth at all costs' policy is followed. Customers may take exception and switch to a competitor.

It is difficult to generalise about the relevance of profit satisficing in transport. Much depends on local situations. Two possibilities are:

● In road haulage there are thousands of small firms, with one or two trucks, trying to earn a living in difficult market conditions. Rising fuel costs affect all businesses and, with very low profit margins, survival is the main objective for many businesses in the short run. The same situation applies in local coach operations, where small firms struggle to meet their costs.

● Although impossible to prove, in some local bus markets there seems to be evidence that firms are unwilling to compete on each other's routes or to enter into a fare-cutting war. Instead, they appear satisfied to earn an acceptable level of profits that will keep them in business.

A third objective of firms is that of **sales revenue maximisation**. This is where a firm produces where marginal revenue is zero and is prepared to accept a lower market price in order to increase its market share. Known as predatory pricing, this is designed to drive rivals out of a market or prevent new firms from entering. This may be good news for consumers in the short run; it is likely to be bad in the long run if the firm uses this tactic to establish a monopoly position and to then raise prices.

This objective is normally a feature of a growing market. Profits will still be earned if total revenue is greater than total costs. Firms may choose this objective as a way of boosting sales, especially if this may help secure cheaper loans or generate large bonuses for its managers.

Predatory pricing was an early feature of markets after local bus deregulation (see below). Large firms, especially, used this tactic to gain market share and force competitors out of business. Such tactics in Chesterfield and Darlington were investigated by the former Office of Fair Trading and subsequently declared to be illegal. What does remain legal, though, in this market is large operators flooding a route with buses in order to force a smaller competitor out of business.

Sales maximisation is a further objective of firms. Here it is the volume of sales that is maximised and not the revenue from sales. Firms increase output up to the break-even level, where total revenue just covers total cost. The only circumstance where this might be justified is where there is **cross-subsidisation** – profit from some activities is being used to support other activities that are not covering their costs.

This practice was prevalent in state-owned transport operations prior to privatisation. In local bus operations, especially, companies felt they had a social obligation to provide a comprehensive network

DEFINITION

Sales revenue maximisation: an objective where a firm produces where marginal revenue is zero

DEFINITIONS

Profit maximisation: the objective of firms that is achieved where marginal cost = marginal revenue

Sales maximisation: an objective that involves the maximisation of the volume of sales

Cross-subsidisation: a business practice where revenue from profitable activities is used to support loss-making ones

of services, both geographically and in off-peak times. To the economist, this practice is inefficient, since some passengers are paying higher fares than they should, while others are paying fares that are below marginal cost. Deregulation sought to remove this practice by providing external subsidy for services that were seen as socially necessary. (See above also with respect to **profit maximisation**.)

Types of profit

An accountant's view of a firm's costs is that they are incurred when a recognised expenditure is made. In transport, this would typically include the various items listed in Table 6.1. **Profit** is what is left when all expenses have been deducted from the firm's income or total revenue.

The economist's definition of profit is rather broader. This is because, when looking at a firm's costs, economists take into account the private costs, as does the accountant, plus an allowance for the opportunity cost of anything else used in the production process. A typical example is the capital that is being used – this could be used in some alternative way to earn an income for its owners. So, there will be a minimum level of profit that the entrepreneur will expect in return for the assets that are tied up in a firm. This is known as **normal profit**. Economists see this as a cost of production, the entrepreneur's minimum reward for risk-taking.

Supernormal profits are those made by firms above normal profits. Where such profits are made in an industry they are likely to attract the entry of new firms, some of which may be operating in similar markets. In contrast, where profits are lower than normal, then this tends to result in some firms exiting an industry.

Market structure

From a simple standpoint, the term **market structure** is one that is used to describe the characteristics of a market. It is concerned with the way in which products are supplied in terms of:

● the number of firms in the market

● the size of firms

● the strength and extent of barriers to entry and exit

● the nature of the product

● whether the firm or firms are price takers or price makers.

It is assumed that firms are profit maximisers although, strictly speaking, this is not a characteristic.

Empirically, an appropriate way of understanding market structure is to establish the pattern of market shares in an industry. This can be measured by what is known as the n-firm **concentration ratio**, where n is usually 4 or 5. So, a 4-firm concentration ratio measures the combined market shares of the four largest firms as a proportion of the total market.

DEFINITIONS

Profit: the difference between revenue and costs

Normal profit: the level of profit that keeps a firm in a particular activity

Supernormal profit: profit that is more than normal profit

DEFINITIONS

Market structure: the characteristics of a market

Concentration ratio: the proportion of the total market shared between the nth largest firms

Table 6.3 shows the market shares of the principal UK scheduled airlines in 2002 and 2006. The measure of market share used is 'seat km available': this covers capacity as well as distance and is a more accurate measure of market share than just aircraft available or services operated.

	2002	2006
British Airways[1]	61	48
Virgin Atlantic	15	15
Ryanair	6	13
easyJet	7	10
BMI Group	4	4
Monarch	1	2
Jet2.com	–	1
Flybe[2]	1	1
Fly Globespan	–	1
Total capacity	**224,398**	**324,391**

[1] Includes franchises. [2] Formerly British European.

Table 6.3 UK scheduled airline capacity (% seat km available)

ACTIVITY ····⦂

Using the data in Table 6.3,

a) Describe the changes in industrial concentration in the UK scheduled airline market between 2002 and 2006.

b) Explain the likely causes of these changes.

STRETCH AND CHALLENGE

c) Explain why seat kilometres available is an appropriate measure of airline capacity.

This measure of market concentration has two main weaknesses. First, it does not necessarily give a true picture of actual market shares. For example, a 4-firm concentration ratio of 76 per cent may have been derived from one firm with a market share of 70 per cent and three firms each with 2 per cent. This market structure is so different from one having two firms with 20 per cent each and two other firms with 18 per cent each. Second, used on its own, it gives no indication of total market size. It is sometimes helpful to know if a market is increasing or declining.

Barriers to entry

A **barrier to entry** is any obstacle that deters new firms from entering a market to compete with existing firms. Such barriers provide incumbent firms with a degree of market power in so far as decisions can be made by them with little or no risk of their market share or profits being challenged by new entrants. They are particularly significant in the analysis of market structures.

DEFINITION

Barrier to entry: obstacle to new firms entering a market

Barriers to entry into transport markets are varied in terms of their strength in restricting the entry of new firms and their importance in determining market structure. They include:

● *high set-up costs.* These are the costs that are necessary to start a business. In some transport markets, they are modest; in others they are restrictive. The capital required to set up a small road haulage business, private hire coach firm or to buy a licensed taxi is relatively modest. In contrast, starting up a new airline or train-operating company requires a substantial amount of capital (see Economics in context).

● *economies of scale.* As referred to earlier, these can arise through falling long-run average costs as the scale of output of a firm increases. Figure 6.4 showed how the LRAC curve for established firms was likely to be lower than that for new entrants.

● *legal barriers.* All types of transport operations are regulated. This is particularly so when firms are transporting passengers. Buses, trains and aeroplanes have to be approved to meet particular standards, public liability insurance is mandatory and the companies involved have to obtain appropriate licences to operate services. (Again see Economics in context.)

● *brand loyalty.* It is invariably difficult for new firms moving into a market to establish themselves

ECONOMICS IN CONTEXT

GRAND CENTRAL RAILWAY – THE TRAIN YOU'VE BEEN WAITING FOR

Grand Central Railway train

On 1 March 2008, after what had seemed to be an incredibly long wait, the first of Grand Central Railway's distinctive black-painted trains hurtled down the East Coast main line from Sunderland to London King's Cross. The company is Britain's newest as well as smallest train operating company. It is also one of the few 'open access' operations, running just three services a day between Sunderland and the capital.

Getting to this stage has been a long, painful and expensive experience. The barriers that Ian Yeowart, its founder, has had to face have been substantial and have included:

● *legal barriers.* GNER, the former franchise holder, fought tooth and nail to block Grand Central's plans, on the basis that it would dilute revenue away from itself. In July 2007, a judicial review in the High Court found in Grand Central's favour. Grand Central, though, is not allowed to pick up or drop any passengers south of York.

● *acquiring rolling stock.* Grand Central paid £1 million for three 30-year-old 125s, formerly part of Virgin Rail's operations. Progress in refurbishing them to Grand Central's specification took far longer than expected.

● *health and safety issues.* Each train has had to be thoroughly inspected before it can be used on the rail network.

● *staffing.* 33 members of staff, drivers and conductors, have had to be recruited and trained at great expense prior to the company becoming operational.

All in all, a long wait.

if competitors have established substantial brand loyalty among customers. They clearly stand a better chance of succeeding if the market is expanding or if existing firms have little or no empathy with their customers.

● *intimidation.* This where an established firm seeks to stop a new entrant through veiled threats or actions that will make it clear that competition is not welcomed. There have reputedly been instances of this in deregulated local bus and taxi markets.

● *predatory pricing.* This occurs when a firm deliberately charges low prices with the intention of preventing new firms from entering a market. In the short run this is good news for customers; in the long run it is unlikely to persist, as a firm that has used predatory pricing may establish a monopoly position to then raise its prices.

Productive and allocative efficiency revisited

Productive and allocative efficiency are important concepts in economics, particularly when evaluating the advantages and disadvantages of particular market structures. Both types of efficiency were introduced in a simple way at AS (see *OCR AS Economics*, pages 53–54 and 56).

Productive efficiency is all to do with using the least possible amount of scarce resources to produce the maximum output. For an economy, this occurs when it is producing on its highest production possibility curve. For firms, it involves producing at the lowest average cost. This is at the bottom of the long-run average cost curve.

In Figure 6.6, the position marked 'X' on AC_3 is the point of productive efficiency. This point is not only at the lowest point on the average cost curve of a firm, it is also on the lowest cost curve. So, here, a firm is producing at the lowest possible average cost.

There would, though, be little point in firms producing goods and services at the lowest possible cost if nobody wanted them or if they gave little or no satisfaction to consumers. Knowledge of **allocative efficiency** can now be developed, in so far as it is all about using scarce resources to produce products

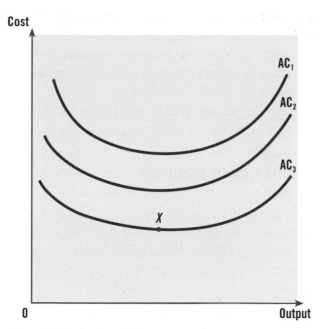

Figure 6.6 Productive efficiency

that are most wanted by consumers, given their cost of production. It occurs where the selling price of a product is equal to its marginal cost of production. Here, the price paid by the consumer represents the true cost of producing the last unit. This should ensure that precisely the right amount of the product is produced.

> **DEFINITION**
>
> **Allocative efficiency:** where price is equal to marginal cost

A simple example will make this important concept clearer. Table 6.4 shows a theoretical situation of the quantity produced, price and marginal cost for a firm.

An output of one unit would not be allocatively efficient. The cost of producing this quantity is less than the value put on it by consumers, as represented by the price they are willing to pay. The

product obviously should be produced but there is scope for more to be made. This is also true when two or three units are produced. At the other extreme, the seventh unit costs £16 to be produced, yet is only valued at £10 by the consumer. The same problem exists with output levels of five and six units. There is only one ideal output and that is when four units are produced – price is equal to marginal cost. This is the allocatively efficient level of output.

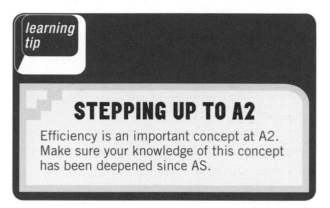

STEPPING UP TO A2
Efficiency is an important concept at A2. Make sure your knowledge of this concept has been deepened since AS.

> **DEFINITION**
>
> **Productive efficiency:** using the least possible amount of scarce resources to produce the maximum output

Monopoly

In theory, in its purest form, a **monopoly** exists when one single firm controls the entire output of

> **DEFINITION**
>
> **Monopoly:** a single firm in a market

Quantity produced (units)	1	2	3	4	5	6	7
Price (£)	10	10	10	10	10	10	10
Marginal cost (£)	4	5	8	10	12	14	16

Table 6.4 Allocative efficiency

an industry. Since by definition there are no close substitutes, this firm is the industry. The power of monopoly is obtained from barriers to entry – this could be in the form of a legal right, a patent or, in some transport markets, a franchise that gives one firm the exclusive rights to provide a particular service. As a consequence, a further feature of monopoly is that supernormal profit is possible in both the short and long run.

The key issue with monopoly is whether the firm dominates its market and, if so, whether it can command a so-called monopoly price. In the UK, the Competition Act (1998) recognises that any firm that has a market share of 25 per cent or more could have the power to act in a monopolistic way. It also recognises that a firm with over 40 per cent market share could be dominant. The legislation seeks to prevent all such firms from abusing their position.

In theory, evidence of monopoly power would be where a firm charged high prices and restricted output in order to make excessive profits (see below). The Competition Act seeks to promote a competitive environment in markets by prohibiting various

agreements in cases where the combined market shares of those firms involved is greater than 25 per cent. Examples of anti-competitive agreements are those that fix prices, share markets or regulate supply. In the case of large dominant firms, the Commission can intervene if firms charge excessively high prices or practice predatory pricing (see above).

EQUILIBRIUM OF MONOPOLY

Figure 6.7 shows the equilibrium position of a monopoly. In theory, the monopolist faces a downward-sloping demand curve. In this situation, the monopolist has to decide on what price to charge or what quantity of output to supply. The firm cannot determine both. The profit maximisation position is where marginal cost is equal to market revenue (see above). This is where output is Q_m and the price that is charged to customers is P_m. The monopolist will obtain supernormal profits as indicated by the shaded area at this equilibrium.

Figure 6.7 can also be used to show what the equivalent price and output would be in a competitive market. This would be at price P_c and output Q_c. So,

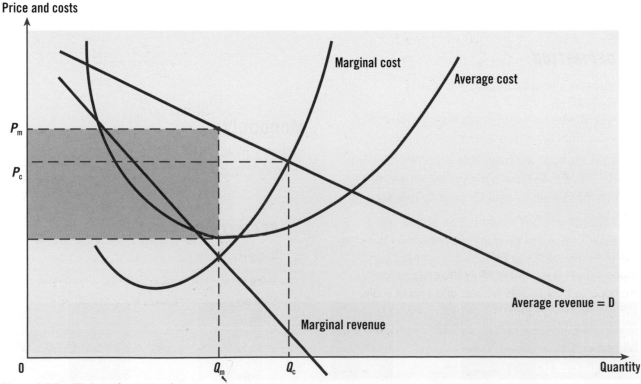

Figure 6.7 Equilibrium of a monopoly

in a competitive market, price is lower and the output supplied is higher, than in a monopoly. Net welfare for consumers is higher – consumer surplus will increase by more than producer surplus.

STEPPING UP TO A2

For explanations of consumer surplus and producer surplus, see *OCR AS Economics*, pages 27 and 34.

It is for the above reason that monopoly is a much maligned market structure. These concerns go even deeper, since at the equilibrium position, the monopoly is not efficient. In terms of productive efficiency, the monopolist is not producing at the lowest point of the average cost curve. The equilibrium output is at a point where the average cost curve is still falling. Allocative efficiency is not being achieved either, since the price that is charged to consumers is greater than the marginal cost of product.

So, all around, in theory at least, a monopoly compares unfavourably with a competitive market. This simple benchmarking conclusion may not be valid for two reasons.

● A competitive market (sometimes known as perfect competition) is a theoretical ideal. It does not occur in a real economy. What is more meaningful is to compare monopoly with other market structures that are observed to occur. These are also not allocatively or productively efficient.

● Figure 6.7 is drawn on the assumption that the costs in monopoly are the same as in a competitive market. This is not necessarily the case, since a monopolist may benefit from economies of scale. Long-run average costs are reduced, and while making supernormal profits, the firm's consumers will be better-off due to lower prices.

In addition to the above reservations, there are other reasons that we need to take into account before

making a sweeping judgement that all monopolies are bad. These include situations:

● where there is a **natural monopoly**. This has particular significance in transport markets and is analysed below.

● where **dynamic efficiency** is being achieved over time. Here the monopolist makes investment in process innovation, product innovation and other ways to protect market position. This is likely to involve some of the supernormal profits being allocated for this purpose. A positive outcome is that consumer choice is widened and unit costs reduced.

● where there is a continued threat of new entrants into a market. This is the principal feature of a so-called **contestable market** (see below) and has particular relevance in many transport markets.

PRICE DISCRIMINATION

Since the monopolist has power over the market, it is able to increase total profits by using **price discrimination**. This occurs where consumers are charged different prices for exactly the same product in different markets. For price discrimination to be effective, the firm must have sufficient power to set

DEFINITIONS

Natural monopoly: where a monopolist has overwhelming cost advantage

Dynamic efficiency: where unit costs are lowered over time

Contestable market: a set of conditions where there is always the threat of new firms being able to enter a market

Price discrimination: where a monopolist charges different prices for the same product in different markets

prices, the markets must be kept separate and, significantly, the product must have different price elasticities of demand in each market.

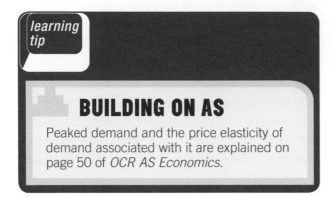

learning tip

BUILDING ON AS

Peaked demand and the price elasticity of demand associated with it are explained on page 50 of *OCR AS Economics*.

The separation of the market in terms of time is particularly important in transport markets where there is a peaked demand (see *OCR AS Economics*, page 50). In the rail passenger market, for example, the price elasticity of demand for commuter travel is more inelastic than for off-peak travel. This is because of the essential nature of peak-period travel. The monopolist will maximise profits by charging a lower price in the market where demand is elastic and a higher price where demand is less sensitive to change in price.

In other transport markets, time is a way of separating the market. Those passengers who travel with airlines can usually get a better deal if they book well ahead of the date of travel; travel much nearer the date of departure is invariably more expensive. This is why, although the product is the same, passengers travelling in adjacent seats could have paid substantially different fares.

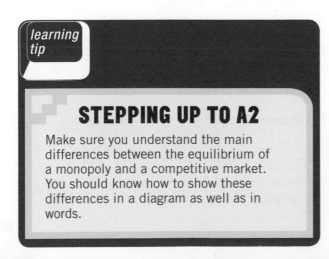

learning tip

STEPPING UP TO A2

Make sure you understand the main differences between the equilibrium of a monopoly and a competitive market. You should know how to show these differences in a diagram as well as in words.

NATURAL MONOPOLY

A natural monopoly is a market situation where a monopolist has overwhelming cost advantage. In theory, this can come about where a monopoly has sole ownership of a resource or where past ownership of capital resources means that it is difficult and extremely expensive for competitors to duplicate these installations. It would also be extremely wasteful to do so.

The natural monopoly case is one that has consistently been put forward in support of public ownership of services such as water, gas and electricity. It is also applicable to railways and canals. In all of these cases, fixed costs are a very high percentage of total costs. As output increases, average costs will fall, offering the prospect of substantial benefits to be gained from economies of scale. With a canal, for example, long-run average costs per vessel using the canal will fall, since the total costs are spread over an increased number of vessels. The same argument applies in the case of rail track.

Figure 6.8 is the usual representation of a natural monopoly. It shows a falling long-run average cost curve, indicative of continuing economies of scale. A monopoly firm would set price at P_1, provide Q_1 output and earn supernormal profits. If it behaved like a competitive firm, the equilibrium position would be where price = long run marginal cost – price would be lower at P_2, the quantity provided higher at Q_2. This is a loss-making position. The problem is that this will only happen if the government is prepared to subsidise the monopoly on the grounds that what it is providing is an essential public service. The alternative is for the service to be provided by the public sector.

TRANSPORT RELEVANCE OF MONOPOLY

The natural monopoly case for railways is particularly strong. When railways were being constructed from 1840s onwards, if rival companies were to construct their own infrastructure, waste and service duplication occurred. There is also the issue of accessibility. Railways are an essential service and even though they may not be provided by the public sector in the UK, their privatisation included

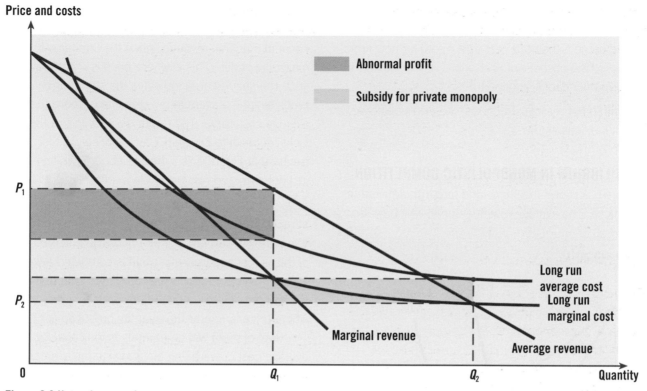

Figure 6.8 Natural monopoly

safeguards with respect to the level and quality of service provided. Returning to Figure 6.8, since it is recognised that services beyond Q_1 are required, the government provides an annual payment to 17 out of the 20 franchises to ensure that services are retained at the levels specified under the conditions of the franchise.

Not all train-operating companies have a monopoly. Competition for passengers is particularly fierce on parts of the East Coast Main Line – First Capital Connect, Cross Country Trains, Hull Trains and Grand Central Trains all compete with the franchisee, National Express East Coast, for passengers along this important route. There are restrictions on where rival services can pick up and drop off passengers and, except for full-fare open ones, tickets are purchased for a particular operator's services.

Monopolistic competition

Monopolistic competition, as its name suggests, combines the features of monopoly and a perfectly competitive market. An essential characteristic of this market structure is that of **product differentiation**,

namely that the goods and services provided by particular suppliers are slightly differentiated. As a result, each firm in the market faces a downward-sloping demand curve that tends to be elastic. Other characteristics are:

● Firms are price makers, as in a monopoly. This exists because of the slight product differentiation.

● There are a large number of firms in the market but none is relatively large in terms of the overall market size.

DEFINITIONS

Monopolistic competition: a market structure with many firms producing a differentiated product and where there are few barriers to entry and exit

Product differentiation: where there are minor variations in the types of products on offer

● There are only low barriers to entry, making it easy for firms to enter this market; if supernormal profit is being earned, then this acts as a signal for new firms to enter. The cost of exit is also low, with firms able to recoup their capital expenditure.

As with other market structures, the firm's objective is profit maximisation.

EQUILIBRIUM IN MONOPOLISTIC COMPETITION

Figure 6.9 shows the short- and long-run equilibrium positions. The average revenue curve, which is also the demand curve, is downward-sloping. The short-run equilibrium position is where marginal cost is equal to marginal revenue, since the firm aims to maximise profits. This is where price is *P* and output is *Q*. The shaded area indicates the supernormal profit, since the average revenue line is above the average cost curve. The upper diagram in this figure looks identical to Figure 6.7 for monopoly – it is, except that Figure 6.9 is the equilibrium position for just one firm and not the whole market.

As explained above, the supernormal profit is an attraction for new firms to enter the market, since there are low barriers to their entry. The outcome of this is that supernormal profit is competed away. The demand curve for any one firm will shift to the left and the long-run equilibrium position will be where price is P_L and the quantity produced is Q_L. The level of profit will be normal, as indicated by the average cost curve being tangential to the average revenue line. The lower diagram in Figure 6.9 is the equilibrium position for all firms in the industry – any firms making losses as a result of new entrants will have exited. Those remaining still possess monopoly power through product differentiation.

Compared to a competitive market, monopolistically competitive markets are inefficient. This can be shown on Figure 6.9.

● In both the short and long run, price is greater than marginal cost. Consumers are being charged a price above what it costs to produce the extra unit of output. Allocative efficiency is not being achieved. In the long run, price exceeds marginal cost by *AB*. By operating at output Q_L, there is a welfare loss to society. This is called the **deadweight loss** (*ABC*). This loss can only be reduced if output expands beyond Q_L.

● Productive efficiency is not being achieved, since in the short and the long run, the firm is operating on the downward-sloping part of the average cost curve. This is at point *D* on the lower diagram in Figure 6.9.

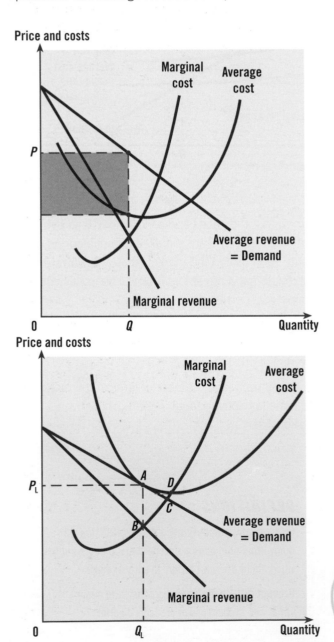

Figure 6.9 Monopolistic competition

> ### DEFINITION
>
> **Deadweight loss:** loss to society of the firm producing where price exceeds marginal cost

With fewer firms in the industry, this inefficiency could be addressed. This form of inefficiency is sometimes called **excess capacity**.

DEFINITIONS

Excess capacity: a consequence of firms producing at above the minimum point on the average cost curve

TRANSPORT RELEVANCE OF MONOPOLISTIC COMPETITION

Given the characteristic of product differentiation, it should be clear that firms in monopolistic competition compete through **non-price competition**. In other

DEFINITION

Non-price competition: competition between firms on the basis of, for example, branding, customer service, location, range of products, advertising

ECONOMICS IN CONTEXT

PUBLIC TRANSPORT IN HONG KONG

Hong Kong ferry service

Hong Kong has a diverse public transport system consisting of a modern surface rail (KCR) and mass transit system (MTR), franchised bus services, tram services, various ferry services, minibuses and public taxis. All are privately owned. In terms of market structure, there are examples of monopoly, natural monopoly and monopolistic competition. Unusually, no subsidies are paid for their operation by the Hong Kong government.

The rail network is a typical example of a natural monopoly. In 2007, the KCR and MTR companies were amalgamated to form a new integrated company. This move was designed to cut out wasteful duplication and competition, while providing scope for the benefits of economies of scale.

Franchised bus services are operated by five companies. Each has its own group of franchised services; fares, frequency levels, types of vehicle, routes and bus stops are all part of franchise agreements with the government. To some extent, the companies have a monopoly in their own geographical area, although there are a few pinch points and stretches of route where they compete with each other.

The famous Star Ferry and Hong Kong Tramways Company have their own monopoly as far as their mode of transport is concerned. What they do not have is a monopoly in their local markets – buses, taxis and the various cross-harbour tunnel companies, as well as private cars, compete with them. Of all Hong Kong's transport services, they have unique brands and a loyal customer base.

Hong Kong has around 4,400 minibuses, known locally as public light buses. The 2,800 green-topped ones carry 16 passengers, all seated, on fixed routes. The remaining red-topped ones are more flexible and not as strictly regulated. The fares charged are competitive and can be determined by the vehicle's driver. Many are owned by their drivers; others are run by small companies.

Finally, Hong Kong has over 15,000 red urban taxis. Fares are strictly regulated by meter and the number of vehicles controlled by the government. Most are privately owned or are leased from local companies by their drivers. As with minibuses, this market provides substantial evidence of monopolistic competition.

words, quality of service, the subtleties of the product on offer, advertising and brand loyalty are indicative of how firms seek to gain market share.

Supporters of deregulation (see below, pages 146–148) believed that removing many of the barriers to entry would lead to transport markets, particularly local ones, becoming like monopolistic competition. This was certainly expected of local bus deregulation. For a while after the 1985 Transport Act became operational, this appeared to happen. In many parts of the country, new small local firms sought to enter the market. Over time, the market has become less competitive. There are exceptions, particularly in many rural areas where demand is low, and in a small number of urban markets. In Manchester, for example, well over 40 different companies run services in and around the city. Most are small local companies, with relatively low fixed costs. They invariably operate older vehicles. The product is differentiated through the services provided as well as more openly through the varied liveries and types of their buses.

Another example of a monopolistically competitive market is in the provision of local taxi services. For both licensed taxis and private hire, the cost of entry is modest and barriers to entry are few. The number of licensed vehicles is restricted, whereas in many areas, there are no quantity restrictions on private hire companies. This latter market is fiercely competitive with little opportunity to make other than a low level of normal profit. Branding and brand loyalty are important ways in which firms compete.

Oligopoly

Oligopoly is a market structure where the total output is concentrated in the hands of a few large firms. There will therefore be a high concentration ratio (see above, page 128). These firms dominate the industry, yet realise they are **interdependent** in so far as the actions of one of these firms will result in counter-actions by others. Oligopoly approximates most closely to the actual state of affairs as it usually exists, and is the most realistic model of market structure yet, but unlike those we have considered so far, does not provide definite predictions about the price and output level of its firms.

Further important characteristics are:

- high barriers to entry
- price rigidity due to risks and uncertainties associated with price competition
- non-price competition in order to gain market share
- profit maximisation may not be the firm's objective.

BEHAVIOUR OF OLIGOPOLISTIC FIRMS

The difficulty in studying oligopoly is that the behaviour of firms can follow two different routes – in some industries there may be cutthroat competition between aggressive firms, while in others there may well be co-operation or tacit evidence of collusion. Consequently, just how one firm actually reacts will depend on how it expects competitors to react. All of this means that it is difficult to put forward one completely acceptable theory of oligopolistic behaviour. There are two main theories that attempt to explain how oligopolists behave. These are the theory of **kinked demand** and game theory.

Oligopolists are price makers. They have the power to set their own prices, but what they are unable to gauge is the reaction of their competitors. This uncertainty means that firms may prefer non-price competition in the form of branding, customer service, location, range of products and so on. The underpinning explanation for this is the kinked demand curve (see Figure 6.10). This can be used to

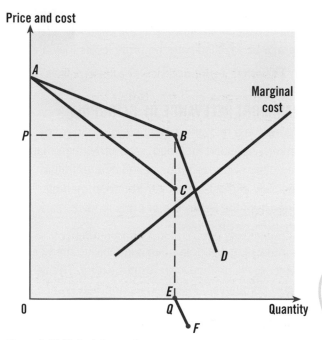

Figure 6.10 Kinked demand curve

explain why prices in oligopolistic markets are often rigid, or stable for relatively long periods of time.

In Figure 6.10, it is assumed that a firm is producing at price *P* and output *Q*. If the firm increases its price above *P*, other firms in the market will not follow. This is because these firms will be able to sell more themselves, attracting customers from the firm that increased its price. So, the firm's demand curve is *AB* and its marginal revenue curve is *AC*. This demand curve is relatively elastic to an increase in price. If the firm lowers its price, it assumes that other firms in the market will follow this lead so as not to lose market share. This starts a price war, the result of which is likely to be that all firms lose out. The demand curve below *B* is relatively inelastic and indicated by *BD*. The marginal revenue curve is *EF*.

So, overall, the oligopolist's demand curve appears to be *ABD*. Price will be rigid at *P* since there is no incentive for a firm to increase or decrease the prices it charges.

The kinked demand curve is in some respects a useful way to explain the behaviour of oligopolists. Empirical evidence unfortunately does not always support what this model tells us. For example, prices in an oligopolistic market may be no more rigid than

in other markets. Also, the reason for price rigidity may have more to do with commercial practices than the firm's awareness of the kinked demand curve.

It is for this reason that in recent years, **game theory** has increasingly been applied in order to understand the behaviour of oligopolists. The 'game' is that firms have to make decisions about the price they charge and their level of output. Decisions are taken based on assumptions about the responses of rival firms; these decisions have particular implications for the profits earned.

> **DEFINITION**
>
> **Game theory:** a means of modelling the behaviour of firms

Table 6.5 shows the game matrix facing two firms, A and B, that have large market shares in an oligopolistic market. Suppose at present there is no price competition and that each firm sells its product for £1. In order to increase market share, both firms are considering reducing their prices by 10 per cent to 90p.

		A's price		The cells show each firm's expected profits
		£1	90p	
B's price	£1	£2m each	£1m B £2.2m A	
	90p	£2.2m B £1m A	£1.5m each	

Table 6.5 An oligopoly game matrix

At £1, each firm is making an annual profit of £2m. If B decided to reduce its price to 90p, its profits would increase to £2.2m. This is not good news for A, which has left its price at £1 and seen profits fall to £1m. Alternatively, A could cut its price to 90p, with B leaving its price at £1. A's profits would increase to

£2.2m, with B's falling to £1m. In this situation, each firm knows what the other is considering – if prices are cut to 90p, then both firms experience a fall in profits to £1.5m. Both firms lose out, so the obvious option is for them to collude to retain their prices at £1 in order to gain higher profits.

Such an agreement, though, is illegal since it is not in the best interest of consumers. Behaviour like this over fuel surcharges resulted in British Airways being heavily fined by the UK's Office of Fair Trading in August 2007.

Tacit collusion, however, is not illegal. It involves unwritten agreement between two firms to not compete with each other through a price war. A typical example might be where two large bus companies in a town agree not to cut fares in order to compete. There may also be a tacit agreement to not develop new routes that duplicate each other's services, since each company's costs would rise and profits decrease accordingly.

The behaviour of oligopolists continues to give concern to regulatory bodies such as the UK's Competition Commission (see above, page 132). A particular cause for concern is the anti-competitive behaviour of firms that collude. This is illegal but very difficult to prove. Such **collusion** is, however, indicative of interdependence.

Examples of collusion are:

● a price agreement or output agreement designed to restrict competition, possibly to scare off new firms looking to enter the market

● price leadership, where when one firm, usually the market leader, increases its price and others follow.

Collusion in some markets is likely to be tacit, whereby rival firms have an unwritten agreement not to compete directly with each other or to engage in a price cutting campaign. Here, the oligopolists would seem to be satisfied with the profit levels they are achieving.

TRANSPORT RELEVANCE OF OLIGOPOLY

Oligopoly is a relevant market structure in many markets, transport included. Over time, there has been clear evidence of increased concentration, especially in most passenger transport markets. Evidence of the behaviour of firms in such markets is sketchy to say the least.

An interesting example of an oligopolistic market is that for crossing the Dover Strait by ferry. The two largest companies, P&O Ferries and Sea France, operate between Dover and Calais. Norfolkline and Speed Ferries have services from Dover to Dunkerque and Boulogne respectively. Prior to the opening of the Channel Tunnel in 1993, there was evidence of price collusion between the companies that operated services at that time. This is no longer the case. Competition is intense and price-driven. P&O remains the largest operator, but in a market that experienced decline up to 2005, it has had

The Dover Strait ferry crossing – an oligopolistic market

> **DEFINITION**
>
> **Collusion:** where firms tacitly or otherwise agree to not compete on prices, service provision and other matters that might adversely affect mutual well-being

	No. of buses	Estimated market share (%)
First Group	9,000	23.0
Stagecoach Group	7,000	17.8
Arriva	6,500	16.6
Go-Ahead Group	3,640	9.3
National Express	2,000	5.1
Others	11,606	28.2
Total	**39,200**	**100.0**

Table 6.6 Leading bus operators in the UK, 2006

to develop the quality of its product to withstand increasing market share from Sea France and the small no-frills, car-only Speed Ferries. This latter company now claims 13 per cent market share.

Following deregulation (see below, pages 146–147), the consolidation of local bus operations has seen the emergence of five major bus companies. Table 6.6 shows these in rank order in terms of the number of buses operated.

At a national level, the market structure would seem to fit that of an oligopoly. In reality, this may not necessarily be a true reflection, since the nature of this market is that it is essentially a local one. A company may have a considerable share of a particular local market, even 100 per cent if it has been able to drive out rival companies. It is only in a limited number of local markets that these large operators compete 'tooth and nail' with each other.

The companies named in Table 6.6 are also major providers of rail passenger transport in the UK. In

2008, they owned 15 out of the 20 franchises that were available following major changes in November/December 2007. Recent government policy would seem to be moving towards concentrating passenger franchises in the hands of a smaller number of companies compared with when the first franchises were awarded in 1995.

The scheduled airline market displays evidence of oligopolistic behaviour through the formation of alliances (see Table 6.7). The strategic purpose of these alliances is to offer extended networks to customers, reduce costs through avoiding unnecessary competition, and share maintenance and operational staff. There are some benefits to consumers in terms of a wider choice of carrier and shorter travel times. It could also be argued that fares on some routes are lower due to the pooling of resources. Passengers, though, may lose out when all competition is removed from a route, with higher fares and less frequent services.

	Star Alliance	Sky Team	Oneworld
No. of partners	17	10	10
Destinations	855	728	692
Passengers (millions)	413	373	320
Fleet size	2,831	2,018	2,453
European leader	Lufthansa	Air France/KLM	British Airways

Table 6.7 Airline alliances, May 2007

Contestability

Most economists now agree that the degree of competition in a market is not necessarily just a function of whether it is a monopoly, oligopoly or monopolistic competition. This may seem surprising, but is argued with justification that what is more important is the extent of **contestability**. This is particularly so in transport markets.

A market is contestable if potential competitors can influence the conduct of firms currently in the market. Potential competitors include similar firms not operating in the market or new firms that could set up if they saw an opportunity to gain market share and operate successfully (see the earlier case of Grand Central Railway). What potential firms have to assess is the extent to which the likely gains from market entry exceed the costs of entry. Barriers to

entry and exit are therefore crucial in determining whether a market really is contestable.

According to the concept, a perfectly contestable market is one where entry and exit are free or costless. This has to be so if potential competitors are not at a relative disadvantage compared with firms already operating in the market. If entry is not free, then new firms will experience higher costs, suffer from a lack of access to technology and be unable to compete effectively because of the brand loyalty that has been built up by incumbent firms. So, the fewer barriers to entry and the lower the cost of entry, the more contestable will be the market.

The cost of exit must also be costless. This means that in a perfectly contestable market, firms will have no **sunk costs** – when they leave the market, they can resell any assets they have used without loss. If this were not possible, then potential entrants might be put off from entering a market. Sunk costs would therefore be seen as a barrier to entry.

The result of costless entry and exit is that contestable markets are characterised by what is known as **'hit-and-run' entry**. A typical example would be the case of a firm attracted to enter a market due to the high level of profits being earned by existing firms. On entry, it would take a share of the profits, but it would then leave once profit levels fell back to normal. In this way, firms are not able to earn supernormal profits in the long run.

A market is perfectly contestable where:

- there is a pool of potential entrants into the market
- entry and exit are costless

- all firms are subject to the same regulations and state of technology

- mechanisms are in place to prohibit responsive or entry limit pricing, as existing firms have lower costs than potential entrants

- incumbent firms are vulnerable to 'hit-and-run' competition.

In theory, as long as entry is free and exit is costless, any market structure could meet the requirements of a perfectly contestable market.

- *Monopolistic competition* has few barriers to entry. Due to non-price competition, it does, though, take small firms time to build up a customer base to obtain brand loyalty. In typical monopolistically competitive markets, transport included, there are also barriers to entry in the form of licensing and regulatory requirements.

- In *oligopolistic markets*, there are high barriers to entry, particularly in the form of the capital costs of entry and expenditure that is essential to build up market share. This is certainly true of transport markets.

- *Monopoly power* can be obtained through a patent or legal right to operate in a market. Where this is so, then the market will not be at all contestable. In other monopoly situations, there could be an opportunity for new firms to enter, although the cost of entry will most certainly not be costless.

So, in each of the above market structures, there could be a high degree of contestability, depending on the cost of entry and exit into the market. Figure 6.11 shows the case of a monopoly and how, if there are no barriers to entry, a new firm moving into the market can have a profound effect on the monopolist's profits. The monopolist is making supernormal profits, shown by the shaded box, and selling output of Q at price P. If the market is perfectly contestable, and there are no barriers to entry or exit, these supernormal profits would be a signal for new firms to move into the market. As a result, the monopolist is forced to reduce price to P_1 while producing the same level of output in order to maximise the volume of sales. Normal profits will now be earned and output will increase to where average cost equals average revenue.

Prices and costs

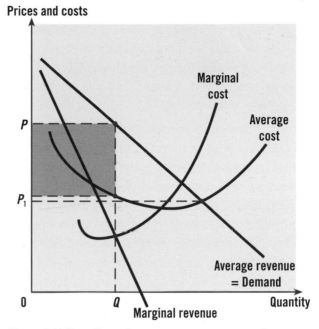

Figure 6.11 The effect of a new entrant on a monopoly

In theory, a perfectly competitive market, which is used to benchmark other market structures, is most similar to a perfectly contestable market. There are no barriers to entry and exit and when this is the case in a perfectly contestable market:

- only normal profits are earned in the long run

- firms are not able to apply cross-subsidisation

- prices cannot be set below average cost to deter new entrants

- allocative efficiency and productive efficiency are being achieved

- the number of firms in the market does not matter.

TRANSPORT RELEVANCE OF CONTESTABILITY

The notion of contestability was developed by the US economist William Baumol in the mid-1970s in the context of domestic airline transport. Baumol believed that if the market was contestable rather than regulated, fare levels would fall, due to the threat of new companies entering the market. An important feature of this particular market was that, in the main, airlines leased their aircraft, meaning that there would be no sunk costs when they left the market. Where airlines had purchased aircraft, these could be transferred to other routes or sold to other companies. Baumol's argument was accepted by the federal government and, following deregulation in 1979, new operators, notably North West Airlines, entered the market. Fare levels fell, new services emerged and, overall, there was increased competition in the market.

The US experience was particularly significant for the UK, since it was the underpinning reason for the radical changes to transport policy that took place under successive Conservative governments from 1979 to 1997. The UK has led the way globally in its intention to achieve contestability in its transport markets. Other countries in the EU, South East Asia and Australia have subsequently removed barriers to entry in many of their transport markets to achieve greater contestability.

Figure 6.12 shows in theory the relationship between barriers to entry and contestability in typical transport markets. It is based on the assumption that when barriers to entry are low and free, the market will

be highly contestable. In contrast, where barriers to entry are high and costly, the market will not be particularly contestable. As the figure shows, in some transport markets, such as road haulage, where barriers to entry are low, it is expected that there will be a high degree of contestability. In contrast, where set-up costs are high, as in rail and air transport, there will be low contestability.

The extent to which reality matches the position shown in Figure 6.12 is debatable. Let us take two examples.

Road haulage

In 2007, there were around 32,500 road haulage businesses in the UK. The number of operators has been declining by 1–2 per cent per year since 2000, resulting in a slight increase in concentration. Profit levels are very low, typically 2–3 per cent. In many respects the market is highly fragmented – there is a small number of large national operations supported

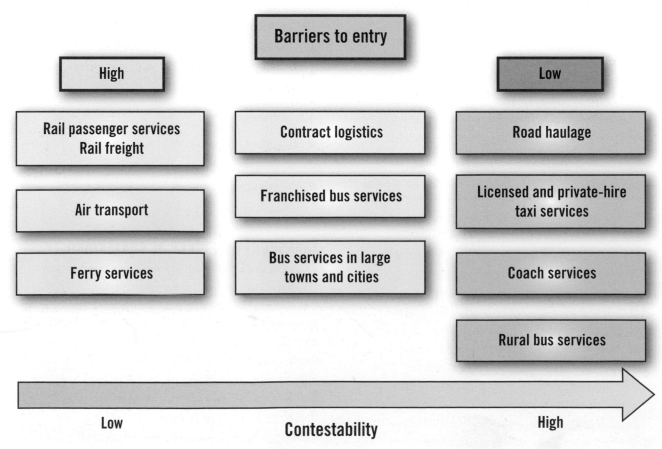

Figure 6.12 Barriers to entry and expected contestability

by a large number of small companies with small fleets serving a highly geographically specific customer base. In 2007, 73 per cent of companies had a turnover of less than £250,000; just 2 per cent of companies had a turnover of above £5m.

As the industry has developed, the nature of barriers to entry has changed. At the early stage of development, the main barrier to entry was the ability to invest in new vehicles. It was a relatively low barrier to entry and one that still applies for small firms. Over the past 20 years, the end user requirement from manufacturers and retailers has been for greater logistics management skills from their hauliers. This has resulted in the phenomenal growth of contract logistics and the emergence of large players such as DHL Exel Supply Chain, Wincanton Holdings and Christian Salvesen. Mergers and amalgamations at the top end of the market have been common, as firms have continuously sought to innovate and at the same time remain competitive from a cost standpoint.

The market is by no means as contestable as it might seem. At a local level, there will always be small firms seeking to set up in the market, particularly where a niche has been identified. The increasing cost of fuel and extremely low profit margins make this a high-risk activity. At the top end of the contract logistics market, when large contracts become available, there is a very small number of firms that can hope to be successful in the bidding process.

Passenger train operations

As stated earlier, the number of passenger train-operating companies has fallen since the early days after privatisation. When franchises have come up for renewal, the successful bidders have usually been existing franchisees. It can be safely concluded that barriers to entry into this market have increased since privatisation, making franchise operation less contestable.

Not all train-operating companies hold franchises. A very small number of companies are open access or non-franchised operators that have elected to set up in businesses to challenge the franchised operator (see above, pages 134–135). Their reasons for this have usually been the high fares that are charged, the poor service provided or a combination of these.

Table 6.8 shows the five open access operating companies in 2008. Two, Hull Trains and Heathrow Connect, are owned by First Group, which has four franchises and is the largest passenger transport company in the UK.

Barriers to entry into the market are substantial (see also Economics in context, Grand Central Railways, page 130) and include:

● a lack of availability of rolling stock

● a shortage of trained drivers and other staff

● a lack of slots at London main line stations, especially on routes into these stations

● restrictions on where services can pick up and drop off passengers.

The assumption that the threat of competition is sufficient to control the behaviour of the franchisee must be questioned. It is not until a competitor has begun to operate that the commercial behaviour of the franchised operator may change.

Given the number of non-franchised operators, it should be very clear that the passenger train market is not very contestable, despite high fares and an expanding market.

Company	Commenced	Services
Grand Central	March 2008	Sunderland–London
Heathrow Connect	June 2005	Paddington–Heathrow
Heathrow Express	June 1998	Paddington–Heathrow
Hull Trains	September 2000	Hull–London
Wrexham and Shropshire	April 2008	Wrexham–London

Table 6.8 Open access train-operating companies, 2008

Deregulation

Deregulation occurs when the government deliberately removes official regulations that act as a barrier to competition in a market. It is a supply-side policy that facilitates contestability. It has a particular relevance in transport markets, many of which have had substantial regulation in the form of various licences and minimum quality standards. This regulation has been used in some markets to protect a public sector monopoly from outside competition.

> **DEFINITION**
>
> **Deregulation:** removal of regulations

Three particular transport markets have been deregulated over the past 25 years or so. They are:

● express buses and coaches (1980) and local bus services (1986)

● domestic and EU air passenger transport (1997)

● EU road freight services (1999).

In all cases, the objective of deregulation has been to improve efficiency through increased competition.

DEREGULATION OF LOCAL BUS SERVICES

Local bus services were deregulated in the Transport Act (1985), which became effective from October 1986. This was a particularly controversial piece of legislation that provoked considerable opposition from trade unions, most public sector bus operators and opposition politicians. It ended a strict system of route licensing that had protected public sector operators for 55 years.

There were two main reasons for deregulation. These were that the market for local bus services had been declining annually since the mid-1950s and in order to maintain services, local authorities were obliged to provide ever-increasing subsidies. After deregulation, the only barrier to entry was that all firms required an operator's licence, largely for safety reasons to ensure minimum quality standards. The system is managed by the regional Traffic Commissioners, who seek to ensure that the behaviour of firms is compliant with the legislation. Fare levels are set by the bus operators. Where a route or service is deemed to be socially necessary, then passenger transport executives go through a tendering process prior to the payment of subsidy. Consequently, there are two distinct types of bus service, those that are commercial and those that require external support.

It was hoped the deregulation would provide a much needed 'shot in the arm' for the local bus industry. Through greater competition, it was anticipated, fares would be lower, service provision and efficiency could increase and cross-subsidisation would be removed. It was also believed that deregulation would provide a new business opportunity for small firms to put on local services in response to local need. This would be consistent with the market structure of monopolistic competition (see above).

Many of the hoped-for benefits from deregulation have failed to materialise. In October 2006, the House of Commons Transport Committee concluded that the current arrangements could 'not be made to work' without overhaul.

In a report, the Committee commented on the poor quality and unreliability of services, the use of old, inaccessible vehicles and the rude attitude of drivers. Other studies on the impact of deregulation have noted that savings are being made by running buses on busy routes, with the result that off-peak services have been cut, along with services on routes where demand is low.

The degree of competition in the market varies. In Bristol, for example, First Group operates 95 per cent of all bus services in and around the city. In

Manchester, by way of contrast, there are around forty companies, large and small, competing for passengers travelling into the city. In Cambridge, Stagecoach has a near monopoly, while in Oxford, the Oxford Bus Company, Stagecoach Oxford and various local companies provide services in and around the city.

ACTIVITY ····⫶

a) Using the criteria stated above, see what statistical information you can find on the national impact of local bus deregulation.

STRETCH AND CHALLENGE

b) For a local bus market known to you, discuss the extent to which the market is contestable.

THE EU'S 'OPEN SKIES' POLICY

Applied to air transport, deregulation is commonly referred to as the realisation of an 'open skies' policy. Within the EU, from April 1997, there has been a single open competitive aviation market for the carriers of member states. Significantly, since May 2004, this market has included carriers in the new member states of central and eastern Europe. (The same model, which is consistent with the Single European Market, has been applied to road freight transport.)

The so-called Third Package consists of three sets of measures that have created this 'open skies' regime.

● Open access, whereby EU airlines can establish themselves in any other member state and operate services with no capacity restrictions.

● Airlines are permitted to fix their own fares and cargo rates, subject to predatory pricing safeguards.

● Common criteria have to be applied for granting operators' licences.

Simultaneously, the European Commission included air transport within the scope of its Competition Policy rules, to prevent various forms of anti-competitive behaviour from carriers that would be detrimental to consumers. Alliances, though, were not considered to be anti-competitive.

ECONOMICS IN CONTEXT

TRANSATLANTIC FARES TO FALL DUE TO INCREASED COMPETITION?

On 30 March 2008, after 30 years of strict regulation, a new 'open skies' agreement between the EU and the USA came into effect. Under this agreement, any European or any American airline is able to fly from anywhere in the EU to anywhere in the USA. By 2010, it is expected that the US 'domestic' markets will be fully opened to competition, otherwise the agreement will be scrapped.

This agreement follows the deregulation of EU air services in 1997. It removes the barrier to entry whereby only four airlines (British Airways, Virgin Atlantic, American and United Airlines) could operate lucrative services from Heathrow to the USA.

Will this be good news for passengers? In theory, this ought to be the case. Delta, Northwest and Air France are all launching new services, which should see the prices of many peak-period tickets falling. Off-peak fares are unlikely to drop unless the price of oil falls, which is most unlikely.

A spokesman for Continental said that his company looked forward to challenging the Heathrow old guard: 'We can finally take them on their own turf. They've been living in a protected commercial environment for many years'.

Industry analysts believe that the most intense competition will be in business class, where British Airways and Virgin Atlantic charge up to £4,000 for a return between Heathrow and JFK. This competition will increase once other American and European giants enter the market.

One substantial barrier to entry remains, namely the availability of slots at Heathrow. At present the airport is operating at near 100 per cent capacity. Any slots that are released in the future will command an even greater price than they do at present. This particular barrier to entry may well mean that the transatlantic market is not quite as contestable as might have been expected following its deregulation.

The effects of deregulation have been substantial, and have included:

● massive growth in passenger numbers, particularly for low-cost carriers. Ryanair, for example, carried over 40 million passengers in 2006, compared to around 15 million in 2002. Overall, passenger numbers have increased by 6–9 per cent per annum since deregulation.

● new entrants tending to be low-cost carriers such as Flybe, Monarch, Jet2.com, Air Berlin, Brussels Airlines and, more recently, SkyEurope, Smart Wings, Wizz and other central European carriers. There are now almost a hundred such carriers in the EU.

● new routes, particularly from smaller regional airports. Due to high landing charges and poor slot availability, low-cost airlines have tended to fly from airports such as Stansted, Luton and Liverpool, other much smaller airports in the UK, and elsewhere in Europe.

● pressure on national airlines to compete with low-cost carriers through competitive fares and services that are more accessible.

Overall, the effects of deregulation have been to make the market more contestable, very much to the benefit of consumers. Whether deregulation has produced the best outcome from an environmental standpoint is a totally different matter. This will be discussed later in Chapter 7.

Franchising

Franchising has been used in some passenger transport markets as a means of promoting competition. It is a system whereby there is a competitive tendering process put in place for the provision of transport services. Unlike deregulation, where the free market decides on what is provided, franchising is much more specific. For example,

> ### DEFINITION
>
> **Franchise:** the outcome of a competitive system to bid for the provision of services

minimum service levels are laid down (railways), or the type of vehicle to be used, acceptance of network tickets and service levels (bus services). As a system, franchising provides the franchise holder with an opportunity to operate with no (or in some cases, limited) competition and to obtain benefits from economies of scale. Much more so than a deregulated market, the franchisees are subject to supervision of their operations, in order to ensure that quality is being maintained.

To amplify this last point, in December 2006, Virgin Rail was successful in extending its West Coast Main Line franchise to March 2012. The franchise agreement from the Department for Transport (DfT) required of Virgin:

● commitment to an enhanced timetable of services between London and Birmingham and London and Manchester by the end of 2008

● a reduction in journey times between London and Glasgow

● improved weekend services between London and Liverpool, Chester and Preston

● Pendolino units to be used on the Birmingham–Scotland service.

Fares would continue to be set in line with current policy, which is determined by the DfT. The franchise agreement also stated the DfT's subsidy payments to Virgin, which peak at £312 million in 2008/09, then fall to around £200 million by the end of the franchise.

Moving on to bus services in London, the decision to franchise rather than deregulate was taken, as it was felt undesirable to introduce competition directly into the market. The bus has a very important function in London, moving people around and keeping unnecessary traffic off the roads. It was feared that in a fully competitive market, as seen elsewhere in the country, there would be excessive supply and hence congestion on main routes, and more limited provision elsewhere. Transport for London keeps the length of franchises short in order to sustain a competitive situation. The main bidders for central London routes have tended to be the large national operators such as First, Arriva and Go-Ahead.

Elsewhere, though, Transport for London remains committed to encouraging new local operators to bid.

Privatisation

Privatisation is the process by which a former publicly owned organisation or activity is sold off to the private sector. This sale can take various forms, including an outright sale to another company, a management and/or employee buyout, or the public sale of shares in a new company. Each of these means has been applied to the transport privatisations that have been made in the UK since 1979 (see Table 6.9)

By any measure, the scale of transport privatisations in the UK has been extensive. It is also unprecedented on a global scale. The early years of the privatisation programme were not particularly controversial. The parts that were privatised were in the main activities that could quite easily be operated by the private sector. Later privatisations, particularly of railways, were much more contentious and provoked considerable opposition from within and outside the industry.

The activities listed in Table 6.9 had been taken into public ownership (nationalised) at various stages since 1947. The reasons this happened are relevant to understanding why not all economists have favoured their subsequent privatisation or *denationalisation*. These reasons included:

- The natural monopoly argument. Economies of scale meant that it made sense to have a single provider of (say) a rail network or local public transport services. It also avoided the problem of duplication and the consequent waste of resources.

- Transport is an essential service that is fundamental to economic and social well-being. This being so, it was argued that it should not be left to the private sector to provide and that a degree of central public control was necessary to develop a meaningful transport policy.

- The transport system produces large external benefits that may not be taken into account by private sector providers when taking decisions.

More recent arguments have included:

- The lack of empirical evidence to support privatisation. This was a particular issue in the privatisation of railways.

- Private monopolies will replace public sector monopolies and some profits that are earned will go back to shareholders.

- The benefits from privatisation are only short term. The longer-term problem is that once privatised, there is the issue of having sold off the 'family silver', with its wider implications.

However, during the mid- to late 1970s, there had been increasing discontent over the traditional

Year	Company	Type of business	Proceeds (£ m)
1982	National Freight Corporation	road haulage	54
1983/4	Associated British Ports	seaports	14
1984	Sealink	ferry services	66
1986	National Bus Company	bus and coach services	260
1987	British Airways	air services	900
1987	British Airports Authority	principal airports	1,281
1996	Railtrack	rail infrastructure	1,930
2002	National Air Traffic Systems	air traffic control	120

Table 6.9 UK transport privatisations

Note: Excludes municipal bus companies, train-operating and rolling stock companies, all of which were privatised over an extended time period.

reasons for state ownership of services such as transport. It was argued that privatisation could produce certain benefits over and above the costs. These arguments included:

● Privatisation would allow businesses to focus more on long-term planning and less on meeting short-term political requirements.

● Public sector transport services are inefficient; private sector organisations are more efficient and likely to operate where price = marginal cost. Cross-subsidisation (see above) would be eliminated under private sector ownership.

● Private sector management would be more motivated and have a greater emphasis on customer service provision.

● Privatisation would provide a new source of investment funding for transport; public sector borrowing was limited, particularly in relation to other demands being placed upon the Exchequer.

At the same time, the political context cannot be ignored.

The Conservative governments of 1979 to 1997, particularly when Mrs Thatcher was prime minister,

Former prime minister Margaret Thatcher

were determined to shrink the size and influence of the public sector. They believed that, if the private sector could provide services such as transport, then it should be allowed to do so, for the reasons given above. A further consideration was that the level of subsidy being given to rail and bus services had continued to increase, with little evidence of improvement in quality. Privatisation was seen as a way of cutting back on this financial commitment.

RAIL PRIVATISATION – HAS IT SUCCEEDED?

At the time rail was, and in some respects it still is, the most controversial as well as the most complex of all transport privatisations. There are compelling reasons why rail should remain in the public sector, since the industry typifies the three classical reasons given above. It is for these reasons, plus the many problems of how to do it, that this has been sometimes referred to as a 'privatisation too far'.

This most certainly was not the prevailing view in the so-called *New Opportunities* White Paper of 1992, which stated that 'public sector ownership is a genuine obstacle … radical change is needed'. The problem with this particular privatisation was its scale and the fact that no other government had attempted to privatise rail networks along the lines proposed for Britain.

The overall objectives were:

● to see better use made of the railways

● to provide greater responsiveness to the customer

● to see a higher quality service

● to give better value for money to rail users

● to generate new capital investment.

These objectives are intended to be realised through the following structure:

● separation of infrastructure from operations, as suggested prior to privatisation by the Adam Smith Institute. This was the most difficult decision that had to be taken – alternative models were for sector separation and geographical separation but with combined infrastructure and operational responsibilities. Railtrack, the track authority, was conceived as a public sector body that was privatised in 1996. (It is now called Network Rail and is effectively back in public ownership.)

● franchising of passenger services, 23 in all, for periods of 7 to 12 years. Most franchises receive a subsidy from the government – a very small number were required to make a premium payment to operate their franchises.

● outright sale of freight services, initially to English, Wales and Scottish Railway (EWS) and Freightliner.

● opportunity for 'open access' companies to compete for passenger and freight services.

● control of track charges by an independent regulator; control of franchise bidding prices by another regulator (now DfT).

● transfer of rolling stock to ROSCOs (rolling stock companies, subsequently privatised).

The above model is a complex one. It mixes a range of different approaches, including outright sales, restructuring, franchising and privatisation, with some regulation.

The view of most economists is that the experience of privatisation has been relatively positive, although not without problems along the way.

ACTIVITY ⋯⋮⋗

a) Go back to the overall objectives of rail privatisation as given in the 1992 White Paper. For each, collect appropriate statistical information from Transport Statistics, Great Britain and use this to evaluate whether the privatisation has been successful.

STRETCH AND CHALLENGE

b) Discuss which of these five objectives is the most important barometer of the success of rail privatisation. Justify your choice.

ECONOMICS IN CONTEXT

CAN HIGHER RAIL FARES BE JUSTIFIED?

Annually, in January, train-operating companies increase their fares. For regular commuters and those travelling at peak periods, the scale of these increases can be eye-watering, well above the rate of inflation. In Britain, we have the highest rail fares by far in the EU. Unlike France, Germany and Spain, there has never been a deeply ingrained culture of public investment in railways in the UK. In those countries and many others, railways are seen as a public service that should not be left to the vagaries of private sector operators. Another difference is that on most other EU rail systems, there are no big differences between peak and off-peak fares.

Why is this? Some critics would argue that, although privatisation was right, the way in which it was done was not sustainable, in the sense that train operators and the track company, Network Rail, have conflicting interests. This is clear to see at weekends and holiday periods, when engineering work takes precedence over the provision of reliable services … and there is little the train operators can do about it. A more logical structure would be one that provides for a vertically integrated railway whereby the trains and track are operated by the same company.

Typical peak-period walk-on standard class open return fares in early 2008 are:

Portsmouth to London Waterloo £49.10
Sheffield to London St Pancras £164

Manchester to London Euston £230
Newcastle to London King's Cross £249.

Can these really be justified? To some extent they can, in so far as:

● post-privatisation, train operating companies and Network Rail have invested heavily in new rolling stock and track upgrades. The better standard of service, with improved reliability, comes at a price.

● the majority of rail travellers – just 6 per cent of the population – are affluent and can afford to pay the higher fares.

● peak-period travellers are basically commuters and business users and not the poor or elderly, who tend to travel off-peak on discount fares.

On the other hand, high fares would seem to be incompatible with:

● the need to get more people to travel by train for environmental reasons. The carbon footprint for car and air alternatives is much greater.

● worsening road congestion. Higher fares will only accelerate gridlock as rail travellers switch back to cars.

● the vast sums of public subsidy that train operators receive to run services.

There is no acceptable answer to this problem, although a structural reorganisation may well be worth evaluating.

7 Market failure and the role of intervention in transport markets

On completion of this chapter, you should be able to:

- describe the negative externalities associated with increased transport use
- explain how and why economists seek to put a monetary value on these negative externalities
- discuss the problems and implications of placing monetary values on negative externalities
- explain the effects on the environment of increased demand for road and air transport
- analyse why the existence of negative externalities is a case of market failure
- discuss the role of the following in cases of market failure:
  - regulation
  - indirect taxation
  - subsidies
- understand what is meant by sustainability in transport
- discuss the extent to which some modes of transport are more sustainable than others
- explain why traffic congestion is a classic example of market failure
- discuss the broad approaches for dealing with congestion
- understand what is meant by road pricing, including congestion charging
- discuss the extent to which road pricing is an effective way of dealing with market failure associated with traffic congestion
- discuss the impact on UK towns and cities and elsewhere in the world where road pricing schemes have been implemented
- discuss how, using case studies of developed and emerging economies, other countries have sought to deal with problems of urban traffic congestion.

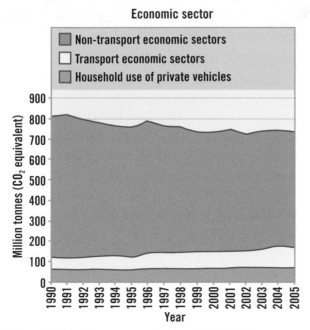

Economic sector

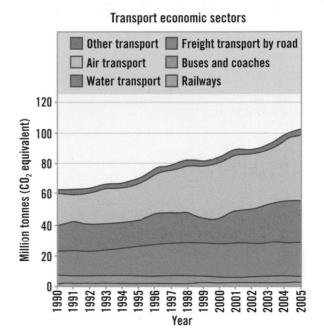

Transport economic sectors

Figure 7.1 Greenhouse gas emissions, 1990–2005

Transport and the environment

In Chapter 5, the ever-increasing demand for passenger and freight transport was analysed; transport forecasts clearly indicated that demand will continue to increase in the foreseeable future. These two undisputed facts have obvious environmental implications, namely that transport is and will continue to be, a major source of atmospheric pollution through greenhouse gas emissions.

It is though important to put the UK's situation in a global context. The USA and China are the world's greatest polluters and, in the case of China, the fastest growing emitter of greenhouse gasses. Emerging economies like those of Poland, the Czech Republic, India, Malaysia, Indonesia and so on, are also growing contributors to global emissions of CO_2, largely through their rapid industrialisation but also as a result of their rising vehicle ownership levels. Overall, the UK is responsible for around 4 per cent of all CO_2 emissions worldwide.

Figure 7.1 shows the trend in greenhouse gas emissions from 1990 to 2005. As this shows, overall there has been a slight fall in total emissions – the emissions from transport, particularly from air transport, in contrast have increased by 38 per cent over the period shown in the figure. In 2005, transport was responsible for 23 per cent of all UK greenhouse gas emissions compared with 15 per cent in 1990.

Household use of private vehicles accounted for 40 per cent of total transport emissions in 2005, a 12 per cent increase on 1990.

In line with the UK's commitment to the Kyoto Protocol, there has been a 'decoupling' of the relationship between the growth in CO_2 emissions, private car use and economic growth as measured by total household spending. This is shown in Figure 7.2. Up to 1993, CO_2 emissions rose more or less in line with the other two variables. After

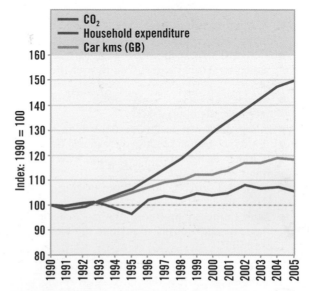

Figure 7.2 Private car CO_2 emissions, car kms and household expenditure, 1990–2005

1993, household expenditure has increased at a much faster rate and there has been a less than proportionate increase in CO_2 emissions relative to the increase in private car use. Tighter regulations on engine and exhaust emissions have been the main reasons for this improvement.

ACTIVITY ⋯⋅⋮⋗

Consider the information in Figures 7.1 and 7.2. Discuss how it might be used to justify a more environmentally acceptable transport policy for the UK.

Negative externalities arising from increased transport use

ATMOSPHERIC POLLUTION

Atmospheric pollution is a negative externality in so far as it has an effect on third parties. At a macro scale, the huge issue of climate change and its effects on the planet should be of concern to all. At a local scale, the external costs have to be borne by members of the community who are not directly responsible for the pollution. A pertinent example is the case of those who suffer from asthma or a similar respiratory complaint. In the UK, it is estimated that one in five of the population are affected in this way. Medical proof of the link between increased road transport use and the increase in asthma is, however,

ECONOMICS IN CONTEXT

THE STERN REVIEW OF CLIMATE CHANGE

In October 2006, Sir Nicholas Stern, former chief economist of the World Bank, produced a report for the government on the devastating consequences of climate change if the world's politicians fail to act as a matter of urgency. 'Climate change is the biggest challenge human civilisation has been asked to meet … dangerous climate change is going to happen … catastrophic climate change is what we have to avoid.'

Key features of the review are:

● Carbon emissions have already pushed up global temperatures by half a degree Celsius.
● There is a 75 per cent chance of global temperatures rising by 2 to 3 degrees Celsius over the next 50 years.
● Rising sea levels could leave 200m people permanently displaced.
● Crop yields will decline, particularly in Africa.
● Extreme weather could reduce global GDP.
● Cleaner energy and better transport technology must be promoted.
● A global market for carbon pricing must be created.
● The European Emissions Trading Scheme must be extended globally to include the USA, China and India.

Globally, transport is responsible for 14 per cent of all greenhouse gases. It is though very worrying, given

Stern's dire warning, that in the USA especially but also elsewhere, greenhouse gases have been increasing at a time when for the future of the planet, they should be falling (see Figure 7.3).

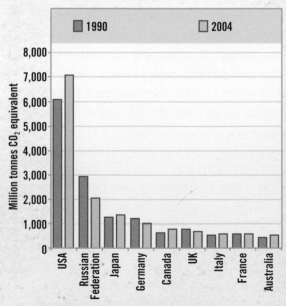

Figure 7.3 Total greenhouse gas emissions by country, 1990 and 2004

sketchy since atmospheric pollution is generated from other sources as well as transport.

Nevertheless, increasing levels of atmospheric pollution result in spillover effects and external costs being imposed on innocent third parties.

NOISE

Noise is a second negative externality arising from the increased use of transport, particularly from air transport and road traffic in towns and cities. As a form of disturbance, noise from both these forms of transport is unwanted by the human ear once it reaches a certain intensity. With road traffic noise, local studies have shown that where people live along a busy road, they are continuously aware of the noise from the traffic. Their lifestyles tend to be determined to some extent by peak and off peak levels of noise – concentration and relaxation are invariably difficult.

Aircraft noise causes much more annoyance. It registers a higher decibel level, and because it is not always continuous, leads to additional pressure on those people who are affected by it. Figure 7.4 shows the population around Heathrow affected by aircraft noise.

The 'Leq' measure used is an assessment of community response to aircraft noise. A measure of 57dB from aircraft noise is seen as being where there is the onset of significant community annoyance. In 2006, 258,000 people lived inside the 57dB area around Heathrow. This is more than six times larger than the population within the 57 Leq contour around

Aircraft noise causes annoyance

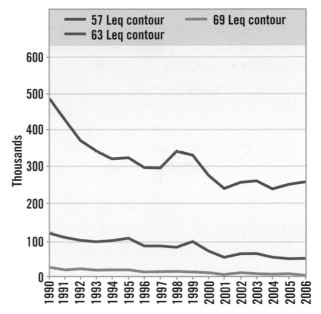

Figure 7.4 Population around Heathrow airport with Leq noise contours

Manchester (see Figure 7.5). The total air traffic movements at Heathrow in 2006 were 471,000, just over twice that at Manchester. Although aircraft are much quieter than fifteen years ago, people's attitude to aircraft noise has changed in this time. The public, particularly in the higher social groups and middle

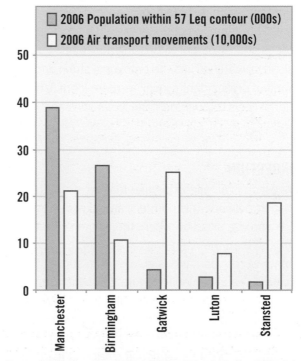

Figure 7.5 Air transport movements and population affected by noise at other major airports 2006

age bands, demand less noise. Given Heathrow's location, the noise problem is a major obstacle undermining the case for a third runway at the UK's main airport.

So, people who live close to a major airport like Heathrow or who live below flight paths experience the spillover effect of aircraft noise. As third parties, they have to bear external costs that are not explicitly included in the prices paid by travellers for their air tickets.

ACCIDENTS

Despite the increase in traffic, fatality rates for all forms of transport in the UK continue to fall. The normal means of measurement is number of deaths per billion passenger kilometres. The highest rates of all the main modes are for car drivers and passengers, 2.6 in 2005. Rates for public transport are much less – over the last ten years, the average for bus and coach passengers has been 0.3 and for rail 0.4. For air travel, the average has been less than 0.1 but of course, this measure reflects the much longer distances that are travelled by air transport passengers.

When someone is killed in an accident, through no fault of their own, external costs arise. These are borne by the families of those killed, by emergency services and by others witnessing accidents. Such costs involve things like the emotional strain and trauma of an accident as well as more identifiable material costs through damage to vehicles and property.

CONGESTION

Congestion is an all too familiar feature of the UK transport network. It is normally associated with roads and is a situation where the volume of traffic is greater than the operating capacity of the road. In other words, demand is greater than supply. This situation is represented in Figure 7.6, which shows the relationship between speed and flow in a typically congested situation. The formula shown holds true for most kinds of traffic conditions – *d* and *f* are constants relating to a particular stretch of road. They will be higher on roads with high capacity.

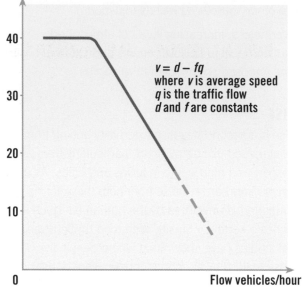

$$v = d - fq$$
where v is average speed
q is the traffic flow
d and f are constants

Figure 7.6 Speed/flow relationship

Traffic congestion occurs when drivers are obliged to travel at less than their desired speed because they are impeded by other vehicles. This imposition is a negative externality since:

● Actual journey times are greater than expected.

● The cost of making a journey is greater than it should be.

● Vehicle emissions are more extensive than if the traffic is free flowing.

● For freight, more vehicles may be required to carry out a particular volume of work.

Road congestion has an adverse effect on the efficiency of the logistics function for manufacturers and retailers. Where 'just in time' production takes place, as in car assembly, then any delay is likely to adversely impact on total production. For retailers, excessive delays may mean that perishable goods do not reach a store in a fit condition to be sold. In such cases, retailers or their suppliers are left not only with this stock but also the additional cost of replacing it.

Congestion is also very much in evidence on other parts of the transport network. Like roads, this is especially so at peak periods. Over 99 per cent of the take off and landing slots are being used at Heathrow

ECONOMICS IN CONTEXT

KUALA LUMPUR – ALL JAMMED UP!

Kuala Lumpur roads are frequently gridlocked

The Malaysian capital of Kuala Lumpur (KL as it is known) has some of the worst traffic congestion of any major city in Asia. At almost every hour of the day, or night for that matter, traffic is likely to be at a standstill. The situation is so bad at times that taxi drivers refuse to take would-be passengers on even short trips because of the time they know it will take.

The jams in KL are indicative of what many people in Asia now want – a prosperous urban life and a car. In KL, as the population has grown then more people have moved out to the many new-build housing complexes that have sprung up on former rubber plantations. A consequence is that they invariably need a car to get to work and to go about their daily affairs. The cheap locally produced Proton cars are everywhere. Malaysians have gone car crazy.

The problem in KL is not helped by its inadequate public transport system, which has not developed in line with changes to where people live and work. In this respect, KL is not atypical of other Asian metropolises such as Bangkok and Beijing. Neither is it atypical in the way that it has sought to build new, high standard public roads and toll roads to relieve its ever-increasing congestion problems.

---

so that when slots become vacant they are traded for many millions of pounds. At Gatwick, the only remaining slots are at times that are not particularly suitable. On the railways, Network Rail is planning to relieve congestion around Birmingham New Street and into some of London's mainline termini where network capacity is stretched. The East Coast Main Line beyond Peterborough, for example, is now operating at full capacity for 18 hours out of 24 each day. Like road congestion, where other modes experience congestion, then negative externalities, particularly in the form of delays, occur, adding to the strain and stress of travel.

OTHER NEGATIVE EXTERNALITIES

These include:

● *visual intrusion*. This is the term used to describe a situation where through providing transport facilities, the quality of the urban or rural landscape is compromised. It can be a particular problem in historic cities where the need to provide signage for road traffic invariably devalues the local environment.

● *blight*. This negative externality is the consequence of poor, unsympathetic planning. Examples could be where neighbourhoods fall into disrepair over plans to build a new road or a new motorway is built close to established properties causing a general deterioration in the physical character of the area.

Negative externalities and market failure

The explanation of negative externalities as an example of market failure was introduced at AS Level. This introductory analysis will now be developed further.

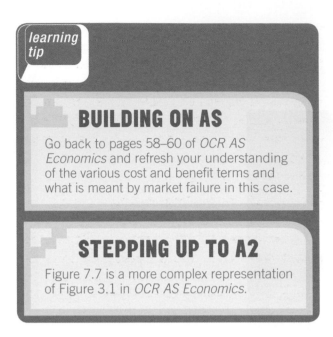

BUILDING ON AS

Go back to pages 58–60 of *OCR AS Economics* and refresh your understanding of the various cost and benefit terms and what is meant by market failure in this case.

STEPPING UP TO A2

Figure 7.7 is a more complex representation of Figure 3.1 in *OCR AS Economics*.

Figure 7.7 shows a market situation where there is a negative externality as there is divergence between private costs and social costs. If external costs are not taken into account, then the market is functioning at point X where the price is P and the quantity produced is Q. Consequently, there is over-production and consumers are not paying the full price. The market is failing at this point.

This is because at output Q, the full (social) cost of production is greater than the value consumers

Costs and price

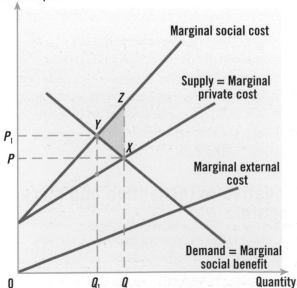

Figure 7.7 Private and social costs divergence

place on it. This is not an efficient use of resources. A welfare triangle loss of *YXZ* occurs. The welfare of consumers could be increased by this amount if output is lowered and the resources saved are used to make other products.

To correct for market failure, the equilibrium should be at point Y (see below). This is where allocative efficiency is achieved, since price is equal to marginal social costs. By producing at Y, the price paid increases to P_1 and the quantity produced falls to Q_1.

Problems of estimating values of negative externalities

In some respects, identifying negative externalities associated with increasing transport use is relatively straightforward. What is much more difficult is to estimate the value of such externalities, either in monetary or in non-monetary terms.

One of the most comprehensive estimates of the social costs of road transport was made by the Adam Smith Institute in 1999. The broad findings are summarised in Table 7.1 below.

Cost element	Estimated cost (£ bn)	% of total costs
Congestion	18	72
Accidents	3	12
Air pollution	3	12
Noise pollution	1	4
Total	25	100

Table 7.1 Social costs of road transport in the UK

The main purpose of this study was to compare the costs road users inflict on society with the benefits they return to society in terms of the taxes paid to use roads. In 1999, road users paid around £32bn in total road taxes and received around £6bn of government spending on roads. Allowing for the social costs shown in Table 7.1, the conclusion was that, on balance, road users are not being excessively charged through taxation. The average taxation would seem to be about right, at an estimated 5.4p per vehicle kilometre.

This is only half a tale, because most road congestion tends to be in urban areas, particularly at the peak. Also, vehicles moving slowly in congested conditions tend to emit more pollutants per kilometre than when travelling at a steady speed. It therefore seems appropriate to recognise that the social costs of peak travel in central urban areas will be much more than the above average suggests. The Adam Smith Institute estimated a typical figure to be over 40p per km for cars and over 80p for diesel-fuelled HGVs (see also below).

Estimates of the costs of road congestion have been made by various organisations. Using current government methods, the present cost of congestion is around £25bn. This is based on:

● the value of time that is lost when road users are stuck in traffic

● the additional fuel costs and maintenance costs of running vehicles in congested conditions

● the additional vehicles required by commercial users as their fleets are not being used efficiently

● the cost to the economy of lost inward investment from firms that would otherwise have invested in the UK.

Estimating these costs is quite difficult and in the case of the valuation of time, rather contentious, given that it uses the opportunity cost argument for a commodity that has no market price. (See Chapter 8 also.)

At a micro level, the marginal cost of congestion can be shown by a simple example. Suppose 1,000 vehicles are travelling on central city roads at say 15 kilometres per hour and that this is regarded by their drivers as a 'desired' speed. Assume the cost per vehicle for this journey is £2. If a further vehicle uses these roads, the speed of traffic will fall slightly, increasing the cost per vehicle to say £2.01. The private cost of the journey to the new driver is £2.01, the same as for all other drivers. The marginal external cost imposed on all other drivers is £10 (1,000 × 1p). The marginal social cost of one more

vehicle is the marginal private cost of £2.01 plus the marginal external cost of £10, namely £12.01. Even from this simple example, it is easy to comprehend why the costs of traffic congestion are substantial. As social cost is greater than private cost, this represents a clear example of negative externality. In the case of a congested motorway, if this is closed and traffic is at a standstill, the congestion cost is around £1 million per minute!

At a national level, the Department for Transport produces estimates of the value of travel time. Table 7.2 shows a selection of these estimates. Since there is no market price for time, a **shadow price** has to be imputed. This is based on the average wage rate per hour and is produced for travel in different types of vehicle and by journey purpose.

DEFINITION

Shadow price: a relative price that is proportional to the opportunity cost for the economy

Type of vehicle and journey purpose	Value of time per vehicle (£ per hour)
Car – in course of work	24.99
Car – commuting	4.75
Car – other	6.81
Goods vehicle	8.42
Bus/coach	59.16
Average – all vehicles	9.30

Table 7.2 Average values of time per vehicle
Source : *COBA Manual*, Department for Transport, 2006

The cost of road accidents is less controversial and a methodology for calculating it has been developed over many years, again by the Department for Transport. As with travel time, this information is an important input into the appraisal of new road schemes (see Chapter 8). Two types of cost are estimated.

● *Casualty costs* based on the severity of an accident. Average costs are calculated depending on the age and current earnings of the person involved. For a fatal accident, the average cost in 2006 was almost £1.25m. For a serious casualty, where emergency treatment and a hospital stay were involved, the average cost was £140,000; for a slight casualty, it was around £11,000. These figures include an estimate of lost output to the economy and the personal distress and suffering involved.

● *External costs* with respect to damage to property, insurance administration and police costs.

It should be clear from these two examples that the task of estimating negative externalities associated with transport use is a complex as well as difficult task. Having said this, such estimates are very important in the evaluation of transport policy and in the appraisal of major road schemes.

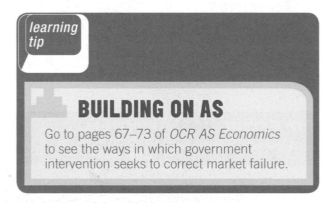

learning tip

BUILDING ON AS

Go to pages 67–73 of *OCR AS Economics* to see the ways in which government intervention seeks to correct market failure.

Policies to correct negative externalities

Of the government policies to correct market failure, the following have specific relevance in correcting negative externalities arising from transport:

● various forms of indirect taxation on transport use

● regulations governing the specification of vehicles and their use

● subsidies to encourage greater use of public transport

● information provision by the government.

A few examples will show how such policies operate and the extent to which they produce a more efficient allocation of resources.

THE LONDON CONGESTION CHARGE AND LOW EMISSION ZONE

The London Congestion Charge is a flat-rate indirect tax levied on all vehicles entering a designated charging zone between 7 a.m. and 6 p.m., Monday to Friday. It was introduced in February 2003 at the rate of £5 per day. It was increased to £8 per day in July 2005. In February 2007, the charging zone was doubled in size to cover a substantial zone in Central London. There are various ways of paying, including online, by telephone or through designated retail outlets and filling stations. The cheapest way is to pay in advance or before 10 p.m. on the day of travel, in which case the standard charge applies. After this, penalty charges apply. The system is managed by a huge network of cameras linked to number plate recognition software that matches details to make sure the charge has been paid. Taxis, motorcycles, disabled badge holders and emergency service vehicles are exempt. Residents in the charging zone receive a 90 per cent discount.

Within the UK, London is an exceptional case, since the elected mayor has explicit powers that enable net revenue from the congestion charge to be retained for use within the capital. This is consistent with the principle of **hypothecation**. The strategy being employed by Transport for London is that most of the new revenue has been used to improve bus services. The European-style bendi-buses, much in evidence in the charging zone, are a highly visible example of this policy.

The London Congestion Charge is an example of **road pricing** (see below also). In principle, it is a way of internalising the external costs of congestion

DEFINITIONS

Hypothecation: a situation where revenue from a tax is directly allocated to some other purpose

Road pricing: a direct charge for the use of a road space and is consistent with the 'polluter pays principle'. Having said this, it is not a particularly exact form of indirect taxation, since it is not directly based on the scale of congestion. Interestingly, the majority of Londoners support the charge, as it has reduced congestion. Although estimates vary, congestion in the extended zone has been cut by around 20 per cent and there are 8 to 12 per cent less vehicles being used on a daily basis than was previously the case.

London's second policy for dealing with negative externalities arising from road transport is the Low Emission Zone (LEZ), which became operational in February 2008. As the name suggests, this policy seeks to improve air quality for people living and working in London. The context is that London has the worst air quality of anywhere in the UK and one of the worst in the EU. The area covered by the LEZ is much more extensive than that for the congestion charge and covers 33 boroughs in Greater London.

The LEZ is an example of the use of regulations to correct negative externalities. It applies 24 hours a day, 365 days a year and initially applied to goods vehicles over 12 tonnes gross vehicle weight used in the zone. These vehicles have to meet at least the 'Euro 3' standard for particulate emissions, or face a daily charge of £200. A late payment and fining system applies, similar to that for the congestion charge. In July 2008, the scheme was extended to vehicles of between 3.5 and 12 tonnes, as well as to buses and coaches. These, too, must meet the above standard, which increases to 'Euro 4' in 2012.

Particulates are just one of the pollutants that are emitted from vehicles. Unlike some other pollutants, particulate matter can be easily measured by a smoke test from the vehicle's exhaust system. The purpose of doing this, and the reason for the LEZ, is to meet EU air quality targets and to reduce the incidence of respiratory problems exacerbated by air pollution among adults and children.

Like the congestion charge, the scheme is monitored by cameras that read a vehicle's registration plate as it passes through the zone. Transport companies who expect to use their vehicles in the LEZ have to register these vehicles with Transport for London. In general, all vehicles registered after October 2001 should meet the required standard. Older vehicles can be subjected to the smoke test and, if compliant, a certificate of compliance is issued. It is therefore very clear that the effects of the LEZ are to improve air quality and also to reduce traffic noise from older, less environmentally acceptable vehicles.

The case of London is unique in the UK, due to the ability of the elected mayor to determine transport

The London mayor determines traffic policy

policies for the capital. The measures described above have been put in place to tackle congestion, encourage drivers to switch to public transport, cycling and walking, and to reduce CO_2 emissions. They are highly applicable examples of policies that can correct some of the negative externalities arising from transport.

ACTIVITY ····⫶

a) i) Redraw Figure 7.7 to show the effects on the market equilibrium of introducing a flat rate tax like the London Congestion Charge.

ii) Discuss whether such a tax has led to an improvement in efficiency in the market.

STRETCH AND CHALLENGE

b) Use Internet newspaper sources to discuss why not all Londoners support the policies that have been described above.

VEHICLE EXCISE DUTY

Vehicle excise duty is the annual tax that is paid by the vehicle's owner to use the road network. Historically, this tax for cars has been charged at one rate, irrespective of the size of the vehicle or mileage travelled per year. From 2008/09, a new banding system is in place, whereby vehicles are classified on the basis of the CO_2 emitted. From 2010/11, a further change to the system is that a first year 'showroom' tax of £115–£950 will be imposed on the purchase of new vehicles emitting above a particular level of emissions. Table 7.3 gives a few examples of how this new tax will be applied.

PUBLIC TRANSPORT SUBSIDIES

A subsidy is a payment that is made to transport operators by central or local government to reduce the market price of the services that are provided. For passengers, it means that the fares they pay are not based on the full cost of the service that is provided. Although not in use to the same extent as in many other EU countries, this form of regulation is an important way in which the UK government seeks to influence the market.

Figure 7.8 shows the effect of introducing a subsidy – a shift to the right of the marginal private cost (supply) curve. As a consequence, the market price falls from P to P_1, with an increase in the quantity of provision from Q to Q_1. The extent of change depends on the amount of subsidy that is paid and on the price elasticity of demand.

There are various arguments for public transport subsidies payments, including:

● *positive externalities.* Here, it is accepted that subsidising a local bus or train service produces an external benefit to the community. This is so in large towns and cities, where subsidising local rail services is a way of reducing road traffic congestion. This has been a particular driving force in West Yorkshire, for example, where the passenger transport executive has consistently invested in new railway rolling stock, in opening new stations and in keeping fares down through payments to train operating companies.

● *social equity.* By subsiding local bus services, as provided for in the 1985 Transport Act, passenger transport authorities are able to ensure that otherwise unremunerative services are retained.

CO_2 emissions (gram/km)	Tax band	1st year tax	2nd year and after	Typical vehicle
Up to 100	A	0	0	VW Polo 1.4Tdi
101–110	B	0	£20	Citroën C1 1.0i
131–140	E	£115	£115	Toyota Yaris 1.3 vwt
171–180	I	£300	£210	Ford Mondeo estate 1.6 (petrol)
Over 255	M	£950	£455	BMW X5 series E70

Table 7.3 Vehicle excise duty rates, from 2010/11

Costs and price

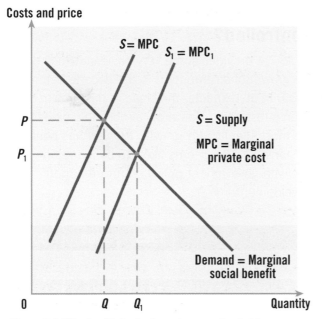

Figure 7.8 Effects of introducing a transport subsidy

In urban areas, such subsidised services tend to be off-peak; in rural areas, it is invariably all services that receive such support. The bus is the only means of transport for some members of the community, particularly non-car owners, older persons and women in one-car households who have to rely on the bus for getting around (see Chapter 5). Through subsidisation, a redistribution of income comes about. Subsidies for rail services are also made for social reasons, for example where cheaper fares enhance the work opportunities for lower paid workers.

In 2005/06, revenue support for local bus services was almost £1bn at current prices, three times the sum paid ten years ago. In addition, over £600m was paid to bus operators for concessionary fare reimbursement, notably for over-60s' half-price off-peak schemes. From April 2008, this scheme came into force at a national level. Bus operators received a further £380m in the form of fuel duty rebates.

The subsidy paid for rail transport is much greater than that paid to bus transport. For 2007/08, it was expected to reach around £5bn, about the same as what passengers pay to travel by train. The positive externality case described above is particularly relevant for subsidising rail commuter services.

The problem with transport subsidies is that the total cost to government is increasing, despite the case that is put forward in support of deregulation and privatisation (see Chapter 6). A further problem is that the nature of subsidies is that it is not possible to target them specifically to those in greatest need. With rail tickets, for example, the price of travel is the same for each passenger – irrespective of the salary earned – dependent upon when the ticket was purchased.

ACTIVITY ⋯⋰

From April 2008, all English residents aged 60 and over have been able to travel free on off-peak bus services anywhere in the country. This is expected to cost around £2bn per year. Discuss the benefits and costs of this policy from:

a) the government's standpoint

b) an older person's standpoint.

Note: off-peak: after 9.30 a.m. weekdays, all day Saturday, Sunday and Bank holidays.

Sustainability and its application to transport

The concept of sustainability has been applied to various types of economic activity, transport included. The most commonly used working definition of sustainable development is that taken from the 1987 Report of the World Commission on Environment and Development. This so-called Brundtland Report stated that 'sustainable development meets the needs of the present without compromising the ability of future generations to meet their own needs'.

As shown at the beginning of this chapter, increased transport use does have an adverse environmental impact. Globally, the growth in vehicle numbers and the distances driven have been consistently increasing. Much demand remains suppressed … but only for the time being. New vehicle registrations in Russia are now the highest in Europe; vehicle ownership in China and India is only just beginning to take off. All in all, on a world scale, the demands on energy, raw materials and space are overwhelming. The increased air pollution and noise pollution arising from millions more vehicles are unprecedented and unknown. It is not a sustainable situation. And this is not to mention air travel or shipping.

Transport is a net user of renewable and non-renewable resources. This latter type of resource includes oil and the various metals and oil-based products that are used in the manufacture of cars and lorries. The essence of a more sustainable transport outcome is when there is a switch from environmentally damaging to more environmentally acceptable modes of transport, alongside a reduction in the distances travelled. Modally, it means a switch of passenger and freight transport away from road-based modes. This, therefore, should be the objective of a more sustainable transport policy (see Chapter 8).

Figure 7.9 shows the average CO_2 emissions for each of the main modes of inland transport. It is clear that, for inland transport, rail is more sustainable than all forms of road transport for moving people and goods. Rail's superiority is particularly evident for freight transport. For passenger transport, it is hardly surprising that air transport is the least environmentally acceptable in terms of CO_2 emissions. When compared to road transport, rail emits fewer pollutants of all greenhouse gases except for sulphur dioxide.

Should air transport growth be controlled?

Table 7.4 provides some very basic statistics on the growth of air transport in the decade before 2005. In all respects, the scale of this growth has been substantial. Heathrow airport dominates; the most spectacular growth, though, has been at Stansted. This seems likely to continue, in line with government policy on future airport development.

	1995	2000	2005
Passenger arrivals or departures (million)			
Total	115.3	161.3	203.1
Heathrow	54.1	64.3	67.7
Gatwick	22.4	31.9	32.7
Manchester	14.4	18.3	22.1
Stansted	3.9	11.8	22.0
Cargo handled ('000 tonnes)			
Total	1,640	2,260	2,294
Heathrow	1,032	1,307	1,306
East Midlands	81	178	267
Stansted	89	166	237
Gatwick	229	319	223

Table 7.4 Air transport growth, 1995–2005
Source: Civil Aviation Authority

Stansted Airport

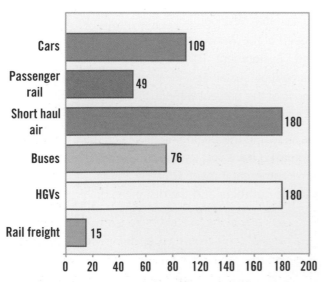

Figure 7.9 Average CO_2 emissions, grams per passenger/ tonne km

Air transport currently accounts for around 5 per cent of all the UK's carbon emissions. By 2050, if airport capacity increases in line with demand and road transport emissions are cut, aviation could account for as much as 25 per cent of all such emissions.

One possible way of controlling the growth of air transport would be to introduce a substantial green tax on flights. Changes to Air Passenger Duty (APD) from 2009 will ensure aviation makes a greater contribution with respect to its environmental impact (see *OCR AS Economics*, page 69). APD also has a role to play in making air passengers aware of the environmental consequences of the flights they are making. From a longer-term point of view, now that aviation is included in the EU Emissions Trading Scheme (see *OCR AS Economics*, page 72), this may well be the most efficient way of ensuring that air travellers pay a fair price and that air transport meets its climate change targets.

ACTIVITY ·····⋮

It has been suggested that one way of controlling air transport growth is to limit the annual number of flights that each person is allowed to take. Make a list of the arguments for and against this form of control.

Combating road congestion

As explained earlier in this chapter, when there is road congestion, the market is failing to produce the best allocation of resources. The social costs to road users are above their private costs. So what can be done about it?

BUILDING MORE ROADS

This is the obvious answer ... or so it seems. If demand exceeds supply, and there is congestion, one possible solution is to increase supply. In other words, build more roads, especially high-capacity roads, like motorways, that can cope with heavy volumes of traffic. Historically, this has been the way in which all countries, rich and poor, have sought to tackle road congestion.

In the UK, this is called 'predict and provide'. As shown in Chapter 5, one reason that statisticians and economists make traffic forecasts is to be able to plan ahead and provide, in principle, the capacity of network that is needed. This was the underpinning reason for the massive investment in a motorway construction programme during the 1960s and early 1970s, followed by a more selective but very expensive continuation during the early 1990s and in the implementation of the 2010 Transport Plan.

When this extensive investment programme started in the late 1950s, there were around 7 million motor vehicles on the roads of the UK. Of these around 4 million were private cars. The decade of the 1960s saw a huge increase in car ownership – by 1970 there were around 10 million cars in a vehicle population of 13.5 million. In 2005, there were over 26 million private cars licensed in the UK, out of almost 33 million vehicles. The corresponding growth in road traffic has been even greater; once households acquire a car, or further vehicles, they are used extensively and greater traffic volumes are generated than previously when there was a greater reliance on public transport.

The problem of congestion has been exaggerated, in so far as the growth in traffic levels has consistently been much greater than the increase in total road length, particularly the construction of new motorways and trunk routes, which can carry the heaviest volumes of traffic.

In recognising the scale of the problem, the Transport 2010 ten-year plan, published in 2000, proposed major new widening schemes for 360 miles of motorways and trunk routes, 100 new bypasses and many local road improvements. At the time, the government's view was that it had seriously underestimated future road congestion and that massive investment was needed to prevent wholesale gridlock on the country's road network.

It must also be recognised that there is an increasingly powerful and vociferous lobby that opposes any plans to build more roads. Although the basis of their protests is environmental concerns, it is also the case that it has now been shown that building new roads to relieve traffic congestion is no more than a short-term solution.

ECONOMICS IN CONTEXT

£5.5BN ROAD-WIDENING PLAN 'WILL NOT EASE CONGESTION'

The Transport Secretary provoked both delight and anger by announcing a £5.5bn package of measures to widen motorways and A roads, alongside local schemes to relieve some of the country's worst congestion problems. Despite warnings from experts, including the chairman of the government's own Commission for Integrated Transport, there was no hint that this latest round of road expansion would be linked to the introduction of new tolls.

The improvement schemes announced were part of the ten-year Transport Plan and included:

- widening of the M6 from three to four lanes between Manchester and Birmingham; widening of the M1 between Chesterfield and Leicester
- major road improvements for the A453, A1, A303 and A30
- bus priority measures in Middlesbrough, Walsall and Wokingham
- up to 1,600 local traffic management schemes
- up to 55 new or extended park and ride schemes
- 1,000 km of new cycle lanes
- other local improvements.

The head of the Confederation of British Industry said that 'this was a sensible long-term package that should help reduce congestion and sustain economic growth'. Others were not as enthusiastic. Transport experts were concerned that the additional capacity created by road-widening schemes would be filled up in as little as a year and that during the building programme, congestion would only get worse.

Source: Financial Times, *11 December 2002 (adaptation)*

PUBLIC TRANSPORT DEVELOPMENT

In theory, public transport is a substitute for the private car. In practice, for the vast majority of the population in the UK, this is not the case. The main exception is London, where public transport is dominant. During the morning peak, almost 90 per cent of the 1.05 million people entering central London do so by some form of public transport. Over the last ten years, the largest growth has been in the number of commuters using the bus, although this total is still much smaller than those travelling by rail (see Table 7.5).

Transport type	1995	2000	2005
Public transport	827	936	939
surface rail	395	465	473
underground & DLR	348	383	342
bus	63	73	115
coach	21	15	9
Private car	145	137	84
Motorcycles and pedal cycles	21	29	33

Table 7.5 People entering central London during the period 7.00–10.00 a.m., 1995–2005 (thousands)
Source: Transport for London

ACTIVITY

Explain how the determinants of demand might be used to explain the main trends found in Table 7.5

Public transport can become a more effective substitute for the private car where the system is efficient, reliable, clean and safe and with a high degree of connectivity. This is true of many urban systems in France, Germany, Netherlands and parts of central Europe. It is particularly the case with modern light rail systems such as Manchester's Metrolink and the more recently opened Croydon Tramlink and Nottingham NET, which opened in 2004. Further investment in similar systems and other innovative forms of public transport are seen as vital in reducing problems of congestion.

Outside London, local rail services provide an important means of transport for commuters travelling into cities such as Birmingham, Leeds and Manchester. These services are subsidised by their respective Passenger Transport Executives (PTE) out of the funding received from Council Tax.

Improving and developing public transport systems provides travellers with more choice in the battle to combat congestion. Investment in public transport, by both the government and the private sector, is now central in moving towards the realisation of a more sustainable transport system for the UK.

ROAD PRICING

As explained in *OCR AS Economics* (page 65), a road or stretch of motorway is a quasi-public good. This is because it exhibits some, but by no means all, of the recognised characteristics of a public good. As road congestion has increased, so the non-rivalry characteristic has become undermined. This is because one additional driver's use of the road will further restrict the use of others. The non-excludability characteristic has also been undermined, but in a slightly different way – as more people obtain driving licences, this, too, contributes to increasing road congestion.

Historically, road users have paid various forms of taxation, including vehicle excise duty, fuel tax and value added tax on new vehicles and vehicle servicing and repairs. The amount of tax any one road user pays is only loosely a function of how much use they make of the road network and when and where their vehicles are used. Relatively, users who drive 100,000 km a year pay less than those using the network for just 30,000 km a year – the price paid by users is not a true cost of the use they make of the road network.

ACTIVITY ····⋮

a) Obtain up-to-date information on
   i) the amount of taxation paid by road users
   ii) the amount of government spending on the road network

STRETCH AND CHALLENGE

b) Comment on any discrepancy you observe.

Road pricing is a system whereby road users pay a direct charge for the use they make of the road network – use of a stretch of road or access to a particular zone. At its most sophisticated level, this should be according to when, where and how much they use the road network. In recent years, **road user charging** and **congestion charging** have been added to the vocabulary in this context. They are forms of road pricing but perhaps best associated with charging regimes whereby road users pay a flat-rate per kilometre travelled in a designated zone or cordon (see London Congestion Charge above, pages 160–162). They are by definition blunter instruments, lacking the more sophisticated basis of a full road pricing scheme.

DEFINITIONS

Road user charging: a form of road pricing where a flat-rate charge is made for the use of a stretch of road or access into a designated charging zone

Congestion charging: a direct charge for access to a designated urban charging zone where the main purpose of the charge is to reduce congestion

To economists, the concept of road pricing is not new. The basis of the case was first put forward by the welfare economist Pigou in the 1920s. This can be shown in Figure 7.10. This is very similar to Figure 7.7, except for the shape of the marginal private cost and marginal social cost curves. These are the same up to point *FF* on Figure 7.10. There is no market failure, since traffic is using a road in 'free flow' conditions. This means there is no congestion and vehicles are being used in an efficient way. Beyond this point, congestion sets in; it gradually gets worse, as shown by the growing divergence between marginal private cost and marginal social cost. As stated earlier, road users are self-interested and do not consider the external cost involved when deciding whether to travel on a stretch of road.

The Pigou effect, as it is known, involves introducing a price that is just sufficient to internalise the externality. This charge is such that the volume of traffic falls from Q to Q_1. Here, all road users

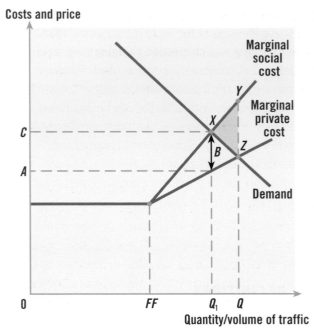

Costs and price

Figure 7.10 Efficient road pricing

Motorways		
	central London	54.5
	inner conurbation	54.5
	outer London	31.5
	outer conurbation	35.6
	rural	4.3
Trunk and principal roads		
	central London	73.8
	inner conurbation	36.4
	outer London	30.3
	outer conurbation	14.4
	rural	9.0
Other roads	central London	190.6
	inner conurbation	62.9
	outer London	42.0
	outer conurbation	2.2
	rural	1.9

Table 7.6 Marginal social cost of private car use by location and type of road (pence per vehicle km, 1998 prices)
Adapted from: Bickel, P. *et al.* (2006) Introducing environmental externalities into transport pricing: measurement and implications, *Transport Reviews* **26**(4): 389–415.

are willing to pay the marginal social cost of their journeys. At this point, they need to pay *C*. This comprises a marginal private cost of *A* and a road price of *B*. The net social gain, the congestion costs saved, is shown by the area *XYZ*.

Determining what a road pricing charge should be is by no means easy, not least because the actual costs of using roads varies according to the type of road and, significantly, between the peak and the off-peak. Table 7.6 summarises research on what could be appropriate charges. As this table indicates, there are huge variations. The implication is that a common flat-rate charge per km would not be efficient, since some road users would end up paying much more and others much less than the true cost of the journeys they are making.

ON OR OFF? ROAD PRICING IN THE UK

Over the last few years a remarkable consensus has developed among economists that 'getting the price right' is the only realistic longer-term way of combating road congestion in the UK. This view has been supported by pressure groups such as the Campaign for Better Transport, independent think-tanks like the Institute of Economic Affairs and the Independent Transport Commission, the government's Commission for Integrated Transport and, most recently, its specialist adviser, Sir Rod Eddington (see below).

In June 2005, after innumerable reports and trials, the government unveiled its plans for a national 'pay as you drive' system of charging for the use of road space. These plans, if fully implemented, would constitute the most ambitious road-pricing scheme ever attempted. A minimum time-scale for implementation was estimated to be by 2015. The main features of the proposals were:

● a charge of £1.30 per mile for using the busiest, most congested roads during peak periods. This charge would typically apply for the use of roads into major cities and on the most congested motorways such as the M25 and the most congested parts of the M1, M4, M6, M60 and M62.

● lower charges elsewhere; as little as 2p per mile or even no charge on the quietest rural roads.

● overall, the scheme would be 'tax neutral'; it would replace the current road taxation system (see above), with 15–20 per cent of road users paying more than at present. Others would pay around the same or even less.

Getting to this stage by 2015 would be preceded by a series of local trials for which the government has already allocated £25.5m. The experience gained from these trials would be used to develop the national system.

Confirmation that road pricing really could reduce road congestion followed in the Eddington Report published in December 2006 (see also Chapter 8). As shown in Figure 7.11, congestion levels would fall by as much as 20 per cent by 2025, following the introduction of road pricing.

Sadly, from the economist's perspective, this is by no means the end of the story! As has consistently happened in the past, following Eddington's report, there was a groundswell of public opinion against the government's plans. By February 2007, over 1.8 million people had signed a petition on the Downing Street website protesting against road pricing. Much of the media and some motoring organisations added weight to these protests.

The result of this opposition was that, in March 2007, the government pulled back from its plans for a complex GPS tracking system to manage road pricing. It announced that any system of road pricing would be a zonal one; the charges would be up to £1.34 per mile in city centres, 14p to 86p per mile in inner suburbs, 4p to 9p in outer suburbs and 2p per mile elsewhere.

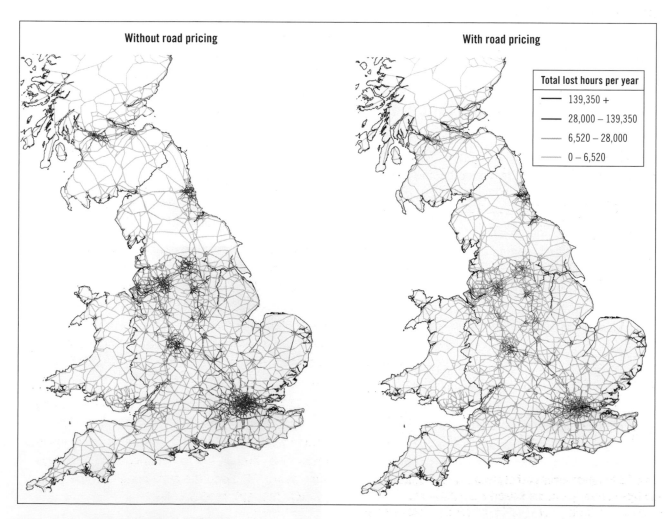

Figure 7.11 Congestion forecasts for 2025

Source: Department of Transport

Finally, in October 2007, plans for a national system were effectively abandoned in favour of a new strategy that gave local authorities discretion to introduce their own road-pricing schemes as part of their strategic plans for dealing with transport problems. Manchester and Cambridge to date have stated their intentions to do so, although in the case of Cambridge, there has been considerable opposition.

So, where has it all gone wrong? In the past, a lack of proven technology has been used as an excuse for treading carefully. The technology via the GPS satellite is now available and could be used to establish a national or a local system. Its implications, though, in terms of invasion of privacy are not acceptable to a high proportion of the population. A second reason is that, politically, road pricing is not acceptable to the millions of disgruntled motorists who mistakenly believe that they are already being charged too highly to use the country's roads.

The international experience of road pricing

SINGAPORE

Singapore is the best-known operational example of road pricing. As early as 1975, the Area Licensing System required the owners of vehicles used in the 'restricted zone' to purchase and display a special licence that entitled them to use their vehicles between 7.30 a.m. and 7 p.m. on weekdays and 2 p.m. on Saturdays. Vehicles with more than two occupants were exempt from the charge, which was collected at the point of entry.

In 1998, this system was replaced by a more sophisticated electronic road pricing (ERP) system. All cars were fitted with an electronic box on the dashboard; drivers have a pre-paid cash card which fits into this unit. As cars drive under various roadside gantries in the charging zone, an amount is automatically deducted from the cash card. The amount of the charge varies by time of day, volume of traffic and the area in which the vehicle is used. The time when charges are at their peak is between 8.30 and 9 a.m. in the central business area.

Charges end at 9.30 a.m. on the outer ring road but apply as above within.

The charge is deducted automatically as a vehicle passes under every gantry on its route. Buses and taxis are not exempt from payment. There is a fining system for drivers who have insufficient credit on their cash cards, which can easily be topped up at petrol stations, local convenience stores and ATMs.

The impact of the ERP has been significant and includes:

● a 16 per cent fall in peak traffic in the first year of operation; a 10–15 per cent decrease in traffic at other times

● a reduction in the number of multiple trips in the charging zone

● improved vehicle speeds

● greater traffic volumes in the morning prior to the start of charging

● road traffic levels have remained reduced since the launch year.

The experience of Singapore shows very clearly that road pricing can reduce congestion, but to put this in perspective, the area covered by the charging zone is less than the original area of the London Congestion Charge. It should also be pointed out that there was no opposition to the introduction of the ERP system.

Road-user charging reduces congestion

ECONOMICS IN CONTEXT

'GREEN' ROAD PRICING BACK ON THE AGENDA

Asia's world city of Hong Kong suffers from two urban maladies, poor air quality and serious road traffic congestion. The combination of heat, tall close-knit buildings and extensive pollution from the manufacturing city of Shenzhen in China are usually given as the main causes of the deteriorating air quality so much in evidence for most of the year. Although buses and taxis are required to use bio-diesel, extensive congestion in Central, Wan Chai, Causeway Bay and parts of Kowloon adds to the problem.

Road pricing was first proposed as a solution to the congestion problem more than 20 years ago. It was, though, abandoned after a brief trial. In 2001, after a massive transportation study, electronic road pricing (ERP) was again put off.

The latest proposals are to use road pricing to encourage the use of environmentally friendly cars by forcing drivers of older cars and those that emit more pollutants to pay a higher fee to enter congested zones. The government must decide whether buses and taxis should be charged, which areas any charges would apply to, how to collect them, penalties for non-payment and whether there should be any alternative routes available for those not wishing to pay a charge.

In terms of technology, one serious suggestion is that tollgates with sensors could check a car's emission levels to assess what charge their drivers need to pay. Vehicles belching dirty exhaust fumes could be barred from entering the charging zones. A leading academic, Hung Wing Tat, believed the proposals were fair, and that from overseas experience few drivers would give up their vehicles because of road pricing. The question of acceptance remains particularly sensitive.

ACTIVITY ⋯⋗

The following data was compiled by the Land Transport Authority in Singapore following an increase in the zonal charge for cars used in the restricted zone in 1998.

Time period	Charge	Price elasticity of demand
7.30–8	$1.50 → $2.00	0
8–8.30	$2.00 → $2.50	–0.35
8.30–9	$2.50 → $3.00	–0.12
9–9.30	$2.00 → $2.50	0.65

a) Account for the variation in the values of price elasticity of demand.

b) How might this information be used by the Land Transport Authority in

   i) Setting charges for the ERP system

STRETCH AND CHALLENGE

   ii) Setting charges to maximise revenue from the ERP?

OTHER EXAMPLES

The Norwegian city of Trondheim holds the distinction of introducing the first electronic urban road pricing system in 1991. The so-called Trondheim Ring consists of eight toll zones around the city. Most vehicles are fitted with an electronic transponder on the windscreen – the toll is deducted automatically for every journey that is made into the zones between 6 a.m. and 6 p.m. Peak and off-peak charges apply. The original purpose of the scheme was as a means of funding the construction of new roads, improvements to public transport and environmental improvement measures. The scheme is set to continue, but with the objective of controlling road traffic.

Also in Norway, the capital Oslo has had a simple road toll system in operation since 1990. Its purpose was to reduce urban congestion and to fund new transport investment, with the emphasis on road construction. The charges apply for all vehicles at any time. Payment is electronic, manual or through a coin-drop facility. The objectives are currently under review. It seems highly likely that more of the receipts from this system will be used to fund public transport developments in the future.

Bergen, again in Norway, introduced a simple road-user charging system in 1986. Like other cities in this country, its original purpose was to raise revenue for new road construction. The original system was a manual one, but from 2004, this was replaced by an electronic system along the same lines as Trondheim's.

The Australian city of Melbourne has a CityLink system that consists of a toll road linking three of the main freeways. Vehicles are fitted with a device that allows charges to be electronically deducted.

Durham became the first place in the UK to introduce a road-user charge, in 2002. This is a small-scale scheme that is in place on just one street in the old city in the vicinity of the cathedral. A charge of £2 per day is payable for vehicles entering between 10 a.m. and 4 p.m., Monday to Saturday. Initially, there was a substantial fall in traffic volumes, so reducing congestion. In June 2008, the government announced that Manchester was to receive £1.45bn for public transport investment, to include the long-awaited extension to Metrolink. This funding was linked to the introduction of a £5-a-day congestion charge to be implemented in 2013.

8 Transport economics and government policy

On completion of this chapter, you should be able to:

● understand the role of public and private sectors in resource allocation in transport

● explain what is meant by cost-benefit analysis

● explain why cost-benefit analysis is needed in the case of investment decisions for new road schemes

● discuss the limitations of the cost-benefit approach and recent modifications to the methodology

● discuss how the cost-benefit approach compares with private-sector methods of appraisal

● explain what is mean by integration in transport policy

● discuss how transport policy seeks to deal with current transport problems and issues such as congestion, in the UK and elsewhere

● discuss how transport policy can meet future needs and requirements, including recent EU policy initiatives in areas such as freight transport.

Resource allocation – role of public and private sectors

As described in Chapter 5, the private and public sectors have responsibilities for the provision of transport services and infrastructure in the UK. Their expenditure can be divided into two main types. These are:

● *capital expenditure.* This is long term and can involve massive sums in the case of motorway construction, rail network upgrades and airport development

● *current expenditure.* This involves smaller sums and is annual or short term in its incidence. Typical examples are for road maintenance, public transport subsidisation and the ongoing replacement of vehicle fleets.

Although the criteria for making decisions may differ (see below), all organisations invariably face the 'economic problem' – there are unlimited wants for transport expenditure yet the resources that are available are limited.

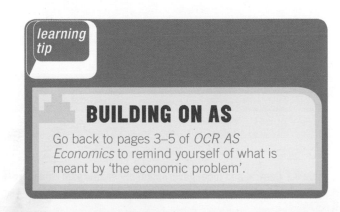

learning tip

BUILDING ON AS

Go back to pages 3–5 of *OCR AS Economics* to remind yourself of what is meant by 'the economic problem'.

One of the consequences of privatisation is that private sector expenditure on transport has increased in importance over the last twenty years or so. This expenditure has typically been on new buses, railway rolling stock, aircraft, ferries and, through the British Airports Authority, airport developments. With the exception of the M6 toll road, there has been no direct investment in roads, unlike in other EU countries.

Public sector investment is more narrow. Road expenditure is by far the largest item, although revenue support for rail and bus services has been increasing over the last few years in real terms and as a percentage of total public spending on transport. This is shown in Table 8.1.

Overall, government expenditure on transport is around 6 per cent of total government spending. This percentage has been relatively stable over the past few years. Total spending, though, has increased in aggregate terms, as GDP has increased. In total, when the private sector's contribution has been taken into account, investment in transport in the UK is at an all-time high.

The benefits of this increased investment can be clearly seen, particularly for rail transport. In 2007, the total passenger miles travelled by rail was 30.1 billion, slightly less than double the figure at the time of privatisation. Further growth of 22 per cent is projected over the next six years. Rail efficiency is improving nationally and train operators are investing more resources in rolling stock, both of which increase the attractiveness of rail transport to passengers.

In contrast, the benefits of increasing spending on roads are less clear. Congestion is getting worse, despite the huge expenditure on motorway widening schemes and the construction of new bypasses. Public investment in roads is back to the level of the

	2002/03	2004/05	2006/07
Central government			
Capital (total)	5,110	4,404	6,162
strategic roads	943	861	1,400
rail	3,254	3,423	4,651
Current (total)	3,603	4,106	6,556
strategic roads	1,265	1,444	1,706
rail	1,462	1,516	2,619
Local government			
Capital (total)	2,757	3,313	4,249
roads	2,279	2,431	2,670[1]
public transport	394	762	1,227[1]
Current (total)	4,021	5,383	5,985
roads	2,413	2,806	2,898[1]
revenue support to public transport	1,440	2,396	2,701[1]
concessionary fares	582	670	701[1]

[1]2005/06.

Table 8.1 Central and local government expenditure on transport (£ m, out-turn prices)
Source: *Transport Statistics*, Great Britain, 2007

mid-1990s and scheduled to increase until the 2010 Transport Plan programme is completed.

One of the main problems with large transport infrastructure projects is the scale of investment that is required. Invariably, there is a long payback period, coupled with high risk and uncertainty. Increasingly, as elsewhere, the UK government has been forced to turn to the private sector for assistance to fund such projects. It has had to do this at a time of growing pressure on the efficiency of the transport network, which is struggling to meet current, let alone future, needs.

For large projects such as the Channel Tunnel High Speed Rail Link, Nottingham's light rail system and the maintenance and upgrading of the London Underground, funding has been through a **Public Private Partnership** (PPP). As the name suggests, this is a contractual arrangement between public and private sector partners. The public sector usually retains ownership but looks to private sector funding to renovate or construct a facility. For this, the private sector partner expects an appropriate rate of return for the risks involved.

DEFINITION

Public Private Partnership (PPP): a contractual arrangement between the public and private sectors in order to fund large-scale projects

This type of arrangement has certain advantages for the public sector. These include:

● an injection of additional resources into transport projects over and above what it would otherwise be able to provide

● a gain in efficiency due to the private sector's participation

● access to innovative techniques and leading-edge technology

● risk transfer to an organisation with proven project management expertise.

Equally, there are potential benefits for the private partner, such as:

● a higher rate of return than if funding the whole of the project

● an opportunity to apply best practices

● some control over assets and user charges

● opportunity for indirect benefits from the management of similar projects.

Returning to the public sector, in the annual spending round, the Secretary of State for Transport has to bid for a share of next year's government spending, like other ministers. Transport may well have a case for a greater share – the increasing level of road congestion is a typical example – but so, too, will other government departments, such as health, education, defence, social security and so on.

Once an overall level of expenditure has been agreed, then resource allocation decisions have to be taken at a lower, more explicit level. For example, in the broad context of the 2010 Transport Plan, these decisions will have included:

● how to decide on which motorways to widen

● which new bypasses should be constructed

● which cities should be selected for public transport improvements

● which parts of the rail network should be upgraded or modernised.

Particularly in the case of road space, but also in the case of other projects where no PPP is feasible, non-commercial criteria have to be applied since no market prices are charged. Decisions that are taken have wider implications, both for the community and for the economy as a whole. In such circumstances, a cost-benefit approach is appropriate. This approach embraces **cost-benefit analysis**.

DEFINITION

Cost-benefit analysis: a technique for assessing the viability of a project, taking into account all of the effects over time

Cost-benefit analysis

Cost-benefit analysis has been widely used as an aid to decision making involving transport expenditure, particularly in the context of motorways and trunk routes. It has also been used to justify subsidies for rail passenger services and to assess the value to the economy of major projects involving huge sums of public investment.

There are four main stages in any cost-benefit analysis:

● *identification of the costs and benefits.* In some ways this is the most important, since it provides the entire framework for the cost-benefit analysis. On the surface, this might seem to be a relatively simple task; in practice it is not so straightforward, as it is often difficult to know where to 'draw the line'. Table 8.2 shows some typical examples of costs and benefits for various types of transport project.

● *enumeration or measurement of the costs and benefits.* This involves putting a monetary value on those that have been identified at the first stage. In some cases, this requires a shadow price (see Chapter 7). In other cases, a normal market price can be used.

● *forecasting the costs and benefits over the length of life of the project.* This is essentially a statistical exercise. Given the long time periods involved in transport investment projects, it is not an easy task (see Chapter 5).

● *establishing the net present value,* the net benefit to cost ratio and any other factors that can help determine whether the project is worthwhile.

ACTIVITY ⋯⁖

Consider a situation where funding for a new light rail transit system is being considered. Using the categories shown in Table 8.2, make a list of the likely costs and benefits. Make a note of any measurement issues you might envisage.

Appraisal of new road schemes

One of the earliest applications of cost-benefit analysis has been in the appraisal of new motorways and trunk roads. A basic methodology was established 50 years ago – this has been progressively developed and refined into a sophisticated computer model (COBA), which is used by the Highways Agency and local authorities. It is necessary for two main reasons:

● Roads are a quasi-public good for which no direct charge is made. Consequently, the market mechanism cannot be used to allocate resources.

● Central and local government expenditure on roads is invariably limited in relation to the many projects that are likely to be proposed. Priorities have to be determined.

The private benefit of building a new stretch of motorway or a bypass to relieve congestion is that there will be an increase in consumer surplus, due to a reduction in travel costs for those using it. This benefit is shown in Figure 8.1.

Private costs and benefits	These accrue to users of a particular project and include travel time savings, accident reduction and vehicle operating cost savings
External costs and benefits	These fall on or accrue to third parties. Examples include noise costs and environmental costs of traffic congestion, loss of amenity or the benefit to road users where some traffic has diverted to another route
Indirect costs and benefits	Spillover or impact effects of a transport project such as regional development, business relocation

Table 8.2 Typical examples of costs and benefits of transport projects

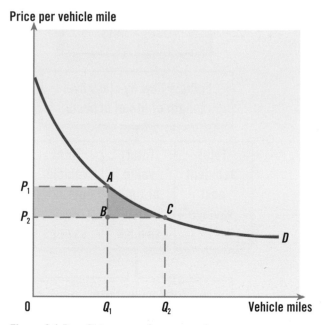

Figure 8.1 Benefit to users of a new road

It is assumed that the market demand curve for travel, *D*, can be derived and that it is downward-sloping, as shown on Figure 8.1. The effect of a road improvement is to reduce travel costs, since vehicles can travel in less congested conditions. This results in the price per vehicle mile falling from P_1 to P_2. At this lower price, there is an increase in the consumer surplus for existing vehicles. This is shown by the rectangle P_1 *AB* P_2. A better-quality road and the prospect of a fall in travel costs will increase demand from other road users. The benefit to this 'generated' traffic is shown on Figure 8.1 by the triangular area *ABC*. Overall, there has been an increase in consumer surplus of P_1ACBP_2. This is the total benefit.

THE COBA MODEL

Within the COBA model, the total benefit is split into three components. These are value of time savings, accident cost savings and vehicle operating cost savings. The first two were discussed in Chapter 7; the third item is the direct cost to road users of fuel cost savings and the savings through there being less wear and tear on the moving parts in the vehicle such as the brakes and clutch. These savings are particularly significant for large goods vehicles (again, see Chapter 7).

Figure 8.2 shows a simplified representation of the COBA model. The left-hand side of the figure shows the two main cost items. These are:

● *capital costs*. These are incurred in the early phase of any major road project and include construction costs, land purchase, design costs and so on.

● *maintenance costs*. These are annual costs to cover the costs of lighting, cleaning and routine resurfacing work. They also include costs for managing a stretch of road by Highways Agency staff and the emergency services.

The right-hand side shows the 'user costs'. This heading is potentially confusing but has come about because the COBA model calculates user cost savings compared to an otherwise 'do minimum' approach. These therefore represent the actual user benefits of constructing a new road scheme. As Figure 8.2 shows, after these preliminary calculations, it is possible to estimate the total costs and total benefits over the lifetime of the project, which can be anything from 30 to 40 years. These totals are then converted to their present values and a net present value is calculated. If this is positive, then there is some overall net benefit of the new stretch of road being put forward for construction.

Whether any project is progressed will depend on the rate of return relative to all other road proposals. This is usually measured by the benefit-to-cost ratio, which is the present value of the benefits divided by the present value of the costs. The value of this measure is that it allows competing projects to be put in rank order according to the benefit they will provide for the community. Subject to funding being available, the schemes that produce the highest benefit to cost ratios will be authorised.

The COBA model is now well understood and is in a standard form that is used by all authorities responsible for the development of the UK's road network. It has also been subject to ongoing updates and amendments since its first use. Having said these things, over the past 30 years or so, the environmental lobby, local objectors and other groups have increasingly voiced their opposition to more or less any major plan to improve the road network. Many of the objections have been against the

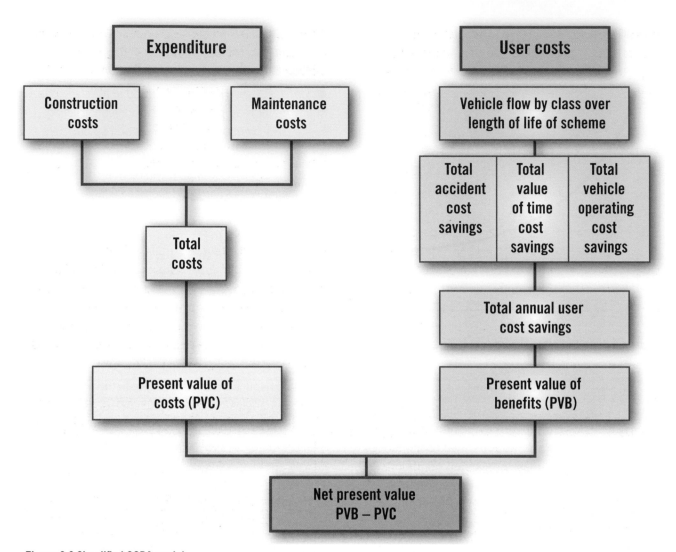

Figure 8.2 Simplified COBA model

principle of building new roads; other objections have been about the limitations of the COBA model.

These criticisms include:

● The COBA model is very difficult to comprehend, which limits the ability of the public to participate fully when there are public inquiries into new road schemes.

● COBA does not recognise all of the benefits and costs involved. It is basically a user-based method of appraisal. It does not, for example, seek to put a monetary value on the external costs and benefits involved, nor does it do so for the indirect costs and benefits of a new road scheme.

● Following from the previous point, the environmental effects of a new road project are

not adequately addressed by COBA. This is largely because of the problem of putting a reasonably robust monetary value on such items. Although the model is unchanged, progress has now been made in tackling this problem by considering environmental impact outside of the COBA model itself.

● Concerns that value judgements have to be made to estimate the total benefits of a road project. These particularly relate to the value of time, which is usually the largest benefit in most cost-benefit calculations.

● The COBA model only applies to roads. What is really needed is a model that applies to all forms of transport. This would provide a level playing-field when taking resource decisions involving government spending on transport.

It was for these and other reasons that a 'new approach to appraisal' has been put in place by the Department for Transport (DfT). The COBA model remains an essential part of this approach, along with an Environmental Impact Assessment (EIA).

A new deal for trunk roads

Research is ongoing to develop and refine what is now a multi-criteria approach to new road schemes. Its purpose is to increase the objectivity and transparency of the resource allocation process. Unlike COBA alone, the approach shows whether small-scale schemes, such as for improved traffic management, can achieve the same or most of the benefits of larger schemes. It can also provide information on whether a less environmentally intrusive proposal would produce the same level of benefit as a much larger scheme.

An important part of this new approach is that, when new road proposals are submitted, they should include what is called an Appraisal Summary Table. This is a one-page summary of the main economic, environmental and social impacts of the proposal. Where more than one option is being proposed, then a summary has to be produced for each. Table 8.3 shows the criteria that constitute the Appraisal Summary Table.

Crossrail

In June 2007, the new LGV-Est line, France's fastest railway link, carried its first passengers between Paris and Strasbourg. This huge project, costing an estimated $4bn (£2.7bn) took just five years to complete. This is in stark contrast to London's Crossrail project, which was first proposed in 1989 and was repeatedly delayed until it was given the go-ahead in September 2007.

Objectives	Qualitative impacts	Quantitative measure	Assessment
Environment	Noise	Number of properties experiencing increase or decrease in noise	Net effect/difference
	CO_2	Number of tonnes added or removed	Net effect/difference
	Landscape	n.a.	To be included in the assessment
	Biodiversity	n.a.	
	Heritage	n.a.	
	Water	n.a.	
Safety	–	Cost of accidents	Present value as % of costs
Economy	Journey time savings and vehicle operating cost savings	–	Present value as % of costs
	Regeneration	Likely further developments	To be included
Accessibility	Pedestrians	n.a.	To be included
	Access to public transport	n.a.	
	Community severence	n.a.	
Integration	–	n.a.	To be included

Table 8.3 Framework of the Appraisal Summary Table for the appraisal of new road schemes

To be fair, Crossrail is a hugely ambitious and in some respects controversial project costing an estimated £16bn. The intention is to link existing rail track between Maidenhead and Heathrow airport in the west to Shenfield and Abbey Wood in the east. To achieve this involves large-scale tunnelling under central London and the construction of seven new stations. These are at Paddington, Bond Street, Tottenham Court Road, Farringdon, Liverpool Street, Whitechapel and Canary Wharf.

Funding Crossrail is a major issue. Although some central government funding will be available, the largest contribution will have to come from the private sector. Cross London Rail Links (CLRL), which is overseeing the project, is currently looking for financial backers. Its cost-benefit appraisal of the scheme provides a convincing case for would-be backers (see below).

Supporters of Crossrail argue that the proposed rail link is of national importance and not just of benefit to the London area. Top of the list was the former mayor Ken Livingstone, who stated: 'Crossrail is vital for the incomes and jobs of Londoners … it is even more important to London's long-term prosperity than our victory in winning the Olympic Games'. The government is also very much in favour of the scheme, for similar strategic reasons.

Not all Londoners, though, are enthusiastic about Crossrail. In East London, for example, residents and politicians are concerned about the physical impact that will result from a six-year construction phase.

They are also concerned about the wider effects on the community, fearing that once operational, Crossrail will result in a rise in house prices, forcing some families out of areas where they have lived for generations. Only time will tell whether, as one local MP has said, Crossrail will be another Millennium Dome.

ECONOMIC APPRAISAL OF CROSSRAIL

The case for Crossrail, like any major new transport infrastructure project, has to be justified through an economic appraisal. As in the case of roads, this is based on cost-benefit analysis.

The projected user benefits of Crossrail are:

● value of time savings for current public transport users and motorists. The rationale for this benefit is that, once the new Crossrail link opens, many users will experience reduced travel times. The opportunity cost of these travel time savings is a benefit to such groups.

● a reduction in crowding and improved journey quality. This benefit will take the form of improved comfort for users transferring to Crossrail from other congested transport modes.

● reduced operating costs for road users and a reduction in accidents. These benefits will accrue to road users who continue to make their journeys by road while a reduction in accidents will also generate some benefits to the local community and to health services.

● benefits to mobility-impaired passengers.

User benefits	£ m	Costs	£ m
Leisure/commuting trips time savings improved quality other	7,985 2,889 355	Capital costs Maintenance costs Operating costs	10,626 1,606 1,670
Business trips time savings other	4,847 17	Total costs	13,902
Total benefits	16,093		

Table 8.4 Projected user benefits and costs of Crossrail (present value)
Source : CLRL, 2005

The costs of Crossrail are easier to identify and consist of:

- capital costs of construction
- maintenance costs
- operating costs.

These costs exclude the likely disruption and effects on the community of Crossrail's construction. They are impossible to quantify.

Table 8.4 summarises the monetary values of these benefits and costs as estimated by CLRL. The benefits are split between trips made in the course of work and those made for leisure and commuting purposes.

As this table shows, Crossrail is expected to generate over £16bn of user benefits, with about one third accruing for business trips, which carry the highest value of time savings per hour of travel time saved. Interestingly, the user benefit from value of time savings is the same as the projected construction costs in 2007.

The cost-benefit analysis also considered the effect of Crossrail on net rail revenue. Crossrail's own revenue is an obvious benefit, but account must also be made of the loss of revenue to other rail operators where passengers switch to Crossrail. There is also a reduced contribution to the Exchequer as motorists switching to Crossrail will pay less indirect taxation through fuel tax in particular.

So far, this summary of the cost-benefit analysis has followed the normal methodology. In planning Crossrail, one of the objectives has been to facilitate the continuing development of London's finance and business services sector. This is an impact effect or secondary benefit arising from Crossrail. Such effects are by no means easy to identify or quantify. Having said this, CLRL has identified four relevant wider benefits. These are:

- *job creation* and a move to more productive jobs in central London. CLRL have estimated that around 5,000 new central area jobs will be created by 2016, rising to 33,000 by 2026. Some workers will be able to move to better jobs, representing a benefit to themselves and to the economy through higher tax revenues.

- *external economies of scale.* Agglomeration benefits will accrue to all central London employment from the move to more productive jobs.

- *increased labour force participation.* More people will enter the labour market, due to the reduced time and costs of Crossrail in accessing central London.

- *imperfect competition.* This is an estimate of efficiency benefits that are not passed on to customers, due to a lack of competition in the local transport market.

The overall value of the wider economic benefits is estimated at £7.2bn. Table 8.5 summarises all of the benefits and costs.

	£ m
Total costs	13,902
Less public transport revenue	–6,149
Plus indirect tax reductions	1,207
Net cost to government	**8,960**
Transport user benefits	16,093
Wider economic benefits	7,161
Total benefits	**23,254**
Total benefits: net costs	2.6:1

Table 8.5 Overall costs and benefits of Crossrail (present value)
Source : CLRL, 2005

ACTIVITY ···▶

a) i) Explain why the valuation of travel time savings is an important item in transport cost-benefit analysis.

ii) Why is 'the opportunity cost of these travel time savings' classified as a benefit?

STRETCH AND CHALLENGE

b) Discuss some of the likely measurement issues in estimating the wider impact effects of a project such as Crossrail.

Objectives of transport policy in the UK

So far, in the preceding chapters and in the early part of this chapter, aspects of transport policy have been discussed. For example:

● how best to forecast future transport demand (Chapter 5)

● how best to organise the UK's transport system (Chapter 6)

● how best to deal with the growing congestion and other negative externalities arising from increasing transport use (Chapter 7)

● how best to allocate government spending on transport (this chapter).

Although rather piecemeal, the common denominator in each of these examples is the use of the term 'how best to'. This sums up the overall objective of transport policy, which is to achieve the best or most efficient allocation of resources in the transport sector.

In practice, this has been very difficult to achieve and, as a consequence, the UK does not have a comprehensive **integrated transport policy**. Policy

DEFINITION

Integrated transport policy: one that encompasses all modes of passenger and freight transport

documents tend to cover all modes of passenger and freight transport, but the overall process of resource allocation lacks the cohesion that an integrated plan would bring. This is largely due to there being no direct charge for the use of roads by private and commercial vehicle users (see Chapter 7).

In striving to achieve the 'best' allocation of resources, the operation of national transport policy has focused on three key areas:

● *structure of transport operations*, involving the determination of responsibilities for the public and private sector. Who should own what has been an important political and social challenge? Today, this responsibility rests very firmly in the hands of the private sector.

● *regulation of transport operations*. The issue here is the extent of the relative roles of government and the market. Deregulation has been prevalent in all transport markets yet, at the same time, the government has had little opposition to its plans to tighten up on vehicle standards and environmental disturbance.

● *control of transport infrastructure*. After a brief flirtation with private ownership, rail track has been back in the hands of the public sector for some time. The provision of road space is predominantly a public sector responsibility; in contrast, airport and seaport ownership is in the hands of private sector providers.

Strategically, transport policy seeks to address these three areas in an integrated way.

The Eddington transport study

Transport policy statements and consultation documents have been produced by the DfT on a seemingly ad hoc basis for many years. In 2000, a controversial ten-year transport plan, Transport 2010, was published, much of which has never been implemented. This was followed by substantial reports on the Future of Air Transport and the Future of Transport in 2004 (see Chapter 6 of *Transport Economics*, for details).

Despite the volume of reports, there were few signs that the UK's transport problems were improving. There was also a view in government that there was a need for a strategic assessment to be made that covered the long-term links between transport, productivity, growth and stability within the context of the government's commitment to sustainable development. The task of doing this was given by the then prime minister, Tony Blair, to Sir Rod Eddington, former chief executive of British Airways.

In producing his report, Eddington consulted some well-known economists and had the full resources and support of the DfT at his disposal. His eagerly awaited report was published in December 2006. It has five main recommendations:

● to focus policy and sustained investment on existing transport networks. This includes increasing capacity on existing railway lines and bus routes. Investing in large prestige transport projects was rejected on account of the diminishing returns that were often experienced. Small-scale investments, according to Eddington, produced a better return. The exception to this general principle was his support for mixed-mode operations at Heathrow which would allow runways to be used for take-off and landing.

● to give priority to relieving congestion in congested and growing city areas. This recommendation was based on the economic significance of such areas for the economy and the projected increase in the city population to 2025.

● to invest in improving the gateways between the UK and, in particular, other parts of the EU with which the country trades. Such investment would include selective improvements to road links to our main ports, modernisation of rail freight routes and other measures to improve port efficiency.

● getting the price right across all modes of transport. In Eddington's opinion, this not only made economic sense but also was necessary for dealing with the various environmental challenges that transport was facing. Having said this, he did not underestimate the problems in achieving a situation where the transport sector, including aviation, met its full environmental costs. There was strong backing for congestion-targeted road pricing. These aspects of the report were seen as giving favourable backing to Stern's warnings on climate change (see 'Economics in context', Chapter 7, page 154).

● to set up a new Independent Planning Commission to take decisions on strategic projects.

Eddington's reasoning in giving his full support for road pricing was rather more to do with the projected benefits to business than for addressing market failure. He estimated that the introduction of road pricing would reduce congestion by 50 per cent below what it would otherwise have been. In turn, this would reduce the need for new road investment by 80 per cent, as well as reducing greenhouse gas emissions. Overall, he estimated that up to £28bn of congestion costs could be wiped out by 2015 when national road pricing would be implemented.

Support was also given to the principle of charging transport users for their relative emissions of CO_2 (see above, page 162). Eddington stated that this could be implemented through green taxes or carbon trading schemes (see *OCR AS Economics*, pages 71–72). A further £20 for short-haul and £50 for long-haul air passengers was suggested. The effect on the number of people travelling was uncertain, as no estimates of price elasticity of demand were made. Having said this, a small increase like that suggested would seem to have little effect in deterring travel on low-cost airlines.

Eddington's proposals for rail were more controversial. In his view, unregulated fares should be increased for peak travel in order to reduce demand and, hence, overcrowding. He was of the view that some commuters could travel later, so saving money.

On efficiency grounds, Eddington rejected the more obvious way forward, of increasing supply. As with air travel, such a policy would only work if demand for peak period travel was reasonably price elastic (unlikely) or some commuters got so fed up that they changed their normal journey to work pattern (also unlikely).

As shown in Chapter 6, unregulated 'walk on' rail fares are not only expensive but have risen above the rate of inflation for the last few years. One effect of this has been that for some domestic trips, for example Edinburgh to London, it is now much cheaper to fly than to travel by rail. Environmentally, as shown in Chapter 7, this is bad news in terms of CO_2 emissions.

Finally, Eddington commented on the difficulty for transport policy makers arising from the ownership structure of passenger transport. He rightly recognised that government was restricted in what could be done to limit the power of the large oligopolists. He did not believe that a return to public ownership would happen – more likely was for the government to exert greater direct and indirect control.

The overall message from this report was that it was essential to get the economics right. For transport users, this can mean just one thing – increased taxes that bring the price paid more in line with the social costs involved.

Towards a sustainable transport system

The government's response to Eddington's study, and to the Stern Review, came in a new transport policy Command Paper in October 2007. This was called *Towards a Sustainable Transport System – Supporting Economic Growth in a Low Carbon World*. The document also set out investment plans for the period to 2013–14 and, significantly, proposals for a new approach for longer-term transport strategy.

The policy document was ground-breaking in so far as it proposed transport goals for delivering CO_2 reduction alongside economic growth. Previously, it had been assumed that this was not possible, due to the apparent incompatibility between the two aims.

The challenge for transport was set out in five broad goals, to:

● maximise the competitiveness and productivity of the economy. As shown in Chapter 7, congestion increases business costs and undermines competitiveness. Unreliability also undermines business confidence. The challenge here for transport policy is to improve the performance of the existing transport network by improving 'predictable end-to-end journey times'. Suggested policy means that might achieve this include better traffic management and getting the prices right, combined with a policy of selected infrastructure development.

● address climate change by cutting CO_2 emissions and other greenhouse gases. Putting a price on

carbon is essential if this goal is to be achieved. Indirect taxation and trading mechanisms can ensure that people are faced with the full social cost of the transport they are using. Alongside these measures, greener alternatives have to be provided; for example, good, innovative public transport.

● protect people's safety, security and health.

● improve quality of life through reducing transport's negative impacts (see Chapter 7).

● promote greater equality of opportunity, in particular through the provision of effective access.

As far as investment plans are concerned, the policy remains more or less as previously – resources will be concentrated on the most congested and crowded parts of the transport system, with additional emphasis on public transport. Significantly, Eddington's advice that small local schemes often represent excellent value for money was supported. So, measures to improve traffic flow (high occupancy lanes for example), bus lanes, park-and-ride schemes and cycle lanes are likely to receive more funding.

Nationally, there is a clear statement of the priority – urban congestion charging backed by investment in public transport. A national system of road pricing is seen as having potential, but no system will be implemented until there has been a full evaluation of local trials (see Chapter 7). There is also a proviso that clear answers are needed to the technological and system challenge involved.

All in all, this transport policy document extensively supports the study made by Eddington, set within the context of Stern's warnings with regard to climate change. It is by far the most forthright statement to be made by the government on the need for a more sustainable national transport policy.

Sustainable freight transport policy

Eddington's study and the resultant transport policy document contained only limited references to freight transport. This is perhaps understandable, as there have been policy initiatives to produce a more sustainable freight transport function since the start

ECONOMICS IN CONTEXT

BIGGER, LONGER, CHEAPER, GREENER: SUPERLORRY IS COMING YOUR WAY

The government is considering allowing a trial of longer, heavier vehicles (LHVs). A study by Heriot-Watt University has found that LHVs would deliver significant benefits in terms of lower costs and CO_2 emissions, without compromising road safety. The vehicle most likely to be approved for a trial is 83 feet long and has a maximum weight of 60 tonnes. This is a massive increase on current maximum levels although well below the 83-tonne road trains that operate in the USA and Australia. If approved, it would match vehicles that are used in the Netherlands and Germany, subject to various conditions.

Public opinion tends to be against heavier lorries. Rail freight companies are bitterly opposed to the proposals, since LHVs could carry two containers and result in customers switching from rail transport. There are also substantial road safety implications – accidents involving current heavy goods vehicles are invariably serious, often leading to a loss of life.

of this century. There is also evidence that these initiatives are beginning to have an effect.

A particularly successful way of producing a more sustainable freight transport policy is where goods carried switch from road to rail transport. As stated in Chapter 5, there has been an unprecedented increase in goods moved by rail since privatisation in 1995 (see also Chapter 6). This has come about largely through competitive forces in the market, since no particular financial incentives have been available from central government for firms switching modes in this way. An

ECONOMICS IN CONTEXT

DO WE REALLY NEED BOTTLED WATER ... FROM FIJI?

Fiji water is fashionable

The market for bottled water in Britain is now worth a staggering £2bn. Thirty years ago, it was virtually nothing – the only bottled water we drank was when we went on holiday to France or Italy. Since then, sales of premium British mineral water brands as well as locally produced types of spring water, which is invariably no more than filtered tap water, have escalated. We have also been inundated with natural and carbonated brands, especially from France. The production of most leading European brands is now controlled by multinational food-processing giants.

The latest craze is for Fiji water, which, as its name suggests, comes from the Pacific. It is sold at Selfridges, Harvey Nichols, Harrods and Waitrose, as well as trendy London restaurants, and quaffed by the likes of Pierce Brosnan, Vin Diesel and Whoopie Goldberg. Those who can afford to taste it claim that they enjoy its 'tropical taste'.

Environmentally, it seems crazy to bring water from the other side of the world when local sources are available. (And of course there is always tap water!) Fiji water, for example, has to travel 10,000 miles by container ship. There are also the internal deliveries to be considered. Overall, delivering a one-litre bottle emits a huge volume of greenhouse gases, without taking into account the plastic bottle and other packaging costs.

A recent report from the Food Commission has been critical of such seemingly unnecessary food miles, while recognising that there is a case for importing exotic treat foods such as mangoes and pineapples. There are also concerns that, while importing Fiji water creates jobs in Fiji, there are still people on those islands who have no clean running water for their own use.

analysis of the changes in goods moved by rail shows that much of the new traffic comes from product types that traditionally have been moved by road; for example, consumer goods, certain types of food and drink, motor vehicles and other manufactured goods. Most of the new traffic has been moved in single container and wagon loads rather than in whole train loads, which has traditionally been the core business of rail freight. Major retailers such as Argos, Superdrug, Sainsbury's and Tesco use some rail freight for primary distribution from ports and via the Channel Tunnel, from EU sources.

In 2002, controversially from a rail freight standpoint, government approval was given to increase the maximum weight of road goods vehicles from 41 to 44 tonnes on six axles. This decision increased the payload of the vehicle, resulting in improved efficiency and significantly less vehicle movements and CO_2 emissions for a given tonnage of goods moved. The government is considering new trials that could see longer, heavier vehicles on the UK's roads (see Economics in context).

The government has also changed the basis of the way in which heavy goods vehicles are taxed, to make it more expensive for hauliers to run trucks that are least environmentally acceptable in terms of their emissions and the damage they inflict on road surfaces. This is the same principle as has more recently been applied to private cars (see Chapter 7).

Another important way in which the freight transport function can be made more sustainable is through cutting down on food miles, the distance that food is moved from where it is grown to where it is consumed. Even for UK produce, the distances over which fresh products such as potatoes and meat are carried can be substantial, due to the ways in which retail supply chains are organised. Public opinion and awareness of this problem is growing, with more consumers taking a responsible attitude to purchasing increasing amounts of locally produced items (see Economics in context).

EU transport policy

Transport provides a very important function in the EU. This involves the movement of goods, consistent with the customs union and Single European Market (SEM), and the movement of people, which is increasingly important with geographical enlargement.

Provision for a Common Transport Policy (CTP) was included in the Treaty of Rome (1957). Its development has been particularly slow, largely due to member states, the UK included, being unwilling to give up their control of this vitally important function. Two key issues have dominated the CTP debate:

● **liberalisation** – the means by which barriers to entry should be removed to give equal access in all national markets to transport providers based within the EU

● **harmonisation** – the means by which 'a level playing-field' is created in EU transport markets. This includes common rates of fuel and vehicle taxation, common standards for vehicle weights and emission levels and common rules for the hours of work by transport drivers and others.

For many years, it was argued by some member states that it was essential that harmonisation was achieved before markets could be liberalised. This has not been so. The push towards completion of the SEM by 1993 began a process of rapid change in the attitudes of member states towards liberalisation. A key issue was that of **cabotage**, the extent to which third-party transport operators can do business

DEFINITIONS

Liberalisation: same as *deregulation*

Harmonisation: establishing a common set of rules and regulations to be followed

Cabotage: the collection and delivery of goods or the transport of people by a truck, plane or other means of transport within a country other than that where that means of transport is registered

in the markets of other member states. This has been particularly controversial in the case of road haulage, where cabotage was illegal before 1992. This meant that the road haulage function was not as efficient as it might be, since empty running was inevitable on most types of intra-EU trip. From 1993 to 1998, a permit system operated, and this provided limited cabotage. From 1998 the market has been fully liberalised, which means that any haulier from any EU member state can do whatever business is available in any other member state.

Cabotage has also been a substantial issue in EU air transport. From 1997 there has been 'a single European sky', whereby the EU has been responsible for issuing a single air transport licence, for setting technical standards and for integrating air traffic control systems. Opening up the market has resulted in the escalation of air passenger services, particularly from low-cost providers. It has meant that airlines based in the EU can operate services from an airport in a third-party country. A particularly successful example of this is how Irish-owned Ryanair has developed a huge network of services from UK airports to other parts of the EU.

The EU has had an important role in funding new transport infrastructure to create Trans-European Networks (TENs). Improvements have been funded for road and rail especially, the most high-profile of which for the UK has been the Channel Tunnel rail link to St Pancras station in London. Additional resources have recently been made available to fund major infrastructure improvements in the new member states in central and eastern Europe.

In recent years, the EU has proposed a range of measures that, like UK national transport policy, should promote a more sustainable CTP. The problems that are faced throughout the EU are very similar to those in the UK. They include congestion on main road and rail routes, increasing concerns about the effects of environmental pollution on health, and wide variations in the use of transport modes between member states. As in the UK, economics is central to the debate – the EU Transport Commission believes that these problems have arisen because not all of the external costs of transport have been included in the cost of transport to users.

Current policy includes:

● support for road schemes that reduce congestion and are consistent with the 'polluter pays' principle

● a tightening of regulations and controls on road freight transport. The EU wants to see harmonisation of fuel taxes, more stringent emissions standards, and more controls over the work done by drivers, particularly those based in the new member states

● a package of measures to open up the market for rail passenger services

● a fully operational 'single sky' policy for air transport.

As things stand, EU transport policy complements that of member states, the UK included. For the future, particularly as some member states progress towards greater economic union, the CTP seems likely to have a more prominent role in EU affairs, to the possible detriment of national transport policies.

ExamCafé
Relax, refresh, result!

Relax and prepare

Alice

I have found transport economics very interesting. I can now see how some of the microeconomics I came across at AS level can be applied to transport. I have tried to answer all of the activities, either for homework or in my own time. When I take the exam, I will try to remember the best advice that I have been given by my teacher – 'Remember Alice, this is an Economics exam, do use economic terms and concepts as much as you can in your answers.' She has also told me to make sure I know all about market structures and how firms behave in transport markets, as somewhere on the paper there will always be at least one question on this topic.

Nick

For AS Economics, I started to read a decent newspaper and got into the habit of surfing the BBC news website. Now I am studying transport economics, I have found that both of these resources have been particularly useful in providing examples of transport problems and issues, both in the UK and elsewhere in the world. My local paper in Cambridge also has relevant articles – recent ones have been on the road pricing debate in the city and on the environmental issues arising from the increased number of flights at Stansted airport. I must try to use up-to-date examples like these in my exam answers.

Emily

I have again found it useful to concentrate my preparation for the exam by spending time answering all of the questions on the exam practice paper in the book. I have also spent time writing answers to the one on the OCR website. My teacher has given me one or two past OCR 2885 papers. I now feel much more confident when tackling the data response questions. A good mark here should help me get a good mark overall on this paper.

Refresh your memory

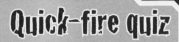
1. How, in official statistics, is transport demand usually measured?
2. What are the main characteristics of an oligopoly?
3. What is meant by deregulation?
4. Why is road pricing an example of 'the polluter pays' principle in economics?
5. What is meant by sustainability and how can it apply in transport?
6. What is cost-benefit analysis and when is it used?

Get the result !

EXAM QUESTION

Discuss whether economists' concerns over monopoly are justified in the case of transport markets.

Charlotte's answer

A monopoly is defined as a situation where a firm is the only one in the market. The firm is the same as the industry. A monopoly therefore is very powerful in the way it can control what it sells, who it sells to and the prices that it charges. For these reasons economists are concerned about monopolies.

In theory, a monopoly can decide what price it charges or it can decide how much it is able to sell. Monopolies also make a lot of profits, since they control their market in this way as they do not have any competition. There are monopolies in some transport markets. Where I live, there is only one bus company. This means we have to rely upon this company if we want to travel by bus. There used to be another firm but Stagecoach got rid of it and is now the only one that runs services. There are plenty of daytime services but if I want to go out at night, I am not able to get the bus home. This is surely wrong — they should be providing a proper service for the public.

There are other monopolies in transport markets. For example, with most rail franchises and certain ferry routes there is only one firm providing services. Here again, firms can charge high prices and make lots of

[Graph: Price level (vertical axis) against Quantity (horizontal axis), showing curves labelled MC, AC, AR, MR, with a shaded area labelled "Profits" bounded by P on the vertical axis and Q on the horizontal axis]

profits. The recent increases in many rail fares have not been well received.

It is for these reasons that monopolies have a bad reputation and this is why economists are concerned.

Comments

It is clear that Charlotte understands the question. She is aware of the general context and its application. The answer, though, is not written in a particularly analytical style, which is the most important thing examiners are looking for at A2 level. There is a very limited discussion and this is confined to an exemplification of economists' concerns; there is no attempt to put the alternative view.

The answer could be improved through:

- a much more explicit statement that in theory the price is higher and the quantity produced (not sold) is lower than in a more competitive market
- reference to the diagram in the written part of the answer; make sure the profits box is correctly drawn and label cost not price on vertical axis
- more substance to the transport examples
- some discussion of the reasons why in certain situations a monopoly may actually be more efficient and the relevance of this to transport markets.

Aakash's answer

In theory, a monopoly exists where one firm controls the whole output of an industry. It can do this for various reasons, in particular where there are high barriers to entry that make it impossible for new firms to enter. In some transport markets, a firm may have a monopoly through virtue of it having a route franchise.

Economists have been concerned about the behaviour of monopolists for a long time. The root cause of this concern is that the price charged is higher and the output produced is lower than in a competitive market. A monopolist also earns supernormal profits in both the short and long run. This is shown in the diagram opposite.

As this diagram shows, the monopolist is not as efficient as if the firm were operating in a more competitive market. This is because it is not producing at the lowest point on the average cost curve (productive efficiency). Neither is the firm

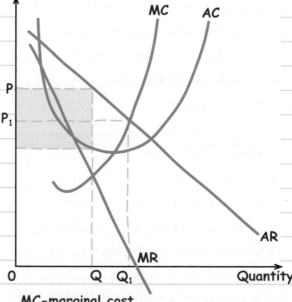

MC-marginal cost
AC-average cost
MR-marginal revenue
AR-average revenue

Supernormal profits

Competitive market equilibrium P₁ Q₁
Equilibrium of a monopolist

allocatively efficient, since the price it charges is not equal to marginal cost. Price is higher than marginal cost and excess or supernormal profits are being made (shaded area).

There is, though, an alternative viewpoint, namely that a monopoly can be more efficient than firms operating in a more competitive market. This is particularly true in the case of a natural monopoly, which is very relevant when looking at transport markets. A good example of this could be in rail passenger transport where it seemingly makes little sense for there to be competitive duplication of resources.

In a natural monopoly, there is a situation where fixed costs are high relative to variable costs. Taking the case of rail, the costs of providing and maintaining rail track are high compared to the variable costs of running train services. As more trains run on a stretch of track, average costs fall, indicative of the benefits that can be gained from economies of scale. Long-run average and marginal costs continue to fall.

To some extent, the privatised rail passenger structure allows franchisees to benefit in this way. At the same time, there is always the threat from open access train operators. A good example is on the East Coast Main Line where Hull Trains, Grand Central Trains and First Capital Connect all compete in some respects with the franchise holder, National Express East Coast.

Another benefit of a monopoly is that it may have the resources to innovate and invest in order to protect its market situation. This has been much in evidence with some of the large train operators such as National Express and First Group. It has also been one of the reasons why they have been awarded particular franchises.

So, to conclude, in economic theory there are concerns about the behaviour of monopolists. These are long standing and will remain. Provided there are regulatory controls and, for transport markets especially, contestability, it is possible that a monopoly may provide a better allocation of resources than a competitive market.

Comments

This is an excellent answer. It is written in a mature, analytical style throughout. Significantly, there is a very clear attempt to put the alternative case, as flagged up by the 'discuss' directive word in the question. There are two aspects of the answer that might be improved. These are:

- examples other than from just rail transport (note the plural 'markets' in the question)
- rather more on contestability and its relevance even in a monopolistic market.

The A2 examination in Transport economics contains two types of question:

- a compulsory data response question (25 marks)
- a two-part structured essay question from a choice of three (35 marks).

To do well in the examination, you need to know what specific skills are required to tackle each of these new question types.

Data response questions

This type of question is so-called because a small number of questions are drawn from information that is provided. This information can take various forms – a data set, a data set with text (as in the exam practice paper) or text that includes some data. In all cases, the early questions tend to be relatively straightforward and carry a small number of marks; they are followed by more demanding questions that have more marks attached to them. Two of these questions will normally have A04 command words such as 'comment' or 'discuss'.

So, here are some 'hot tips':

- Be familiar with the main sources of transport data, for example, *Transport Statistics, Great Britain* and *Transport Trends* (annual and on the DfT's website). Features on the BBC news website often contain data, as do transport articles in good newspapers.

- Make sure you know what the data means. Look carefully at the units and variables used. See if a source is given.

- Watch out for forecast data. These are often used in this type of question. Remember that not all forecasts, especially over a long time period, are accurate.

- With time series data, look for annual changes in the level and for the trend over the entire period.

You need to spend about 50 minutes on this question. For a start, though, spend up to 10 minutes reading through the information provided. Look at the data – make sure you understand it and what it shows. Underline any economic concepts contained in the

text. Then look through the questions before writing your answers. And remember … if you cannot answer a particular question, then move on. And above all, remember that only short answers are asked for. The time you spend writing them should be broadly in line with the marks available.

Structured essay questions

This type of question is so called because it consists of two interrelated parts. For both you are required to write a short essay. Questions may or may not include what is called a 'stem'. This is an introductory sentence. Where there is a stem, this should help you understand the context of both parts.

The first part of this question is worth 15 marks. A typical command word is 'explain' – this means that you are required to give a reasoned account of a particular problem or issue. An alternative command word might be 'analyse'. This indicates you need to pick out the main elements in a particular topic.

Before choosing which question to answer, look also at part b). It is no good answering a question unless you can make a reasonable attempt at both parts. Remember also that part b) will seem harder than part a), but it should follow on from it.

So here are some 'hot tips' for part a):

- Try to write in an analytical way. To do this, you need to use key economic terms (as defined in the book) and, above all, avoid what is unnecessary description.

- A diagram may support your answer, particularly if the question draws upon the content of Chapter 6. But remember to actually use your diagram in your answer – in other words, refer to it. And if you do decide to use a diagram, make sure you can draw it correctly.

- Stick to the point and spend around 30 minutes on this part of your answer.

The second part of the question is worth 20 marks, the largest mark allocation of any question on the paper. A typical command word is 'discuss' – this means that you need to consider two sides of an issue or argument. If you do this, you will reach Level 4 for which a massive 10 marks are available.

So, here are some 'hot tips' for part b):

● Think very carefully about what this question requires; write your answer in a logical way.

● Make sure your answer is balanced; try to write about the same volume of writing for each side of the topic.

● Your discussion should be underpinned with relevant economic analysis.

● Use diagrams where appropriate to analyse issues.

● Avoid making rash, opinionated statements.

● For a very good mark of 16 and over, try to make a reasoned judgement on the topic, based on the evidence you have provided in your answer.

● Where possible, refer to relevant transport examples or things you have read. These can enhance the currency of an answer.

● Spend around 40 minutes on this part and pay particular attention to the last paragraph. This should be a concise summary of your discussion.

Exam practice paper

Section A

Answer all questions.

Passenger transport demand – is it becoming more sustainable?

It has been government policy for the last decade or so to promote a more sustainable transport policy. Just how effective this has been is difficult to assess. At a simple level, it could be seen as when the overall demand for transport falls from one year to another or, alternatively, when the rate of growth of demand for transport is lower than the annual rate of economic growth.

Table 1 below shows the demand for the three main modes of passenger transport in Great Britain from 1998 to 2006. Table 2 shows how the percentage change in total passenger transport (which largely consists of the three modes from Table 1) over this period compares with the annual percentage change in real GDP growth.

	Cars*	Buses/Coaches	Rail
1998	636	45	44
1999	642	46	46
2000	640	47	47
2001	654	47	47
2002	677	47	48
2003	673	47	49
2004	678	48	50
2005	674	49	52
2006	686	50	55

* Includes light vans and taxis

Table 1 Passenger transport demand, 1998 –2006 (billion passenger km)

	Passenger transport	Real GDP
1998	1.0	3.0
1999	1.5	3.4
2000	−0.3	3.8
2001	2.1	2.3
2002	3.3	2.1
2003	−0.1	2.5
2004	0.9	3.2
2005	−0.1	2.0
2006	2.1	2.6

Sources: *Transport Statistics*, 2007 edition; HM Treasury

Table 2: Annual percentage change in passenger transport demand and real GDP, 1998–2006

1 a) Using the data in Table 1, which mode of transport experienced

    i) the greatest percentage increase in demand

    ii) the least percentage increase in demand over the period from 1998 to 2006? (2)

  b) State and explain <u>two</u> possible determinants of the increase in demand for passenger transport by car from 1998 to 2006. (6)

  c) i) Describe why the demand for passenger transport is a derived demand. (2)

    ii) Explain the expected relationship between the annual change in real GDP and the annual change in passenger transport. (3)

    iii) Comment upon the extent to which this relationship is evident in Table 2. (4)

  d) Using the data in Tables 1 and 2, discuss whether there is any evidence that the demand for passenger transport is becoming more sustainable. (8)   (Total 25 marks)

Section B

Answer <u>one</u> question.

2 a) Explain how firms compete in oligopolistic markets. (15)

  b) Using examples, discuss the extent to which transport firms really do compete in oligopolistic markets. (20)

3 a) Explain how the negative externalities arising from the increased use of air transport are typical examples of market failure. (15)

  b) Discuss how effective fiscal measures such as Air Passenger Duty are in reducing such negative externalities. (20)

4 a) Explain why cost-benefit analysis is often used to justify major new transport projects. (15)

  b) Discuss the underlying principles that have been used to justify the Crossrail project for London. (20)

The global economy

This part of the book revisits the idea of macroeconomic performance. It extends what you have studied in the AS course by considering more advanced economic analysis of the national economy. It also sets this performance in regional and global contexts. Overall, this part emphasises the ways in which individual economies and regional blocs are interdependent through trade, the process of economic integration and the increasing globalisation that characterises current economic activity.

Chapter 9 focuses on the causes and consequences of economic growth. You will find some of what is presented familiar from the AS course, but the depth of analysis and evaluation will be deeper. Aggregate demand and supply analysis is the key to understanding economic growth in the short and the long run. The learning tips in this chapter refer you back to what you have studied before to help you to make links to what you studied in Part 2 of the AS textbook. The chapter also introduces the issues of economic stability and international competitiveness and how macroeconomic policies can promote them. The emphasis throughout this chapter is on a range of different national contexts.

Chapter 10 revisits international trade and employs new concepts to explain the benefits of trade. You will be encouraged to look critically at these benefits from the perspective of a range of different economies and explore examples of the world's major trading 'blocs'. You will see how exchange-rate fluctuations and imbalances in the balance of payments might create problems for economies. The issue of economic integration is explained in the context of the European Union (EU), the North American Free Trade Area. (NAFTA) and the Association of Southeast Asian Nations (ASEAN). The chapter, therefore, introduces a regional context to macroeconomic performance.

Chapter 11 gives you an insight into some of the economic issues that affect the lives of the 80 per cent of the world's population who live in developing countries. It looks at what we mean by economic and human development, how this can be measured and how it can be promoted. The focus is on the process by which economic growth can be made to improve human well-being both now and in the future. You will see how the impact of economic growth on the environment, on resources and on people is important in making development sustainable.

Part 3 concludes by considering the increasing globalisation of economic activity. You will be able to take a critical look at the role of multinational companies in the global economy and the major international institutions such as the World Bank, the International Monetary Fund (IMF) and the World Trade Organization (WTO).

When you have completed this part you should be able to:

- analyse and evaluate the causes and consequences of economic growth

- assess the effectiveness of policies to promote economic growth and stability and international competitiveness

- analyse the effects of international trade and understand global trade patterns

- assess the strengths and weaknesses of different exchange rate systems

- analyse the causes and consequences of imbalances on the balance of payments

- explain the different stages of economic integration and evaluate their effects

- explain what economic development is, and the relationship between growth and development, and assess different measures of development

- evaluate the different policy approaches to promoting development

- understand the idea of sustainable development and assess how it can be measured and promoted

- assess the causes and consequences of different international financial flows

- evaluate the causes and consequences of globalisation

- explain the roles of the WTO, the IMF and the World Bank

- comment upon the issues surrounding current international trade negotiations and trade disputes.

9 Macroeconomic performance

On completion of this chapter, you should be able to:

- show an awareness of the recent performance of the UK economy
- distinguish between short-run and long-run economic growth
- describe and understand the different stages of the economic cycle
- analyse the nature and significance of output gaps
- evaluate the causes of economic growth in the short and long run
- define the multiplier and discuss its interaction with the accelerator as determinants of the economic cycle
- evaluate the consequences of economic growth for the main indicators of macroeconomic performance
- understand the nature of policies to promote economic stability and growth
- evaluate the effectiveness of policies to promote economic stability, growth and international competitiveness
- analyse and evaluate the significance of policy rules, targets and constraints in promoting economic stability, growth and international competitiveness.

The recent macroeconomic performance of the UK economy

Towards the end of the first decade of the twenty-first century, the talk in the UK is of a worsening of macroeconomic performance as the global economy enters a slowdown. It is easy to forget that in 2004, UK economic performance was being praised highly by organisations such as the Organisation for Economic Co-operation and Development (OECD). In its economic survey of the UK, the OECD began by saying, 'The performance of the UK economy has been impressive in recent years.'

How are we to judge the performance of an economy such as the UK?

There are four key indicators that build up into a picture of macroeconomic performance. These are:

- **real GDP growth**

DEFINITION

Real GDP growth: a measure of the total output, expenditure or income of an economy after adjusting for changes in the price level. The growth of real GDP is the percentage change in output during a particular time period, often measured over a year

- inflation

- and the **balance of payments** (usually the **current account**).

> **DEFINITION**
>
> **Inflation:** the sustained increase in the general level of prices, measured in the UK by changes in the cost of a basket of goods and services bought by a typical household (Consumer Price Index or CPI), weighted according to the expenditure on each item in the basket

- unemployment

> **DEFINITION**
>
> **Unemployment:** arises when someone is out of work and actively seeking employment. Measured as the total number of people unemployed (the level of unemployment) or as a percentage of the workforce (the rate of unemployment). Comparisons of unemployment internationally use a standardised measure of unemployment found from a survey of the labour force. Measuring unemployment in the UK by the number of people claiming Job Seekers' Allowance (JSA) tends to underestimate the true level of unemployment

> **DEFINITIONS**
>
> **Balance of payments:** records money flows into and out of a country over a period of time
>
> **Current account** (in balance of payments): includes money flows due to trade (the trade balance – broken down to trade in goods and trade in services), transfers of interest, profit and dividends (the investment income balance) and transfers of money by governments and international organisations (the transfers balance)

Figures 9.1–3 give an overview of UK economic performance after 2000.

Figure 9.1 shows the growth in real GDP from 2000 to 2006. What this shows is a consistent period of rising real GDP, with an average growth rate of around 2.7 per cent – slightly above the UK's historical trend rate of growth. Compared to other groupings of economies, such as the EU27 and the G7 major industrialised countries, the UK's recent growth record is strong too.

The UK's recent inflation performance is shown in Figure 9.2. By historical standards, the UK's rate of inflation has been low and is below that of the other groupings. What is noticeable, though, is that the UK's lower relative rate of inflation has all but disappeared since 2004 due to the inflation rate

learning tip

A common mistake among students is to confuse the *rate of change* of a set of data on GDP or inflation with the *level* of GDP and prices. For example, a student might say that in Figure 9.1 GDP has fallen in the UK from 2000 to 2006 when they mean that the GDP is growing less quickly. Similarly, a student might say that, in Figure 9.2, prices in the EU27 fell between 2000 and 2003, when in fact the prices are simply rising less rapidly.

Sort out the difference between rates of change and levels before you receive the pre-issued stimulus material for your exam!

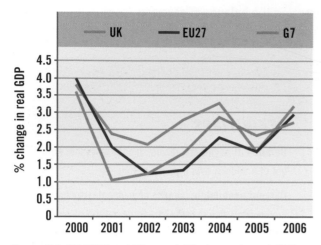

Figure 9.1 UK, EU27 and G7 growth (% change in real GDP), 2000–06

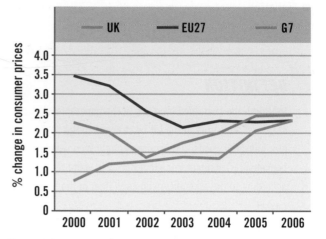

Figure 9.2 UK, EU27 and G7 inflation (% change in consumer prices), 2000–06

rising and creeping over the government's target rate of 2 per cent. Riding a slowdown in global economic activity at a time of rising inflation presents real challenges for policy makers in the UK.

Unemployment in the UK was on a downward trend until 2006, as Figure 9.3 shows, and was half the rate that it was in the early 1990s. There have been sharp falls in both long-term unemployment and in youth unemployment. The UK's record on unemployment has been one of the best in the European Union, where unemployment rates in some countries only just fell below 10 per cent of the labour force in the same period.

While the UK's deficit on the current account of the balance of payments improved from 2000 to 2003,

there has been a significant worsening of the deficit since 2003 (see Figure 9.4). The explanation lies in a significant deterioration in the UK's trade in goods deficit, which has more than offset a growing surplus in trade in services and incomes balance.

Returning to examine the performance of the UK economy in 2007, the OECD was still upbeat. It noted that the UK's GDP per capita had risen from bottom of the G7 league table to third from the top as a result of its more stable and high economic growth. Three key explanations for the UK's strong economic performance were identified by the OECD:

- a willingness to adapt and embrace globalisation

- well-managed monetary and fiscal policy

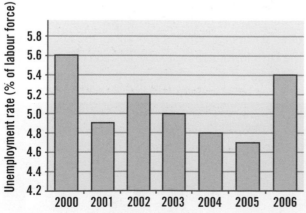

Figure 9.3 UK unemployment (% of workforce), 2000–06
Source: Labour Force Survey

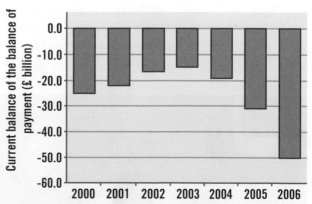

Figure 9.4 Current account of the balance of payments (£ billion), 2000–06

● the benefits of economic growth in the economies of the UK's major trading partners.

Some of these themes are picked up later in Part 3, after the economics of growth has been examined.

ACTIVITY ····⋮

Since 2004, UK economic growth has fallen and the rate of inflation has risen.

a) Using your knowledge of AD/AS analysis from the AS course, discuss the relationship you might expect to see between economic growth and the rate of inflation.

STRETCH AND CHALLENGE

b) Discuss whether a deterioration in the UK's current account of the balance of payments, such as that experienced from 2003, is a cause for concern.

ACTIVITY ····⋮

There is no single agreed measure of the standard of living – GDP per capita is commonly used but is supplemented with measures such as doctors per 1,000 of the population, or broadband connections per 1,000 households.

a) Make a list of five indicators that you think might be useful to judge a nation's standard of living.

b) Use the World Bank's Quick Query. Go to www.heinemann.co.uk/hotlinks, insert the express code 2230P, and click on 'World Bank Quick Query' to compare the standard of living in two countries of your own choosing.

c) What conclusions do you reach?

STRETCH AND CHALLENGE

d) To what extent is it meaningful to compare the standard of living of two countries?

Economic growth in the short run and long run

If a country has increased its real GDP, then there are more goods and services for people to consume. A growing economy is often taken to mean that the **standard of living** of the country's inhabitants has improved. China's economic growth record over the last ten years has been impressive, yet its growth rate does not come close to matching that of Azerbaijan, which experienced 31 per cent growth in real GDP in 2007. So economic growth rates differ markedly throughout the world, but they also vary over time for individual economies. An economy might grow rapidly in some years, slowly in others and may even slip into periods when the rate of economic growth is negative.

There are two issues that need explanation. Why do some economies grow more rapidly than others and why does the rate of economic growth fluctuate over time? The 'answers' to these questions lie in the distinction economists make between **short-run economic growth** and **long-run economic growth.**

DEFINITION

Standard of living: a measure of the material well-being of a nation and its people

DEFINITIONS

Short-run economic growth: the actual annual percentage increase in an economy's output, sometimes referred to as *actual economic growth*

Long-run economic growth: the rate at which the economy's potential output *could* grow as a result of changes in the economy's capacity to produce goods and services, sometimes referred to as *potential economic growth*

ACTIVITY ⋯⋯⋗

China's economy and society have undergone rapid change over the last twenty years, due mainly to impressive annual rates of economic growth of approaching 10 per cent in the last ten years.

A report to China's National People's Conference in 2007 stated that, in the last year:

● retail sales of consumer goods had increased by 13.7 per cent

● average incomes had increased by 7.4 per cent in rural areas and by 10.4 per cent in urban areas

● minimum wage rates had been raised

● more people in rural areas had access to old age pensions, basic medical, unemployment and maternity insurance

● methods of compensating farmers for compulsory purchase of land to build reservoirs had improved.

a) Explain one way in which economic growth in China might have contributed to an increase in the standard of living.

b) Explain one way in which economic growth in China might have contributed to a decrease in the standard of living.

STRETCH AND CHALLENGE

c) To what extent can rapid economic growth, such as that in China, be expected to raise the standard of living in countries such as the UK?

Figure 9.5 helps to explain the difference between the two types of economic growth. A shift in the production possibility curve from PPC to PPC_1 shows long-run, or potential economic growth, because the economy's maximum possible output has increased. Economic growth in the short run can occur from point *a* to point *b* or to points *c* or *d* so long as the economy's capacity to produce is being increased by long-run economic growth.

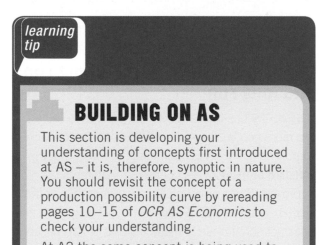

learning tip

BUILDING ON AS

This section is developing your understanding of concepts first introduced at AS – it is, therefore, synoptic in nature. You should revisit the concept of a production possibility curve by rereading pages 10–15 of *OCR AS Economics* to check your understanding.

At A2 the same concept is being used to help you to distinguish between short-run and long-run economic growth.

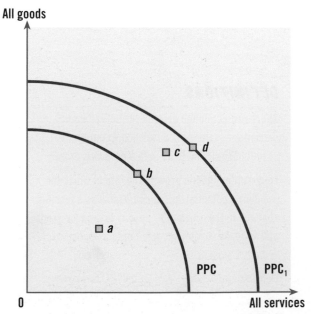

All goods

0   **All services**

Figure 9.5 Production possibility curves (PPCs), short-run and long-run economic growth

Short-run economic growth, then, comes about because more of an economy's resources are being used. For example, if fewer people are unemployed or more plant and machinery is being used to produce goods and services, the total output of the economy moves closer to its PPC. Long-run economic growth can only happen if there is an increase in either the quantity or the quality of a nation's resources of land, labour, capital or entrepreneurship, increasing the potential output of the economy.

The distinction between short- and long-run growth is important, as Table 9.1 shows. Australia and the USA both had a real GDP in 2006 that was over three times bigger than it was in 1970. In comparison, Italy and the UK had a real GDP that had increased much less – their 2006 real GDP was just over 2.2 times bigger. If real GDP is related to the standard of living, the citizens of Australia and the USA have become significantly better off relative to Italians and the British. Yet the differences in their annual growth rates were not huge. This shows that, if sustained over a long time period, small differences in growth rates matter. Mathematically, a real GDP growth rate of 1 per cent per annum results in a doubling of real GDP in 72 years. This is the so-called '72 rule' – dividing 72 by the annual rate of economic growth gives the approximate number of years in which real GDP will double. If these differences in growth rates persist, it will not be long before Australia's GDP outstrips those of Italy and the UK.

GDP at constant 1990 prices, millions of local currency			
Country	1970	2006	% increase per year
Australia	228,366	712,256	3.21
Italy	387,710	862,336	2.25
USA	3,037,076	9,276,652	3.15
UK	356,535	822,296	2.35

Table 9.1 A comparison of real GDP and growth rates
Source: UN National Accounts database

The difference between actual and potential GDP is known as the **output gap**. If actual output exceeds the economy's potential level of output, a positive output gap is said to exist. This will tend to indicate that there is very little, if any, **spare capacity** in the

ACTIVITY ⋯⋯⃗

a) Use the estimates of the output gap in Figure 9.6 to identify periods in which the UK may have suffered inflationary pressures.

STRETCH AND CHALLENGE

The statement below was made in 2006 by Mervin King, governor of the Bank of England, to the UK Treasury Select Committee:

> 'The output gap is an abstract concept that economists find useful but it does not correspond to anything you could go and measure.'

The Committee concluded that:

> 'The concept of the output gap has significant measurement problems, particularly given the growing economic importance of immigration.'

b) Discuss the usefulness of estimates of the output gap for the management of the UK economy.

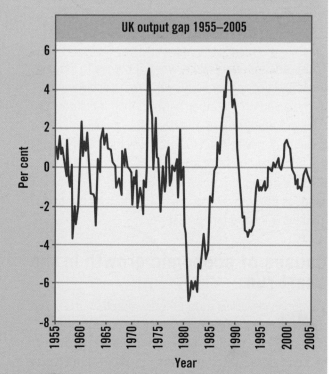

Figure 9.6 Treasury estimates of the UK output gap (%)
Source: HM Treasury, evidence to the Treasury Select Committee, July 2005

economy. The result will be that actual economic growth is likely to generate inflationary pressures. If actual output is below the economy's potential output, then the economy has clearly got spare capacity that will allow output to expand further without generating inflationary pressure. Therefore it is said that a negative output gap exists.

DEFINITIONS

Output gap: the difference between the actual and potential output of an economy. It is common practice to refer to a situation where actual output is below potential output as a *negative output gap*. A *positive output gap* occurs when, in the short term, actual output exceeds the economy's potential output

Spare capacity: exists when firms in the economy are capable of producing more output than they are actually producing

These are important ideas when it comes to judging the impact of economic growth on the economy as a whole and on the other performance indicators of inflation, employment and the current account of the balance of payments. However, it is hard to measure the potential output of an economy accurately and the output gap can only ever be an estimate. This reduces the reliability of the output gap as a measure in judging inflationary pressures.

Causes of economic growth in the short run

Economic growth is much more variable in the short run than in the long run. Over short periods of time, GDP can vary by quite a large amount as Figure 9.7 shows. Quarter by quarter, the real GDP of the Italian economy has risen and fallen by as much as 4 per cent from the end of 2004 to the middle of 2007. In comparison, economic growth in Germany (Figure 9.8) has been much more stable. The **trend rate of**

growth (shown by the dotted line) over the period is different, too. It is worth noting that over almost three years the Italian economy has grown by less than the German economy – in fact the German economy has grown nearly twice as fast, with a 6.3 per cent increase in real GDP compared to 3.5 per cent in Italy.

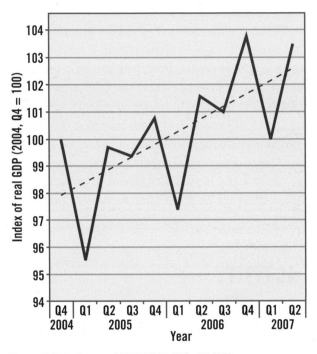

Figure 9.7 Italian real GDP, 2004 (Q4)–07 (Q2)
Source: HM Treasury, Pocket Databank, 23 January 2008

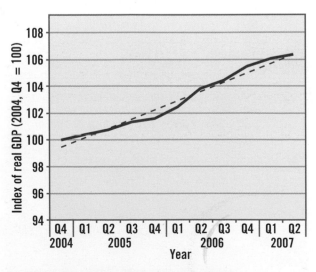

Figure 9.8 German real GDP 2004 (Q4)–07 (Q2)
Source: HM Treasury, Pocket Databank, 23 January 2008

DEFINITION

Trend rate of growth: the average rate of economic growth measured over a period of time, normally over the course of the economic cycle (from peak to peak or trough to trough). See page 207 for an explanation of the economic cycle

learning tip

Data on macroeconomic performance is often reported and presented over time. Keep a close eye on the time period over which changes are being measured. It would be possible for real GDP to rise in April 2008 compared to March 2008, but to have fallen compared to April 2007!

In general, the shorter the time period over which changes are being measured the more volatile macroeconomic performance will appear to be.

Quarterly data split the year into four three-month periods.

CHANGES IN AGGREGATE DEMAND

What causes these variations in economic growth in the short run? On pages 112–115 of *OCR AS Economics*, you learned that the equilibrium level of

learning tip

BUILDING ON AS

At AS you studied the equilibrium level of national income using aggregate demand (AD) and aggregate supply (AS) analysis. At A2 you are expected to examine the causes of economic growth in more depth, but the tools of AD and AS are obviously highly relevant. It would be worthwhile revisiting these concepts by rereading Chapter 4 of *OCR AS Economics*.

national income was determined by the interaction of aggregate demand (AD) and aggregate supply (AS). These tools of economic analysis can now be applied to the causes of economic growth in the short run.

Figure 9.9 gives a quick reminder of what happens to real GDP if there is a change in AD. An increase in aggregate demand from AD to AD_1 results in real GDP rising from Y to Y_1 – there is positive economic growth. Reductions in AD would obviously have the opposite effect. It is reasonable to conclude, therefore, that economic growth in the short run can result from changes in the factors that affect the demand side of the economy.

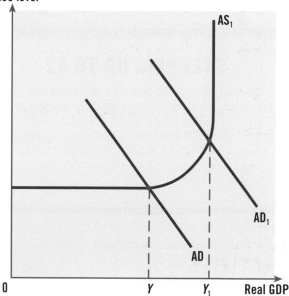

Figure 9.9 Changes in real GDP caused by changes in aggregate demand

You learned in Chapter 4 of *OCR AS Economics* that aggregate demand has five main components – consumer spending (*C*), investment expenditure by firms (*I*), general government expenditure (*G*) and net foreign/external demand made up of expenditure by foreigners on domestically produced goods (exports, *X*) minus expenditure by domestic consumers, firms and the government on foreign produced goods (imports = *M*). In short, aggregate demand can be summarised by the following equation:

$$AD = C + I + G + (X - M)$$

The first three components of the AD equation are known as domestic demand (*C* + *I* + *G*) and the last two as net external demand (X – M). Economic growth in the short run can be driven by changes in the domestic economy or by changes in the international economy.

BUILDING ON AS

The components of aggregate demand were covered in detail on pages 83–90 of the AS textbook. Don't forget to review what you learnt at AS, as well as reading the summary below.

STEPPING UP TO A2

At A2 the emphasis is on evaluating the causes of economic growth. This means making judgements about the importance of changes in the components of AD. For example, in the case of the UK economy, consumer spending makes up over two-thirds of AD.

ACTIVITY

Over the whole of 2007, UK real GDP grew by 3.1 per cent, according to figures published by the Office for National Statistics in February 2008. However, in the last three months of 2007, there was a slowdown in the growth of consumer spending. Spending by consumers grew by 0.2 per cent in the fourth quarter of 2007, having grown by 0.9 per cent in the third quarter of 2007.

The Bank of England cut interest rates to 5¼ per cent in February 2008, despite concerns about inflation. The deputy governor of the Bank of England, Rachel Lomax, warned that UK growth was likely to slow down, due to a squeeze on credit following the Northern Rock crisis.

a) Analyse two reasons why in the last three months of 2007 there had been a slowdown in consumer spending in the UK.

STRETCH AND CHALLENGE

b) Comment on whether a reduction in interest rates will always stimulate short-run economic growth.

ACTIVITY

The euro has risen dramatically against the dollar over the past two years. In 2006, its value rose by 8.2 per cent; this was followed by a further 9.1 per cent rise in 2007. In February 2008, the euro had appreciated by 12 per cent against the dollar compared with a year earlier. But there is no sign of any action to curb the euro's appreciation. Indeed, the inflation hawks at the European Central Bank may welcome the policy mix of a strong currency and relatively low interest rates.

A stronger euro should undermine the competitiveness of euro zone goods on international markets and should reduce net external demand, which has been a supporting factor for the region's growth. Yet net exports contributed 0.4 per cent to overall euro zone growth last year, despite a strong euro and slowing US growth. Part of the explanation lies in low wage growth, large productivity gains, strong growth in world demand, the price elasticity of demand for euro zone exports and the benefits of lower import prices.

Source: adapted from 'Don't Expect a Rate Cut', Natascha Gewaltig, Spiegel Online International

a) Explain why a stronger euro should reduce short-run economic growth in the euro zone.

b) Analyse two reasons why the euro zone's net exports have risen despite the euro's appreciation against the dollar.

STRETCH AND CHALLENGE

c) The exchange rate of the Singapore dollar has been deliberately managed by the Monetary Authority of Singapore to appreciate over time. On some measures it has appreciated by over 90 per cent in 20 years. Discuss the case for such a policy towards the exchange rate.

CHANGES IN SHORT-RUN AGGREGATE SUPPLY

You learned in pages 114–115 of *OCR AS Economics*, that aggregate supply refers to the relationship between the total output of the economy and the general or average level of prices, and that this relationship is a positive one. As the general price level increases, firms respond by raising production. The aggregate supply curve is, therefore, upward sloping. **Short-run aggregate supply** simply refers to the idea that there will be a time period in which labour costs and other factor input costs do not or cannot respond to changes in the macroeconomy. So, wage rates might not rise immediately following an increase in labour demand and the existing workforce may be used more intensively, by working overtime. The short-run aggregate supply curve is drawn as a simple upward-sloping line, as in Figure 9.10.

Changes in the costs of production, then, cause the short-run aggregate supply (SRAS) curve to shift. Rising costs shift the SRAS curve to the left and falling costs shift it to the right. Changes in the costs of production arise from changes in:

● *labour costs*. Labour costs can change for a number of reasons, but the most obvious cause is a change in wages rates. Lower wage rates reduce the cost of production for firms, allowing them to reduce

DEFINITION

Short-run aggregate supply: shows the level of production for the economy at a given price level, assuming labour costs and other factor input costs are unchanged

prices. This will result in a rightward shift of the SRAS curve (to *SRAS₁* in Figure 9.10), increasing real GDP to Y_1.

● *other input prices*. A term that covers a wide range of factors, including raw material prices, the price of components and the price of plant and machinery. If these prices fall, firms will experience lower costs of production and will be able to lower prices. The SRAS curve again shifts right and real GDP increases.

● *taxes and regulation*. Changes in the taxation or regulation of business will have an impact on business costs and, therefore, shift the SRAS curve. Most regulation increases business costs rather than reducing them, so it is likely that the SRAS curve shifts left and real GDP is reduced.

The economic cycle

Real GDP, then, can rise or fall due to changes in AD and SRAS. Economists have observed that the rises and falls of real GDP tend to follow a regular pattern or cycle. This has become known as the **economic cycle**.

DEFINITION

Economic cycle: fluctuations in the level of economic activity as measured by GDP. Typically, there are four stages in the cycle: recession, recovery, boom and slowdown

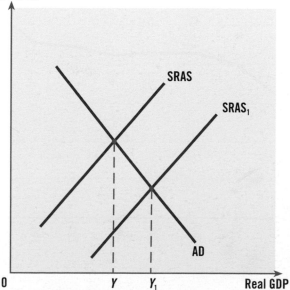

Figure 9.10 The impact of a change in SRAS on real GDP

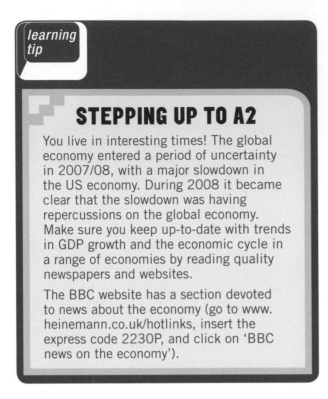

learning tip

STEPPING UP TO A2

You live in interesting times! The global economy entered a period of uncertainty in 2007/08, with a major slowdown in the US economy. During 2008 it became clear that the slowdown was having repercussions on the global economy. Make sure you keep up-to-date with trends in GDP growth and the economic cycle in a range of economies by reading quality newspapers and websites.

The BBC website has a section devoted to news about the economy (go to www. heinemann.co.uk/hotlinks, insert the express code 2230P, and click on 'BBC news on the economy').

Figure 9.11 shows the economic cycle in Germany from 1992 to 2006. The dotted line represents what would have happened to real GDP had the German

economy grown by 1¾ per cent per annum over the period. This could be used as an estimate of the potential output of the Germany economy – it represents a rate of economic growth above the trend growth rate over the period. There are two years in which the rate of economic growth is negative – 1993 and 2003. It is clear that the consequence of this is that actual output falls below potential output. More significantly, it will take a period of economic growth higher than the potential rate of growth for the economy to return to its previous growth path.

Some economists have argued that economic instability such as this can itself influence the rate at which the economy grows. Their argument is rooted in the hysteresis effect of unemployment you learnt about on page 124 of the AS textbook. Long periods of unemployment lead to the deskilling of the workforce and a consequent loss of **human capital**. When the economy returns to a period of positive economic growth, it does so at a slower rate of economic growth as there is a loss of productivity and it becomes more difficult to raise output. The result is that the economy's trend rate of economic growth

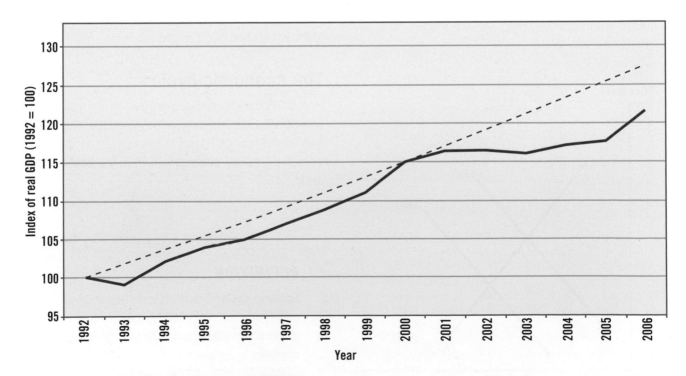

Figure 9.11 The economic cycle in Germany, 1992–2006
Source: HM Treasury, Pocket Databank, 23 January 2008

may be reduced. There is some, albeit limited, evidence in Figure 9.11 that the German economy may have suffered from this effect since 2003.

Economists divide the economic cycle into four stages. Figure 9.12 represents the economic cycle and the four stages in a stylised way. The four stages are:

● *the recovery*, when economic growth becomes positive after a recession

● *the boom*, when the rate of economic growth exceeds the rate of growth of potential GDP so that the output gap is narrowed

● *the slowdown*, when the rate of economic growth begins to fall and approach zero

● *the recession*, when the rate of economic growth becomes negative and real GDP actually falls.

In reality, the economic cycle is not as regular as Figure 9.12 suggests. This is because each of the stages will vary in length and severity. For example, some recessions can be short-lived and output may not fall by a significant amount. At other times, the recession can be very prolonged and deep. It remains to be seen whether the 2008 economic slowdown in the USA will become a recession and, if so, how long this period of negative economic growth might last. The actions of the Federal Reserve Board to try to promote greater economic stability and economic growth in 2008 suggest that the concerns about a prolonged and severe recession are very real among economic policy makers.

It is not surprising, therefore, that economists have tried to understand and analyse the causes of the economic cycle. Different economists have offered different explanations of the economic cycle, which emphasise the importance of different determinants of economic growth. Broadly there are three explanations offered as to the causes of the business cycle:

● the *multiplier* and *accelerator* effects and their interaction

● the role of stocks (inventories)

● monetary explanations of the economic cycle.

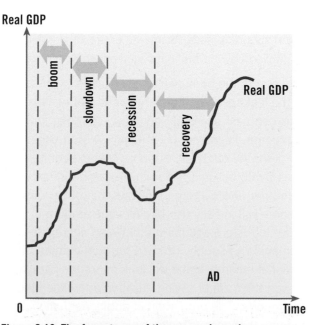

Figure 9.12 The four stages of the economic cycle

The multiplier, the accelerator and their interaction

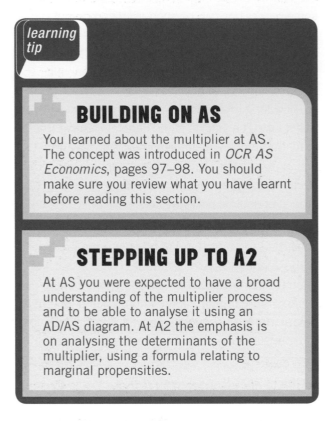

learning tip

BUILDING ON AS

You learned about the multiplier at AS. The concept was introduced in *OCR AS Economics*, pages 97–98. You should make sure you review what you have learnt before reading this section.

STEPPING UP TO A2

At AS you were expected to have a broad understanding of the multiplier process and to be able to analyse it using an AD/AS diagram. At A2 the emphasis is on analysing the determinants of the multiplier, using a formula relating to marginal propensities.

The multiplier effect is the process by which any change in a component of aggregate demand results in a greater final change in real GDP. The idea that one person's spending becomes another person's income captures the essence of the concept. So, when spending rises, its impact on national income is multiplied beyond the initial increase in spending.

The size of the multiplier is determined by the size of the leakages from the circular flow of income. This can best be visualised using a circular flow of income diagram such as Figure 4.9 on page 96 of the AS textbook. Suppose that expenditure rises by £5 billion. Tracing this expenditure around a circular flow diagram, it follows that output and income will initially rise by the same amount in order to restore equilibrium between aggregate demand and supply. Of this £5 billion increase in national income, some will leak out of the circular flow in the form of saving, taxation and expenditure on imports. The proportion of additional national income that goes to leakages is known as the

marginal propensity to withdraw (MPW) and is made up of:

- the **marginal propensity to save** (MPS)
- the **marginal propensity to tax** (MPT)
- the **marginal propensity to import** (MPM).

If half of any increase in income leaks out of the circular flow in saving, taxation and import expenditure, half must be spent on domestically produced goods and services and output and incomes will rise by a further £2.5 billion. Half of this next rise in output and income will leak out of the circular flow and a further £1.25 billion will be spent on goods and services produced domestically. At this point, you can see that national output and income has risen by £8.75 billion (the initial £5 billion + £2.5 billion in the second round of expenditure + £1.25 billion). The multiplier process will continue until national output and income have risen by a total of £10 billion. The initial increase in expenditure has been multiplied by a factor of two, which is the value of the multiplier. This can be calculated using the formula:

$$k \text{ (the multiplier)} = \frac{1}{\text{marginal propensity to withdraw (MPW)}}$$

DEFINITIONS

Marginal propensity to save (MPS): the proportion of additional national income that is saved $= \frac{\Delta s}{\Delta Y}$, where s is savings, Y is national income and Δ is the change in s or Y

Marginal propensity to tax (MPT): the proportion of additional national income that is taxed $= \frac{\Delta t}{\Delta Y}$, where t is taxation

Marginal propensity to import (MPM): the proportion of additional national income that is spent on imports $= \frac{\Delta m}{\Delta Y}$, where m is imports

$$= \frac{1}{\text{MPS} + \text{MPT} + \text{MPM}}$$

Since half of any increase in national income leaks out of the circular flow, the MPW is 0.5.

So, k (the multiplier) $= \frac{1}{0.5} = 2$.

It follows that any change in expenditure in the national economy will cause national income to be amplified (or multiplied). This concept goes some way to explain the upswings and downswings of the business cycle. But it leaves open the question as to what causes expenditure to change in the first place.

This is where the concept of the **accelerator** comes into play. The accelerator is a theory of investment that relates the total level of investment to the rate of change of national income. Investment is needed for two purposes. First, to replace the capital stock that is wearing out, and second, to provide new capital stock to give additional productive capacity to meet rising demand. When the economy is in a recession, there is clearly no need for firms to undertake investment to raise productive capacity – demand for output is falling, after all. There may be no need for investment to replace worn-out machinery, either, if demand has fallen significantly. Hence, there is likely to be little if any investment taking place in the economy. In times of rising national income, on the other hand, firms will require additional capacity and investment will rise. This increase may be larger in percentage terms than the increase in national income. The key point is that investment depends on the *rate of change of national income* and not on its level. As a result, investment will tend to be a volatile component of aggregate demand. Investment can, for example, fall when the rate of growth of the economy slows down and this, of itself, will tend to lower domestic demand.

DEFINITION

Accelerator: the theory of investment that states that the level of investment depends on the rate of change of national income

---

This last point illustrates the way in which the multiplier and the accelerator may interact to generate periods in which real GDP rises more and more rapidly (the boom phase of the economic cycle) and situations in which a slowdown in economic growth becomes a period of falling real GDP (the recession phase of the economic cycle). The links in the chain are summarised in Figure 9.13.

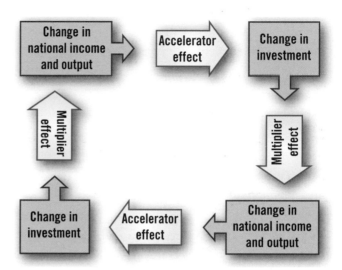

Figure 9.13 The interaction of the multiplier and accelerator

Once actual output approaches the economy's potential output, the economy reaches its 'ceiling' and economic growth must slow down. Similarly, there must be a 'floor' to economic activity as firms must invest a minimum amount to replace worn-out or obsolete capital and there is a minimum level of consumption for households. These ceilings and floors represent the turning points in the economic cycle – booms and recessions eventually come to an end.

It is important to note that the interaction of the multiplier and the accelerator is a theoretical explanation of the determinants of the economic cycle. In practice, the economy never works in the mechanical way that economic theory predicts. The economic cycle is far from predictable and the fluctuations in economic activity not as regular as Figure 9.12 would suggest. The accelerator is not a description of economic reality. There are a number of limitations to the theory and to the interaction of the accelerator and the multiplier as an explanation of the economic cycle. These limitations include:

- If firms have spare capacity, rising demand can be met without rising investment.

- The theory of the accelerator ignores the crucial role that confidence and expectations play in investment decisions – firms will not respond immediately to rising demand by raising investment if they are uncertain about whether rising demand will be sustained in the future.

- Firms can exercise choice over investment to replace machinery that is wearing out and they may delay such investment.

- Investment decisions are planned well in advance of changes in economic activity and can be difficult to halt or postpone.

- The multiplier effect of changes in investment may be small, so that although investment is volatile, it does not have a large impact on aggregate demand and, therefore, on economic growth.

- External or random shocks to the economy can be just as important a cause of the economic cycle as the relationship between the accelerator and the multiplier.

- Fiscal and monetary policy changes may help to smooth out the economic cycle and policy makers may be able to over-ride the accelerator and multiplier effects.

These limitations focus mainly on the size of the accelerator and multiplier effects and the extent to which they are predictable. The effects, however, are still important in determining the course of the economic cycle. Changes in demand in the economy do influence firms' investment decisions and the evidence points to the fact that investment is a very variable component of aggregate demand. The interaction of the multiplier and the accelerator is not the only determinant of the economic cycle, however.

OTHER EXPLANATIONS OF THE ECONOMIC CYCLE

Another plausible explanation of the economic cycle concerns the behaviour of **stocks**. With time lags in production, it is not always possible for firms to immediately increase output in order to meet higher demand. As a result, firms hold

> ### DEFINITION
> **Stocks:** the amount of finished goods that firms hold in order to be able to satisfy increases in demand

stocks of finished and semi-finished goods. As with investment, the amount of stocks held by firms tends to fluctuate over the course of the economic cycle and this fluctuation contributes to the cycle itself.

When the economy is recovering from a recession, the level of confidence of firms is fragile. Firms will be reluctant to take on new workers or to increase investment when they are unsure about whether demand will continue to rise in the future. As a result, they will tend to sell their stocks of finished goods instead of producing new output. The recovery phase of the economic cycle will see a rise in output that is less than the rise in demand, and the output growth will, therefore, be slow. But the stock of finished goods is limited. As demand continues to rise, the confidence of firms will grow and they will start to build up their stock levels from current production. This will boost output and create additional demand in the economy through the multiplier effect. During this time the growth of output will exceed the growth of demand as firms re-stock. Once stock levels have been rebuilt, output growth will slow down to match the growth in demand. This slowdown in output growth will bring about the end of the growth phase of the economic cycle in line with the multiplier–accelerator theory above. Stock levels will now start to increase as demand falls. Eventually, firms will cut back production to stop stock levels growing, the economy will enter the recession phase of the economic cycle and firms will run down their stocks of finished goods. The cycle will start all over again once firms cannot satisfy demand from their dwindling stocks.

Both theories of the economic cycle suggest that the pattern of rising and falling real GDP is inbuilt into the economic system. The economic cycle occurs because of regular fluctuations in aggregate demand. In a very important way, this is the result of the decisions of consumers and firms based on their expectations of the future. Economists and policy makers attempt to measure these expectations, using surveys of consumer and business confidence, to try to predict the next turning point in the economic cycle.

What the theories don't explain is why for some economies the economic cycle is more severe than for others, or why some economies like the UK have appeared to enter a phase of greater economic stability where the cycle of boom and recession is less evident than it has been in the past. This issue of economic stability is examined later on in this unit.

Causes of economic growth in the long run
CHANGES IN LONG-RUN AGGREGATE SUPPLY
Economic growth in the long run has nothing to do with changes in aggregate demand and everything to do with changes in aggregate supply. To distinguish short-run economic growth from economic growth in the long run, economists use the concept of the **long-run aggregate supply curve.**

> **DEFINITION**
>
> **Long-run aggregate supply (LRAS) curve:** the relationship between total supply and the price level in the long run. The LRAS curve represents the maximum possible output for the whole economy – its potential output

There is some disagreement among economists about how best to represent LRAS. This disagreement centres on the shape of the LRAS as Figure 9.14 shows.

Classical economists believe markets clear in the long run, with prices adjusting to ensure that demand equals supply. They argue that if there is unemployment in the labour market, wages will fall so that the excess supply of labour is

> **DEFINITION**
>
> **Classical economists:** economists who believe that markets will 'clear', that prices and quantities adjust to changes in the forces of supply and demand so that the economy produces its potential output in the long run

eliminated. All those who are willing to work at the equilibrium wage rate will be employed. The same is true for the markets for the other factors of production, land and capital. The output of the economy in the long run equals the maximum potential output, as all the factors of production will be fully employed. The economy's LRAS curve is, therefore, vertical, according to this group of economists.

Keynesian economists believe that there is no mechanism that guarantees that the maximum potential output will be supplied in the long run. They take this view because of a belief that, in practice, markets fail. For example, they would say that labour market failure will mean that unemployment is likely to persist in the long run, due to wages not being flexible (so-called 'sticky wages'), the existence of minimum wage legislation, trade unions, the system of welfare benefits for the unemployed and the segmentation of labour markets through geographical and occupational immobility of labour. The economy's long-run equilibrium could be at any level of real GDP, and that full employment of the factors of production is a very special case. Keynesian economists believe that there are three sections of the LRAS curve. First, long-run aggregate supply is perfectly elastic when there is a deep recession as output can be increased without wages and prices increasing. Beyond this, LRAS is upward-sloping as firms will have to pay higher wages to recruit more labour. Finally, the LRAS curve is vertical when all factors of production, including labour, are fully employed.

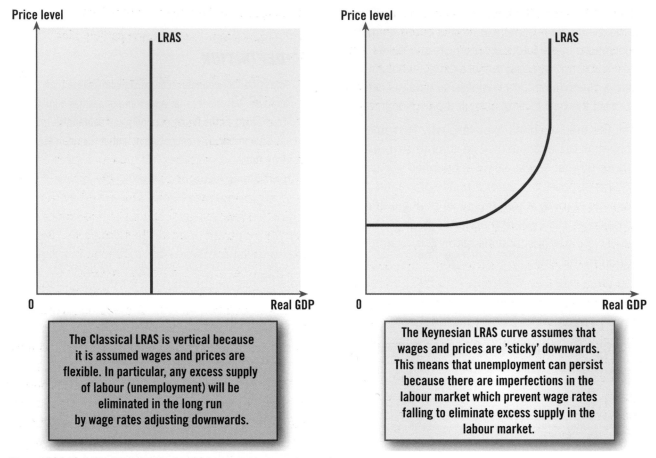

The Classical LRAS is vertical because it is assumed wages and prices are flexible. In particular, any excess supply of labour (unemployment) will be eliminated in the long run by wage rates adjusting downwards.

The Keynesian LRAS curve assumes that wages and prices are 'sticky' downwards. This means that unemployment can persist because there are imperfections in the labour market which prevent wage rates falling to eliminate excess supply in the labour market.

Figure 9.14 The Classical and Keynesian long-run aggregate supply curves

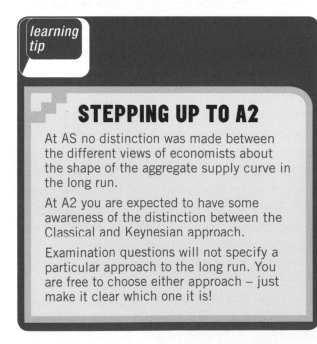

learning tip

STEPPING UP TO A2

At AS no distinction was made between the different views of economists about the shape of the aggregate supply curve in the long run.

At A2 you are expected to have some awareness of the distinction between the Classical and Keynesian approach.

Examination questions will not specify a particular approach to the long run. You are free to choose either approach – just make it clear which one it is!

DEFINITION

Keynesian economists: economists who believe that market failures will result in price and quantity rigidities such that the economy's equilibrium output in the long run may be less than its potential output

is determined by both the quantity and quality of the factors of production, economic growth is caused by increases in both the quantity and the quality of land, labour and capital. Sources of these improvements in quantity and quality are examined in the sections that follow.

Economists are agreed that long-run economic growth results in a shift to the right in the LRAS curve. If there is an expansion in the labour force, for example, it will be possible for the economy to produce a higher level of potential output.

Economic growth in the long run is caused by factors that increase the potential output of the economy. Since the potential output of the economy

Figure 9.15 shows the impact of economic growth in the long run on both the Classical and Keynesian LRAS curve. The Classical LRAS and the Keynesian LRAS both shift right. In both cases, the shift in LRAS represents the idea that the economy is able to produce a higher level of output at any given level of prices.

INCREASES IN THE QUANTITY AND QUALITY OF RESOURCES

Long-run economic growth, then, is all about increasing the economy's capacity to supply goods and services. Right at the start of your study of economics, you came across the basic economic problem of scarcity (Chapter 1 of *OCR AS Economics*). The limit to output in the long run is related to the quantity and quality of the four factors of production: land, labour, capital and entrepreneurship. Long-run economic growth is generated by increasing the quantity and the quality of these factors of production. Some of the ways of achieving these increases are examined below.

The quantity of the labour force

Increasing the size of the **labour force** can be achieved in a number of ways:

- increases in the size of the population
- increases in the **labour force participation rate**
- increases in the flow of workers into an economy (immigration).

The first of these happens when the birth rate exceeds the death rate. This not only results in a larger labour force, but also increases the proportion of younger people in the labour force. This might increase geographical and labour mobility. However, as a source of economic growth, population growth has problems. One of these is that for output per person to increase, the rate of economic growth generated by population growth needs to be bigger than the rate of population growth. There is no guarantee that this will happen. In addition, the birth rate is influenced by social and cultural factors and may be difficult to influence, whereas the death rate falls as the economy gets richer through economic growth. Economic growth itself is likely to reduce population growth and to cause an ageing of the population. Population growth is unlikely to be an important contributor to economic growth. Indeed, economists have found little relationship between population growth rates and growth of GDP per capita.

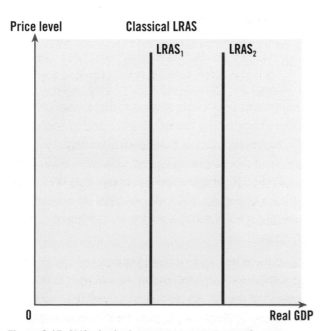
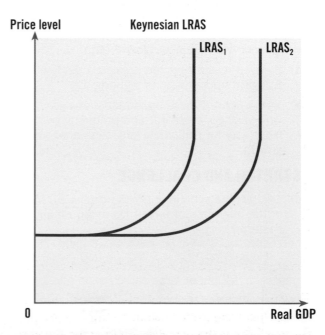

Figure 9.15 Shifts in the long-run aggregate supply curve

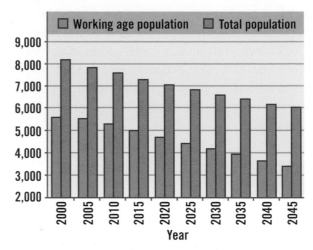

Figure 9.16 Population projections (thousands) for Bulgaria
Adapted from: Quintanilla, R. *et al.* (2005) *Bulgaria: The Road to Successful EU Integration – The Policy Agenda,* World Bank, Washington, DC.

ACTIVITY

Bulgaria and Romania's full membership of the European Union (EU) from the beginning of 2007 brought the total number of member states of the EU to 27. This followed a major enlargement of the EU in 2004.

Prior to its membership of the EU, Bulgaria had made impressive progress towards long-term stability and sustained growth. However, Bulgaria is significantly poorer than the central and eastern European economies that joined the EU in 2004. To narrow the income gap and facilitate convergence with the rest of the EU, Bulgaria needed to increase employment and productivity. Raising investment and productivity is necessary for long-term economic growth. This is particularly critical given the long-term population projections for the country shown in Figure 9.16. As Bulgaria approached EU accession, it had the opportunity to act on these challenges and set the economy on a higher growth path.

a) Suggest reasons for the projected decline in Bulgaria's population of working age.

b) In the light of these projections, analyse why raising investment and productivity is necessary for Bulgaria's long-term economic growth.

STRETCH AND CHALLENGE

c) Discuss the economic effects on the EU15 of the migration of labour from central and eastern Europe.

Increases in the labour force participation rate are a much more important cause of economic growth, as the experience of the USA and Europe shows. In America and Europe, the biggest growth in labour force participation has come from an increase in the number of women entering the workforce. Changes to the tax and benefit system in the UK have also encouraged people to seek work by making more and more welfare benefits (such as the Child Tax Credit and the Working Families Tax Credit) dependent on employment. This has been a deliberate and high-profile strategy of the New Labour government since 1997 – making work pay. Ireland's rapid economic growth over the last twenty years has, in part, been possible because of a significant increase in labour force participation – employment of those aged 15–64 increased by 52 per cent between 1993 and 2000.

Faced with an ageing population, many European governments are looking at ways to discourage older workers from leaving the labour force and to encourage firms to employ older workers and discourage them from discriminating against older workers in recruitment. Raising the retirement age may be politically unpopular but it may become an economic necessity in Europe in the not too distant future.

Immigration increases the size of an economy's labour force but also increases the size of the population. Unless immigration contributes to an increase in output per worker (productivity) there might be little benefit in terms of GDP per person, even though GDP rises. Recent enlargements of the EU have increased the size of the labour force for those economies, like the UK and Ireland, that have not restricted the free movement of labour from central and eastern Europe. Whether this will be a source of economic growth in the long run depends on whether the flow of immigrant workers is permanent or temporary. If immigrant workers stay on a temporary basis, there may be no long-term increase in the productive capacity of the economies to which such workers migrate.

The quality of the labour force

Increases in the quality of the labour force are probably more important for economic growth in the long run than the size of the labour force. The quality of the labour force is closely linked with productivity. Increasing output per person employed allows the capacity of the economy to produce output to grow.

The labour force can be made more productive through education and training. This raises workers' human capital by equipping people with more skills and technical knowledge. Human capital can be gained through formal education, by providing workers with training on the job or by giving people access to opportunities to retrain for new jobs. Human capital is important because it enables workers to cope with the demands of employment (from relatively low level skills such as numeracy and literacy, through intermediate skills required for particular jobs to highly technical skills and knowledge). Of increasing importance is the ability of the labour force to be flexible in the tasks that they can do (functional flexibility) and being able to adapt

to changes in the labour market by acquiring skills for new jobs (occupational flexibility).

The challenge for many economies is to equip their labour force with the skills needed for a knowledge-based economy. As economies have experienced economic growth, the balance of production has changed. The primary and secondary sectors have shrunk relative to the tertiary sector. Within the secondary sector, output and employment is growing most rapidly in high-technology industries such as computers, electronics and aerospace. A growing part of the tertiary sector in affluent economies is based on the production, distribution and use of knowledge and information. The employees most in demand no longer produce physical products, but provide information services – marketing specialists, business, economics and IT consultants and technicians. Growth industries require a labour force with increased human capital.

The problem for policy makers is how this increased human capital can be delivered. First, there is the cost of education and training, which can be very high. Second, there is the issue of whether this should be provided by the government or by the market – education and training involve positive externalities (benefits to the wider economy as well as individuals and firms) and may be under-provided by the market. Third, there is the question of what kind of education and training should be provided. Figure 9.17 suggests that the UK's skills problems lie in too high a proportion of the labour force with low level qualifications and too few with intermediate qualifications, relative to its major competitors. The

ACTIVITY ····⫶

Systems of support for the unemployed differ markedly in different economies. At one extreme, the unemployed in the USA receive benefits that are very low in comparison to average earnings. Some economists believe that such systems of support discourage the unemployed from remaining on benefits and encourage them to seek work.

In comparison, unemployment benefit is much more generous relative to average earnings in countries such as Germany and France. The same

economists would argue that this contributes to high unemployment and a labour market that adapts slowly to economic change.

a) What impact might the generous unemployment benefits available in Germany and France have on these economies' long-run aggregate supply curve?

b) Would you expect these economies to have higher or lower rates of economic growth compared to the UK and the USA? Explain your answer.

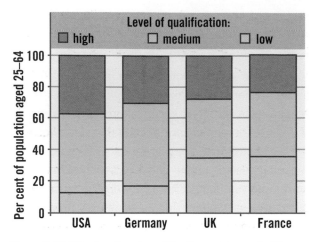

Figure 9.17 UK educational qualifications compared with those of its major competitors

Source: *Productivity in the UK 6*, HM Treasury, March 2006

UK compares favourably with Germany and France in terms of the percentage of the labour force with the highest qualifications (such as university degrees). Fourth, there is the issue of who should pay for education and training – the government, firms or individuals. These tensions can be seen in recent UK education policy, which has attempted to shift the financial burden of higher education to students in the form of tuition fees.

Increasing the quality of the labour force through investment in human capital, therefore, is important for economic growth in the long run but it is not clear what should be provided, how it should be provided and for whom. There are also time lags to consider. The benefits of measures to increase the quality of the labour force may take some time to materialise, but the costs are borne immediately. This may cause an under-investment in human capital and limit economic growth in the long run.

The quantity and quality of the capital stock

The potential output of an economy depends on the quantity and quality of the plant, equipment and machinery used to produce output – its capital stock. Increasing the quantity of the capital stock will enable an economy to produce more output. This requires investment in various forms of capital. But it is not just the amount of investment that determines the potential output of the economy. The quality of investment matters

too. This is determined by the rate of technological advance. The productivity of investment is measured by the economy's **capital output ratio**. This is the amount of capital needed to generate each unit of output. Technological advance increases the productivity of investment because it results in less capital being required to produce each unit of output.

These ideas can be formalised in a model of economic growth known as the Harrod–Domar model. The model makes a number of simplifying assumptions:

saving (S) is a fixed proportion (s) of national income (Y)

$\quad S = sY$ [assumption 1]

investment (I) is the change in the capital stock (ΔK)

$\quad I = \Delta K$ [assumption 2]

in an economy with no trade and no government, national income equilibrium occurs when withdrawals equal injections

$\quad S = I$ [assumption 3]

It follows from these three assumptions that

$\quad sY$ (savings) $= \Delta K$ (investment) [equation 1]

Rearranging this equation gives an equation for the equilibrium level of national income (Y)

$\quad Y = \dfrac{\Delta K}{s}$ [equation 2]

If the capital output ratio (k) is the amount of additional capital (ΔK) required to produce an additional unit of output (ΔY), then it follows that

$\quad k = \dfrac{\Delta K}{\Delta Y}$ [equation 3]

which, rearranged, gives an equation for the growth of national output

$\quad \Delta Y = \dfrac{\Delta K}{k}$ [equation 4]

> **DEFINITION**
>
> **Capital output ratio:** the amount of capital needed to generate each unit of output

The rate of economic growth can be written as

$$\frac{\Delta Y}{Y} \qquad \text{[equation 5]}$$

Substituting equations 4 and 2 into 5 gives

$$\frac{\Delta Y}{Y} = \frac{\Delta K / k}{\Delta K / s} \qquad \text{[equation 6]}$$

which simplified gives an equation for the rate of economic growth

$$\frac{\Delta Y}{Y} = \frac{s}{k} \qquad \text{[equation 7]}$$

The maths is nothing more than a tool to analyse the determinants of economic growth in the long run. The conclusion is the important point to remember (equation 7). This says that, in order to increase economic growth in the long run, there must be either more savings (s) to fund higher levels of investment or technological advance to increase the productivity of investment and lower the capital output ratio (k).

For many economies the low level of domestic savings constrains economic growth in the long run. This is especially true for some developing economies (see Chapter 11). However, economies can grow faster than the Harrod–Domar model would suggest if they can 'plug' the savings gap. Foreign multinational investment, for example, breaks the link between domestic savings and investment by allowing a higher level of investment than domestic savings would imply is possible. Also,

in an increasingly global economy (see Chapter 12) domestic firms can access the capital they require for investment outside their own economy. So, the link between savings and economic growth in the long run is not as strong as the Harrod–Domar model predicts.

Modern growth theory (so-called endogenous growth theory) stresses the importance of the second of the two determinants of growth in the Harrod–Domar model of growth. The theory focuses on knowledge and innovation as two of the key drivers of technological change. Policies that are often recommended to increase the growth of knowledge and innovation include:

● government subsidy of research and development by firms, for example, into nano-technology in the USA

● promoting, supporting and funding science education in schools and scientific research at universities

● increasing the supply of highly skilled workers through immigration (for example, Germany encourages Indian software engineers to enter the country)

● tax incentives to encourage innovation and to reward those who innovate.

It is difficult, however, to quantify the benefits of such policy measures as, if they work, they do so only in the long run.

ACTIVITY ····

The ratio of capital to annual output for the US economy is roughly 2.8:1

In a typical developing economy, such as Kenya, the ratio is approximately 6.8:1

a) Calculate the proportion of national income which needs to be devoted to saving in order for the US and Kenyan economies to achieve economic growth of 2.5 per cent per annum.

b) Due to low levels of income in developing economies, the savings rate tends to be low. Are developing economies, such as Kenya, doomed to low rates of economic growth in the long run? Explain your answer.

learning tip

Be careful not to fall into the trap of thinking that the solution to raising economic growth in the long run is for the government to 'spend more and do more'. Try to think of the role of the government in terms of what you learnt at AS about market failure. Governments have two roles:

● to make markets work better

● to intervene where markets would otherwise fail.

Look back over your notes on market failure and government intervention and reread Chapter 3 of *OCR AS Economics* (pages 55–73).

ECONOMICS IN CONTEXT

PRODUCTIVITY

Changes in the global economy, commonly referred to as globalisation, are allowing production to take place across the world and reducing the barriers to trade. Developed countries are increasingly outsourcing labour-intensive manufacturing and assembly to low-cost economies, and focusing on knowledge-based activities, such as research and development and design. This explains the rise of so-called emerging economies, such as China and India, which between them are responsible for almost 50 per cent of the growth in world output from 2001 to 2004 and are predicted to be producing over 25 per cent of world output by 2015. The challenge for developed economies, such as the UK, is to raise productivity so that they can remain competitive and benefit from globalisation.

The output of an economy in the long run is determined by two things: the amount of resources it has and the efficiency with which it uses them.

Productivity is a measure of how well an economy uses its given resources and is the key determinant of living standards in the long run. There are many different measures of productivity, but the most commonly used measures relate to the productivity of labour – output per worker and output per hour worked. Other measures such as total factor productivity attempt to take into account the productivity of capital, although this is difficult to estimate.

On any measure of productivity there is a productivity gap between the UK and its main competitors in the global economy, as shown in Figure 9.18. Although the UK has narrowed the gap, its main competitors are 30–40 per cent more productive in their use of labour measured by output per worker, and 12–16 per cent more productive measured by output per hour worked.

The present UK government's response to this productivity gap is to focus economic policy on what it calls the 'five drivers' of productivity growth:

- competition
- innovation and technological progress

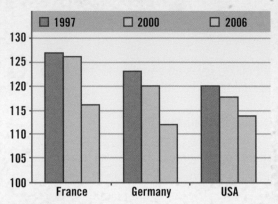

Figure 9.18 Relative output per hour worked (UK = 100)
Source: Productivity in the UK 7, HM Treasury, November 2007

- investment in physical capital
- skills of the labour force
- enterprise.

The government sees its roles as follows:

- to encourage competition through active competition policy
- to fund basic scientific research that involves positive externalities and to give incentives to the private sector to innovate
- to fund or provide investment in the UK's infrastructure and to create a stable macroeconomic environment to encourage investment
- to improve educational standards in order to reduce the high percentage of the UK working population with low skills (including basic literacy and numeracy), to encourage training at the firm level
- to promote enterprise through creating institutions that support business and by correcting market failure in the provision of finance to new businesses.

ACTIVITY ····⋗

a) Identify a range of market failures that would justify government intervention to raise the UK's productivity.

b) In each case, suggest a policy the government might use to raise productivity and show how this would reduce the market failure you have identified.

Consequences of economic growth

The concepts introduced in this chapter are important in considering the consequences of economic growth for the key performance indicators of inflation, employment and unemployment and the balance of payments. If governments are to pursue economic growth as a policy objective, they need to be aware of any conflicts it may have with other objectives. This is so that economic growth can be managed to maximise its benefits relative to its costs. In addition, the consequences of economic growth for the government's fiscal position should be examined. There are, unfortunately, no hard and fast 'laws' here – much depends on the nature of economic growth and other factors that affect the key performance indicators.

GROWTH AND INFLATION

The consequences of economic growth for inflation depend very much on the nature of economic growth. China's economic growth has averaged around 9.6 per cent over the last two decades, yet until 2007 its inflation rate remained below 3 per cent. In 2008, the US growth rate began to decline, yet its inflation rate increased. To understand why seemingly contradictory relationships between economic growth and inflation exist in the global economy, you need to bring together the macroeconomic concepts you have studied at AS and A2.

learning tip

BUILDING ON AS

You came across the key performance indicators at AS. Reviewing your understanding of these indicators would be useful before you read this section. Make a list of the key influences on each of the performance indicators or create a mind map summary of the topic using pages 105–8 of *OCR AS Economics*. In your list or mind map, it would be worthwhile to include the causes of inflation, unemployment and current account deficits and surpluses using pages 118–22 of the textbook.

Economic growth will be a cause of higher rates of inflation, if growth is generated by increases in aggregate demand (AD) that are not matched by increases in aggregate supply. At the simplest level, a rise in aggregate demand causes a movement up the long-run aggregate supply curve, causing the price level to increase (to P_1 as in Figure 9.19).

The closer the economy comes to its maximum capacity, the more that higher AD causes prices to rise. This is because shortages of inputs push up production costs, increasing numbers of firms have little or no spare capacity to meet demand and labour shortages result in higher wage bills for firms. The key to understanding these inflationary pressures of rising demand is the size of the output gap. As the gap between actual and potential output narrows, so inflationary pressures build up in the economy. It is possible to avoid this consequence by increasing the economy's productive capacity. If the aggregate supply curve can be shifted to the right (to $LRAS_1$), AD can rise without inflationary pressures building up (the price level stays at P). To avoid the inflationary pressures of economic growth, it is necessary to make sure that the growth in actual output is sustainable. So, non-inflationary economic growth is the goal of macroeconomic policy.

China's economic growth was, until recently, sustainable because of the very high growth in investment in physical capital to increase productive capacity. The concern in 2008, expressed by China's premier, Wen Jiabao, was that the balance

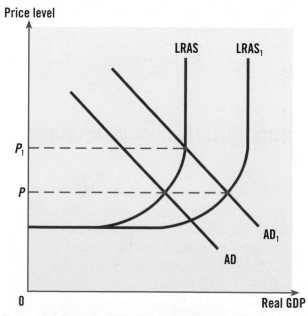

Figure 9.19 Non-inflationary economic growth

of aggregate demand had shifted towards consumption and away from investment. The rate of growth of potential output had slowed, while the growth of actual output had accelerated and inflationary pressures had built up. In 2007, China's official rate of inflation more than trebled and many economists were expecting it to increase to over 6 per cent in 2008.

ACTIVITY ···⋮›

Chinese inflation reached an 11-year high of 7.1 per cent in January 2008. The root cause of this inflation was China's policy of export-led growth, encouraged by under-valuation of its exchange rate. Increases in global commodity prices played their part too, but the effect was made worse by an exchange rate that was too low. As a result of rapid growth in exports, surplus labour had become a thing of the past and export industries were being hit by higher wages. Export earnings had flowed into China, but had been channelled into assets such as stocks and property. Property prices had boomed as a result and fuelled a boom in construction, generating further inflationary pressures.

a) Explain how the under-valuation of China's currency had promoted the growth in Chinese exports.

b) Analyse the consequences of China's economic growth for inflation.

STRETCH AND CHALLENGE

c) Comment on the policies the Chinese government could use to reduce the inflationary impact of economic growth.

GROWTH, EMPLOYMENT AND UNEMPLOYMENT

The link between economic growth and employment is recognised by policy makers as central to improving macroeconomic performance. The European Union is just one example where growth and jobs have taken centre stage in terms of economic policy. In 2005, the EU relaunched its Lisbon Strategy as a growth and jobs strategy, committing member states to raising investment in research and development and labour force participation rates.

A comparison of economic growth and employment between two EU members states since 1995 illustrates the nature of the relationship between these two key performance indicators. Figure 9.20 shows that by 2006 the number of people in employment in Ireland had increased by almost 60 per cent since 1995, whereas over the same period employment in Belgium increased by only 11 per cent. It is not difficult to find the reason for this stark difference – the Irish economy grew by an average of 7.3 per cent per annum over the period, while average annual economic growth in Belgium was barely over 1 per cent. Figure 9.21 shows that, in terms of real GDP, the Irish economy had doubled in size, compared to a mere 11 per cent growth in Belgium.

Since the demand for labour is a derived demand, the number of people employed in an economy is closely related to output. Increases in real GDP will tend to increase the demand for labour and so the level of employment will rise. Even in the long run, where economic growth may be generated by higher productivity or capital investment, the consequences for employment are positive. The relationship between output and jobs can be represented with an inverted employment curve on an AD/AS diagram, as shown in Figure 9.22. In the short run, increases in output (Y to Y_1) increase the number of people employed (L to L_1). In the long run, raising labour force participation rates or increasing productive capacity through capital investment would shift LRAS to the right and raise employment (the employment curve would be extended downwards). Increasing labour productivity may result in some reduction in employment in the short run, because firms may choose to produce the same output but with fewer workers. This can be represented by pivoting the employment curve in Figure 9.22 to show less labour employed at each level of GDP. In the long run, however, it is likely to generate more jobs as aggregate demand increases.

The impact of growth on unemployment is less mechanical, however. Higher employment might be expected to reduce unemployment, but this is not always the case when the labour force itself is changing. Increases in the population of working age

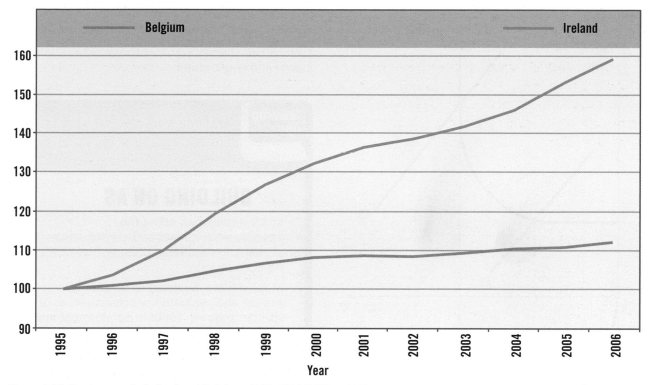

Figure 9.20 Employment in Ireland and Belgium, 1995–2006 (1995 = 100)

Source: European Central Bank website, Statistical Data Warehouse

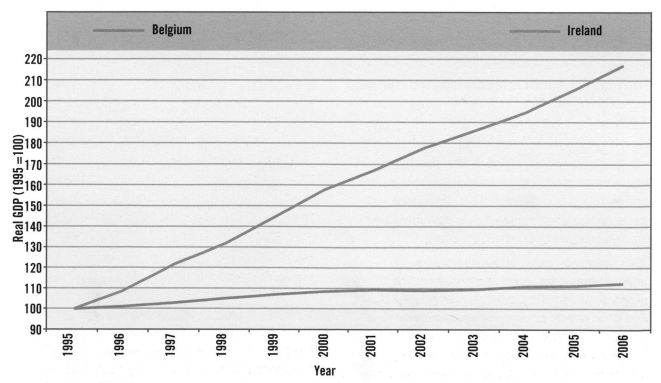

Figure 9.21 Real GDP in Ireland and Belgium, 1995–2006 (1995 = 100)

Source: European Central Bank website, Statistical Data Warehouse

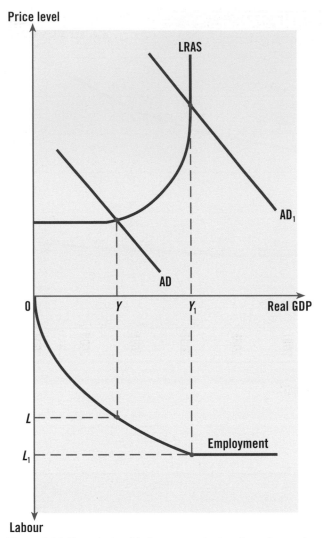

Figure 9.22 **The relationship between output and employment**

to acquire the skills necessary for the jobs being created. Hence, the emphasis in the EU's growth and jobs strategy is on supply-side measures to promote growth and employment.

learning tip

BUILDING ON AS

At AS you learned about the measurement, causes and consequences of unemployment (see Chapter 5 of *OCR AS Economics*).

At A2 you are expected to be able to analyse and evaluate the consequences of economic growth for both employment and unemployment. Some of the concepts you learnt at AS are useful in evaluating these consequences. You should review your understanding of these concepts referred to in this section.

GROWTH AND THE BALANCE OF PAYMENTS

Economic growth can have a number of consequences for an economy's balance of payments, depending on the nature of growth. An increase in AD caused by rising consumption is likely to affect the balance of payments negatively. This is because rising consumption is likely to increase the demand for imports, worsening the current account balance of the balance of payments. This effect will be more pronounced the higher the income elasticity of demand for imports. If growth is export led, on the other hand, the current account of the balance of payments will show an improvement. Supply-side improvements, such as increases in productivity, innovation and capital investment, which contribute to long-run economic growth, are less likely to worsen the current account of the balance of payments. Increases in productivity, for example, will tend to improve an economy's international competitiveness by lowering unit labour costs and reducing the impact of growth on imports. Higher capital investment will increase the productive potential of an economy, resulting in a greater ability of domestic

and in the number of people actively seeking work can mean that rising employment coincides with rising unemployment. Figure 9.23 shows the rate of unemployment in Belgium rising from 2001 to 2005 and in Ireland from 2001 to 2003. If you look back to Figure 9.20, you will see that in both these periods employment was rising in each country.

The consequences of economic growth for unemployment also depend upon the nature of growth and on the causes of unemployment. Economic growth generated by increases in AD is likely to reduce cyclical unemployment, but may have little impact on unemployment arising from problems related to the supply of labour, such as structural and frictional unemployment. Job creation must be accompanied by measures to assist the labour force

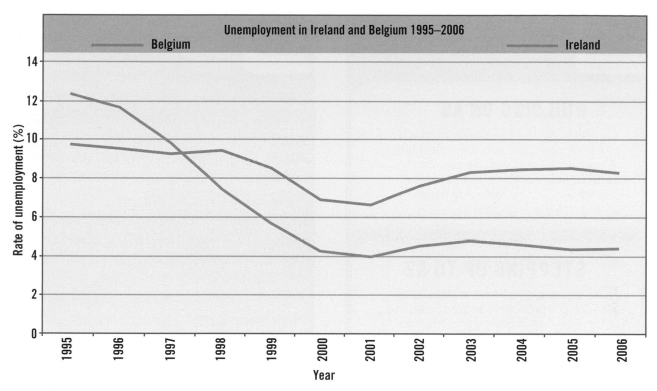

Figure 9.23 Unemployment in Belgium and Ireland, 1995–2006 (1995 = 100)
Source: European Central Bank website, Statistical Data Warehouse

firms to meet higher levels of domestic demand. The source of investment also determines the impact of economic growth on the balance of payments. Direct investment by foreign firms represents a long-term capital inflow that improves the **capital account of the balance of payments**. Even if growth causes the current account to worsen, this may not be a problem if it is matched by a capital account surplus.

Traditionally, the balance of payments has been viewed as a constraint on economic growth. A simple analogy might help to explain this concept. As a student, you can spend more than you earn because you are likely to be able to repay debts in the future through higher earnings. If you didn't have this future earnings potential, your ability to live beyond your means would be limited. The same is true of countries. Countries can only spend more on imports than they earn from exports if their future earnings potential is good. Otherwise, they must live within their means and the balance of payments must be in equilibrium. This can be captured in a simple equation known as Thirlwall's Law. This states that

DEFINITIONS

Capital account of the balance **of payments**: the section of the balance of payments that records long-term flow of capital into and out of an economy. It records purchases and sales of assets and is split into two sections, **long-term capital flows** and **short-term capital flows**

Long-term capital flows: flows of money used for investment in assets (for example *direct investment* by a company in setting up production facilities or *portfolio investment* through buying shares in companies)

Short-term capital flows: flows of money that occur to take advantage of differences in countries' interest rates and changes in exchange rates; sometimes referred to as *hot money*

BUILDING ON AS

You learnt about the balance of payments at AS, in particular about the structure of the current account. Review your understanding of the elements of the current account by rereading pages 116–17 of the AS textbook.

STEPPING UP TO A2

At A2 you are introduced to the capital account of the balance of payments and to the idea that the two accounts must balance in order for the overall balance of payments to be in equilibrium. Make sure that you are clear about how the current account and the capital account differ.

learning tip

The balance of payments can be a confusing area of economics for students. Knowing the structure of the two main accounts (current and capital) helps you to understand what goes where.

Understanding the significance of changes in the balance of payments is a bit more tricky, but it does help to think in terms of exports earning the foreign currency to pay for a nation's imports.

Students often think that exports are 'good' and imports are 'bad'. If you think of why an economy imports goods and services you might be able to see why this way of looking at the balance of payments is unhelpful.

If you are still puzzled, try to check out the IMF's 'back to basics' explanation of the balance of payments in its *Finance and Development* magazine. Go to www.heinemann.co.uk/hotlinks, insert the express code 2230P, and click on 'IMF Finance and Development'.

the rate of economic growth consistent with balance of payments equilibrium is equal to:

$$\frac{\text{the rate of growth of exports}}{\text{the income elasticity of demand for imports}}$$

So, if an economy's exports normally grow by 2 per cent per annum and the income elasticity of demand for imports is 0.2 (inelastic), then annual growth of

$$\frac{2}{0.2} = 10\%$$

will be possible without causing balance of payments problems. However, if the income elasticity of demand is more elastic, for example if YED = 1, then the rate of economic growth consistent with balance of payments equilibrium is much lower:

$$\frac{2}{1} = 2\%$$

ACTIVITY ····>

Read the IMF's 'back to basics' explanation of the balance of payments in its *Finance and Development* magazine (see learning tip above) and then answer the questions below.

a) What has happened to the US current account balance of its balance of payments since 1993?

b) What has happened to the US capital account balance of its balance of payments since 1993?

c) What has happened to the balance between savings and investment in the USA since 1993?

STRETCH AND CHALLENGE

d) Discuss the extent to which the current account deficit of the USA is a cause for concern.

GROWTH AND THE GOVERNMENT'S FISCAL POSITION

The government's fiscal position refers to the balance between government expenditure and revenue from tax receipts. The difference between the two is known as the **public sector net cash requirement (PSNCR).** The existence of the economic cycle results in changes in both government expenditure and tax receipts over which governments have no control.

DEFINITION

Public sector net cash requirement (PSNCR): the difference between the spending of general government (central and local government) and their revenue. If expenditure exceeds revenue, there is a budget deficit. If expenditure is smaller than revenue, there is a budget surplus. A budget deficit requires government to borrow money to make up the shortfall of revenue over planned expenditure

In a booming economy, tax receipts will tend to rise even without any action by the government to raise tax rates or widen the tax base. The reason is that the higher level of economic activity will bring the government more tax revenue. A higher level of employment results in more income tax revenue, higher expenditure by consumers results in more revenue from expenditure taxes and higher levels of profit result in greater levels of corporation tax receipts for the government. Government expenditure, on the other hand, will tend to fall when the rate of economic growth rises. This is because there is likely to be lower unemployment in the boom phase of the economic cycle. This reduces the amount that needs to be spent on unemployment benefits. In addition, if economic growth raises average incomes, the amount needed to be spent on income-related benefits will tend to fall too. It follows that, in a recession, tax receipts will fall and government expenditure rise. These changes in expenditure and receipts take place with no action by the government. They are automatic, not discretionary, changes. They are sometimes referred to as

automatic stabilisers because they have the effect of dampening down a boom and cushioning the effect of a recession. A bit like stabilisers on a bike stopping you from falling off when you were learning to ride!

DEFINITION

Automatic stabilisers: changes in government expenditure and taxation receipts that take place automatically in response to the economic cycle. For example, expenditure on unemployment benefits rises during the recession phase of the business cycle

The consequence of these automatic stabilisers is that the government's fiscal position (or stance) will change over the course of the economic cycle. A budget surplus will tend to emerge during the boom phase of the economic cycle and a deficit materialise in a recession. Governments will have to borrow to make up the shortfall during recessions but, in principle at least, they should be able to repay this borrowing during the boom years from the budget surplus. The PSNCR (a measure of the government's fiscal stance) will, therefore, vary over the economic cycle. This is shown in Figure 9.24.

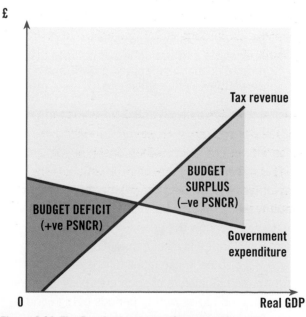

Figure 9.24 The fiscal stance over the economic cycle

The cyclical nature of the government's fiscal position means that, to know what the 'underlying' fiscal position is, budget deficits and surpluses have to be adjusted for the effects of the cycle. In addition, the existence of the 'fiscal cycle' reduces the size of the multiplier and dampens down the economic cycle, if the automatic stabilisers are allowed to work. The role of fiscal policy in dampening the economic cycle will be examined in detail in the next section of this chapter.

Policy issues – growth, economic stability and international competitiveness

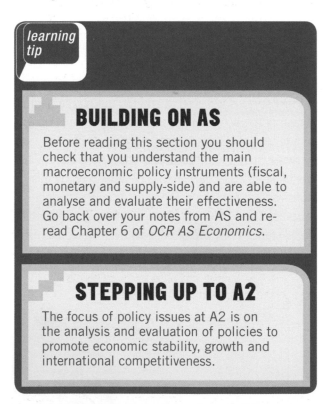

learning tip

BUILDING ON AS

Before reading this section you should check that you understand the main macroeconomic policy instruments (fiscal, monetary and supply-side) and are able to analyse and evaluate their effectiveness. Go back over your notes from AS and re-read Chapter 6 of *OCR AS Economics*.

STEPPING UP TO A2

The focus of policy issues at A2 is on the analysis and evaluation of policies to promote economic stability, growth and international competitiveness.

Government policies can promote economic growth both in the short and the long run, but over the last ten years attention has switched to **economic stability** as an objective of macroeconomic policy. You have seen how the economic cycle creates fluctuations in the level of economic activity. There will also be implications for the other key performance indicators of such instability. Inflation rates will tend to rise during periods of high and unsustainable growth. Employment will rise and

DEFINITION

Economic stability: the avoidance of volatility in economic growth rates, inflation, employment and unemployment and exchange rates, in order to reduce uncertainty and promote business and consumer confidence and investment

unemployment will fall. The current account of the balance of payments will deteriorate if growth raises the demand for imports relative to export demand. On the other hand, recession will see the indicators moving in the opposite direction. This is what economists mean by economic instability – fluctuations in the key performance indicators caused by the economic cycle.

Economic stability has become a more prominent objective of macroeconomic policy in recent years because of what are perceived to be the consequences of instability. It is argued that instability in any of the key performance indicators creates uncertainty, which damages long-term economic performance. For example, uncertainty about demand and prices will undermine both consumer and business confidence. A lack of consumer confidence discourages consumption, which may make the economic cycle more pronounced – recessions could be more prolonged and recoveries less strong because of a lack of demand in the economy. Businesses are likely to under-invest in times of uncertainty and this will reduce the economy's long-term rate of economic growth. Economic stability, then, is the key to improving macroeconomic performance.

Macroeconomic policies to promote stability and growth have focused on:

● a 'prudent' approach to management of the economy

● taking fiscal and monetary policy decisions on the basis of the long-term interests of the economy rather than short-term political considerations

- ensuring that fiscal and monetary policies support each other

- bringing openness and transparency to decision making through putting in place rules and targets

- improving the supply-side performance of the economy.

FISCAL POLICY ISSUES

You have seen that the government's fiscal position varies with the economic cycle. The government's budget will move into surplus in time of economic boom and into deficit in time of recession as a result of automatic stabilisers. Governments must avoid the temptation to spend surpluses and to try to claw back deficits in order to 'balance the books'. Such action can contribute to a more pronounced economic cycle. For example, if governments raise spending and cut taxes simply because the budget is in surplus they run the risk of raising AD during the course of the boom phase of the economic cycle. In addition, high levels of government borrowing can reduce the amount of finance available for private sector investment. The private sector is then **crowded out** by the government and private sector investment falls, reducing the economy's long-term rate of economic growth. High government borrowing will also tend to push up rates of interest, as governments have to persuade the money markets to 'buy' government debt. These higher rates of interest contribute to low levels of private sector investment by increasing its cost.

To promote economic stability, fiscal policy in the UK is 'prudent'. The aim of UK fiscal policy is to balance the government's budget, but over the course of the economic cycle rather than at any one point in time. Short-term political considerations are not supposed to drive decisions on government expenditure and taxation. The government bases fiscal policy decisions on a cautious estimate of the economy's long-term rate of economic growth. To promote economic growth, UK fiscal policy focuses on measures that will raise the productive capacity of the economy by shifting out the LRAS curve. In times of slowdown or recession, the government will have to borrow money to make up for the shortfall of tax receipts over government expenditure. But they should not borrow more than this **cyclical deficit** to fund current expenditure. In other words, UK government borrowing is only justified if it arises automatically because of the economic cycle or is used for investment. This has become known as the **golden rule** of fiscal policy.

DEFINITIONS

Cyclical deficit: a budget deficit that arises because of the operation of automatic stabilisers

Golden rule: a commitment by the UK government that, over the economic cycle, it will borrow only to invest and not for current expenditure

DEFINITION

Crowding out: when government borrowing reduces the funds available for private sector investment or raises the cost of investment by raising market interest rates

learning tip

There are lots of resources on the nature of UK fiscal policy on the Treasury's website. For a brief summary of the UK's approach to fiscal policy setting out the government's five principles of fiscal management, go to www.heinemann.co.uk/hotlinks, insert the express code 2230P, and click on 'Treasury 5 fiscal principles'. To check out the UK government's Code for Fiscal Stability, click on 'Code for Fiscal Stability'.

Different governments, however, have different approaches to designing fiscal policy to promote economic stability and growth. This shows that there isn't one set of rules around which agreement can be sought. While there might be broad principles (these are often stated to be **credibility**, **flexibility** and **legitimacy**), there are different approaches to what the rules and targets should be.

DEFINITIONS

Credibility (principle of fiscal policy): a credible fiscal policy framework is one where the government's commitment to economic stability is trusted by the public, business and financial markets

Flexibility (principle of fiscal policy): a flexible fiscal policy framework is one that has the flexibility to deal with macroeconomic shocks, such as sudden and unexpected changes in AD and/or AS

Legitimacy (principle of fiscal policy): a legitimate fiscal policy framework is one that has widespread support and about which there is general agreement among the public, business and politicians

DEFINITION

Stability and Growth Pact (SGP): an agreement by members of the EU about the way in which fiscal policy should be conducted to support Europe's single currency. It requires those countries adopting Europe's single currency (the eurozone states) to abide by the following rules:

- a budget deficit of 3 per cent of GDP or less
- a government debt of 60 per cent of GDP or less

The problem with the UK's approach is that it requires accurate estimation of the productive capacity of the economy and the economy's long-term rate of economic growth. Such things are difficult to estimate. In addition, governments would have to be able to forecast the likely trend in actual economic growth to set spending and taxation for the years ahead. In contrast, the members of the eurozone have to abide by the **Stability and Growth Pact**, which limits budget deficits to 3 per cent of GDP and government debt to 60 per cent of GDP. Such rules are simpler to interpret and to measure, but they lack flexibility. If an economy is in recession, its government's budget deficit will rise and may fall foul of the 3 per cent limit. The EU's

Stability and Growth Pact includes a financial penalty for economies that breach the rules – this would add to their credibility and legitimacy. Perversely, however, the penalties make it harder for an economy to bring its deficit down and, because they lack flexibility, might make the economic cycle more pronounced than it otherwise would be if the automatic stabilisers of fiscal policy were allowed to operate.

Fiscal policy rules, such as those contained in the UK government's Code for Fiscal Stability, are no guarantee that governments will get these things right or, indeed, stick to their own rules. Unless fiscal policy is run independently of government, there is always the risk that politicians will take risks with fiscal policy and destabilise the economic cycle. It would take a very principled Chancellor of the Exchequer to avoid the temptation of raising government expenditure and cutting taxation in the run-up to an election if polls showed them at risk of losing. In choosing between economic stability and political success, politicians are likely to be vote maximisers and favour fiscal expansion over fiscal prudence. To be effective, there must be 'costs', or penalties, attached to the rules – costs or penalties for breaking or amending them. Where governments themselves judge whether they have met the rules, there are clear government failures that might arise – information failures, asymmetric information and moral hazard.

Fiscal policy rules and targets may also encourage 'creative fiscal accounting', whereby governments find ways around the rules by changing the way in which expenditure is measured, for example. It may be that, over time, people lose confidence in the commitment of governments to sticking to the rules, or the rules themselves come to be seen as worthless. If this happens, then the whole credibility of government fiscal policy is eroded and the exercise becomes self defeating.

MONETARY POLICY ISSUES

Monetary policy can promote economic stability and growth in several ways. Changes in interest rates impact on domestic demand, through consumption and investment, and on net external demand, through the exchange rate. The way in which it does this is known as the **monetary transmission mechanism** and is summarised in Figure 9.25. Rapid economic growth and accelerating inflation can be dampened by increases in interest rates, and an economic slowdown and falling rates of inflation can be tackled with reductions in interest rates. Monetary policy could, in principle, be used to manage the economic cycle and to smooth out the fluctuations in short-run economic growth that bring with them instability in the other key performance indicators. In short, monetary policy could be used to manage aggregate demand.

> ### DEFINITION
>
> **Monetary transmission mechanism:** the way in which monetary policy affects the inflation rate through the impact it has on other macroeconomic variables

ACTIVITY ⋯⫶

Using your knowledge of monetary policy from AS (see pages 143–45 of *OCR AS Economics*) and going to the Bank of England's website by going to www.heinemann.co.uk/hotlinks, inserting the express code 2230P, and clicking on 'Bank of England monetary policy', explain how changes in the rate of interest affect:

a) market rates of interest

b) asset prices

c) expectations/confidence.

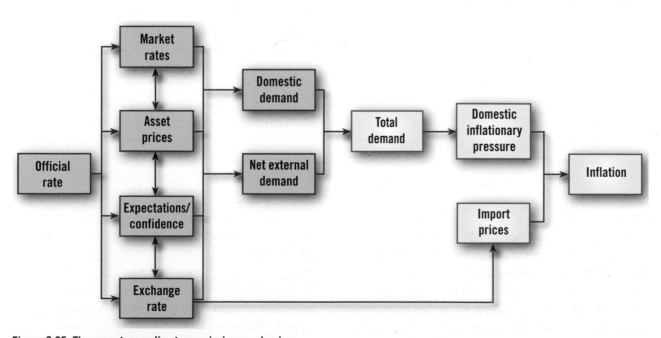

Figure 9.25 The monetary policy transmission mechanism
Source: Bank of England

> **DEFINITION**
>
> **Price stability:** when the general price level does not change or, if it does change, the rate of change is low enough not to significantly affect the decisions of firms and households

> **DEFINITIONS**
>
> **Purchasing power of money:** what a unit of currency will buy in terms of goods and services
>
> **Signalling function:** changes in demand and supply of goods and services are signalled to producers and consumers through changes in absolute and relative price levels

But the primary objective of monetary policy is to deliver **price stability**. It is argued that low and stable rates of inflation provide a framework for economic stability. Inflation erodes the **purchasing power of money**. In doing so, it damages the heart of any economic system – the exchange of money for goods and services. If wage growth starts to increase to compensate for the fall in the value of money, there is a very real danger that inflation will get out of control. Prices also serve a **signalling function** in a market economy. Changes in prices should reflect changes in demand and supply and send out messages for resources to be allocated and reallocated to the goods and services that consumers most want. Inflation is sometimes described as 'noise' in the economic system – it stops the messages being

heard and the market system does not function so well. Variable rates of inflation also coincide with the economic cycle and create economic uncertainty that discourages savings and investment, crucial for long-term economic growth. High relative rates of inflation also damage international competitiveness in the longer term, affecting output and jobs.

The role of monetary policy is, therefore, to deliver low and stable rates of inflation. In recent years, many countries have adopted inflation targets to achieve this objective. First introduced in New

ACTIVITY ⋯⋗

A variety of fiscal frameworks and rules operate within the EU, reflecting different needs at the national level.

Denmark. The Danish government focuses on ensuring sustainable public finances in the medium and long term by maintaining budget surpluses of the order of 1.5–2.5 per cent of GDP on average towards 2010.

Estonia. The Estonian government focuses on maintaining a balanced central government budget. The only exception allowed to this general rule is the cost incurred in financing pension reform.

Poland. The Polish constitution caps government debt at 60 per cent of GDP. It states that the government may not contract any additional borrowing if this would involve breaching that level.

United Kingdom. The UK has two fiscal rules: the golden rule, that over the economic cycle

the government will borrow only to invest and not to fund current spending; and the sustainable investment rule, that public sector net debt as a proportion of GDP will be held over the economic cycle at a sustainable and prudent level. Other things being equal, net debt will be maintained below 40 per cent of GDP over the economic cycle.

Source: adapted from an HM Treasury discussion paper, 2004

a) Explain the difference between government debt and government borrowing.

b) What are the advantages and disadvantages of the fiscal policy rule adopted by Estonia?

STRETCH AND CHALLENGE

c) Discuss the effectiveness of fiscal policy rules in promoting economic stability.

Zealand in 1990, over twenty countries have now adopted inflation targets. In addition, central banks have been given responsibility to deliver price stability and have been given **operational independence** from governments. It is argued that this makes monetary policy less susceptible to short-term political considerations and more likely to operate in the long-term interest of the economy.

DEFINITION

Operational independence: when a central bank is given responsibility for the conduct of monetary policy independent of political interference. The target for inflation, however, is normally set by governments

---

The inflation target itself varies between countries. Some countries have a target range for inflation, for example that inflation should be kept within a range of 1–3 per cent. In others, there is an explicit target inflation rate within a range – so the target might be to achieve an inflation rate of 2 per cent but within a range of 1–3 per cent. In some cases, the target is for inflation to be below a certain rate – the European Central Bank aims for inflation below 2 per cent. Targets, therefore, can be **symmetric** or **asymmetric**. Differences in the way in which the target is set can be important in terms of delivering growth and stability, as you will see later in this section.

DEFINITIONS

Symmetric inflation target: when deviations above and below the target are given equal weight in the inflation target

Asymmetric inflation target: when deviations below the inflation target are seen to be less important than deviations above the target

---

Inflation targeting has a number of benefits for growth and stability:

● *transparency and accountability* – an inflation target makes the conduct of monetary policy clear. There is a firm commitment to price stability that is communicated to firms and households. Transparency and accountability are further enhanced when central banks publish reasons for the decisions they make.

● *expectations* – an inflation target that is credible directly affects expectations of inflation. If people expect the inflation target to be met, they will build this expectation into their behaviour and this will do much to bring about the rate of inflation they expect – expectations become self-fulfilling. For example, if workers expect inflation in the future to be low, they will moderate their wage demands and this will reduce cost–push inflation. Firms will be more confident in their investment plans if they expect future inflation to be low. This will raise the productive capacity of the economy and reduce the likelihood of demand–pull inflation.

● *flexibility* – the design of symmetric inflation targets gives as much weight to low inflation as it does to high inflation. This means that a degree of flexibility is built into monetary policy, which can contribute to economic stability. For example, if inflation is predicted to fall below the bottom of the range set, then the central bank is likely to reduce interest rates to raise AD. Without this symmetry, there might be a bias towards reducing inflation at the cost of slower economic growth, lower employment and higher unemployment. This is a criticism levelled at the European Central Bank's inflation target and is particularly relevant at a time of global economic slowdown. Some argue that the eurozone's relatively sluggish economic macroeconomic performance is, in part, due to the way in which monetary policy puts a greater emphasis on the control of inflation than it does on the real economy.

There are a number of problems with inflation targeting. Whether it promotes economic stability, growth and international competitiveness depends, mainly, on the central bank bringing credibility to the target. To be credible, the central bank has to build up a reputation for meeting its target. Some economists have argued that, in the short run, this can lead to central banks trading off low economic growth for low inflation.

In order to be successful in hitting its target, a central bank has to be good at forecasting inflation. Monetary policy works with time lags. So an increase in today's interest rate might not have its full effect on inflation until up to two years later. This means that a central bank will have to set today's interest rate to affect the rate of inflation it expects in two years' time. Inflation targeting has to be guided by forecasts of inflation and by all the macroeconomic variables that affect inflation, including the size of the output gap. Inflation targeting, then, is only as successful in delivering low inflation as the central bank is at forecasting.

learning tip

As the global economy enters a period of instability, watch out for how central banks throughout the world respond. Already in 2008, some central banks aggressively cut interest rates to stimulate AD, while others did not, citing price stability as their primary objective.

Stephen King, chief global economist at HSBC, has been critical of inflation targeting in the present global economic climate. Check out what he had to say in the *Independent* newspaper at the end of March 2008. Go to www.heinemann.co.uk/hotlinks, insert the express code 2230P, and click on 'inflation targeting'.

Even the best forecasts cannot anticipate unforeseen events. Until recently, the economies

ACTIVITY ⋯⋗

In the last quarter of 2006, solid output growth was maintained in the UK. Market interest rates rose, sterling appreciated and asset prices remained buoyant. The underlying trend in household spending appeared firm, while the upturn in business investment was sustained.

The world economy expanded briskly. In the Bank of England's Monetary Policy Committee's central projection, GDP continued to grow at a rate close to its average over the past decade shown in Figure 9.26.

The margin of spare capacity within businesses appeared limited and unemployment flattened off.

The pressure on businesses' energy and import costs eased, but early indications point to a modest increase in pay growth. There are signs that businesses are more confident in their ability to raise prices. CPI inflation picked up to 3 per cent in December. In the central projection, inflation remains above target in the near term and then falls back, settling around the 2 per cent target over the medium term. The risks to growth are balanced, while those to inflation are weighted to the downside in the near term and to the upside further out.

a) Explain **two** determinants of the UK's long-run economic growth rate.

b) Analyse the significance of the limited 'margin of spare capacity within businesses' for the UK's Monetary Policy Committee.

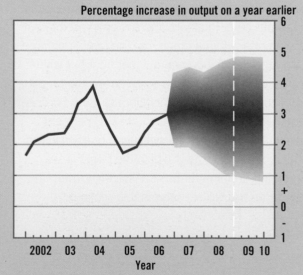

Percentage increase in output on a year earlier

Figure 9.26 GDP projection based on market interest expectations
Source: Bank of England, Inflation Report, February 2007

STRETCH AND CHALLENGE

c) Comment upon the extent to which an inflation target, such as that in the UK, promotes economic stability.

that have used inflation targeting have been remarkably stable. That stability may not be due to inflation targeting, as some would argue, but it may have made it easier for central banks to meet their targets. The real test of inflation targeting is whether it can deliver economic stability and growth at a time when global economic conditions are themselves unstable.

SUPPLY-SIDE POLICY ISSUES

Supply-side policies aim to increase AS in order to increase the economy's productive capacity, thereby helping to prevent inflation, reduce structural and frictional unemployment and improve the economy's long-run rate of economic growth and its trade position.

Earlier in this chapter, you learnt how long-run economic growth could be promoted by shifting out the LRAS (see pages 213–215). The effect of supply-side policies on economic stability and growth are analysed in Figure 9.27. The shift in LRAS increases real GDP to Y_1 and allows future increases in AD, raising real GDP still further to Y_2. All of this occurs without any increase in the price level – there is no trade-off between growth and inflation or price stability. In terms of the economic cycle, then, supply-side policies allow for sustained periods of non-inflationary growth. This is consistent with what you have learnt about economic stability. Some economists argue that the period of sustained,

non-inflationary economic growth in the UK since 1992 has been the consequence of supply-side improvements to the economy.

However, supply-side policies are not the panacea that some economists believe them to be. It is little use expanding the productive capacity of the economy, improving work incentives, making markets work more efficiently through deregulation or raising productivity, if there is insufficient demand in the economy. For example, if AD were at AD_0 in Figure 9.27, supply-side improvements would have no effect on real GDP or the price level in the Keynesian analysis of LRAS. Of course, this is not the case in the Classical analysis of LRAS (see pages 213–215). Despite this, supply-side policies are increasingly seen as important to deliver improved macroeconomic performance in the long run and to improve **international competitiveness**.

> ### DEFINITION
>
> **International competitiveness:** the ability of an economy's firms to compete in international markets and, thereby, sustain increases in national output and income

---

learning tip

STEPPING UP TO A2

At AS you learnt about the impact of supply-side policies on the economy and looked at a range of different examples (see pages 145–48 of *OCR AS Economics*). At A2 the focus of your study of supply-side policies should be on analysing and evaluating their role in promoting economic stability, growth and international competitiveness.

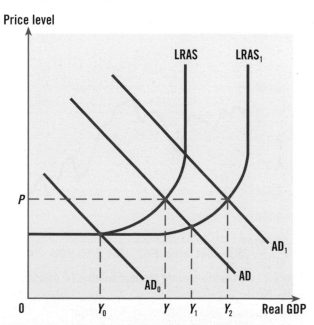

Figure 9.27 Supply-side policies, growth and stability

If there was an EU prize for 'most improved macroeconomic performer' in the last two decades, there would be few on the panel of judges who would not award the prize to the Irish economy. During the 1990s, Ireland attracted high levels of investment from multinational companies, its exports grew markedly, its economic growth rate exceeded that in the rest of the EU, living standards rose and long-term unemployment all but disappeared. As Ireland's national income increased, however, the pattern of its economic growth changed as rising confidence boosted household and government spending. The Irish economy continued to grow rapidly, but this growth hid an emerging competitiveness problem from about 2000. The extent of this problem can be seen in Ireland's growing current account deficit in Figure 9.28.

A country's international competitiveness is determined by both the prices and the quality of its goods and services relative to those of other countries. A number of factors affect the relative prices of a country's goods and services. These include:

● the costs of production

● productivity

● the exchange rate.

Relative unit labour costs can, therefore, change for three reasons:

● a change in the cost of labour compared to other countries

● a change in productivity (output per unit of labour) compared to other countries

● a change in the exchange rate.

DEFINITIONS

Unit labour costs: the cost of labour per unit of output (including the social costs of employing labour as well as the wage costs)

Relative unit labour costs: the cost of labour per unit of output of one country relative to its major trading partners

The problem with this measure of international competitiveness is that it takes no account of quality factors. For example, a country might improve its relative unit labour costs but its current account balance may still worsen if the quality of its goods and services worsens relative to those of its competitors. Quality factors that could affect international competitiveness might include:

● design of products

● delivery dates

● after-sales service

● reliability

● marketing.

In the case of Ireland, declining international competitiveness appears to boil down to problems related to poor growth in productivity, high growth in inflation and costs, and a rising exchange rate. Ireland's National Competitiveness Council approaches the country's international competitiveness using the pyramid in Figure 9.29.

At the top of the pyramid is sustainable growth in living standards. This comes from past improvements in competitiveness. Next in the pyramid are the factors that determine current competitiveness, including business performance (such as trade and investment), productivity, prices and costs and labour supply. Last in the pyramid are the policy inputs.

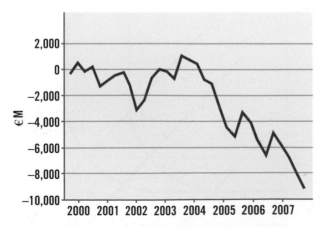

Figure 9.28 Ireland's current account balance (€ million), 2000–2007

Source: National Competitiveness Council, Annual Competitiveness Report, 2007

These are the three key things that the Council believes determines future productivity:

● *the business environment* – this determines the 'cost' and ease of doing business in Ireland and includes the impact of taxation, regulation, the degree of market competition, the extent of labour market regulations, the cost of raising finance on business.

● *physical infrastructure* – this determines productivity and costs and includes transport, energy and IT infrastructure that is affected by levels of investment by firms and government.

● *knowledge infrastructure* – education, training and research and development affects the quality of the labour force and of the products firms are able to produce.

Supply-side policies are key to improving the business environment, a nation's physical infrastructure and its knowledge infrastructure.

If you are in any doubt, look back to where this chapter started in distinguishing between short-run and long-run economic growth (pages 201–207). Some of these supply-side policies might require higher government expenditure but some require fiscal and monetary policy to deliver the conditions for long-run economic growth and a stable macroeconomic environment. These policies, however, will not deliver immediate results. Improving macroeconomic performance has no quick fixes!

ACTIVITY ⋯⋮

a) Using the examples of supply-side policies in the AS textbook (see pages 145–48, *OCR AS Economics*) and the section in this chapter on long-run economic growth (pages 201–207), explain how three supply-side policies might improve an economy's international competitiveness.

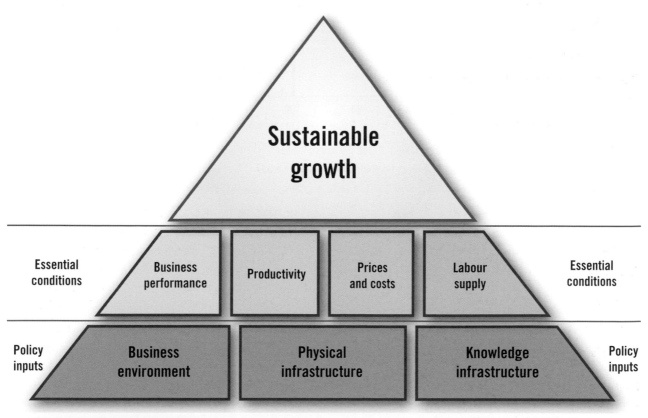

Figure 9.29 Ireland's competitiveness pyramid
Source: National Competitiveness Council, Annual Competitiveness Report, 2007

ACTIVITY ···⁑

Price levels and inflation vary markedly in the EU as Figure 9.30 shows.

a) Explain the difference between the price level and inflation.

b) Which member state of the EU would you expect to have the greatest competitiveness on the basis of the figure below? Explain your answer.

c) Analyse one supply-side measure that would improve the international competitiveness of a high cost, high inflation economy such as Ireland.

STRETCH AND CHALLENGE

d) Comment on the implications for monetary policy of the introduction of effective supply-side policies.

For a speech by the ex-president of the European Central Bank that you may find useful, go to www.heinemann.co.uk/hotlinks, insert the express code 2230P, and click on 'speech by ex-president of ECB'.

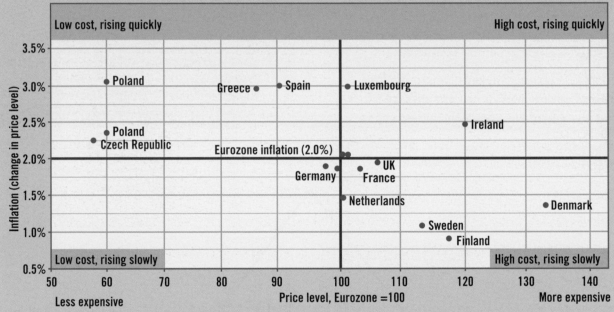

Figure 9.30 Price level (2006) and inflation (2003–07) in eurozone states

Source: National Competitiveness Council, Annual Competitiveness Report, 2007

10 Trade and integration

On completion of this chapter, you should be able to:

- understand the terms absolute and comparative advantage and use them to analyse the basis of international trade and the gains from trade
- define, measure and analyse the significance of the terms of trade and changes in the terms of trade over time
- outline the pattern of global trade and evaluate comparative advantage as an explanation of global trade patterns
- explain how exchange rates are determined and evaluate the relative merits and drawbacks of alternative exchange rate systems
- explain purchasing power parity
- evaluate the causes and consequences of exchange rate fluctuations
- analyse the causes of imbalances on the balance of payments and evaluate policies to correct these imbalances
- understand and explain the stages of economic integration
- be familiar with different examples of economic integration
- evaluate the internal and external consequences of economic integration.

learning tip

BUILDING ON AS

At AS you learnt about the pattern of UK trade, the advantages that may be gained from international trade and restrictions to the free movement of goods and services between countries.

At A2 you will revisit some of these themes, but will explore them using more advanced economic models and theories.

Before you start reading this chapter, it would be a good idea to review your understanding of international trade by rereading pages 158–63 of *OCR AS Economics*. Creating a mind map summary of what you already know will help you to make links between AS and A2.

According to the **World Trade Organization**, a staggering $14,838 billion of goods and services were traded globally in 2006, an increase of 14 per cent from 2005. Trade is a significant contributor to world GDP, and this contribution is increasing – trade represented 26 per cent of world GDP in 2006. Whether we realise it or not, trade touches all of our

DEFINITION

World Trade Organization (WTO): an international body responsible for negotiating trade agreements and 'policing' the rules of trade to which its members sign up. Trade disputes between members are settled by the WTO

lives. This textbook has been written and edited in the UK but printed in another country. The paper may well come from wood logged somewhere else, the inks be made in another part of the world and the printing machinery in yet another. The price and variety of goods we, as consumers, are able to buy is determined by international trade, either directly or indirectly. Many firms face competition in world markets, which affects their prices, output and ultimately employment, wages and incomes in the economies in which they operate.

ACTIVITY ····:·

Find out what it might be like to be an ambassador to the WTO. Go to www.heinemann.co.uk/hotlinks, insert the express code 2230P, and click on 'BBC interactive quiz'.

To find out more about the WTO, click on the WTO Profile link on the right of this page.

Record three of your key findings about the WTO.

This chapter looks at a number of issues related to international trade:

● economic theories of trade

● exchange rates

● the balance of payments

● regional integration and trading blocs.

Absolute and comparative advantage

ACTIVITY ····:·

Go to www.heinemann.co.uk/hotlinks, insert the express code 2230P, and click on 'CIA World Factbook'. Choose three countries with different levels of GDP per capita.

a) List the main exports and imports for each country.

b) What reasons can you give to explain what you have found out for each country?

The basis of some trade is easy to understand. For example, the bananas you eat are imported because the UK doesn't have the climate required to produce them. Australia, Canada, Africa and South America export uranium because this is where the world's deposits of uranium ore are found. To understand the economics of international trade, however, requires you to understand the concept of specialisation. Countries specialise in the production of certain goods and services which they can produce relatively efficiently. By exporting these goods and services they can earn revenue to import the goods and services that they cannot produce so efficiently.

The goods and services that countries should specialise in are determined by their absolute and comparative advantages. These are the basic forces that determine the pattern of global trade. A country is said to have an **absolute advantage** in the production of a good or service when it can produce it at a lower unit cost than other countries. This unit cost advantage arises because it uses fewer resources to produce a good or service than other countries.

DEFINITION

Absolute advantage: where one country is able to produce more of a good or service with the same amount of resources, such that the unit cost of production is lower

Figure 10.1 illustrates this idea of absolute advantage with the use of production possibility curves (PPCs). If we assume that the USA and Japan have the same resources of land, labour and capital, then the USA's ability to produce more wheat (ten units) than Japan (five units) must mean that it uses fewer resources to do so. Assuming that the cost of resources is the same in each country, the USA produces wheat at a lower unit cost than Japan. It has the absolute advantage in wheat production. Similarly, because Japan can produce more electronic goods (fifteen units) than the USA (seven units) it has the absolute

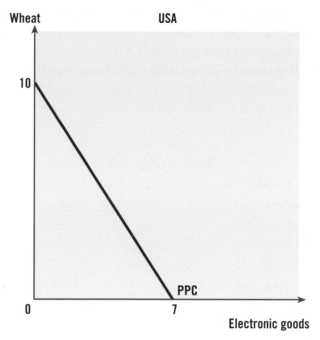

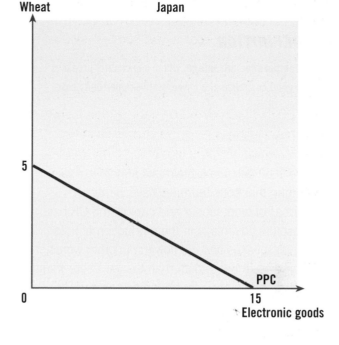

Figure 10.1 A model of absolute advantage

advantage in electronic goods production as its unit cost is lower. There is a clear basis for trade – each country's absolute advantage complements the others. This is known as **reciprocal absolute advantage**. The USA should export wheat and import electronic goods, whereas Japan should export electronic goods and import wheat.

of as a relative concept as well as an absolute concept. Ricardo understood international trade in terms of the opportunity cost of resource use. This gave rise to the principle of **comparative advantage**, which underlies the economic theory of trade to this day.

DEFINITION

Reciprocal absolute advantage: where, in a theoretical world of two countries and two products, each country has an absolute advantage in one of the two products

A more tricky situation to understand is when a country does not possess an absolute advantage in the production of any good or service. Surely, there is no basis for trade? This was a problem that David Ricardo, an economist writing at the beginning of the nineteenth century, set out to solve. According to Ricardo, there is still a basis for international trade because cost can be thought

---

learning tip

BUILDING ON AS

Students frequently have difficulty explaining the difference between absolute and comparative advantage. The key to understanding the difference is the concept of **relative opportunity cost**. Opportunity cost is a concept you first came across at AS (see *OCR AS Economics*, pages 6–7). Can you define it? Can you show opportunity cost on a PPC diagram? If you can do both of these it will help you to get to grips with how comparative advantage is different from absolute advantage.

Figure 10.2 helps to explain this principle. Again, assuming that both countries have identical resources of land, labour and capital, the UK has an absolute advantage in the production of both financial services and cut flowers. In other words, it can produce more of both than Kenya. There would appear to be no basis for trade because the UK uses its resources more efficiently than Kenya. Why would

the UK trade with a country less efficient than itself? The answer lies in the relative opportunity costs of production. In the case of the UK, the opportunity cost of producing one unit of financial services (F) is one unit of cut flowers (C). The opportunity cost ratio for the UK is:

$$1F: 1C$$

For Kenya, the opportunity cost ratio is:

$$1F: 2C$$

Although Kenya is relatively inefficient at producing financial services, it is relatively more efficient than the UK in producing cut flowers. The opportunity cost ratios are:

for the UK $1C: 1F$
for Kenya $1C: \frac{1}{2}F$

What this means is that Kenya can produce cut flowers with a smaller sacrifice in the production of financial services than is possible for the UK. When a country has a lower relative opportunity cost of production in one good or service than another, it is said to have a comparative advantage. Now there is a basis for trade. The UK would make better use of its scarce resources if it specialised in the production of financial services and traded these with Kenya for cut flowers.

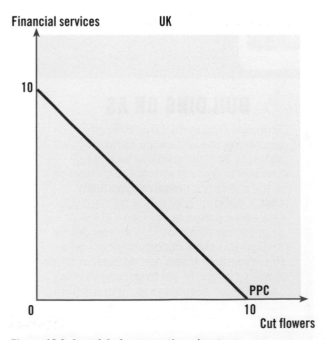
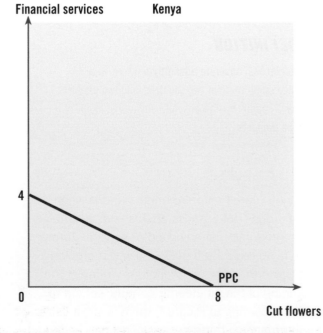

Figure 10.2 A model of comparative advantage

In the example above, for the two countries to benefit from specialisation and trade, they must agree prices at which financial services and cut flowers should be traded. These prices are known as the **terms of trade**. In exporting financial services, the UK needs to be able to buy more than one cut flower for each financial service it exports. Otherwise, it might as well produce cut flowers itself. On the other hand, Kenya would not want to sell more than two cut flowers to buy one financial service – it can produce financial services itself at this cost. So the terms of trade will have to lie in-between the relative opportunity cost ratios for each country to benefit.

Let us assume that the terms of trade are 1 financial service for 1½ cut flowers. At this price, the UK could in principle buy 15 cut flowers if it specialised in financial services and sold them all to Kenya. Kenya could buy 5.3 financial services (i.e. 8/1.5 = 5.3) if it specialised in producing cut flowers and sold them all to the UK. What you should notice is that, if this were to happen, each country could consume outside its production possibility curve (PPC). The consumption combinations possible through specialisation and trade at these terms of trade are shown by each country's **trading possibility curve** (TPC) in Figure 10.3. Through specialisation and trade, each country

DEFINITION

Terms of trade: the price of a country's exports relative to the price of its imports. The terms of trade can be measured using the formula:

$$\text{Terms of trade} = \frac{\text{Index of average export prices}}{\text{Index of average import prices}} \times 100$$

DEFINITION

Trading possibility curve (TPC): a representation of all the combinations of two products that a country can consume if it engages in international trade. The TPC lies outside the production possibility curve (PPC), showing the gains in consumption possible from international trade

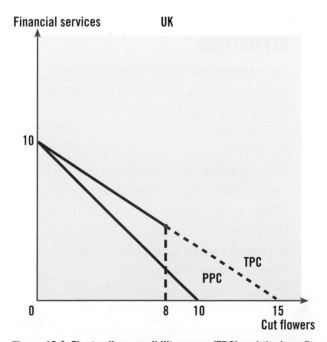

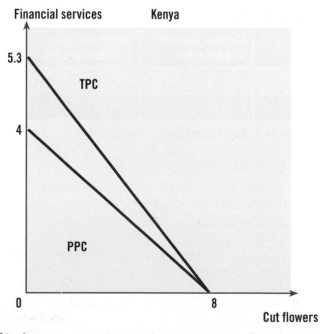

Figure 10.3 The trading possibility curve (TPC) and the benefits of trade

can consume more than it could produce itself. This is the great insight into trade offered by the principle of comparative advantage. Even if one country has an absolute advantage in the production of all goods and services, another country will have a comparative advantage in something and trade will benefit both.

Of course, in this simple model Kenya is unable to produce more than eight cut flowers, so the UK would not be able to consume along the dotted section of the TPC. However, this does not change the conclusion of the model. For those who engage in international trade, trading possibilities exist that exceed domestic production possibilities. In other words, countries do better engaging in trade than trying to produce everything themselves – trade allows a more efficient use of global resources.

ACTIVITY ····⁞

The table below shows the maximum production possibilities for clothes and motor vehicles for two countries, Italy and China, assuming all resources are used for the production of each good.

	Maximum output using all resources for each good	
	Clothes (number of garments)	Motor vehicles (number of cars)
Italy	1,000	4,000
China	5,000	5,000

Table 10.1 Maximum production possibilities

a) Draw the PPC for each country.

b) Which country has the absolute advantage in the production of clothes?

c) What should each country specialise in producing and exporting and why?

d) What terms of trade would benefit from both countries?

e) Construct a trading possibility curve (TPC) for each country based on the terms of trade you have chosen.

THE SOURCES OF COMPARATIVE ADVANTAGE

So far we have simply assumed that each country has a comparative advantage. A big question for economists is what gives countries these relative productive efficiencies.

The answer to this question is to look at the resources that each country has. Economies differ in the quantities of land, labour and capital that they have – they have different **factor endowments**. For example, China has abundant supplies of cheap labour, Europe and the USA have abundant supplies of capital, and so on. The production of different goods requires different amounts of each of the factors of production – they have different **factor intensities**. Different factor endowments and intensities lead to the conclusion that countries with lots of labour supplies will have a comparative advantage in **labour-intensive production** and countries with abundant capital a comparative advantage in **capital-intensive production**. Obviously, there will be differences, too, in the skills of the labour force and so human capital endowments will differ. So, a country such as the USA, with lots of skilled labour and physical capital, will have a

DEFINITIONS

Factor endowments: the mix of land, labour and capital that a country possesses. Factor endowments can be determined by, among other things, geography, historical legacy, and economic and social development

Factor intensities: the balance between land, labour and capital required in the production of a good or service

Labour-intensive production: any production process that involves a large amount of labour relative to other factors of production

comparative advantage in the production of aircraft. China, with lots of unskilled labour, may well specialise in the production of clothing and textiles. This is the **Heckscher–Ohlin theory of international trade,** named after two Swedish economists.

DEFINITIONS

Capital-intensive production: where the production of a good or service requires a large amount of capital relative to other factors of production

Heckscher–Ohlin theory of international trade: a theory that a country will export products produced using factors of production that are abundant and import products whose production requires the use of scarce factors

A country's comparative advantage is not set in stone, however. It will tend to change over time. As a country's GDP rises, higher levels of saving will result in the accumulation of more capital, and more expenditure on education will raise the skill level of the workforce. Encouraging entrepreneurship may allow comparative advantages to emerge in new industries over time.

The effects of international trade

International trade has a number of effects, which are outlined below.

INTERNATIONAL TRADE AND GLOBAL GDP

You have seen that specialisation and trade lead to a more efficient use of global resources. An efficient use of resources is clearly important because resources are scarce. Through international trade, global production is increased. To see how this happens, you should refer back to Figure 10.3 and take a look at Table 10.2. If, before trade, each country devoted half

ECONOMICS IN CONTEXT

INDIA'S CHANGING COMPARATIVE ADVANTAGE

It is all too easy to stereotype developing countries as having particular factor endowments – abundant natural resources and supplies of labour might easily spring to mind. Prior to the 1990s, this might have been an accurate picture of the Indian economy. Its exports were dominated by resource-intensive commodities, such as agricultural products (35 per cent of total exports) and minerals (23 per cent of total exports), and unskilled labour–intensive goods (22 per cent of total exports), such as textiles.

But India's comparative advantage is changing. Human capital and technology-intensive exports have doubled their share of total exports to 35 per cent. Agricultural and mineral-intensive exports have declined from 58 per cent of total exports to 35 per cent.

In recent years, India has become the world's leading exporter of IT services, with Indian companies such as Infosys, TCS and WIPRO, nicknamed the Bangalore Tigers, challenging established western multinational companies. As a result, companies such as Virgin and HSBC are now running their airline-booking systems and banking transactions through Indian IT companies based in Bangalore.

Part of the explanation for this changing comparative advantage lies in the 4–5 million science and engineering graduates coming out of Indian universities every year. Part of the explanation also rests

with growth in entrepreneurship encouraged by reduced government regulation. Narayan Murthy, co-founder of Infosys, says: 'It is the task of the government to create an environment where business thinks that it has enough incentives to create more and more jobs'. Significant economic reform and market liberalisation by the Indian government has provided this pro-business environment since the 1990s. Infosys has seen its revenues grow dramatically, from under $100 million in 1996 to over $2 billion in 2006. In the same period, the number of Indians employed by the company has increased from around 3,000 to over 60,000.

	Production before trade		Production after trade	
	Financial services	**Cut flowers**	**Financial services**	**Cut flowers**
UK	5	5	8	2
Kenya	2	4	0	8
World total	**7**	**9**	**8**	**10**

Table 10.2 Production increased by international trade

of its resources to the production of financial services and half to cut flowers, global production would be seven units of financial services and nine units of cut flowers. Trade allows each country to specialise. After trade, Kenya uses all of its resources to produce cut flowers and the UK uses 80 per cent of its resources to produce financial services and 20 per cent to produce cut flowers (partial specialisation). The result is that the world is now able to produce one more unit of financial services and one more unit of cut flowers. World production has increased – global GDP is higher.

INTERNATIONAL TRADE AND ECONOMIES OF SCALE

Without international trade, the production of goods and services would be limited by the size of the domestic market. By being able to supply global markets, firms and industries can benefit from economies of scale. Higher production for global markets will reduce average costs of production. This is a particular benefit for small countries and explains why exports can be a larger percentage of GDP for small countries than for large countries. Initially, however, some industries may lack the economies of scale to compete in global markets. These are sometimes referred to as **infant industries** and a case

DEFINITION

Infant industries: industries in an economy that are relatively new and lack the economies of scale that would allow them to compete in international markets against more established competitors in other countries

can be made for their temporary protection, through tariffs and quotas on imports.

INTERNATIONAL TRADE AND COMPETITION

Trade increases competition for domestic firms and, as a result, will put downward pressure on prices. These lower prices will squeeze firms' **profit margins**. This provides an incentive for firms to lower average costs by seeking efficiencies in production and eliminating waste. Exposed to international competition, domestic firms will be forced to be more productively efficient or face bankruptcy or merger. This raises the possibility that international trade can lead to job losses and reductions in the output of some industries. Overall, there is still a net gain from international trade, but there will be winners and losers within each country.

DEFINITION

Profit margin: the difference between a firm's revenue and costs expressed as a percentage of revenue

This point can be illustrated with the market demand and supply diagram in Figure 10.4. Let us say that this is the European Union market for clothing and textiles. Without trade, the price of the good or service is determined by the interaction of domestic demand and supply at Peu. International trade lowers the price of the good or service to P_1, which raises domestic demand to Qd but reduces domestic supply to Qs (Qd – Qs represents the imports from a relatively more efficient foreign producer). There are gainers and losers from this change. Consumers

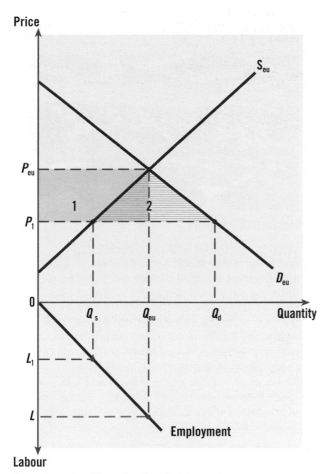

Figure 10.4 The EU market for clothing and textiles

to allow the economy to adjust to international competition and for resources to be re-allocated.

INTERNATIONAL TRADE AND DYNAMIC EFFICIENCIES

Dynamic efficiencies relate to changes that occur over time. According to the World Bank, countries that are more open to trade grow faster over the long run than those that remain closed. There are two possible reasons for this. One is that, as the global economy grows, there is an increase in the demand for an economy's exports. This growth in demand may exceed the growth in global GDP for income elastic goods and services. The growth in exports creates an increase in AD for exporting countries. In addition, it is argued that international trade gives rise to **knowledge and technology transfer**, which impacts on AS. This happens through collaboration with foreign firms, **licensing arrangements**, foreign direct investment and the outsourcing of production. The dynamic benefits of trade can be seen in India's toy industry, which is currently expanding by 15–20 per cent per annum, despite competition from Chinese imports (which make up 70 per cent of the Indian

have gained from lower prices and the ability to increase consumption. This gain is represented by area 1 + 2, which is the increased consumer surplus arising from lower prices. Domestic producers, along with workers in the industry, are the losers, with a reduction in output to *Qs* and a fall in labour employed to L_1. This loss is represented by area 1, the reduction in producer surplus caused by the lower price. Overall, there is a gain in economic welfare because area 1 + 2 (the gain in consumer surplus from international trade) is bigger than area 1 (the reduction in producer surplus from international trade). Resources are freed up to move to industries in which the EU is relatively more efficient.

However, this requires labour, in particular, to be mobile between industries. This may take time and there may be structural unemployment in the short term. This may require government intervention to ensure that workers have the skills to move into other occupations or may justify some temporary protection

DEFINITIONS

Dynamic efficiencies: efficiencies that occur over time. International trade can lead to changes in behaviour over a period of time that can increase productive and allocative efficiency

Knowledge and technology transfer: the process by which knowledge and technology developed in one country is transferred to another, often through licensing and franchising

Licensing arrangements: an agreement that ideas and technology 'owned' by one company can be used by another, often for a charge

market) and is beginning to change away from small-scale, labour-intensive production of low-value and poor quality products. As well as lowering prices, competition also encourages innovation, adding to the supply-side benefits of knowledge and technology transfer. For these reasons trade is thought of as the engine of economic growth.

INTERNATIONAL TRADE AND FACTOR PRICES

If the source of comparative advantage is differences in factor endowments, then over time trade will tend to equalise the prices of the factors of production. China's comparative advantage in labour-intensive production will lead to an increase in the demand for its exports. This will increase the demand for labour in China due to it specialising in the production of labour-intensive goods. Over time, this will cause wage rates in China, and other low-wage economies, to increase and the gap in income between the rich developed world and the poor developing world will narrow. This effect has been seen particularly where **regional trading blocs**, such as the North American Free Trade Area (NAFTA) and the European Union (EU), have been formed. In the case of NAFTA, trade has increased wages in Mexico and decreased the wages of unskilled workers in the USA as the structure of production changes to reflect the comparative advantages of the two countries. In countries with an abundance of cheap capital, an increase in capital-intensive production caused by trade will tend to increase the price of capital. The differences in factor prices, which encouraged trade in the first place, will disappear over time.

DEFINITION

Regional trading bloc: countries in a region that have formed an 'economic club' based on abolishing tariffs and non-tariff barriers to trade, e.g. the European Union (EU), the North American Free Trade Area (NAFTA) and the Association of South East Asian Nations (ASEAN)

ACTIVITY ····⟫

Lesotho textile workers

Lesotho is a small and poor developing economy in Africa with a population of 1.8 million. Over 45,000 people work in its textile industry, supplying garments to companies such as Gap and Levi Strauss. In 2006, export revenue from the sale of textiles to the USA was worth $385 million. The future for the industry, however, is uncertain as a result of competition in international markets from China where labour costs are at least a third lower than in Lesotho. In addition, almost all of the fabric used to make garments in Lesotho is imported.

a) What are the benefits of trade in textiles for Lesotho?

STRETCH AND CHALLENGE

b) Comment on the ways in which the textile industry in Lesotho might respond to the competition from China in international markets.

The terms of trade

You first came across the terms of trade in the model of comparative advantage on page 242. A country exports and imports a wide range of goods and services, so the calculation of the terms of trade in practice is complex. In principle, they are calculated using the formula below:

$$\text{Terms of trade} = \frac{\text{Index of average export prices}}{\text{Index of average import prices}} \times 100$$

The terms of trade tell you the volume of exports needed to purchase any given volume of imports. So, if export prices on average are rising more than import prices, a lower amount of exports will be needed to buy a certain quantity of imports. For this reason, a rise in the terms of trade is referred to as an 'improvement'. If export prices rise less rapidly than import prices (or if they fall relative to the average price of imports), then a country will have to export a larger volume in order to pay for the same quantity of imports – in this situation the terms of trade are said to have 'deteriorated'. The terms of trade, therefore, give some indication of the extent to which an economy will benefit from international trade.

For economies dependent on a narrow range of imports, changes in the terms of trade can be highly significant. Since 2000, there have been dramatic increases in the price of **primary commodities**, such as oil, copper, zinc, tin and platinum. These price increases have created a short-term boost to the

economies dependent on these commodities for their export revenue, particularly since the demand for primary commodities tends to be price inelastic. Export revenues from these commodities have increased sharply over the last seven years. However, over a longer period of time there is some evidence that primary commodity prices tend to follow a downward trend. Figures 10.5 and 10.6 show the monthly price (solid line) of tin and of robusta coffee and the trend in prices (dotted line) from January 1980 to January 2008.

The long-term trend in the price of coffee is bad news for the 95 developing economies that earn at least 50 per cent of their export revenue from coffee beans. According to the economists Raul Prebisch and Hans Singer, the long-term deterioration in the terms of trade for primary commodities severely limits the gains from trade for economies whose structure is dominated by the primary sector. Instead of relying on their comparative advantage in primary products, developing economies should seek to change the structure of their economies in order to avoid the development trap created by declining terms of trade.

DEFINITION

Primary commodities: goods produced in the primary sector of the economy, such as coffee and tin

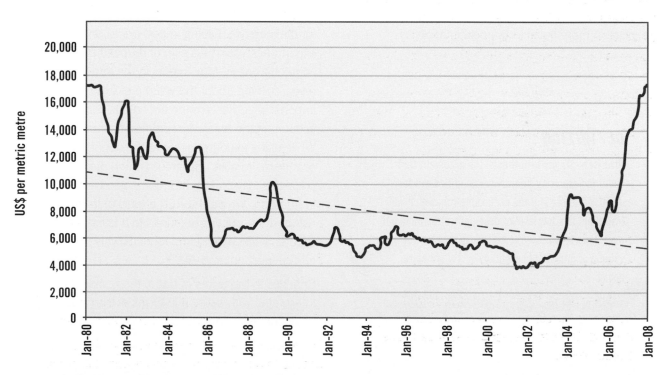

Figure 10.5 World price of tin, January 1980–January 2008
Source: IMF

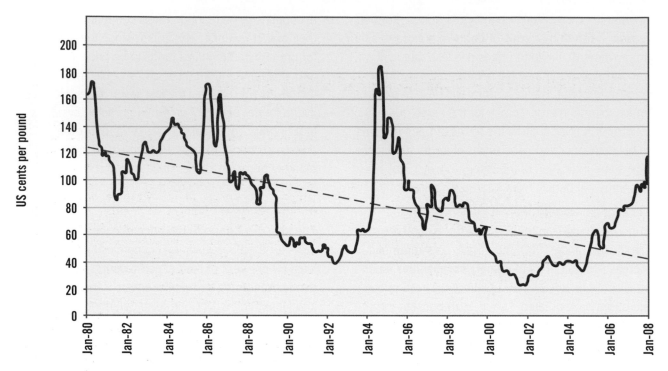

Figure 10.6 World price of coffee (robusta), January 1980–January 2008
Source: IMF

This has become known as the **Prebisch–Singer hypothesis**. The problems created by international trade for developing economies is a theme you will explore in more detail in the next chapter.

DEFINITION

Prebisch–Singer hypothesis: the argument that countries exporting primary commodities will face declining terms of trade in the long run, which will trap them in a low level of development as more and more exports will need to be sold to 'pay for' the same volume of imports of secondary sector or capital goods

'Improvements' in the terms of trade, however, are not without their problems too. Whether rising terms of trade create a benefit depends upon the reasons for the increase. Falling import prices and rising export prices can be a sign of reduced international competitiveness. Movements in the terms of trade reveal nothing about the volume of exports and imports, which determine the effects on the current account of the balance of payments and AD. While rising export prices give the opportunity for economies to gain from trade, much depends on the price elasticity of demand for the goods or services in question. Where the PED is elastic, for example, rising export prices could lead to a fall in the value of exports, which would impact negatively on both the current account and AD.

Changes in the terms of trade, then, should be interpreted with caution in terms of their impact on an economy.

ECONOMICS IN CONTEXT

ETHIOPIAN COFFEE – TURNING A BEAN INTO A BRAND?

Ethiopia has licensed its coffee 'brands'

The £3 cup of latte or iced moccachino at Starbucks, Coffee Republic or Costa Coffee has become an affordable luxury in the UK. But for the 20 million families whose livelihoods depend on growing the coffee beans for our latte, the swings in the world price of coffee beans really do matter. Coffee beans are the second largest source of export revenue for developing countries. For Ethiopia, revenues from the export of coffee make up 36 per cent of total export earnings.

The world price of coffee beans is determined by market forces of demand and supply and is highly volatile. Back in 2002, the world price hit an all-time low, falling almost 90 per cent from its peak six years earlier.

What brought this about was a glut of coffee beans on the world market. Global production exceeded consumption by 300 million kg in 2002. The increase

in world supply, particularly in Vietnam, was a response to the earlier high prices. Vietnam's coffee plantations underwent massive expansion. Between 1990 and 2000, Vietnam increased its production of coffee beans by 1,400 per cent and become the world's second largest producer of coffee beans.

Coffee consumers in the West are not very sensitive to price changes – demand is price inelastic. So when supply increased, there was no significant change in consumption and prices dropped dramatically. The terms of trade for countries heavily dependent on coffee beans for export revenue turned against them.

Coffee producers fear that the current rising price of coffee beans could set off another expansion of supply and are finding ways to avoid the next downturn in prices. But changing consumption habits in the West might work in their favour. Not all lattes are the same – consumers now demand high-quality coffee. For Ethiopia, that is good news: 40 per cent of its production is high-quality coffee beans that command a high price. So much so, that the Ethiopian government has tried to trademark the names of three of the world's finest varieties – Harar, Yegarcheffe and Sidamo. It is reported that Starbucks objected and the National Coffee Association in the USA sought to block the trademark application through the US courts. To get around the problem, Ethiopia has licensed its 'brands' to seventy suppliers, including Starbucks.

Ethiopian coffee beans, then, have moved up-market in order to try to avoid the wild swings in the world price and the consequent problems related to their terms of trade with the rest of the world.

The pattern of global trade

A striking feature of the pattern of global trade is its uneven distribution. Figure 10.7 shows the extent to which **developed economies** dominate world trade. Almost two-thirds of world trade is accounted for by the world's richest economies. This suggests inequality in the distribution of the gains from trade identified by the theory of comparative advantage. However, this is not surprising if developed

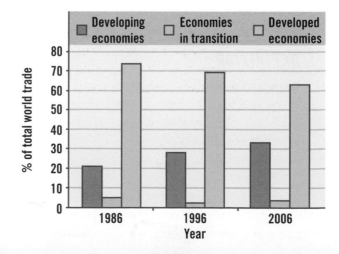

Figure 10.7 Shares of total world trade
Source: *UNCTAD Handbook of Statistics*, 2007

economies hold a comparative advantage in capital-intensive production. These goods and services will tend to command a high price and, therefore, the value gained from their trade will tend to be higher than that of trade in the labour-intensive products traded by **developing economies.**

DEFINITIONS

Developed economies: countries with a high income per capita and diversified industrial and tertiary sectors of the economy. Examples of developed economies would include the USA, the UK, Japan and South Korea

Developing economies: countries with relatively low income per capita, an economy in which the industrial sector is small or undeveloped and where primary sector production is a relatively large part of total GDP

This dominance of global trade by rich countries, however, is declining and developing countries have benefited from a rising share of world trade over the last thirty years. This is due to the **liberalisation** of world trade and the greater exploitation of comparative advantage. Despite this, there are some patterns of global trade that do not appear to fit the economists' theory of international trade based on comparative advantage.

DEFINITION

Liberalisation: reductions in the barriers to international trade, in order to allow foreign firms to gain access to the market for goods and services that are traded internationally

What is surprising is that rich economies tend to trade with other rich economies. Comparative

advantage would suggest that this should not be the case. Trade should take place where relative opportunity costs are widest. In other words, rich nations should trade with poor nations, given the differences in their factor endowments. Figure 10.8 shows that this is not the case. With the exception of **transition economies**, countries appear to trade within their own group (intra-group trade) rather than with countries whose income level is different. Given that factor prices will tend to be similar within these income groups, this suggests that comparative advantage is a weak explanation of the pattern of global trade.

DEFINITION

Transition economies: economies in the process of changing from central planning to the free market

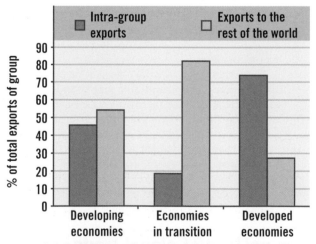

Figure 10.8 Destinations of exports by groups of economies
Source: *UNCTAD Handbook of Statistics*, 2007

Figure 10.9 gives a more detailed picture of the flows of world trade and shows that trade is concentrated not just among economies of similar income levels but also geographically. A key observation you can make is that 55 per cent of the world's trade in goods takes place within the regions identified on the map (**intra-regional trade**). By far the biggest source of intra-regional trade is in Europe: 31.4 per cent of the world's trade in goods takes place between European

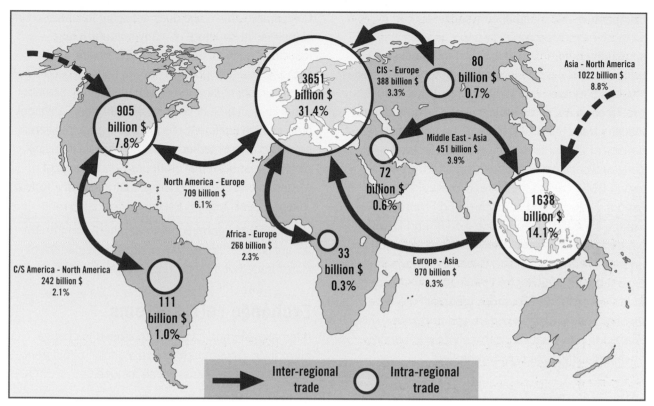

Figure 10.9 Selected inter- and intra-regional trade in goods, 2006
Source: International Trade Statistics 2007, World Trade Organization

countries. This seems to be at odds with comparative advantage theory, until you think that the theory as presented took no account of transport costs. Small differences in opportunity costs may be cancelled out by significant transport costs. This could explain why trading partners tend to be geographically close. Alternatively, it could be argued that the world is divided up into trading blocs, such as the EU, NAFTA and ASEAN. Such regional integration often involves tariffs against trade with non-member countries and

this will go some way to explaining the geographical concentration of trade you can observe in the map.

DEFINITION

Intra-regional trade: trade between countries in the same geographical area, for example trade between the UK and Germany or the USA and Canada

ACTIVITY ···

The Doha round of WTO negotiations, launched in 2001, has been called the 'Doha Development Round' because it is trying to reduce the tariffs imposed by rich countries on imports of agricultural commodities. In 2008, France and Germany proposed that imports of food into the EU must comply with EU rules on hygiene, animal welfare and labour laws, or be subject to high import tariffs. They claim that this will protect EU consumers.

a) Use a demand and supply diagram to show how tariffs affect international trade.

b) With reference to your diagram, identify the winners and losers from the use of tariffs.

Comparative advantage theory suggests that, if a country exports a good or service, it will import something different. This is called **inter-industry trade**. In reality, a very high proportion of global trade involves countries exporting and importing products produced in the same industry. This is termed **intra-industry trade** and is a feature of the trade between nations of the same income level and in the same geographical area. So, for example, Germany will export BMW cars to the UK and France, the UK exports Nissan cars to Germany and France, and France exports Citroën cars to the UK and Germany. Nations in Europe (and elsewhere) are exporting and importing the same things. Table 10.3 shows the extent of intra-industry trade in automotive products in 2006 – of the ten countries/groups in the table, eight appear as both exporters and importers. This is at odds with what you learnt about comparative advantage at the start of this chapter.

Comparative advantage does not seem to take account of the market structure of many manufacturing industries, such as the automotive industry. Such industries are oligopolies. They are characterised by a small number of large producers, high entry barriers and a large degree of product differentiation. Different firms produce different products to appeal to different segments of the market. In the automotive industry, each car manufacturer produces a wide range of models of cars. This encourages intra-industry trade as variety appeals to consumers.

As a theory of international trade, then, comparative advantage goes some way to explain the pattern of global trade but it has shortcomings.

Exchange rate systems

International trade gives rise to a need to change currencies. Governments have a choice of different exchange rate systems, which include:

● **freely floating exchange rate**

DEFINITIONS

Inter-industry trade: trade involving the exchange of goods and services produced by different industries

Intra-industry trade: trade involving the exchange of goods and services produced by the same industry

DEFINITION

Freely floating exchange rate: a system whereby the price of one currency expressed in terms of another is determined by the forces of demand and supply

Exporter	Share of world exports (%)	Importer	Share of world imports (%)
European Union (EU25)	52.6	European Union (EU25)	43.8
Japan	13.7	USA	21.5
USA	9.4	Canada	6.1
Canada	6.5	Mexico	2.8
Republic of Korea	4.2	Russian Federation	2.0
Mexico	4.2	China	1.8
China	1.4	Australia	1.5
Brazil	1.3	Japan	1.4

Table 10.3 Leading exporters and importers of automotive products, and share of world exports/imports, 2006
Source: International Trade Statistics 2007, World Trade Organization

- **fixed exchange rate**
- **semi-fixed/semi-floating exchange rate**.

The choice of exchange rate system is dependent on the nature of the economy and government policy and policy objectives. Each system has its relative merits and drawbacks.

DEFINITIONS

Fixed exchange rate: an exchange rate system in which the value of one currency has a fixed value against other countries. This fixed rate is often set by the government

Semi-fixed/semi-floating exchange rate: an exchange rate system that allows a currency's value to fluctuate within a permitted band of fluctuation

FREELY FLOATING EXCHANGE RATE

In a freely floating exchange rate system, the value of the currency is determined solely by the forces of demand and supply and there is no government intervention in the **foreign exchange (FOREX) markets**. The demand and supply of a currency on the FOREX markets is affected by three things:

DEFINITION

Foreign exchange (FOREX) market: a term used to describe the coming together of buyers and sellers of currencies

- trade – for example, UK goods and services sold in the USA create a demand for the pound, whereas UK spending on imports from the eurozone results in pounds being supplied to the FOREX markets to buy euros.

- **short-term capital flows** – funds flow in and out of countries in the form of deposits in bank accounts. These flows can be highly volatile and depend upon actual and expected interest rates and exchange rates.

- **long-term capital transactions** – flows of money related to buying and selling of assets, such as land or property or production facilities (direct investment) or shares in companies (portfolio investment).

DEFINITIONS

Short-term capital flows: flows of money in and out of a country in the form of bank deposits. Short-term capital flows are highly volatile and exist to take advantage of changes in relative interest rates

Long-term capital transactions: flows of money related to buying and selling of assets, such as land or property or production facilities (direct investment) or shares in companies (portfolio investment)

learning tip

BUILDING ON AS

You have studied the determination of exchange rates at AS. Check that you can analyse, using a demand and supply diagram, how changes in demand and supply of a currency lead to changes in the exchange rate – this is synoptic knowledge and you are expected to be able to use it at A2.

STEPPING UP TO A2

The emphasis at A2 is on comparing different exchange rate systems and their advantages and disadvantages.

Changes in any of these factors lead to a change in demand or supply of a currency and a rise (appreciation) or fall (depreciation) in the exchange rate.

A freely floating exchange rate system has a number of merits over other exchange rate systems.

● Governments are free to set domestic economic policy to achieve the key policy objectives. There is no need to set interest rates to achieve an exchange rate target, for example. The central bank is, therefore, free to use the interest rate to achieve price stability and the exchange rate ceases to be a constraint on economic policy.

● Monetary policy is more effective in controlling AD and inflation under a freely floating exchange rate system. Suppose that the central bank wishes to increase interest rates to decrease inflation and to reduce AD. The higher interest rate will cause the exchange rate to appreciate. This appreciation of the currency will lower import prices, which will reduce inflationary pressure. Lower import prices will also raise the demand for imports, which will decrease AD. Export prices will be raised by the currency's appreciation, which will further reduce AD. The exchange rate effect, therefore, reinforces domestic monetary policy.

● Balance of payments problems are corrected automatically by freely floating exchange rates. An underlying deficit on the balance of payments means that there is more money leaving the economy than entering it. This must mean that the exchange rate is in disequilibrium, as in Figure 10.10, because the supply of the currency (the value of imports + capital outflows) exceeds its demand (the value of exports + capital inflows). The exchange rate will automatically depreciate. This depreciation will reduce export prices and raise import prices, raising export demand and reducing the demand for imports. The balance of payments deficit will be eliminated.

● A freely floating exchange rate provides a mechanism for adjusting to **external economic shocks**. If the global economy goes into recession, an economy such as the UK would find that the demand for its exports would be reduced. But this would reduce the demand for pounds on the FOREX markets,

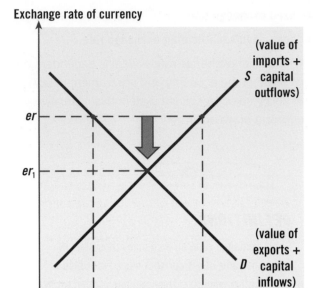

Figure 10.10 Automatic correction of balance of payments deficit under freely floating exchange rate

causing the pound's exchange rate to depreciate. This depreciation would cushion the reduction in demand for exports by lowering their price.

● There is reduced speculation over the value of a currency when it is freely floating. There will be a tendency for freely floating exchange rates to reflect **purchasing power parity (PPP),** and so it is unlikely

DEFINITIONS

External economic shocks: unexpected events coming from outside the economy that cause unpredicted changes in AS or AD. Examples might include rapid rises in oil prices or a global slowdown

Purchasing power parity (PPP): the exchange rate that equalises the price of a basket of identical traded goods and services in two different countries. PPP is an attempt to measure the true value of a currency in terms of the goods and services it will buy

to be over- or undervalued. Currency speculators have little to gain as a result and this will encourage greater stability in the exchange rate over time. An exchange rate is at its purchasing power parity rate when it will buy the same volume of internationally traded goods and services at home as abroad. So, if the market exchange rate is £1 = $2, this will be the PPP rate if $2 buys the same quantity of goods and services in the USA as £1 buys in the UK. It is argued that an increase in domestic inflation will cause the exchange rate to depreciate to offset the increase in the price of goods and services bought domestically.

The merits of a freely floating exchange rate can be overstated, however. The freedom to set domestic economic policy does not necessarily guarantee that governments will choose to prioritise price stability above other objectives. Automatic adjustment mechanisms may lead to governments pursuing short-term economic growth at the expense of higher inflation. The reliance on exchange rate depreciations to offset domestic inflation is likely to be unsustainable in the long run. A depreciation of the exchange rate raises import prices, which will make the domestic inflation problem worse over time

and require further currency depreciation to maintain international competitiveness. There is a danger that a lack of control over inflation could create a run on the currency, which could result in economic crises such as that experienced by Argentina from around 1999 to 2002, when a crisis of confidence in the economy resulted in massive withdrawals from the banking system. In panic, people converted pesos into dollars and took money out of the country, causing the value of the currency to fall dramatically. The shortage of cash in the economy created a major recession; GDP fell by almost 20 per cent by 2002 and unemployment rose to 25 per cent of the workforce.

Depreciation of the exchange rate does not always improve balance of payments problems, especially in the short run. If the demand for imports is price inelastic, rising import prices will raise the value of imports, making trade and current account deficits worse, not better. This would mean that the supply of the currency was actually downward-sloping. That is, a lower exchange rate would increase the quantity of the currency supplied, not reduce it. As a result, the exchange rate would become unstable, continuing to fall, rather than finding a new equilibrium.

ECONOMICS IN CONTEXT

IS CHINA'S CURRENCY TOO CHEAP?

China's success in international markets and the growth in its exports have brought accusations that its currency, the yuan, is seriously undervalued. The view has been expressed strongly by EU politicians, including the French president, Nicolas Sarkozy, the president of the European Central Bank (ECB) and by US senators.

The eurozone's growing trade deficit has been blamed on the undervaluation of the yuan. This deficit increased by 25 per cent in the first eight months of 2007 to reach €70 billion. The US trade deficit with China reached $233 billion in 2006, almost 30 per cent of the total US trade deficit. In the USA, the issue is creating pressure for protection of domestic industry against what is considered to be the artificially low price of imports from China. It is argued that these low prices are causing jobs in the USA to be lost. Some US politicians have called for

tariffs as high as 27.5 per cent on imports from China to offset the undervaluation of the yuan against the dollar.

In judging whether the yuan is undervalued, a useful source of information on purchasing power parity (PPP) is *The Economist*. The magazine regularly publishes its Big Mac Index to crudely estimate whether market exchange rates are over- or undervalued. It uses the price of a McDonald's Big Mac in local currencies to calculate a Big Mac PPP. The Big Mac PPP is the exchange rate that equalises the price of a hamburger in the USA and elsewhere.

According to *The Economist*'s July 2007 Big Mac Index, China's currency is undervalued by 58 per cent.

For a short video guide to the Big Mac Index, go to www.heinemann.co.uk/hotlinks, insert the express code 2230P, and click on 'Economist Big Mac Index'.

DEFINITION

J-curve effect: shows the trend in a country's balance of trade following a depreciation of the exchange rate. A fall in the exchange rate causes an initial worsening of the balance of trade, as higher import prices raise the value of imports and lower export prices reduce the value of exports due to short-run price inelasticity of the demand for imports and exports. Eventually the trade balance improves. An appreciation of the currency causes an inverted J-curve effect

If the price elasticity of demand for exports is also inelastic, falling export prices would reduce the value of exports sold, further reinforcing the tendency of the trade and current account to worsen. This is known as the **J-curve effect** of a depreciation and is shown in Figure 10.11. In the diagram, the depreciation takes place at time *t*, following a deficit on the current account of the balance of payments. Because the price elasticities of demand for imports and exports are inelastic, the current account deficit worsens before it starts to improve.

The extent to which a freely floating exchange rate system provides the economy with an adjustment mechanism, therefore, depends on the degree of the responsiveness of imports and exports to price changes. This is captured in the **Marshall–Lerner condition**, which states that a depreciation will improve the balance of payments only if the price elasticities of demand for imports and exports are greater than one when added together.

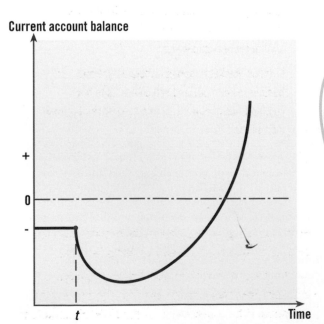

Figure 10.11 The J-curve effect of an exchange rate depreciation

DEFINITION

Marshall–Lerner condition: states that for a depreciation of the currency to improve the balance of trade the sum of the price elasticities of demand (PEDs) for imports and exports must be greater than 1

FIXED EXCHANGE RATES

In a fixed exchange rate system, the value of the currency has a fixed value against another currency or a basket of other currencies. The choice of currency is often determined by the pattern of trade. So, Argentina may choose to fix the exchange rate of the peso against the dollar because a significant amount of its trade is with the USA. This is sometimes known as a currency peg.

In order to fix its exchange rate, a country will have to be prepared to intervene in the FOREX markets to buy and sell its currency, to restrict currency flows or to abandon the use of monetary policy to maintain price stability. Referring to Figure 10.12, if the exchange rate is fixed at er but the demand and supply of the currency is D_0 S_0 there will be an excess supply of the currency. Without government action, the exchange rate would depreciate. To maintain the exchange rate at er, either the demand for the currency must be raised to D_1 or its supply must be reduced to S_1. To do this, the central bank will need to use its reserves of foreign currency to buy its own currency on the FOREX markets. Alternatively, it may have to limit the amount of the currency that leaves the country – this is known as using exchange controls (limits to the amount of currency that can be taken out of the country). Or it may be forced to raise interest rates to attract currency inflows and raise the demand for the currency.

A fixed exchange rate system is argued to have important advantages over freely floating exchange rates:

● reduced exchange rate uncertainty – a fixed exchange rate reduces the risks of trade and investment by reducing exchange rate uncertainty. Fixed exchange rates allow the price of exports and imports to remain more stable. As a result, it is argued, countries operating fixed exchange rates will enjoy higher levels of trade and investment.

● reduced cost of trade – under freely flowing exchange rate regimes, businesses face a risk that movements of the exchange rate can undermine the profitability of trade. As an insurance against movements in the exchange rate, firms engaging in international trade **hedge** their risks by buying currencies in the **futures markets**. Fixed exchange rates reduce the need for hedging and this lowers the cost of international trade.

● imposes discipline on domestic firms – if the exchange rate cannot depreciate, domestic firms will have to make sure that they match the productivity improvements of their foreign competitors and do not allow unit labour costs to increase.

DEFINITIONS

Hedging: business strategy that limits the risk that losses are made from changes in the price of currencies or commodities

Futures markets: markets where people and businesses can buy and sell contracts to buy commodities or currencies at a fixed price at a fixed date in the future

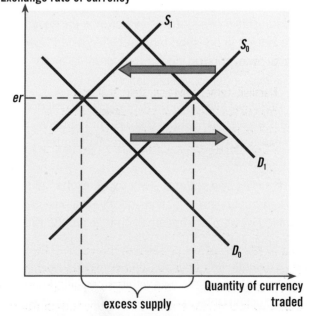

Exchange rate of currency

Figure 10.12 Intervention required to maintain a fixed exchange rate

Fixed exchange rate systems are not without their problems, however. These problems include:

● the need to maintain high levels of **foreign currency reserves** – reserves of foreign currencies are needed for intervention in the FOREX markets to maintain the exchange rate. Such reserves have an opportunity cost. They represent money that could

DEFINITION

Foreign currency reserves: foreign currencies held by central banks in order to enable intervention in the FOREX markets to affect the country's exchange rate

have been used to finance government expenditure on health, education or infrastructure. This may put a constraint on the kinds of economic policies that would contribute to economic growth in the long term.

● the loss of control over domestic monetary policy – under a fixed exchange rate system, interest rates have to be set to maintain the exchange rate. In situations where the interest rate needs to be reduced to prevent the exchange rate from appreciating, this may lead to a conflict with the objective of maintaining price stability. When the interest rate needs to be increased to prevent the exchange rate from depreciating, there is a conflict with the objective of maintaining economic growth.

● speculative 'attacks' on the currency – under fixed exchange rate systems, currencies can become over- or undervalued. In the event of persistent over- or undervaluation, currency speculators are likely to sell or buy the currency, causing volatility in the exchange rate. In the Asian financial crisis of 1997, large capital outflows put downward pressure on the exchange rates of many East Asian economies. The International Monetary Fund had to intervene, committing $40 billion to stabilise the currencies of South Korea, Thailand and Indonesia. East Asian economies themselves were forced to raise interest rates to very high levels in an attempt to stem capital outflows. These high interest rates did much to damage the economies affected and, in the end, could not halt the depreciation of the currencies affected. Indonesia's currency lost half of its value in one year, there were riots in Jakarta in response to higher import prices and Indonesia suffered a 14 per cent fall in GDP during the crisis.

● international retaliation – countries have much to gain in the short run by deliberately fixing their

exchange rate below the market rate. They are likely to benefit from high growth in export volumes, aided by the low price of their goods abroad and low growth in imports. In the longer term, however, this may cause a rise in protectionist measures against their exports. US companies have argued that China's fixed exchange rate system amounts to a massive subsidy of its exporters. They cite the growing US trade deficit with China (in 2007 this had reached a record $256 billion) as evidence of the undervaluation of the Chinese currency (the yuan). There is mounting pressure, in both the USA and the EU, to impose trade restrictions (so-called anti-dumping tariffs and quotas) against Chinese exports of shoes, textiles and steel products.

SEMI-FIXED/SEMI-FLOATING EXCHANGE RATES

Semi-fixed or semi-floating exchange rates include a range of exchange rate systems somewhere between floating and fixed exchange rates. The idea of these hybrid systems is to try to achieve the advantages of both fixed and floating systems and to minimise their disadvantages. So, they are either closer to a fixed exchange rate system with an element of floating or they are more like floating systems with some degree of intervention to limit fluctuations. Economists have distinguished between these different systems or regimes as follows:

● *adjustable peg systems* – where the exchange rate is fixed in the short term but is adjusted upwards or downwards in the long term in order to avoid sustained under- or overvaluation.

● *managed floating systems* – where the exchange rate is allowed to float but there is central bank intervention to prevent large fluctuation in the exchange rate.

● *crawling peg systems* – where the exchange rate is fixed but large revaluations or devaluations are avoided by frequent but small changes to the fixed exchange rate.

● *exchange rate band systems* – where the exchange rate floats freely within a permitted band of fluctuation. Intervention only occurs when the exchange rate reaches its upper or lower limit (ceiling or floor).

ECONOMICS IN CONTEXT

THE HONG KONG DOLLAR

The Hong King dollar (HK$) is an example of a semi-fixed exchange rate. For almost twenty-five years its value has been pegged to the US dollar (US$). Currently the currency is fixed within a permitted range of fluctuation of HK$ 7.75–7.85 to US$ 1. During 2007 there was strong upward pressure on the currency, resulting in intervention in the foreign exchange markets in October to keep the currency within its permitted range. The authorities had to buy over US$ 1 billion to stop the exchange rate rising.

A semi-fixed exchange rate has been good for Hong Kong because of the importance of international trade. The value of exports of goods and services represents over 200 per cent of GDP. Exporters have benefited from greater certainty and reduced risk because of the very narrow band of permitted fluctuation of the HK$. This has encouraged investment and enabled Hong Kong to experience high rates of economic growth.

But the exchange rate policy has had its costs too. Because the exchange rate cannot adjust to external shocks, domestic output and prices have to take the strain. In addition, Hong Kong cannot pursue an independent monetary policy and must set interest rates in line with those in the USA. This has had damaging effects on the Hong Kong economy in the past. Before the Asian financial crisis of May to July 1997, annual inflation in Hong Kong averaged almost 9 per cent. Interest rates could not be increased without the exchange rate appreciating outside of its permitted range. During the Asian crisis, Hong Kong suffered severe deflation (prices fell by 14 per cent and GDP declined by 5 per cent) but it was unable to reduce interest rates to stimulate aggregate demand.

With interest rates falling in the USA in response to the downturn in the economy, Hong Kong in 2008 is once again faced with a policy dilemma because of its semi-fixed exchange rate. During 2007, the economy was growing above its trend rate of growth and labour market conditions were tightening. With unemployment at around 4 per cent, labour shortages were beginning to push up wages. The normal policy response would be an increase in interest rates. But this would put further upward pressure on the HK$, especially since US interest rates were being cut so aggressively.

In short, Hong Kong's semi-fixed exchange rate has provided stability and certainty in its international trade (external stability) but at the cost of problems in the management of the domestic economy (internal instability).

Exchange rate fluctuations

Freely floating exchange rates, in particular, will fluctuate over time. These fluctuations can be quite large, as Figure 10.13 shows. For example, between 1999 and early 2001, the euro/pound exchange rate had fallen by almost 20 per cent, yet from the end of 2007 the rate appreciated by roughly 20 per cent through 2008. It might be expected that **bilateral exchange rates** show greater fluctuation than measures of **effective exchange rates** based on averages of a basket of currencies. Figure 10.14, however, shows that the euro's effective exchange rate index has shown as much fluctuation as, if not more than, its bilateral exchange rate against the pound.

DEFINITIONS

Bilateral exchange rate: the exchange of one currency against another

Effective exchange rate: the exchange rate of one currency against a basket of currencies of other countries, often weighted according to the amount of trade done with each country

CAUSES OF EXCHANGE RATE FLUCTUATIONS

Exchange rate fluctuations are caused by changes in the demand and supply of the currency on the FOREX markets. When the demand for a currency exceeds its supply, the exchange rate will appreciate (rise in value) and when supply exceeds demand it will depreciate (fall in value).

In the longer term, changes in demand and supply of a currency are related to changes in the value of exports and imports and long-term capital flows, as explained on page 255. The determinants of exports, imports and long-term capital flows change slowly over time. These determinants centre on differences between economies, including:

ACTIVITY ⋯⋮

Using newspapers or the Internet:

a) Keep a record – for about four weeks – of selected exchange rates for a currency of your own choosing. This could be done in a spreadsheet.

b) Keep a 'clippings' file of news related to the economy and its exchange rate.

c) Explain the trend in the selected exchange rates you observe.

For a good source of exchange rate data, go to www.heinemann.co.uk/hotlinks, insert the express code 2230P, and click on 'BBC website exchange rates'.

The *Economist* allows you to chart daily exchange rates for currencies back to 1990 and hosts an interactive exchange rate map. Go to www. heinemann.co.uk/hotlinks, insert the express code 2230P, and click on 'Economist website exchange rates':

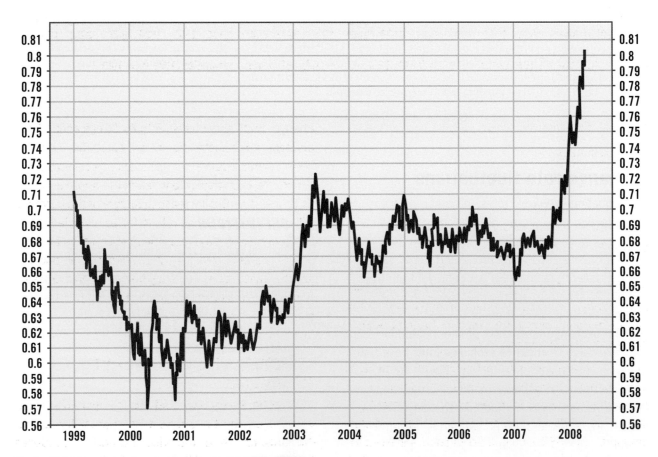

Figure 10.13 Euro/pound exchange rate (daily) 1999–2008
Source: European Central Bank, Statistical Data Warehouse

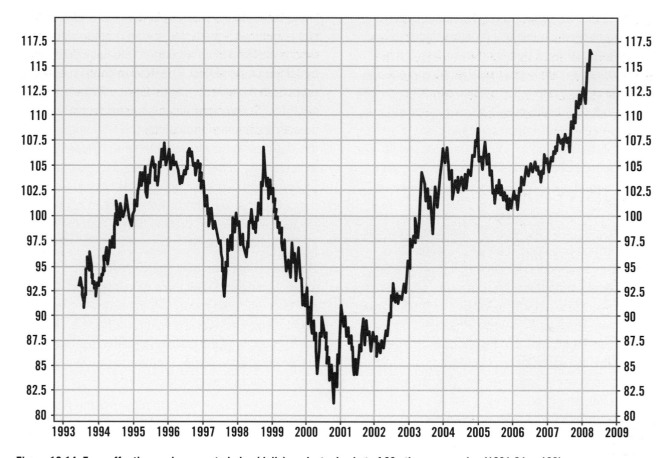

Figure 10.14 Euro effective exchange rate index (daily) against a basket of 22 other currencies (1991 Q1 = 100)

● rates of inflation

● interest rates

● rates of economic growth

● labour productivity

● measures of international competitiveness generally.

These are sometimes referred to as the economic fundamentals. This suggests that exchange rates will move slowly towards their long-term equilibrium. This long-term equilibrium will be the purchasing power parity, introduced on page 256.

In the short term, however, exchange rate fluctuations owe much to speculation. According to recent research by the Bank for International Settlements, the average daily turnover on global FOREX markets amounted to US$3.2 trillion. Speculators will react to news about economic performance and buy or sell currencies in the expectation that exchange rates will

change. Such speculation actually brings about the changes in the exchange rate expected. So, if the central bank reduces interest rates, speculators will expect the exchange rate to fall in the future and sell the currency – this increase in supply of the currency will cause the exchange rate to fall as expected. Confidence can play a big role in speculative buying and selling of currencies – it is difficult to pin down exactly what causes currency traders to gain or lose confidence in a currency, beyond changes in the economic fundamentals listed above.

CONSEQUENCES OF EXCHANGE RATE FLUCTUATIONS

Changes in the exchange rate have important effects on the economy. For example, an appreciation of the exchange rate raises the price of exports and reduces the price of imports. Higher export prices can have an adverse effect on the macroeconomy. Higher export prices will reduce the demand for exports. The extent to which this is a problem depends on the price elasticity of demand for exports. If the demand for exports is price elastic, an appreciation of the exchange rate will lower the value of exports, which in turn will reduce AD, economic growth and employment. Lower import prices will add to these effects if the demand for imports is price elastic. The consequence could, therefore, be a deterioration in the current account balance of the balance of payments.

However, currency appreciation also brings benefits. Lower import prices are a benefit for consumers and for those producers that import raw materials, components and machinery. Consumers benefit from an increase in living standards as their income buys more goods and services. Producers benefit from lower input costs and higher profit margins or are able to reduce prices to raise demand. An appreciation of the exchange rate can, therefore, reduce inflationary pressures.

Depreciation of the exchange rate has the opposite effects to those above.

Fluctuating exchange rates, though, are a different matter. The important thing about fluctuating exchange rates is the regular movements up and down in the value of the currency. These movements create uncertainty and risk.

Suppose, for example, an American retailer signs a contract to buy 1,000 T-shirts in four months' time from a supplier in Pakistan. The supplier in Pakistan quotes a cost for the contract of 130,000 Pakistan rupees. At the current market exchange rate (US$1 = 65PKR), the cost to the American supplier is US$2,000 or US$2 per T-shirt. Given other costs for the US retailer and the US retail price of T-shirts in

Table 10.4, the US retailer plans to make US$1 profit per T-shirt if all T-shirts are sold. If, in four months' time, the dollar/rupee exchange rate has depreciated by 10 per cent to US$1 = PKR58.5, the US retailer's profit from the sale of T-shirts falls by 22 per cent to US$0.78. Pakistan's fluctuating exchange rate creates uncertainty and risk for the US importer – in this case, profit may turn out to be significantly less than planned. If the exchange rate had risen, the profit for the US retailer would have been greater than expected. You should notice that, in relative terms, the variation in profit is bigger than the change in the exchange rate.

Uncertainty and risk may, therefore, deter international trade. The more a country's exchange rate fluctuates, the more risky trade is with that country and the lower the volume of trade is likely to be. This is one of the main arguments that have led some countries to favour fixed exchange rate systems over floating exchange rates.

There are, of course, ways to minimise the risks from fluctuating exchange rates. In the example above, the US retailer could pay for the contract up front, completely avoiding any risk from depreciation of the dollar. However, this involves an opportunity cost – the sacrifice of interest that could have been earned over the four months before the T-shirts are delivered. Another option is to use futures markets. Futures markets are a way for firms to guarantee an exchange rate by buying currencies at a fixed rate at some point in the future. These methods of dealing with exchange rate risks are not without cost, however.

Despite the risks and uncertainties created by fluctuating exchange rates, world trade volumes are remarkably stable. The major reason for this is that

T-shirts	Cost in Pakistan rupees (PKR)	Exchange rate	Cost in US$	Cost in US$ per T-shirt	Other costs in US$ (transport and retailing)	Market price in US$	Profit per T-shirt in US$
1,000	130,000	US$1 = PKR65	2,000	2	2	5	1
1,000	130,000	US$1 = PKR58.5	2,222	2.22	2	5	0.78

Table 10.4 Impact of fluctuating exchange rates on a US importer and retailer

exporters appear to price their goods and services for their export markets, absorbing changes in exchange rates in their profit margins. So, faced with a depreciating US dollar, the supplier in Pakistan would cut their price in rupees to maintain stable prices in US$. This is not to say that exchange rate fluctuations don't matter, but that they do not have the impact on the volume of international trade that some supporters of fixed exchange rates argue.

Nevertheless, the argument for exchange rate stability was a very powerful argument supporting the creation of a **single currency** among some members of the EU. These countries believed that, with a large majority of trade taking place with other members of the EU, trade and investment in the EU would be increased if exchange rates were permanently fixed and countries shared the same currency. So, the fluctuation of the euro exchange rate you saw at the beginning of this section has less impact than might at first be supposed. This is because the majority

of trade of those economies using the euro is with others in the **euro area** and not with the UK or the 22 other countries accounted for by the euro's effective exchange rate index.

DEFINITION

Euro area, eurozone: term to describe the combined economies of the countries using the euro

DEFINITIONS

Single currency: a currency that is shared by more than one country. The euro is shared by 15 countries in the European Union (EU)

Balance of payments problems

If the balance of payments balances, how can there be balance of payments problems? This is an understandable question posed by many students. Balance of payments problems are best understood as imbalances between the different sections of the accounts. The main focus is on the current account. Table 10.5 shows the countries with the largest current account imbalances (both deficits and surpluses), measured in US$. These may not be the largest imbalances when expressed as a percentage of GDP, as evidenced by Singapore's surplus and Eritrea's deficit, both of which are much larger percentages of GDP than the other countries listed. The extent to which these imbalances matter is a source of debate among economists.

Country	Current account balance (US$) + = surplus – = deficit	World ranking (largest surplus to largest deficit)	Current account balance (% of GDP)
China	+363,300,000,000	1	11.0
Japan	+195,900,000,000	2	3.8
Germany	+185,100,000,000	3	5.7
Singapore	+41,390,000,000	10	26.9
Eritrea	–343,100,000	92	24.1
UK	–111,000,000,000	162	4.0
Spain	–126,300,000,000	163	8.9
USA	–747,100,000,000	164	5.4

Table 10.5 Current account surpluses and deficits for selected economies, 2007 (estimates)
Source: CIA World Factbook

Understanding the causes and consequences of imbalances in the balance of payments helps you to understand the circumstances in which problems may arise.

CAUSES OF IMBALANCES ON THE BALANCE OF PAYMENTS

The structure of the current account of the balance of payments shows how imbalances on the balance of payments might come about. We will concentrate mainly on imbalances due to current account deficits, but you should recognise that a current account surplus is an imbalance too.

Both the UK and the Czech Republic have current account deficits as Tables 10.6 and 10.7 show. The cause of these deficits is different, however. The UK's current account deficit arises because of a deficit on the balance of trade in goods. The Czech Republic's deficit has a different cause – a negative income balance. The latter reflects interest, profit and dividends flowing out of the Czech Republic due

	£ bn
Trade in goods	−87.6
Trade in services	+38.8
Income balance	+5.3
Current transfers	−13.9
Current account balance	−57.4

Table 10.6 UK current account, 2007
Source: HM Treasury, Pocket Data Bank, 16 April 2008

	€ m
Trade in goods	+4,227.8
Trade in services	+1,989.8
Income balance	−9,154.2
Current transfers	−285.1
Current account balance	−3,221.7

Table 10.7 Czech Republic current account, 2007
Source: Czech National Bank website, Monthly Balance of Payments – key items

to the ownership of assets by foreigners. The capital account shows foreign direct investment of €5,731.9 million in 2007 alone.

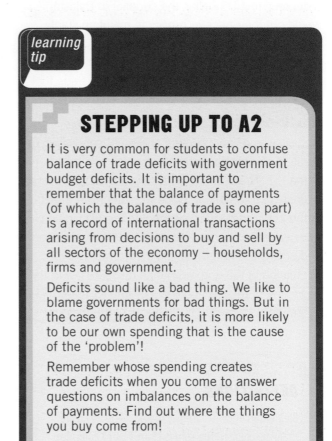

STEPPING UP TO A2

It is very common for students to confuse balance of trade deficits with government budget deficits. It is important to remember that the balance of payments (of which the balance of trade is one part) is a record of international transactions arising from decisions to buy and sell by all sectors of the economy – households, firms and government.

Deficits sound like a bad thing. We like to blame governments for bad things. But in the case of trade deficits, it is more likely to be our own spending that is the cause of the 'problem'!

Remember whose spending creates trade deficits when you come to answer questions on imbalances on the balance of payments. Find out where the things you buy come from!

How might a trade deficit (either in goods or services or both) come about? There are a number of possible reasons:

● high levels of consumption causing excessive spending on foreign-produced goods and services

● high levels of investment spending causing capital goods being imported from abroad

● a change in comparative advantage causing cheaper goods and services being imported rather than produced domestically

● a high or over-valued exchange rate causing consumers to switch away from domestically produced goods and services to those produced abroad

● structural weaknesses in the economy resulting from domestic firms losing competitiveness against imported goods due to a lack of investment, high labour costs or low productivity.

You can see that not every cause of a deficit on the current account of the balance of payments is a sign of economic weakness. Often a current account deficit can be a sign of economic strength.

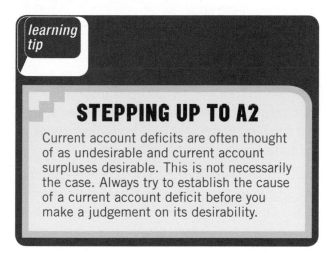

learning tip

STEPPING UP TO A2

Current account deficits are often thought of as undesirable and current account surpluses desirable. This is not necessarily the case. Always try to establish the cause of a current account deficit before you make a judgement on its desirability.

POLICIES TO CORRECT IMBALANCES ON THE BALANCE OF PAYMENTS

If an imbalance on the balance of payments caused by a current account deficit is not necessarily a bad thing, then why does anything need to be done about it? There is a long-running debate among economists that centres on exactly this question. Both the UK and the USA have run large current account deficits for years with no policy to correct them. Why?

The answer lies in the way in which imbalances on the balance of payments are 'financed'. You have seen that a current account deficit must be matched by a capital account surplus. What this means is that, if more money is flowing out of the economy on the current account, then more money must flow in on the capital account, otherwise there will be downward pressure on the exchange rate. Both the UK and the USA manage to 'finance' current account deficits because their economies are seen to be fundamentally 'sound'. As a result they have attracted foreign investment, which counts as a credit in the capital account of the balance of payments. So the first policy to correct an imbalance on the balance of payments is 'do nothing'.

Where the fundamentals of the economy are not sound, and the imbalance represents an underlying weakness in the economy, there needs to be some kind of policy response to correct the imbalance. There are two reasons for this. Both relate to the fact that, in these circumstances, a current account deficit becomes unsustainable. The first reason is, basically, that the economy is living beyond its means. It is spending more abroad than it is earning from abroad. It needs to borrow the difference. This borrowing may be done by the private sector or the public sector, but it will result in a build-up of foreign debt. If an economy is not generating the income to repay that debt, then a financial crisis can emerge. The second reason is that, where an economy operates a fixed or semi-fixed exchange rate, it will not be able to afford to support its currency indefinitely by using reserves of foreign currency to intervene in the foreign exchange markets.

To correct the imbalance under these circumstances there are two broad policy approaches that can be adopted: **expenditure-switching** and **expenditure-reducing policies**.

DEFINITIONS

Expenditure-switching policies: policies that increase the price of imports and/or reduce the price of exports in order to reduce the demand for imports and raise the demand for exports to correct a current account deficit on the balance of payments

Expenditure-reducing policies: policies that reduce the overall level of national income in order to reduce the demand for imports and correct a current account deficit on the balance of payments

EXPENDITURE-SWITCHING POLICIES

To encourage a switch in expenditure away from imports towards domestically produced goods and services requires the relative price of imports to rise and the relative price of exports to fall. This can be achieved by:

- a fall in the exchange rate
- tariffs on imports
- subsidising exports.

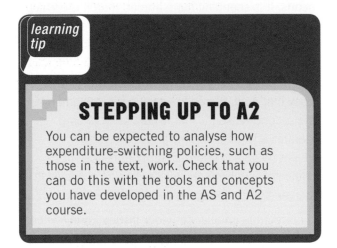

learning tip

STEPPING UP TO A2

You can be expected to analyse how expenditure-switching policies, such as those in the text, work. Check that you can do this with the tools and concepts you have developed in the AS and A2 course.

The main problems with expenditure-switching policies are related to their effectiveness and to their impact on the domestic economy. The effectiveness of the policies is dependent on the price elasticities of demand for imports and exports. Raising the price of imports may have little impact on the volume of imports demanded if the price elasticities of demand (PED) for imports is inelastic. If domestic output is not a good substitute for imported goods and services because of its inferior quality or reliability, expenditure-switching policies will be ineffective. They may also make the situation worse, as an increase in price combined with a less than proportionate reduction in demand will raise the *value* of imports. The increased price of imports may itself be a problem. Higher-priced imports will add to domestic inflation by raising both retail prices and the costs of production. Subsidising exports and placing tariffs on imports risks retaliation from the countries affected and would be against the rules of the World Trade Organization. The policies will also take time to affect spending patterns, so that there will be a J-curve effect on the current account of the balance of payments.

EXPENDITURE-REDUCING POLICIES

An alternative approach is to dampen spending in the economy by reducing the level of national income. This can be achieved by:

- raising the level of taxation
- reducing government expenditure
- raising interest rates.

The problem with this approach to correcting an imbalance in the balance of payments is obvious. There is a large cost to the domestic economy and to individual firms and consumers of reducing aggregate demand and output. It may require a large and sustained period of recession in order to bring the current account deficit under control.

Both expenditure-switching and expenditure-reducing policies can also be criticised as aiming at the wrong target. If the cause of the imbalance in the balance of payments is a fundamental weakness of the economy, then policy should be directed at the cause and not the symptom. Reducing domestic inflation, raising levels of productivity, reducing unit labour costs and raising levels of investment would be more appropriate policy responses. These require, admittedly, a longer-term approach to the problem, but by tackling the economic fundamentals they will allow the economy to avoid imbalances on the balance of payments in the future or ensure that any imbalance is sustainable.

Economic integration

The pattern of global trade is very heavily concentrated geographically and dominated by intra-regional trade. One explanation given earlier in this chapter was that the world is divided up into trading blocs through regional economic integration. But what exactly is **economic integration**?

DEFINITION

Economic integration: refers to the process of blurring the boundaries that separate economic activity in one nation state from that in another

The free movement of goods, services and the factors of production between economies is often reduced by tariff and **non-tariff barriers (NTBs)**. The result of these barriers is to separate economic activity in one country from other countries. So, tariffs raise the price of imports relative to domestic goods and services, government subsidies help domestic producers to compete against foreign competition, exchange rates create additional costs for exporters and importers and the existence of national product standards makes it difficult for exporters to access foreign markets.

DEFINITION

Non-tariff barriers (NTBs): things that restrict trade other than tariffs

Economic integration seeks to remove these barriers to trade. Countries join together in 'economic clubs' that blur the boundaries separating economic activity between them. Examples of such clubs include the North American Free Trade Area (NAFTA), the Association of South East Asian Nations (ASEAN) and the world's largest trading bloc the European Union (EU).

ACTIVITY ····❖

a) Add to the types of non-tariff barriers (NTBs) mentioned in the text.

b) Explain how each NTB restricts trade.

c) How might economic integration seek to eliminate such NTBs?

STAGES OF ECONOMIC INTEGRATION

The main stages or levels of economic integration that economists refer to are outlined below.

Free trade areas (FTAs)

The members of a free trade area (FTA) agree to remove tariffs and quotas on trade between themselves, but they keep the right to decide their own trade policy towards countries that do not belong to the FTA. This is the weakest form of economic integration and free trade can often be restricted to a limited range of goods and services. In addition, trade can get 'deflected' if imports from non-members come into the FTA through the country with the lowest tariffs and then get re-exported tariff-free into other countries in the FTA. A country's independent trade policy can, therefore, be undermined by joining a FTA. To prevent this, complex rules need to be drawn up to determine the origin of goods traded within the FTA. For example, in the North American Free Trade Area (NAFTA), coats made in Mexico from imported fabric are not allowed to be exported tariff-free to the USA.

DEFINITIONS

Trade deflection: where one country in a free trade area imposes high tariffs on another to reduce imports but the imports come in from elsewhere in the free trade area

Free trade area: an agreement between two or more countries to abolish tariffs on trade between them

Customs union (CUs)

The problem of **trade deflection** is avoided by strengthening economic integration by agreeing a common external trade policy. Members of a **customs union** (CU) remove tariffs and quotas on trade between themselves and agree on a common external tariff on trade with non-members. This

DEFINITION

Customs union: an agreement between two or more countries to abolish tariffs on trade between them and to place a common external tariff on trade with non-members necessarily involves a loss of economic sovereignty. Trade is not completely free because the existence of non-tariff barriers (NTBs) may still exist which limit or distort the flow of goods and services between the members of the CU.

Single markets (SMs)

A **single market** (SM) removes restrictions on the free movement of labour and capital between countries, removes NTBs through agreeing a common approach to product standards, employment laws, taxation policies, competition policies and state aid to industry. In addition, members of an SM may adopt common policies in key industries. This involves more than just removing barriers (so-called negative integration) as it requires integrating a large range of economic policies (so-called positive integration). Instead of national markets for goods and services being separated or segmented, they begin to form part of a larger SM. Flows of goods, services, labour and capital between the members of the CU become significant and price disparities between the member states narrow.

> **DEFINITION**
>
> **Single market:** deepens economic integration from a customs union by eliminating non-tariff barriers to trade, promoting the free movement of labour and capital and agreeing common policies in a number of areas

Economic unions (EUs)

An **economic union** (EU) involves an extension of the degree of integration in a single market. Economists are not agreed on the definition of an EU, though many would say that economic policy making becomes more centralised. It might, for example,

> **DEFINITION**
>
> **Economic union:** deepens integration in a single market, centralising economic policy at the macroeconomic level

involve a common approach to macroeconomic policy particularly in the area of personal and business taxation.

Monetary unions (MUs)

This stage or level of economic integration takes the idea of macroeconomic policy co-ordination one step further by agreeing a common approach to monetary policy. Countries may agree to fix their exchange rates or they may go as far as abolishing national currencies and replacing them with a single, common currency. This form of economic integration eliminates exchange rate uncertainty and, in the case of a single currency, takes away the cost of changing currencies (transaction costs). A single currency also makes comparing prices in the MU easy (price transparency), as all prices are expressed in the same currency. A **monetary union** strengthens a single market by increasing the flow of goods and services and increasing competition between member states. It requires a common monetary policy that sets the interest rate for the whole single currency area and a single central bank. To create stability for the currency, governments must limit their borrowing and co-ordinate, harmonise or centralise their fiscal policy.

> **DEFINITION**
>
> **Monetary union:** the deepest form of integration in which countries share the same currency and have a common monetary policy as a result

STEPPING UP TO A2

Economic integration is best thought of as a process, because of the many different boundaries between countries. Economists think of integration in terms of stages or levels, from very weak forms of integration to very strong. This does not mean that countries need to move through each stage one after the other. It is simply a way of judging the degree of integration by creating labels or categories for what we see in the real world.

EXAMPLES OF REGIONAL ECONOMIC INTEGRATION

North American Free Trade Area (NAFTA)

NAFTA is a free trade agreement between the USA, Canada and Mexico. It has been in existence since 1994, yet still creates controversy and debate in all three countries. NAFTA has abolished most of the tariffs on trade between the three countries, including those on cars, textiles and computers. However, some tariffs have only been reduced gradually, notably on agricultural commodities, and will not be eliminated completely until 2009/10.

Debate on the impact of NAFTA continues to pit those in favour of free trade against those hostile to it. Free traders argue that NAFTA has increased trade between the three countries, boosted foreign investment and helped to raise growth in Mexico in particular. The critics of NAFTA point to the loss of manufacturing employment in the USA as firms have moved to Mexico and the plight of Mexican farmers unable to compete against cheap corn imports from the USA (where farmers receive in excess of $10 billion of subsidies for the production

of corn). What is clear is that free trade agreements such as NAFTA create winners and losers, as the theory of trade you have studied in this chapter predicts. This is the consequence of resource reallocation.

Association of Southeast Asian Nations (ASEAN)

ASEAN was created in the late 1960s by Thailand, Singapore, Malaysia, Indonesia and the Philippines. It has since expanded to ten members and now includes Brunei, Vietnam, Laos, Burma and Cambodia. ASEAN was created to bring about peace and security as well as economic growth. It has reduced tariffs on trade between the ten member states and in 2007 committed itself to creating a single market by 2020 with the free movement of goods, services, capital and labour. Air travel will be the first industry to be deregulated and liberalised in this process.

However, ASEAN's free trade zone involves exemptions for too many goods and services and there has been little success in reducing NTBs. The result is that, while trade between the members of ASEAN has grown, trade with non-ASEAN countries has grown much more rapidly. Currently, 75 per cent of the trade by ASEAN countries is with non-members. ASEAN has some way to go down the path to economic integration.

European Union (EU)

The EU has its roots in the signing of the Treaty of Rome by six western European countries in 1957. Through a series of enlargements, starting in the 1970s, the EU has grown to a club of twenty-seven western, central and eastern European economies. The EU started life as primarily a customs union, but economic integration has both widened and deepened. More markets have been opened up to competition through agreement on common product standards and the lifting of NTBs, and more countries have joined the club. This is a widening of economic integration. Deepening has come about through the adoption of a wide range of common policies on agriculture, fishing, the environment and competition, among others. The EU's greatest achievements have been the significant free movement of goods, services and capital achieved through the **Single European Market (SEM)** and the adoption by fifteen member states of a common currency (the euro). The latter has, however, not been without controversy, as some members of the EU, such as the UK, Sweden and Denmark, have been reluctant to sacrifice their **monetary policy sovereignty** and have stayed out of this deeper level of economic integration.

DEFINITIONS

Single European Market (SEM): a process adopted in the EU that promoted the free movement of goods, services and capital by harmonising product standards and removing remaining non-tariff barriers to trade

Monetary policy sovereignty: the ability of a country to pursue an independent monetary policy

The impact of economic integration

The impact of economic integration differs according to its depth or level. A free trade area, for example, gives some of the benefits of trade that you have learnt about in this chapter but they are limited by the fact that the agreements only involve a small number of countries.

Deeper levels of economic integration, such as a customs union, represent only a step towards free trade, as tariff and non-tariff barriers are erected against non-members. The EU, for example, promotes free trade among its members but has been described as 'fortress Europe' because of its discrimination in trade with the outside world. The effects of such economic integration are not so straightforward to analyse.

TRADE CREATION

Economic integration creates trade among those who sign up to free trade areas and customs unions. This arises because high-cost domestic production is replaced with imports from a more efficient partner within the FTA or CU. Trade between countries in an economically integrated area increases. This benefits consumers through lower prices and higher consumer surplus. Domestic producers suffer and there may be reductions in output, lower producer surplus and lower employment. The impact of **trade creation** is similar to that of free trade – overall, economic efficiency is raised but there are winners and losers. The benefits from trade creation, however, are not as great as might be the case if tariffs against all countries were removed. Nevertheless, at least in theory, the overall impact is positive.

DEFINITION

Trade creation: where economic integration results in high-cost domestic production being replaced by imports from a more efficient source within the economically integrated area

TRADE DIVERSION

Trade diversion refers to a situation where economic integration results in trade switching from a low-cost supplier to a less efficient supplier within the FTA or CU. This arises because tariffs on trade are eliminated within the economically integrated area but remain on trade from outside.

DEFINITION

Trade diversion: where economic integration results in trade switching from a low-cost supplier outside the economically integrated area to a less efficient source within the area

An example of trade diversion is the UK's imports of lamb, before and after it joined the EU. Before joining the EU, the UK imported lamb from New Zealand, even though there were tariffs placed on such imports. On joining the EU, tariffs on imports of lamb from France were removed but the UK had to agree to a EU-wide tariff on lamb imports from outside the EU. This made imports from France cheaper than those from New Zealand. The result was that trade was diverted from New Zealand and created with France.

This coincidence of trade creation and diversion can be analysed using Figure 10.15. Before joining the EU, the UK imports $Q_2 - Q_1$ lamb from New Zealand at a price P_{NZ+t} that includes a tariff, as this is cheaper than importing from France at the tariff inflated price of P_{F+t}. After joining the EU, the price of lamb imported from France falls to P_F due to the removal of tariffs and the UK's tariff on New Zealand lamb is replaced with a common EU tariff. The UK now imports $Q_4 - Q_3$ lamb from France. UK consumers gain consumer surplus of area 1+2+3+4, but UK farmers lose area 1 in producer surplus. In addition the UK government losses tariff revenue of areas 3+5. Overall, economic welfare has increased by areas 2+4 but fallen by area 5. It is difficult to say

whether economic integration involving trade creation and trade diversion is of any economic benefit to the UK. It is clearly of no economic benefit to New Zealand, which has lost a valuable export market.

The impact of economic integration on the UK depends on:

● the relative efficiencies of EU and non-EU producers (the more inefficient the UK's new trading partners are, the bigger will be area 5)

● the price elasticities of demand and supply of the goods and services affected by integration (the more price inelastic they are the smaller will be areas 2 and 4).

Economic integration can, therefore, be expected to affect a country's pattern of trade but it is unclear whether the changes in trade will raise economic efficiency. This is very different from the conclusion reached about free trade earlier in this chapter.

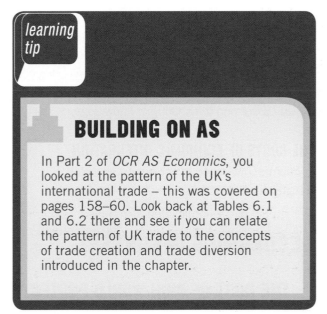

learning tip

BUILDING ON AS

In Part 2 of *OCR AS Economics*, you looked at the pattern of the UK's international trade – this was covered on pages 158–60. Look back at Tables 6.1 and 6.2 there and see if you can relate the pattern of UK trade to the concepts of trade creation and trade diversion introduced in the chapter.

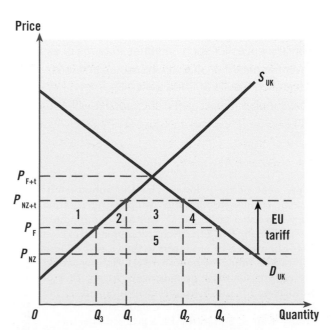

Figure 10.15 Trade creation and diversion effects of a customs union

THE DYNAMIC EFFECTS OF ECONOMIC INTEGRATION

Trade creation and trade diversion are sometimes referred to as the short-run or static effects of economic integration. In the longer term, economists expect there to be other consequences of economic integration, which are known as the dynamic effects because they occur over time. These effects include the following three.

A reduction in monopoly power

Economic integration erodes the power of domestic monopolies, leading to increased choice for consumers, lower prices and greater allocative efficiency.

Greater innovation and R&D

Competition between producers in an economically integrated area can bring benefits in terms of more product and process innovation and expenditure on research and development. This will have benefits not just for consumers but also for the long-term rate of economic growth in the economically integrated area.

A larger market and economies of scale

The removal of barriers to trade within an economically integrated area and the creation of a single market allow firms within that market to raise the scale of production and to benefit from both internal and external economies of scale. Over time, there may be regional concentration of industry, which will bring cost advantages in terms of access to specialist suppliers, skilled labour and the sharing of knowledge.

THE COSTS OF ECONOMIC INTEGRATION

Economic integration is not without its costs. Geographical concentration of industry risks the emergence of regions that attract the lion's share of investment and jobs and other regions that lag behind. This has been described as a 'core–periphery' problem and could result in significant regional and structural unemployment within an economically integrated area. In deeper levels of integration, it may be necessary to have a common regional policy to ensure that the benefits from integration are spread widely among regions.

Integration may also, over time, result in the emergence of oligopolies and monopolies. Deeper levels of economic integration may require agreement on competition policy to tackle the abuse of market power that spans national boundaries. So, for example, the European Competition Commission has investigated and found guilty EU producers of glass, synthetic rubber, vitamins, elevators and escalators, and hydrogen peroxide for engaging in price-fixing cartels. The number of anti-competitive behaviours uncovered by the Commission has almost doubled in the last five years and fines imposed for operating price-fixing cartels rose from €405 million in 2003 to €3.3 billion in 2007.

THE EXTERNAL IMPACT OF ECONOMIC INTEGRATION

Trade diversion represents a potentially significant loss in income for those countries outside free trade areas and customs unions. This can have severe economic consequences for such countries in terms of export revenue, output of affected industries and jobs.

ECONOMICS IN CONTEXT

THE COST OF RICH WORLD PROTECTION

According to the International Food Policy Research Institute (IFPRI), the trade policies of developed nations cause great harm to the economies of many developing nations, which depend heavily upon agriculture, for example. They claim that Latin America and the Caribbean lose about $8.3 billion in annual income from agriculture, Asia loses some $6.6 billion, and sub-Saharan Africa close to $2 billion. The IFPRI is especially critical of the EU, which it claims is most guilty of trade-distorting measures, accounting for 50 per cent of these losses. The EU subsidises its domestic farmers through the Common Agricultural Policy and levies tariffs on agricultural commodities from outside the EU. Effectively, economic integration closes EU markets to producers in the world's poorest nations. The lifting of trade barriers globally would raise exports for these nations, with 70 per cent of this increase for sub-Saharan economies and 50 per cent for Latin American and Caribbean economies coming from an end to the EU's protection alone.

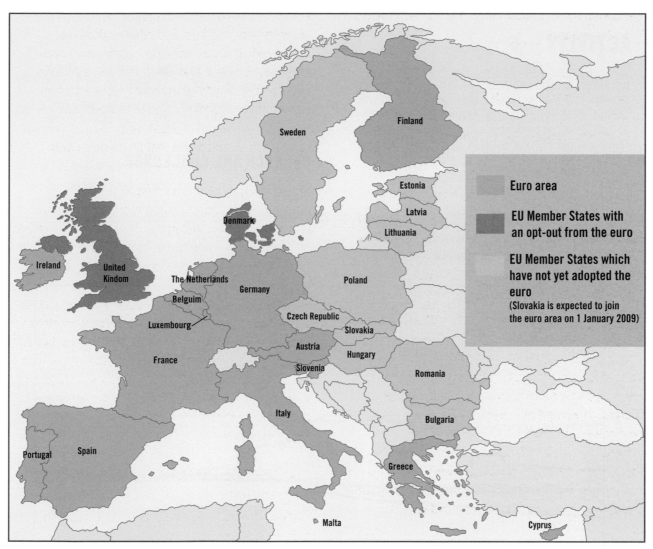

Figure 10.16 The euro area (eurozone)

Legend:
- Euro area
- EU Member States with an opt-out from the euro
- EU Member States which have not yet adopted the euro
(Slovakia is expected to join the euro area on 1 January 2009)

Poor countries suffer most from this aspect of economic integration because of the importance for them of agricultural exports. For more economically developed nations, the difficulties of exporting to economically integrated areas, such as the EU, are surmountable. Japanese car manufacturers, for example, have been able to locate production of cars in the EU and take advantage of the EU's single market. Such foreign direct investment (FDI) is not open to economies whose economic structure is dominated by primary sector production. For them, regional economic integration poses a threat. For others, such as Japan, the USA and Korea, economic integration brings an opportunity to share in the benefits we have looked at in this section.

THE IMPACT OF MONETARY UNION

The consequence of the deepest level of economic integration, monetary union, is to enhance the benefits of trade through distinct microeconomic effects but it also has important consequences for macroeconomic policy.

At the microeconomic level, a single currency has three key advantages:

● Reduced **transaction costs**. Trade between countries using the same currency eliminates the costs of changing currencies, making trade cheaper and lowering prices.

● Elimination of exchange rate risk. A single currency eliminates the risk and costs that come from changes

ACTIVITY ···⃗

Every year the European Commission (EC) produces a report on car prices in the European Union. The annual report was launched in the 1990s, following complaints from consumers about differences in car prices between member states of the EU and obstacles placed in the way of those consumers who wished to buy in another EU country.

The latest report, published in April 2008, found that the cheapest pre-tax prices in the euro area were in Finland, Greece and Slovakia. Within the EU as a whole, pre-tax prices were cheapest in Denmark. Pre-tax car prices were most expensive in the Czech Republic at 10.8 per cent above the EU average.

a) Identify and explain two reasons why the retail price of cars differs between countries in the EU.

STRETCH AND CHALLENGE

b) Comment on the extent to which economic integration tends to lead to the convergence of the prices of consumer goods such as cars.

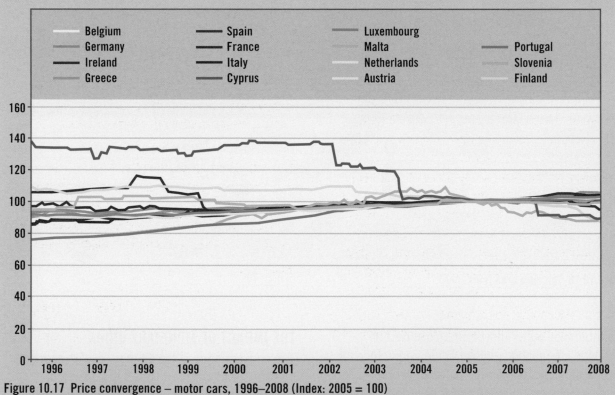

Figure 10.17 Price convergence – motor cars, 1996–2008 (Index: 2005 = 100)
Source: European Commission

in exchange rates. Businesses no longer have to worry that exchange rate movements will reduce profit margins on trade with other countries or 'hedge' against these risks through complex financial instruments such as futures, options or swaps. This stimulates trade between members of the single currency.

● Increased **price transparency.** Prices in an economically integrated area involving a single currency are easy for consumers and producers to compare. As a result, it is harder for firms to 'hide' price differences and to engage in price discrimination between markets in different countries.

At the microeconomic level, a single currency should bring lower prices for consumers, lower costs for producers, increase the degree of competition in markets and encourage investment across national boundaries. However, these benefits might be limited by the ability of consumers to engage in cross-border shopping. The benefits of greater competition may be limited by cross-border acquisitions and mergers that result in greater market concentration. There are short-term costs, too, which firms and consumers might have to bear. These include the costs of changing over to a new currency (including menu costs) and an opportunity for firms to take advantage of confusion on the part of consumers by raising prices. For firms, the costs of changing over to a new currency are largely fixed and, as a result, will impact especially hard on small and medium-sized businesses. However, these are one-off costs and some of them will be faced by firms outside the monetary union that do trade with countries in it.

The macroeconomic consequences of monetary union may bring benefits for the currency union as a whole but may involve substantial costs for individual countries within the union.

At the level of the currency union, a single currency should raise AD by increasing trade, investment and international competitiveness. In addition, there should be an increase in AS resulting from lower production costs, greater factor mobility and higher productivity stemming from increased competition. Figure 10.18 shows how, in theory, the euro area economy should benefit from the introduction of the euro. The combination of higher AD and AS increases real GDP (Y to Y_1) and, in the long run, allows for higher rates of GDP growth without the consequences of inflation.

For individual economies within the monetary union, the consequences of this type of economic integration are not so clear cut. Possible costs of membership of a monetary union are outlined below.

The loss of monetary policy sovereignty

With one currency, there is one monetary policy conducted by a single central bank. So, in the euro area, the European Central Bank (ECB) sets the euro interest rate. This interest rate may not suit the individual circumstances of a particular country. For example, a low interest rate may not suit an economy whose GDP growth is so rapid that it is experiencing demand–pull inflation. In addition, countries cannot offset losses in competitiveness through exchange rate depreciation. This loss of monetary policy sovereignty places a bigger burden on fiscal policy and supply-side policy. Fiscal policy is the only tool left for short-term management of the economy and supply-side policies must be used to bring long-term improvements in economic performance.

The constraint on fiscal policy

It is likely that in a monetary union there will need to be rules to limit the public sector borrowing by individual governments. If this does not happen, fiscal policy of individual nations might undermine

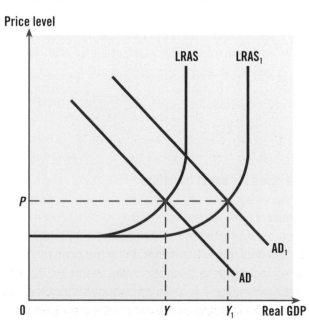

Figure 10.18 Potential impact of the euro on the euro area economy

monetary policy for the whole currency area. In the euro area, these fiscal policy constraints are known as the **Stability and Growth Pact** and they limit public sector borrowing to 3 per cent of GDP and the national debt to 60 per cent of GDP. Depending where these limits are set, it is possible for membership of a monetary union to limit the operation of **automatic stabilisers** in individual economies and to cause the business cycle in some countries to be more pronounced as a result.

> ## DEFINITION
>
> **Stability and Growth Pact:** limits agreed to public sector borrowing and the national debt for those EU countries that are part of the euro area

> ## DEFINITION
>
> **Automatic stabilisers:** elements of fiscal policy that cushion the impact of the business cycle without any need for corrective action by the government. For example, higher spending on unemployment benefits and welfare payments and lower taxation receipts provide an automatic fiscal stimulus in times of economic slowdown

The need for fiscal transfers

A monetary union requires a mechanism for **fiscal transfers** between member states to compensate for the constraints on national fiscal policy and its reduced effectiveness in stabilising the economy at key points of the business cycle. Without such a mechanism, there is a risk that countries lack the macroeconomic policy instruments to manage their economy when its performance diverges from the 'average' of the rest of the monetary union.

> ## DEFINITION
>
> **Fiscal transfers:** occur where taxation raised in one country is used to fund government expenditures in another country

Deflationary bias

In order to create credibility, it is argued that a new currency requires 'tough' monetary policy by the central bank in its early years in order to build a track record for low inflation. Only if this is done will inflationary expectations for the new currency be low. This could result in monetary policy 'overkill', where interest rates are so high as to hold back economic growth. Alternatively, interest rate management may be very conservative, with the central bank slow to adapt to a global slowdown. This was the criticism made of the European Central Bank in 2008.

These costs of monetary union are greatest when there is a lack of **economic convergence** between member states. A lack of economic convergence could occur when one country is in the boom phase of the economic cycle when others are in the recession phase. In this situation, one country requires interest rates to rise and the others need interest rates to fall. The lack of business cycle convergence therefore means that one interest rate does not 'fit all'.

Different economic structures also cause a lack of convergence. Changes in interest rates can have very different effects in different economies, depending on the nature of their borrowing and the interest elasticity of demand. Countries where borrowing tends to be at variable rates of interest will show much more response to interest rate changes than countries where borrowing is at fixed rates. Different economic structures can also lead economies to experience different kinds of external shocks – oil-importing countries will be affected differently by rising oil prices from countries, such as the UK, for example, which is a major oil producer.

DEFINITION

Economic convergence: the process by which economic conditions in different countries become similar. Economists distinguish between monetary convergence (for example, similarities in inflation and interest rates) and real convergence (for example, similarities in the structure of economies). Membership of the euro area only requires monetary convergence to have taken place

differences in economic performance that arise from the loss of monetary policy sovereignty. They are the characteristics of what has become known as **optimal currency areas**. Of these characteristics, some economists argue that the most important are those that impact on the supply-side performance of the economy. This is because, as you learnt in Chapter 5, economic policy instruments such as the interest rate, exchange rate and fiscal policy are of little consequence in determining long-term economic performance.

To combat the problems created by a lack of economic convergence, countries belonging to a monetary union need flexible labour markets, high degrees of labour and capital mobility and a mechanism to redistribute money to countries or areas adversely affected by the problems of a single currency. These requirements help to smooth out

DEFINITION

Optimal currency area: refers to conditions that need to be met to avoid the costs of monetary union. These conditions include: a high degree of labour market flexibility, mechanisms for fiscal transfers, and the absence of external shocks that impact differently on different economies (asymmetric shocks)

Figure 10.19 Ten success stories of the euro
Source: European Commission

11 Development and sustainability

On completion of this chapter, you should be able to:

● distinguish between growth and development and explain the relationship between the two

● understand the details and limitations of GDP per capita and the HDI (Human Development Index) as measures of development

● recognise the common and diverse features of developing economies as they develop

● evaluate the effectiveness of policies to promote development, including the role of international trade and economic integration

● discuss the relative importance of the different constraints on development, both internal and external

● understand and explain the meaning of sustainable economic development and analyse the social, environmental, resource and demographic impacts of growth at different stages of development

● explain the use and limitations of indicators, such as GDP and the ISEW (Index of Sustainable Economic Welfare), in measuring sustainable economic development and evaluate their usefulness as indicators in policy-making contexts

● evaluate the usefulness of national and regional policies and international agreements in promoting sustainability.

The meaning and measurement of economic development

The economist Jeffrey Sachs begins his book, *The End of Poverty*, by asking his readers to consider the headline that could appear in our newspapers every morning:

'More than 20,000 people perished yesterday of extreme poverty.'

This startling fact, which actually goes unreported every day, arises from the stark contrast between our lives and the lives of the 80 per cent of the world's population who live in developing countries. That 80 per cent live off less than $16 a day, according to the

United Nation's 2005 *Human Development Report*. According to this report:

● the richest 20 per cent of the world's population have 75 per cent of the world's income

● the poorest 20 per cent have 2 per cent of the world's income

● the poorest 19 per cent (1.2 billion people) live off less than US$1 a day at purchasing power parity (PPP)

● 66 per cent of Africa's population (420 million people) live off less than US$1 a day at PPP.

These stark facts do not tell the story of change, however. Almost 40 years ago the majority – 86 per cent – of the world's poor lived in East and South

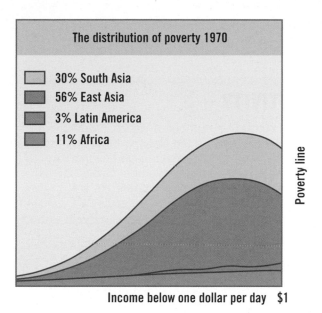

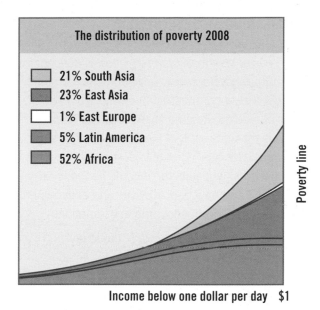

Figures 11.1 and 11.2 The regional distribution of the world's poor in 1970 and projected distribution in 2008
Source: Gapminder

Asia, as Figure 11.1 shows. Since then, the number living in **poverty** in South Asia has fallen and most of the world's poor now live in Africa. Clearly something has happened in one part of the world that has reduced poverty, something that hasn't happened elsewhere.

This something is the process of **economic development**, which you will explore in this chapter.

DEFINITION

Poverty: when income is below the level that would allow someone to enjoy some agreed minimum standard of living. The World Bank defines 'extreme poverty' as living on less that US$1 per day (at PPP) and 'moderate poverty' as living on less than US$2 per day (at PPP)

DEFINITION

Economic development: the process of improving people's economic well-being and quality of life

learning tip

Examiners are not going to test you on your knowledge of facts and figures about economic development, so you don't have to worry about learning lots of numbers about the global distribution of income!

However, it helps in your study of economic development if you have a feel for indicators of economic development and broad trends. Both the World Bank and the United Nations publish data on key indicators.

A really useful and visual source of information is this presentation of the UN's 2005 *Human Development Report.* Go to www.heinemann.co.uk/hotlinks, insert the express code 2230P, and click on 'Human Development Report 2005'.

For lots of interactive resources useful for developing your understanding of some of the other concepts introduced in this chapter, go to www.heinemann.co.uk/hotlinks, insert the express code 2230P, and click on 'UN Human Development Reports'.

THE MEANING OF DEVELOPMENT

Comparing income levels between countries is a much easier task than comparing levels of economic and human development. Development is a broad concept that encompasses much more than just levels of income. Income levels (GDP per capita) show us the end result of the use of a nation's resources. But they don't tell us what the resources were used for, who gets the income generated from production and how people's lives and environments are affected by production and consumption.

These issues are at the centre of the study of economic and human development. First, development is a process it is not a one-off event. Second, development focuses on the outcomes of economic activity and resource allocation. These outcomes have one thing in common: improvements in people's well-being. While traditional economics looks at how scarce resources can best be allocated to maximise the output of goods and services, the study of development is much broader. There is a need to agree what human well-being means and how it can be measured.

A well-known development economist, Michael Todaro, has said that the process of development must seek to achieve the following three things:

● *an increase in the availability and distribution of basic life-sustaining goods*, such as food, shelter and health

● *an increase in standards of living* (material and non-material), which should include higher incomes, more jobs, better education and enabling people and societies to feel a greater sense of worth and self-respect

● *an expansion of the economic and social choices available to people*, which frees people from poverty and misery, ignorance and a dependence on others.

Unlike other terms and concepts you have met in this textbook, the concept of development is open to much interpretation. There is no single agreed measure of development (see pages 284–287 below), and different people will stress the importance of different indicators of development. In short, there is a normative element – an element of value judgements – to the study of development

that distinguishes it from some other branches of economics.

ACTIVITY ····⟩

As a result of a number of world summits in the 1990s, the United Nations drew up a list of goals and targets which have become known as the Millennium Development Goals (MDGs). Developing and developed countries are committed to achieving these goals by 2015. The goals are:

● eradicate extreme poverty and hunger

● achieve universal primary education

● promote gender equality and empower women

● reduce child mortality

● improve maternal health

● combat HIV/AIDS, malaria and other diseases

● ensure environmental sustainability

● global partnership for development.

a) Use the UN website to research further the MDGs and the targets that go with them. In each case explain how, if achieved, it would help to raise economic development.

b) For a developing country of your own choosing, research its progress in achieving four targets referred to in the MDGs. Produce a factsheet of your findings.

STRETCH AND CHALLENGE

c) Using your findings, comment on economic development in the developing country you have chosen to investigate.

For your research, go to www.heinemann.co.uk/hotlinks, insert the express code 2230P, and click on 'UN MDG website'.

THE RELATIONSHIP BETWEEN ECONOMIC GROWTH AND DEVELOPMENT

The three objectives Michael Todaro sets out can, in part, be achieved by economic growth. Growth raises a nation's income and it is, therefore, possible to provide more health care, better education and more jobs, and to reduce poverty. Growth is a necessary condition of development. Without it, development cannot take place. It provides the conditions that allow development to take place. But economic growth is not enough on its own. Some examples might help you to understand why.

● Economic growth will raise a nation's total income (GDP), but the additional income might be unequally distributed, so that a large number of people see little or no increase in their individual income. In this situation, affluence and poverty could exist alongside each other.

● Economic growth might deplete natural resources, so that future generations are unable to achieve the same level of income. In this case, economic growth has made future generations worse off. In this way, development cannot be said to have happened and is described as unsustainable.

● Economic growth might be achieved by the use of capital-intensive methods of production that generate few additional jobs. This growth might be concentrated in a single sector of the economy, such as the oil industry, which has little positive impact for the vast majority of the population. In these scenarios, the nation's overall income may have increased but unemployment and poverty will have remained high.

● Economic growth might be achieved by methods that result in high levels of pollution. The environmental damage caused would damage health and reduce levels of living, therefore conflicting with the objectives set out above.

So, economic growth can promote development, but the wrong kind of growth can limit or reduce it. Economic growth is, then, necessary for development but it is not sufficient.

ECONOMICS IN CONTEXT

INDIA: GROWTH OR DEVELOPMENT?

Once a synonym for stagnation, India is now tracking China at the top of the world economic growth super league. From information technology to steel, cement and automotive parts, Indian companies are world-beaters. Symbols of the new prosperity are everywhere. The relentless expansion of gleaming shopping malls reflects a surge in the prosperity of India's middle class – some 250 million people. Mobile phone connections are growing by 5 million every month. Stock markets are booming, and foreign investors are lining up for a slice of the action.

By any measure of economic success, India's credentials as a five-star performer speak for themselves. When it comes to human development, it is trundling along in the slow lane. Comparisons with neighbours make painful reading. Bangladesh is poorer than India and its economy is growing far more slowly. But over the past decade, child deaths have been falling at an annual rate 50 per cent faster than in India, and Bangladesh now has a better child survival record.

So what is holding India back? This is a country defined by division. Inequalities exist between economically dynamic states in the south and the slow-growing, impoverished north; between urban areas and agricultural ones; between rich and poor; between women and men. Economic reform and global integration have done little to break down these divides, with the result that high growth has been grafted on to mass poverty.

– Kevin Watkins, director of the UN's Human Development Report Office, Guardian, 3 October 2006

ACTIVITY ⋯⋗

The chart below represents three different categories of objectives that the process of development might seek to achieve.

a) What objectives might be added to each of the categories?

b) Give a reason why in each case.

STRETCH AND CHALLENGE

c) Comment on one conflict between economic growth and economic development.

Economic objectives

- Growth
- _____ ?
- _____ ?
- _____ ?

Social objectives

- Equity
- _____ ?
- _____ ?
- _____ ?

Environmental objectives

- Conserve non-renewable resources
- _____ ?
- _____ ?
- _____ ?

THE MEASUREMENT OF DEVELOPMENT

Given the potentially positive relationship between economic growth and development, it is not surprising that some measures of development include GDP. Adjustments are always made for population size and purchasing power, by using GDP per capita at purchasing power parity. Other measures try to take a different approach to reflect the broader meaning of development.

GDP per capita

Dividing the income generated from a nation's resources (GDP) by its population gives GDP per capita. Comparisons between countries' levels of development are frequently made using this figure. For example, the World Bank divides countries into the following groups:

- **low-income countries**
- **lower middle-income countries**
- **upper middle-income countries**
- **high-income countries**.

DEFINITIONS

Low-income countries: countries with a GDP per capita of $905 or less

Lower middle-income countries: countries with a GDP per capita of $906–$3,595

Upper middle-income countries: countries with a GDP per capita of $3,596–$11,115

High-income countries: countries with a GDP per capita of $11,116 or more

It is necessary to express each country's GDP per capita in dollars, in order to make international comparisons. However, using market exchange rates does not give a true picture of differences in living standards. This is because market exchange rates do not reflect what different currencies will buy in terms of goods and services. In Chapter 10, you learnt that adjusting for such differences involves calculating the purchasing power parity (PPP) of a currency. Classifications of countries based on their GDP per capita, therefore, make use of data adjusted for PPP.

Even with these adjustments, GDP per capita has limitations as a measure of development. These relate to the broader meaning of development. GDP per capita takes no account of the distribution of income, pollution, environmental degradation, resource depletion, unpaid work and unmarketed or unrecorded economic activity. GDP per capita also gives no value to leisure time (unless there is expenditure on leisure activities) and doesn't put a value on human freedom.

Human Development Index (HDI)

The United Nations Development Programme (UNDP) has produced an alternative measure of development that recognises the limitations of GDP per capita. This is known as the **Human Development Index (HDI)**. It was an early attempt to produce a measure that combined some of the outcomes that might be valued in the development process.

The HDI is made up of three components:

● *life expectancy at birth* as an indicator of the health of the population and longevity

● *the adult literacy rate* (*weighted two-thirds*) and the *percentage of the relevant population enrolled in primary, secondary and tertiary education* (*weighted one-third*) as an indicator of knowledge and education

● *GDP per capita in US$ at PPP* as an indicator of the standard of living.

For each component, there are maximum and minimum values ('goalposts'). The components are scored relative to these goalposts. If only the minimum goalpost is achieved a score of 0 is recorded. Achieving the maximum goalpost gives a score of 1. The minimum and maximum goalposts for life expectancy at birth are 25 and 85 years, for example. A country in which life expectancy was 55 years would score 0.5 on the first component of the HDI. The scores for each component are then combined into a single indicator by taking a simple average of the three values for life expectancy, education and living standards.

Countries are ranked according to the value of their HDI and grouped into three categories:

● **high human development**

● **medium human development**

● **low human development**.

> **DEFINITIONS**
>
> **High human development:** where the HDI is 0.8 and above
> **Medium human development:** where the HDI is between 0.5 and 0.8
> **Low human development:** where the HDI is less than 0.5

The HDI successfully focuses attention on the outcomes of development, rather than on economic growth. It also stimulates debate about the policy choices made by national governments by showing how countries with the same level of GDP per capita can have very different levels of HDI. There should be a positive relationship between the two, with higher average incomes resulting in higher life expectancy, lower rates of infant mortality and higher literacy rates. If a country's HDI ranking is lower than its ranking on GDP per capita, this indicates that resources need to be redirected towards raising human development.

> **DEFINITION**
>
> **Human Development Index (HDI):** a measure that, recognising limitations of GDP per capita as a measure, combines outcomes that might be valued in the development process: life expectancy at birth; adult literacy rate and percentage of the relevant population enrolled in primary, secondary and tertiary education; and GDP per capita in US$ at PPP

Another advantage of the HDI is that it allows judgements to be made on a country's development over time. On the basis of the 2005 HDI (published in 2007), all but one of the twenty-two countries with low human development improved their level of development between 2004 and 2005. The HDI also focuses attention on the countries with the lowest level of human development, which might help to guide the allocation of international aid.

But the HDI does have limitations. The first is that it focuses on only three aspects of development. As a result, the HDI does not give a complete picture of the level of development. It might be argued, however, that adding more and more indicators reduces the value of a composite indicator of development. This is because the more indicators there are in the index the more insignificant each becomes in the overall measure. Perhaps the HDI's selectivity is its real strength. But this selectivity must be recognised in any interpretation of the HDI. An improvement in a country's HDI is only a narrow indicator of improved development.

There is also an issue related to the weighting of the three indicators. There is no economic or social justification that supports the three indicators being given equal weight. The choice of a simple average of the three components of the HDI is arbitrary. Different weights would give a different outcome and may make a difference to how the HDI changes over time.

Related to this issue is the question of opportunity cost and value. To improve its HDI, a country may be advised to reallocate resources to health care and education. This reallocation involves an opportunity cost. There is a value judgement to be made about allocating more resources to health care and education. Large expenditures on health and education may be required to raise life expectancy by one year or the school enrolment rate by 10 per cent. Is this additional expenditure justified? How can higher life expectancy and higher school enrolment rates be valued? Would resources be better diverted to improving access to clean water, to investment in transport infrastructure or to irrigation projects in rural areas? These are difficult, if not impossible, questions to answer.

ACTIVITY ····▸

Table 11.1 shows the GDP per capita and the Human Development Index for eight countries in 2005.

	GDP per capita PPP (US$) 2005	HDI 2005
Pakistan	2,370	0.551
Gambia	1,921	0.502
Haiti	1,663	0.529
Uganda	1,454	0.505
Chad	1,427	0.388
Benin	1,141	0.437
Yemen	930	0.508
Sierra Leone	806	0.336

Table 11.1 GDP per capita and HDI for eight countries, 2005
Source: United Nations Development Programme, Human Development Reports website

a) Relatively low HDI values are usually related to low GDP per capita.

   Identify two countries for which data in the table least support this relationship. Explain your choices.

b) Uganda and Chad have a similar GDP per capita. Explain some possible reasons why their HDI values are substantially different.

c) Use the UNHDP website (go to www.heinemann.co.uk/hotlinks, insert the express code 2230P, and click on 'UN HDP website') to find out about the Human Poverty Index (HPI). Compare the ways in which the HDI and the HPI are measured.

The HDI also suffers from the criticism that it says nothing about the quality of the two non-economic measures of human well-being. A greater percentage of the population enrolled in education says nothing about the 'quality' of that education. Living one extra year may not be an improvement in human well-being if the quality of life is dismal.

These limitations of the Human Development Index remind us that the HDI is only an indicator of development and that it should not be taken too literally or in isolation from other indicators of human well-being. Some of these may be difficult to quantify, but that does not mean that they are unimportant. The distribution of the outcomes of development are important, too. Raising GDP per capita, life expectancy, literacy and enrolment rates in urban areas or for men would raise the HDI but might not be thought of as a widespread improvement in human well-being.

ECONOMICS IN CONTEXT

DEVELOPMENT DIAMONDS

The World Bank uses 'development diamonds' to examine the relationships between socioeconomic indicators of development, such as GDP per capita, life expectancy at birth, primary (or secondary) school enrolment rates, and access to safe water for an individual country compared with the average for low-income countries.

The World Bank also produces 'economic diamonds' for countries on a similar basis. These compare a country's trade, investment (capital formation), indebtedness and domestic savings with the average for low-income countries.

Figure 11.3 shows Chad's economic ratios for 2006. Compared with other low-income countries, there are a number of positive economic factors which should assist Chad's economic development. There is a high level of domestic savings, an openness to international trade and a low level of international debt that might constrain its development. Investment, however, is lower than average for low-income countries.

You have already seen that Chad has a low HDI relative to its GDP per capita, in the Activity on page 286. The World Bank's development diamond for Chad, in Figure 11.4, presents some socioeconomic indicators that might explain the relative low level of human development. These include life expectancy, primary school enrolment and access to safe water lower than average for the low-income group of countries. Exploring the reasons for these outcomes may help to guide policies for raising the level of development in the future.

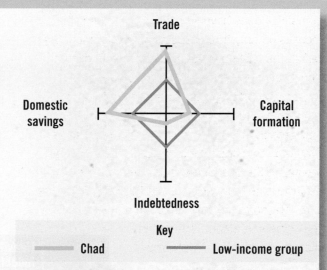

Figure 11.3 World Bank 'economic diamond' showing Chad's economic ratios for 2006

Source: Chad at a Glance, World Bank

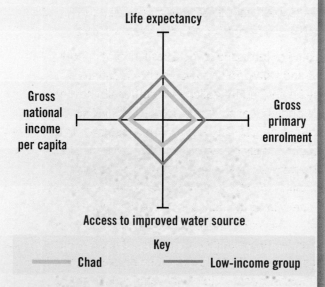

Figure 11.4 The World Bank's development diamond for Chad

Source: Chad at a Glance, World Bank

The common and diverse characteristics of developing countries

Developing countries share a number of similar characteristics, which, together, help to define their lack of development. These common characteristics make it possible to view this group of countries as facing similar problems. But right from the outset, you should recognise that there is a danger of making generalisations. Despite the shared characteristics, there is a great deal of diversity in the developing world. The differences between developing countries mean that the problems they face are as different as they are similar. This is important when it comes to thinking through the policies that might be appropriate for individual countries.

COMMON CHARACTERISTICS

There are six key similarities between developing countries:

● low living standards

● low levels of labour productivity

● a high rate of population growth

● an economic structure dominated by primary sector production

● a high degree of market failure

● a lack of economic power in international markets and dependence.

Low living standards

A low level of development is characterised by low living standards. Low living standards are related to low income, poor health, high infant mortality, malnutrition, a lack of access to clean water and

	Year	Heavily indebted poor countries (HIPCs)	Low-income	Lower middle-income	Upper middle-income	High-income
GDP per capita PPP (current international $)	2006	1,047	1,860	4,899	10,879	34,933
Internet users (per 100 people)	2005	2	4	8	18	56
Life expectancy at birth (years)	2006	53	60	71	70	79
Births attended by skilled health staff (% of total)	2006	43	43	86	94	99
Infant mortality rate (per 1,000)	2006	151	112	36	26	7
Malnutrition (% of children under 5)	2006	28	35	11	–	–
Measles immunisation (% of children aged 12–23 months)	2006	74	69	90	94	93
% of urban population with access to improved sanitation facilities	2004	50	60	76	89	100
% of population with access to improved water source	2004	56	75	81	93	99

Table 11.2 Indicators of low-level standards for selected income groups of countries
Source: World Bank

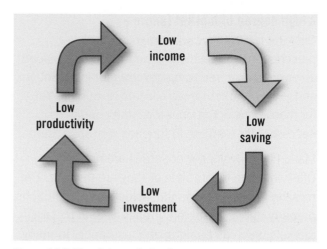

Figure 11.5 The vicious circle of poverty

to goods and services that many people in more developed nations might take for granted.

These problems of low living standards are often made worse by low rates of growth in income per capita, a highly uneven distribution of income and a large percentage of the population living on subsistence income (less than US$1 per day).

ACTIVITY ···

a) Explain the relationships between GDP per capita and two of the other indicators in Table 11.2.

b) Explain the view that economic growth is a necessary but not sufficient condition for economic development.

Low levels of labour productivity

Output per worker (labour productivity) in developing countries tends to be very low, especially compared

to that in developed economies. This is partly because of the shortage of physical capital in these countries. The low level of GDP limits investment in machinery and infrastructure, such as roads, railways and electricity generation and distribution. Low investment in physical capital is related to the lack of domestic savings, as you saw in the Harrod–Domar model of economic growth in Chapter 9. Low GDP and savings also contribute to the lack of investment in human capital, as you have seen in terms of enrolment rates in education. On top of this, poor health and malnutrition reduce the productivity of labour. The result is a vicious cycle of low income, poverty and low economic growth as Figure 11.5 summarises. Low incomes and low productivity feed into each other, creating a cycle of poverty that developing countries find difficult to break out of. The two things together create the biggest obstacle to development, as they tend to reinforce each other. Developing countries have low incomes *because* they have low productivity and they have low productivity *because* they are poor.

A high rate of population growth

84 per cent of the world's population lives in developing countries (low and middle income). The poorest countries also have the highest rates of population growth. The reason for this is very high birth rates in these countries in excess of death rate. This is part of the demographic transition, whereby birth rates in developing countries have remained high at the same time as death rates have fallen as a result of improved health conditions and control of infectious diseases.

The high rate of population growth is the cause of a large dependency burden in these countries. This

	Year	Heavily indebted poor countries (HIPCs)	Low-income	Lower middle-income	Upper middle-income	High-income
Total population (millions)	2006	603	2,420	2,276	811	1,031
Population growth (annual, %)	2006	3	2	1	1	1

Table 11.3 Total population and population growth rates, by country income group
Source: World Bank

dependency burden is both different in nature from that in developed countries and also higher overall. The workforce of developing countries has to support large numbers of children under the age of 15. This is in contrast to developed countries, where the elderly population is the focus of the dependency burden.

ACTIVITY ···⁝

Explain how the domestic population problems of developing economies weaken their ability to develop.

An economic structure dominated by primary sector production

There is a clear relationship between the structure of the economy and development. As an economy develops, the importance of its primary sector diminishes.

Large numbers of people in developing countries live in rural areas and are engaged in agriculture. In the very poorest nations, this output is often not marketed but is produced for own consumption – it is small-scale, subsistence agriculture. In addition, agricultural productivity is low because of the large number of people relative to the land available, poor irrigation and little use of physical capital.

Typically, primary products make up a large percentage of the exports of developing countries. Yet, as you have seen in Chapter 10, these exports have low value, have been subject to declining terms of trade over the long term and, in some instances, face tariffs from developed nations that protect their own agricultural sector.

A high degree of market failure

Over the last two decades, many of the prescriptions for developing countries have placed an emphasis on reducing government intervention and letting market forces allocate resources. Yet, for many developing countries, the conditions necessary for markets to function well are absent.

Markets in developing countries are not perfect. Often they are incomplete or they are missing. The reasons for this include the lack of legal institutions, property rights, a stable currency and financial markets, such as banking and insurance. In many rural areas, for example, there is a single village 'money lender', operating much like a monopolist, charging high rates of interest for small sums of money. Natural resources such as land are often not owned by individuals but are a common resource, leading to overuse and depletion over time. Where land is owned, it is either fragmented, as it is divided when passed down from generation to generation, or is owned by large landowners who rent it out at monopoly rents. Market failure is, therefore, rife in developing countries.

ACTIVITY ···⁝

a) Explain how the balance between the different sectors of an economy indicates its level of development.

STRETCH AND CHALLENGE

b) Comment on the problems that might be faced by a developing country in changing the structure of production.

	Year	Heavily indebted poor countries (HIPC)	Low-income	Lower middle-income	Upper middle-income	High-income
Agricultural output as % of GDP	2005	30	22	12	6	2

Table 11.4 Agricultural output by country income group (% of GDP)
Source: World Bank

ECONOMICS IN CONTEXT

MICRO CREDIT – A SOLUTION TO MARKET FAILURE?

In 2006, the Nobel Peace Prize was awarded to a Bangladeshi economist, Muhammad Yunnus, founder of the Grameen Bank. In response to the market failures in financial markets in Bangladesh, Yunnus set up a system of 'micro credit' in order to provide banking services for the rural poor. Traditionally, this group has been unable to access credit or has had to pay interest at rates well above 'market' rates because of the monopoly power of village money lenders; their poverty meant that they could not provide any collateral to guarantee loans from traditional banks.

Loans from the Grameen Bank require no collateral, so even beggars can borrow money. The Bank operates by lending small amounts of money (typically less than £50) to the rural poor, mainly women, in order for them to be able to lift themselves and their families out of poverty by starting up in business, paying school fees or buying a mosquito net.

The Grameen Bank currently has 7.5 million borrowers (97 per cent of whom are women) and 2,500 branches, and works in 82,000 villages. Since its foundation in 1976, it has lent out US$7 billion, 98 per cent of which has been paid back at low rates of interest by the borrowers.

Some commentators, however, are critical of micro-credit schemes such as the Grameen Bank. They say that entrepreneurship in developing countries is limited by the size of markets, that money borrowed is often diverted into consumption rather than investment, that money has not gone to the poorest in rural areas and that, while it may help poor people to survive, it is not the key to development.

For links to useful case studies, articles and short videos for you to research the issues surrounding micro credit, go to www.heinemann.co.uk/hotlinks, insert the express code 2230P, and click on 'Micro credit 1–4'.

A lack of economic power in international markets and dependence

The low value of the exports of developing countries and the market structures in which they operate give them little economic power in international trade. This contrasts with developed countries, where firms operate in oligopolistic markets and have a greater degree of control over the prices they can command for their products. Even where developing countries might be thought to have a comparative advantage, the world trading system is dominated by multinational companies based in developed nations. This dominance takes many forms. Multinationals are both dominant producers and dominant buyers in international markets. So, for example, 90 per cent of internationally traded bananas are grown on plantations owned by just five companies. Cargill, a US multinational, accounts for 25 per cent of world trade in grain and has a 40 per cent market share of world cocoa trade.

Some economists also argue that developing countries are dependent on developed countries through the legacy of colonial rule. This may be responsible for a narrow economic structure, infrastructure that served the needs of colonial rulers and inappropriate political, educational and administrative systems. To such economists, underdevelopment is a function of the history of developing countries, which has created domestic élites resistant to change.

DIVERSE CHARACTERISTICS

Developing countries are every bit as different as they are similar. There are marked differences in their resource endowment, the size of their economies and the level of income, their historical background and their economic structure, including the balance between the state and markets.

ACTIVITY ⋯⋮⋅

The price of rice, like other primary commodity prices, is volatile. In 2007 rice prices increased by 50 per cent, and they tripled during 2008. Thailand, the world's biggest rice exporter, has called for the creation of a rice cartel among the world's South East Asian producers, such as Thailand, Laos, Cambodia and Vietnam. It argues that a rice cartel will give countries more control over international rice prices. The recent price rises have been caused by poor harvests, rising demand and hoarding of supplies in anticipation of future price increases.

a) Using a demand and supply diagram, explain why primary commodity prices are volatile.

b) Explain what is meant by a cartel of rice producers.

STRETCH AND CHALLENGE

c) Assess the benefits of a rice cartel to net exporters and importers of rice.

Use these links to the BBC website to find out more about the problems facing developing countries as a result of the rising price of rice: go to www.heinemann.co.uk/hotlinks, insert the express code 2230P, and click on 'BBC News Business – rice' and 'BBC News South Asia – rice'.

Some developing countries are fortunate in having natural resource endowments that favour development. This might include fertile land or deposits of oil or minerals. Others, such as Bangladesh, are less fortunate, with few natural resources and land that is difficult to cultivate. Yet there is no clear link between natural resource endowment and development. Singapore, a former British colony and an independent republic since 1965, has no significant natural resources. Yet it is a success story of development, recording an HDI of 0.992 in 2007. Zambia, rich in deposits of copper, has seen its GDP per capita fall by 50 per cent since independence from British rule in 1964. With average life expectancy of only 40 years and one of the lowest average incomes, its HDI was only 0.434 in 2007.

Developing countries differ, too, in their human resources. Population size is an obvious source of diversity in the developing world. Large populations would seem to indicate a large potential market for goods and services, yet there are as many developing countries with large populations as there are with small populations. Population size makes little difference to development and growth. For example, Singapore's population of 4.7 million is less than half that of Zambia's (11.7 million),

yet China and India, the growth success stories of recent years, have populations of over 1 billion.

There is diversity too in historical background. Singapore and Zambia are examples of countries which were once colonies. Their independence from colonial rule is relatively recent compared to countries in Latin America. Colonial rule has left different legacies in different countries. In many respects the colonial legacy in Singapore has been a positive one, yet in much of Africa it is argued that the legacy is a negative one.

Finally, there are differences in the structure of economies in the developing world and in the role of the state and markets in the economy. The role of the state in African economies has traditionally been prominent compared to the greater role of the private sector in Latin America and South East Asia. The result has been a wide variation in economic policies in these regions. Planning and state investment have dominated development policies in Africa in the past. In South East Asia, the approach to development has been much more about giving incentives for market-driven development, particularly in encouraging foreign direct investment (FDI) and entrepreneurship. In terms of economic structure, agriculture is much more dominant in Africa than it

ECONOMICS IN CONTEXT

AFRICA'S ECONOMIES CONFRONTED BY PROBLEMS

Professor Nicholas Stern, former director of policy and research at the UK's Commission for Africa, has identified these causes of Africa's low level of economic development:

- a lack of investment in infrastructure and transport links, with the result that it costs about twice as much to take goods out of Africa relative to other countries
- the legacy of colonial rule, which focused on a narrow range of economic activities surrounding the extraction of natural resources such as copper, timber and gold
- the political fragmentation, with 48 sub-Saharan African countries creating economic as well as political barriers
- barriers to trade created by developed nations.

For useful weblinks (articles, audio and video links) to follow up the issues raised here, go to www.heinemann.co.uk/hotlinks, insert the express code 2230P, and click on 'Development issues in Africa 1–4'.

ACTIVITY ····⁝➔

a) Choose two developing countries in the same continent and research the similarities and differences between them. Use the similarities and differences identified on pages 288–293 as a guide to your research.

b) Summarise your findings on one side of A4. You could create a case study booklet if you are doing this activity with other students.

STRETCH AND CHALLENGE

c) To what extent is it useful to view developing countries as a group of countries with similar characteristics?

A COMMON PATTERN OF CHANGE?

You have seen that development involves more than just economic growth. However, it does involve economic change. This change relates to the balance between the primary, secondary, tertiary and quaternary sectors of the economy. Economists call this structural change. Along with structural change comes change in formal and informal economic activity and in the rural and urban sectors.

As economies grow, the balance between the different sectors of the economy changes. A common pattern of structural change is that initially primary sector output falls as a percentage of output and secondary sector output rises. This is known as industrialisation. Further growth in the economy is associated with a reduction in the secondary sector as a percentage of total output, and with growth in the contribution made by the tertiary sector output. This is known as deindustrialisation. Within the service sector of the economy, high levels of economic development seem to be generating rapid growth in knowledge- and information-related services (quaternary sector). Examples of such services include education, research and development (R&D), modern communications (telephones and the Internet) and business services. This is known as the 'knowledge revolution'. Evidence for this common pattern of change in the structure of the economy can be seen in Figure 11.6.

is in Latin America and South East Asia. This is in part due to differences in the level of development and to the change in economic structure away from the primary sector and towards industrialisation brought about by the more rapid development in these regions.

Developing countries, then, should not be viewed as a homogeneous group. The great diversity between them means that you should be wary of making generalisations. The development process is not a blueprint that can be transferred from country to country. Policies to promote economic development need to take note of the unique circumstances of each country.

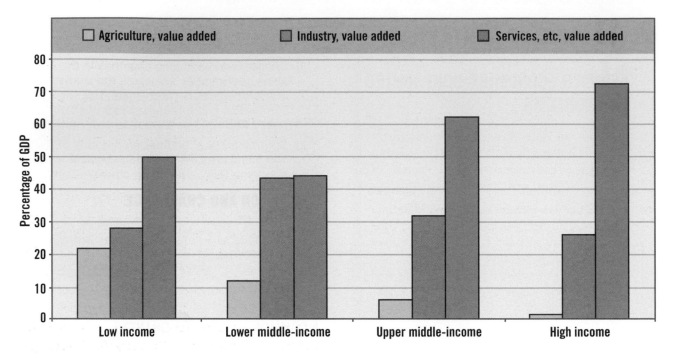

Figure 11.6 Output of selected sectors of the economy, by country income group (% of GDP)
Source: World Bank website

As this structural change occurs, formal economic activity eventually takes over from informal activity. But it is common for the informal sector of the economy to grow to begin with. In the early stages of structural change, the small size of the urban industrial sector generates relatively high wages for those in formal sector employment. This creates a 'pull factor' for the rural population, contributing to a high degree of rural–urban migration. Internal migrants find access to formal sector jobs difficult either because of a lack of education and training or because of the inability of the formal sector to absorb the volume of migrants. The growth of urban shantytowns in developing countries results from a modern, industrial sector that is relatively small in size and offers little in the way of employment to migrants. The consequent high unemployment in developing countries (in Namibia approximately 35 per cent) drives people into the informal sector, swelling its size and diversity – shoe cleaning, 'waste' collection and recycling, errands, street entertaining, vending and prostitution, to name but a few activities. The lack of structures and institutions makes the

obstacles to entry into the formal sector even greater. Lack of access to clean water, to health care and education make the prospects dismal for the average migrant from rural areas and serve to perpetuate a large informal sector.

There are economic forces that drive changes in the structure of the economy. As incomes rise, the demand for food grows, but less slowly than incomes grow. The demand for food is income inelastic. The demand for secondary sector output, on the other hand, is income elastic. As a result, industry grows more rapidly than agriculture. In addition, increases in agricultural productivity reduce the price of food and the value of output of the agricultural sector falls relative to the output of the secondary sector of the economy. Higher agricultural productivity creates surplus labour in rural areas. The migration of labour to urban, industrial areas keeps wage rates there low. The emerging industrial sector's profits rise, allowing investment to create self-sustaining growth. Finally, higher incomes generate higher levels of savings, which, according to the Harrod–Domar model of growth (see page 218), further stimulates economic growth.

The pattern of change in the structure of the economy need not be common to all countries, however. As you saw in Chapter 10, the Indian economy is experiencing rapid growth in revenues, jobs and export earnings from its IT service companies, nicknamed the Bangalore Tigers. There is no reason to suppose that the historical pattern of structural change is a process that is inevitable. India's supply of well-educated labour has attracted multinational investment in service sector activities such as call centres and its increasingly affluent middle classes are attracting investment by major retailers such as Wal-Mart.

ACTIVITY ····⫶

Explain the importance of industrialisation for developing countries.

The constraints on development

Before looking at the policies to promote economic development and their effectiveness, you should understand the constraints facing countries in their quest for development. These constraints are a mixture of internal and external factors and processes.

One way of looking at these constraints is to consider the reasons for the economic structure of low-income economies identified in the last section. This economic structure has, for many countries, persisted over long periods of time. The primary sector of the economy has remained large and dominant. Economic development is obviously being held back or constrained. In one respect the continuing dominance of the primary sector in developing countries can be argued to reflect the particular resource endowments of many developing countries. For example, while agricultural output only accounts for 12 per cent of Namibia's GDP, mining contributes 20 per cent. Namibia is 'blessed' with high-quality diamond deposits, is the fifth largest producer of uranium and produces large quantities of lead, zinc, silver, tin and tungsten. This kind of wealth of natural resources has become known as the 'resource curse', as the structure of the economy

becomes trapped in a low level of development because of a nation's resource endowment.

The continued dominance of the primary sector of developing countries, however, also results from their low level of development. With a large proportion of the population living on low incomes (in Namibia 35 per cent living on less than $1 a day and over 55 per cent on less than $2 a day), subsistence farming is the norm for many – almost 50 per cent of the population in Namibia are engaged in agriculture. The result of low incomes is low levels and rates of saving. Low levels of savings constrain the ability of the secondary sector to grow, since it is essentially starved of funds for investment. Furthermore, the lack of developed financial markets and financial intermediaries mean that what savings exist are not efficiently channelled into the secondary sector. Rich élites in developing countries tend to invest savings outside the domestic economy (capital flight), further limiting the development of the secondary sector. The primary sector, therefore, remains large.

The constraints on structural change reinforce a dependence on primary sector activity generated by, in some cases, the legacy of colonial rule and, in most cases, the nature of international trade. Nations colonised in the past specialised in primary production and trade. Colonial infrastructure facilitated this specialisation. Following free trade principles, on independence many developing countries sought to develop by exploiting their comparative advantage in primary production through trade. With low-income elasticities of demand and rising world production of many primary commodities, however, the price of primary exports decreased relative to that of goods imported. Developing countries became caught in a trade and development trap, whereby more and more primary commodity exports were required to prevent foreign currency earnings from falling. Promotion of capital-intensive industrial production became ever more difficult, since it required the importation of capital paid for in foreign currency.

These constraints on development impede the transfer of the factors of production into the secondary or tertiary sectors of the economy.

Only some of the many constraints identified by development economists have been explored here. Some of the others include:

- inequalities in the distribution of income and wealth
- inequalities in the distribution of the ownership of land
- insufficient and inadequate infrastructure, including electricity, water, communications, ports, roads and rail
- the lack of financial markets, including banks and stock markets
- an education system that is insufficient, inadequate and inappropriate, including a neglect of primary education and over-allocation of resources to higher education
- poor governance, corruption and patronage generating élites resistant to change
- market failures that distort the allocation of resources and reduce competition
- an inability to access international markets because of regional trading blocs such as the EU and NAFTA and the protection of domestic markets by developed countries
- the policies of international organisations such as the World Bank and the IMF
- high levels of external debt.

Policies to promote economic development

The desire to promote economic and human development is for many students what draws them to study development economics. But there needs to be a recognition from the beginning that there are no simple solutions to improving the lives of the many millions in the world whose human development deserves to be raised. You should not expect to find a policy blueprint for economic development by working your way through this section!

DIFFERENT APPROACHES TO PROMOTING ECONOMIC DEVELOPMENT

Four approaches to promoting economic development are looked at here:

- state ownership, government intervention and import substitution
- export promotion
- filling the savings gap through international aid
- the Washington Consensus and the role of markets.

State ownership, government intervention and import substitution

Thinking about policies to improve economic development has divided economists over the years. To start with, thoughts focused on the failure of markets. Many early policies emphasised a big role for government intervention through large-scale economic planning, high levels of public investment, state ownership of firms, and controls on the private sector. Common approaches have been to set up state-owned enterprises in the manufacturing sector, set maximum prices for agricultural commodities and control the export and import of goods and services. This has become known as the 'big push' approach to economic development, practised in much of Latin America until the 1960s and in India and Africa after independence.

The emphasis of this approach to economic development was to provide massive investment in infrastructure and rapid industrialisation through a policy of import-substituting industrialisation (ISI). This involved countries imposing tariffs on imported manufactured goods in order to allow domestic industry to grow. In this way it was hoped that the structure of the economy would become less reliant on the primary sector and that a new comparative advantage would be created. This would, it was argued, free the economy from the constraint of declining terms of trade and the development trap created by free trade.

Countries following such policies to promote economic development experienced rapid rates of economic growth, at least in the early years. However, growth rates eventually began to stagnate. The approach suffered from a number of problems. A very important issue was the bias created towards the urban, industrial sector and the neglect of agriculture and rural areas. While GDP per capita increased, this was not equally distributed and income inequalities rose dramatically.

Human development was not advanced because state funds were not directed towards education and health. For many countries, protection stifled growth in the long term because of the small size of the domestic market. Firms lacked the economies of scale to generate lower unit costs and productive efficiencies. Some countries found that growth was hindered by shortages of capital or that imports of consumer goods were replaced by imports of capital goods creating severe balance of payments problems. The use of subsidies, quotas and tariffs distorted market prices and led to resources being misallocated. Protection from international trade resulted in a lack of competition, which, over time, bred inefficiencies. Powerful élites emerged that had an interest in maintaining protectionism, state ownership and subsidies.

ECONOMICS IN CONTEXT

DEVELOPMENT POLICY: MARKET OR STATE?

In May 2008 a major report was published by the independent Commission on Growth and Development. *The Growth Report: Strategies for Sustained Growth and Inclusive Development* concluded that relying on market forces alone to produce growth in developing countries would not reduce poverty. Instead, the report suggested that some degree of government intervention and protectionism is necessary, at least in the early stages of development.

'*No country has sustained rapid economic growth without also keeping an impressive rate of public investment in infrastructure, education and health. Far from crowding out private investment, this type of spending crowds it in.*'

Market failures are too severe in developing economies to allow markets to function well. The Commission was critical, however, of import substitution, which they said limited growth in the long term because of the small size of the domestic market.

(For useful weblinks related to policies to promote economic development, go to www.heinemann.co.uk/hotlinks, insert the express code 2230P, and click on 'Economic development policies 1–2'.)

Export promotion

Among the countries following the ISI approach to economic development were a number of countries that quickly switched to the promotion of exports. The most successful of these countries were South Korea, Singapore, Hong Kong and Taiwan. These countries have since become known as the high-performing Asian economies (HPAEs) as a result of their spectacular rates of economic growth from the 1960s through to the 1990s. These economies focused on developing a comparative advantage in goods for export to the developed world. The role of the state in export promotion is very different from its role in ISI. The HPAEs focused government investment on strategic industries, sometimes with state ownership, but always exposed to international competition. Protectionism still played a role in the development of these economies. But protection was quickly removed. Entrepreneurs soon learnt to adapt to international trade and dynamic efficiencies were created. Initially, they found success in the export of labour-intensive manufactured goods. At the same time, there was heavy investment in education (particularly primary education) in order to raise labour productivity.

Despite the success of the HPAEs, the export promotion approach to economic development does not provide a blueprint for development. There is still wide variation in the growth rates of economies that have followed this approach. For example, India's rate of economic growth has been much faster than Brazil's, even though the two countries have followed similar policies. It is also important to recognise that success is not due to a single policy, such as the liberalisation of trade. Some economists have argued that other factors are as important in explaining the successful development of the HPAEs. Some cite a stable macroeconomic environment and others the high levels of savings characteristic of these economies.

There is a danger that export promotion policies make economic development dependent on growth in demand in developed nations. It might also encourage countries to seek to engage in competitive devaluations of their currency in order to maintain competitiveness. In addition, the HPAEs are currently losing their comparative advantage to economies such as India and China, which have substantially lower labour costs.

ECONOMICS IN CONTEXT

DEVELOPMENT BLOOMS IN ETHIOPIA

Flower-growing is not the most obvious business you would associate with Ethiopia, but the conditions are ideal. On the outskirts of Addis Ababa lies a sprawling Ethiopian-owned rose farm covering 15 hectares. In vast, fabric-covered hothouses the size of meadows, thousands of roses bloom. Computer-linked sensors open and close the roof awnings according to changes in the weather and turn a regiment of sprinklers on and off in a closely climate-controlled environment. It is a very sophisticated operation.

'We can grow 150 to 180 stems per square metre all year round, so that's 10,000 roses per hectare per year,' says Adane Gebru, the young farm manager. 'We sell direct to Germany and Sweden and also through the huge flower auctions in the Netherlands.'

This bright-eyed, optimistic entrepreneurialism is a relatively new feature of Ethiopia. Mr Gebru makes a painful face at the mention of the country's former soviet-style socialism. 'Before, the government didn't like market economics, they confiscated private property, restricted the markets and told you where you could sell and where you couldn't. But now we can sell our product anywhere, we can utilise the market.'

Globalisation, he argues, can work in Ethiopia's favour. 'We can't avoid globalisation – it's the same for everyone. But there are no import tariffs on flowers and that helps.'

The 550 workers here may earn only a dollar a day, but this is a huge advance on their prospects of just a few years ago. The dairy farm previously on the site employed only 50 people – this new enterprise is improving the economic, health, welfare and educational opportunities for local families.

Adane Gebru has a vision of Ethiopia buoyant on trade: 'In 20 years time, education will reach everyone. The infrastructure will be built properly, there'll be roads and schools and hospitals. We won't be a developed country, but we will be on the right track.'

Adapted from: Doney, M. and Wroe, M., 'A good year for the roses', *Developments,* Department for International Development, London, www.developments. org.uk

Filling the savings gap through international aid

Another popular approach to promoting economic development is rooted in the Harrod–Domar model of growth introduced in Chapter 9. According to the Harrod-Domar model, economic growth is held back by a lack of domestic savings, which in turn is related to low levels of income created by a lack of development. Appropriate policy responses are to find ways of making up for this gap in domestic savings. One of these is to seek international aid.

Foreign aid is any flow of capital to developing countries that meets two criteria:

● its objective is non-commercial from the point of view of the donor

● it is characterised by concessionary terms; for example, interest rates lower than the market rate, or longer repayment periods.

Aid can come in many different forms. These include:

● *grants*, for which no repayment is required; including money for development projects, free technical help and expertise, free university education in donor country

● *loans* for which repayment is required – to qualify as aid, loans must be 'soft', i.e. not at market rates

● *tied aid* given in return for the purchase of donor country goods or services

● *bilateral aid* direct from one country to another

● *multilateral aid*, which is money from international agencies such as World Bank, UNICEF or IMF, or from more than one country

● *food aid*, often in the form of emergency relief aid.

Governments of developed nations can help to promote economic development by a policy of giving aid (or overseas development assistance, ODA) to developing countries. The World Bank exists to provide aid to developing countries in the form of loans, which in 2005 totalled $22 billion. ODA is concentrated in the poorest regions of the world. Yet, when the distribution of aid is looked at in more detail, there are a number of worrying observations:

● 50 per cent of the world's poorest people live in South Asia, yet they receive only $4 per person in aid

● the top twenty aid recipients receive more than 50 per cent of aid

● only 31 per cent of aid goes to the ten developing countries with 66 per cent of the world's poorest people

● the richest 40 per cent of developing countries receive more than twice the aid of the poorest 40 per cent.

What these observations show is that the policy of aid is not driven entirely by need. While aid may, on the surface, help to promote economic and human development by being channelled into education, health and rural areas, in many respects it serves to promote the interests of the donor. So, for example, Israel receives 100 times more aid per person from the USA than does Bangladesh.

The evidence on the effectiveness of aid is even less positive. There is little evidence that aid promotes economic growth (average incomes in Africa have fallen over the past twenty years despite the region receiving over $500 billion in aid). Aid has also contributed to the macroeconomic problems of developing countries by raising levels of debt and worsening the balance of payments. In total, developing countries have external debt of over $2 trillion, which costs them over $300 billion in interest and repayments (debt service) each year. Aid has often been misdirected into schemes that do little to improve human well-being, might not reach the intended recipients because of corruption,

and may contribute to a bias in economic growth towards the urban, industrial sector. Finally, countries may become dependent on aid as the major source of government expenditure or as the largest contributor to GDP. In Mozambique, for example, official development assistance represents around 60% of GDP.

The Washington Consensus and the role of markets

The perception that planning, trade protection and aid had all failed to promote economic development led to a belief that developing countries needed to make major policy changes. This view strengthened in the 1980s and 1990s, focusing on a set of policies that became known as the 'Washington Consensus'. The policy prescription was handed out to developing countries by the World Bank, the International Monetary Fund (IMF) and the US Treasury Department as based in Washington. The common theme in the mix of policies prescribed was the emphasis on increasing the role of market forces.

The Washington Consensus made ten policy recommendations (see Table 11.5), but it can be summarised under three main headings:

● *fiscal discipline* – the elimination of budget deficits, limits on government spending and the development of a reliable tax base

● *market liberalisation and privatisation* – the ending of government intervention in markets, including the sale of state-owned industries and the end of price controls

● *trade liberalisation and the encouragement of foreign investment* – the scrapping of tariffs and other protectionist measures, including those that created barriers to foreign investment.

Many developing countries had no option but to adopt these policies. Loans and aid to developing countries from the IMF, the World Bank and others became dependent on them making such 'structural adjustments'. The economic logic was that, without these structural

	Fiscal discipline	Market liberalisation and privatisation	Trade liberalisation and the encouragement of foreign investment
Policy recommendations of the Washington Consensus	Avoidance of budget deficits and balanced budget over the economic cycle	Privatisation of state-owned enterprises	Trade liberalisation, reduction of tariffs and removal of non-tariff barriers to trade
	Redirection of public expenditure towards health, education and infrastructure	Deregulation of markets and removal of entry barriers to promote competition	Removal of barriers to and restriction on foreign investment
	Reform of the tax system to widen the tax base and lower marginal rates of taxation	Legally supported property rights	Competitive exchange rates
	Market-determined interest rates	–	–

Table 11.5 The ten policy prescriptions of the Washington Consensus

adjustments, development aid had little chance of success. So, governments should create macroeconomic stability and control inflation by limiting and controlling public expenditure. Market liberalisation and privatisation would ensure that resources were allocated efficiently, reduce government failure, eliminate productive inefficiencies and allow the profit motive to raise levels of investment, including investment by foreign multinational companies. Trade liberalisation would expose domestic firms to international competition and encourage developing countries to earn export revenue. Scarce resources would then be allocated more efficiently and the maximum possible output would be produced from a nation's limited resources. It was, above all else, a policy prescription aimed at maximising the rate of economic growth of developing countries. The benefits of this higher growth, it was assumed, would 'trickle down' to the bulk of the population and living standards, over time, would improve.

There is fierce debate among economists about the effectiveness of Washington Consensus policies. Supporters point to the success in reducing inflation in many developing countries, arguing that this has created a stable macroeconomic climate. They point to the high rates of economic growth experienced by countries such as Brazil, to the jobs created by multinational companies in the more open developing economies and to the reduction in debt in such economies.

The views of critics are not far removed from those expressed in the portrayal of IMF structural adjustment programmes in Figure 11.7. They argue that many of the policies have increased poverty in developing countries. For example, the end of price controls on food, subsidies on fertilisers, trade liberalisation and currency devaluations have raised the price of food in developing countries and contributed to higher malnutrition. Domestic food production has been replaced by imports from countries, such as the USA, where agriculture is heavily subsidised. The rush to earn export revenue from 'cash crops', such as peanuts and coffee, has raised world supply and reduced prices, so that developing countries need to export greater volumes of primary commodities to stay still in development terms. Fiscal discipline has been achieved by cuts in expenditure on health and education, which have worsened human development.

Criticism of the Washington Consensus has not been confined to charities such as Oxfam and anti-globalisation campaigners. The former chief economist of the World Bank and Nobel Prize winner for economics, Joseph Stiglitz, is among those who have argued that World Bank and IMF policies have done much to retard economic and human development. In his books, *Globalisation and Its Discontents* and *Making Globalisation Work*, he has argued that the Washington Consensus has focused on the wrong problem. The problem is not too much government intervention but market failure: developing economies lack the infrastructure to allow markets to work efficiently; financial institutions and markets are poorly developed, so cannot channel funds from savings to investment; the lack of a developed legal system undermines private property rights and holds back private sector investment; and there is a lack of entrepreneurial culture in developing countries as a result of low incomes, subsistence and the legacy of colonial rule. According to Stiglitz and others, the focus of policies to promote development should be on tackling these fundamentals rather than be set by a belief in the power of markets.

Figure 11.7 A critical view of Washington Consensus policies
Source: Polyp, c/o *New Internationalist,* www.newint.org

What can be concluded from all of this? Perhaps the most important conclusion is to re-emphasise the observation made at the beginning of this section. There is no policy blueprint for developing countries to follow. There does seem to be a new consensus emerging, however, even in the World Bank and the IMF. The World Bank has publicly reflected on its policies of the 1980s and 1990s in its 2005 report, *Economic Growth in the 1990s: Learning from a Decade of Reform*. There seems to be a new emphasis on strengthening institutions, investing in human capital and promoting social equity as ways of promoting development. The IMF has moved away from structural adjustment programmes to focus on poverty reduction.

ACTIVITY ···⁝›

To qualify for a World Bank or IMF loan, developing countries such as Peru, Ethiopia, Tanzania and Zimbabwe have had to agree to sign up to structural adjustment programmes (SAPs).

a) What is meant by 'structural adjustment programme'?

b) Explain why the World Bank believes that some developing countries require structural adjustment.

STRETCH AND CHALLENGE

c) Discuss the extent to which structural adjustment programmes necessarily promote economic development.

For a weblink to a useful video interview with Martin Kohr, director of the Third World Network, go to www.heinemann.co.uk/hotlinks, insert the express code 2230P, and click on 'Structural adjustment explained'.

	Period of high growth	Per capita income at start (US$)	Per capita income, 2005 (US$)
Botswana	1960–2005	210	3,800
Brazil	1950–80	960	4,000
China	1961–2005	105	1,400
Hong Kong, China	1960–97	3,100	29,000
Indonesia	1966–97	200	900
Japan	1950–83	3,500	39,600
Korea	1960–2001	1,100	13,200
Malaysia	1967–97	790	4,400
Malta	1963–94	1,100	9,600
Oman	1960–99	950	9,000
Singapore	1967–2002	2,200	25,400
Taiwan, China	1965–2002	1,500	16,400
Thailand	1960–97	330	2,400

Table 11.6 Thirteen countries that have sustained annual economic growth rates of 7% over 25 years
Source: Commission on Growth and Development, Growth Report: Strategies for Sustained Growth and Inclusive Development, May 2008

What we do know is that some countries have been able to achieve consistently high rates of economic growth over a number of years (see Table 11.6). But we also know that over the last decade, income inequality *within* very many developing countries has increased. Most importantly, we know that, unless economic growth raises human well-being, true development cannot be said to have taken place.

Sustainable development
THE MEANING OF SUSTAINABILITY
Sustainable development is rooted in a desire to reduce the economic, social and environmental costs of economic growth. The phrase was first coined by the United Nation's World Commission on Environment and Development (the Brundtland Commission) in 1983. At the UN's 1992 Conference on Environment and Development in Rio de Janeiro, 179 governments agreed to adopt national strategies and to take global action to achieve sustainable development.

The definition of sustainable development used by the Brundtland Commission is now generally used by economists and governments to describe development that:

'meets the needs of the current generation without compromising the ability of future generations to meet their own needs'.

Sustainable development, then, is all about ensuring that economic growth improves living standards and the quality of people's lives, both now and in the future. To achieve this, there should be a balance between economic, social and environmental objectives.

● *Economic objectives* of growth tend to focus on making better use of scarce resources so that there is an increase in the goods and services available for households to consume. This requires an increase in the output of the primary, secondary and tertiary sectors of the economy. To be sustainable, however, this growth should also ensure that sufficient resources are allocated to investment in human and physical capital to raise the productive capacity of the economy. In other words, economic growth should concentrate on improving the supply-side performance of the economy, as you discovered in Chapter 9.

● *The social objectives* of growth concern the distribution of the benefits of growth. Certain basic goods and services are needed by all people, in order that their lives are healthy and productive. These might include food, shelter, health and education. An education system in which girls had unequal access to schooling would not meet the social conditions of sustainability. There are important external benefits (positive externalities) to raising school enrolment rates for girls. These include reduced fertility rates (reducing population growth), reduced infant and child mortality rates, increased labour force participation rates and reduced HIV/AIDS infection rates. Social objectives, then, can and do have important economic benefits. An economic system that did not provide women with adequate family planning services or adequate health care for the elderly would not meet these social conditions either. An economic system that did not provide pensions for the elderly would be failing to meet an important social objective of growth.

● *The environmental objectives* of growth focus on ensuring that future generations do not inherit a stock of natural capital that will reduce their quality of life or reduce their ability to produce goods and services. There are environmental concerns associated with current economic growth, both in developed and in developing nations. Some of these concerns you have examined in Chapter 3 of *OCR AS Economics*. They were introduced as examples of negative externalities, resulting in over-production and -consumption and market

failure. In developing countries, poverty itself is a major cause of environmental damage. Poverty leads to agricultural land being over-farmed. This results in soil degradation, which reduces the productivity of land over time. Often the lack of clearly defined property rights contributes to this over-use of land. There are no incentives to make efficient use of land or to invest in improving its productivity if land is in common ownership or if ownership of land is not clearly defined. Natural resources, such as mineral deposits, may be depleted in order to raise current GDP. Urban water supplies are often contaminated by the lack of investment in sanitation infrastructure. Poor countries cannot afford expensive clean technologies for production, common in developed nations. Rainforests may be destroyed to provide land for cultivation (for only a few years) or to provide an income from 'logging'. The external cost of such environmental degradation is either a global cost or a cost borne by future generations. It does not enter the calculations of the present generation. Environmental degradation persists without national, regional or global action to internalise the costs. But, as you will see, such action raises a number of difficult issues.

It is worth pointing out that there is a popular misconception about many of the problems referred to above. These problems are often blamed on high population growth. It is true that in many parts of the world rapidly growing populations have contributed to problems in both rural and urban areas. Shortages of land and water in villages and health problems from poor sanitation in urban areas are not helped by rapidly growing populations. But high population growth and environmental problems that make growth unsustainable share one thing in common. The underlying cause of both is poverty. Raising the standard of living is a way of delivering sustainability in the long term.

ACTIVITY ⋯⋇

The activities of multinational corporations create much controversy and debate. The two extracts below capture some of this.

> Since the fall of communism in 1989, eastern Europe has attracted some $300 billion of foreign direct investment. But the multinationals that arrived did much more than just invest money. They provided technology, know-how and access to foreign markets and, most importantly, introduced higher standards of performance, ethics and practices that have spread across the region.

Source: *International Herald Tribune* website, 16 February 2005

> Sales of bottled water worldwide are worth a staggering $35 billion. Multinational corporations are, therefore, keen to buy up springs in order to source mineral water. Nestlé, which accounts for over 30 per cent of bottled sales in the USA, has recently come into conflict with the residents of McCloud, a town in the shadows of California's snow-capped Mount Shasta. Pristine spring water comes from Shasta's glaciers and feeds some of the world's best fly-fishing rivers. Nestlé have acquired the rights to the water and intend to build a 1 million-square-foot water-bottling facility in McCloud. Residents have campaigned against the development. 'There is concern about traffic, air pollution, what is going to happen to our water,' said Debra Anderson, head of the local campaign group. 'What if there is a drought? They have the right to continue to pump. What happens to the town of McCloud, the people in it?'

Adapted from: www.biomedicine.org

a) Explain why sustainable development is desirable.

STRETCH AND CHALLENGE

b) Discuss the extent to which the actions of multinational companies are likely to promote sustainable development.

ECONOMICS IN CONTEXT

THE MILLENIUM ECOSYSTEM ASSESSMENT

In 2000 the Secretary General of the United Nations, Kofi Annan, called for an assessment of the impact of economic activity on the world's ecosystem. The Millennium Ecosystem Assessment started its work in 2001, involving more than 1,300 experts worldwide. Some of its findings, published in 2005, are summarised below.

Water

- Water withdrawals from rivers and lakes for irrigation, household and industrial use doubled in the last 40 years.
- Humans now use between 40 and 50 per cent of the freshwater running off land to which the majority of the population has access.

Conversion and degradation

- Since about 1980, approximately 35 per cent of mangroves have been lost, while 20 per cent of the world's coral reefs have been destroyed and a further 20 per cent badly degraded or destroyed.

Nutrient use and levels

- Human activities now produce more nitrogen than is produced by all natural processes combined, and more than half of all the manufactured nitrogen fertilizer ever used on the planet has been applied since 1985.

Fisheries

- At least one quarter of marine fish stocks are overharvested.
- The quantity of fish caught by humans increased until the 1980s but is now declining because of the shortage of stocks.

Source: *Millennium Ecosystem Assessment, Living Beyond Our Means, 2005*
www.millenniumassessment.org/documents/document.429.aspx.pdf

THE MEASUREMENT OF SUSTAINABILITY

Development is only sustainable if future generations are left with a stock of capital that is at least equal to the stock of capital used to generate today's output. That stock of capital should include not just man-made capital (such as machinery) but also natural or environmental capital (such as forests, air quality and soil quality) and human capital (such as knowledge and skills). If any of this capital is used up (depreciates) in the production of goods and services, this affects the ability of future generations to meet their needs. Deducting this depreciation from national income gives us a picture of what is called sustainable national income.

Economic indicators, such as GDP, are clearly limited when it comes to assessing the costs and benefits of increased production of goods and services. GDP measures the market value of consumption, investment, government expenditure on goods and services and net trade. It makes no distinction between output that raises human well-being and output that generates environmental damage, for example. It says nothing about the distribution of the nation's income and cannot, therefore, capture what is happening to the social objectives of development. GDP treats all expenditure as a 'positive'. So, for example, higher expenditure on double glazing to reduce the impact of noise pollution by residents close to airports raises GDP. The quality of life of these residents isn't higher as a result of this expenditure. It simply restores their quality of life to what it was before. It is a 'defensive' expenditure necessary to compensate for the lower quality of life caused by noise pollution. Expenditure by the government treating respiratory diseases caused by air pollution raises a nation's GDP. But the nation's quality of life hasn't increased. It has been restored. Polluted rivers and lost biodiversity reduce the quality of life. But the production and consumption that brought them about raises GDP. GDP, therefore, measures the level of economic activity rather than well-being. Comparisons of GDP over time are misleading. They do not allow sensible resource allocations to be made or allow genuine progress to be measured.

Measures of sustainable development have tried to capture elements of these wider costs and benefits of

ISEW	=	total personal consumption
	minus	defensive expenditures by the private sector
	minus	losses arising from income inequality
	minus	the costs of environmental degradation
	minus	depreciation of natural capital
	plus	increases in the stock of man-made capital
	plus	the value of domestic labour
	plus	non-defensive expenditure by the public sector

Table 11.7 The component parts of the Index of Sustainable Economic Welfare (ISEW)

economic growth. One of these measures is the Index of Sustainable Economic Welfare (ISEW). It was first constructed in 1989 by two economists, Herman E. Daly and John B. Cobb. There are versions of the ISEW published by campaigners, such as Friends of the Earth, and by national governments. The creators of the ISEW have also refined and added to the measure to create what they call the Genuine Progress Indicator (GPI). All of these measures have a common method. They add or subtract from national expenditure things which raise the quality of life (or well-being) and deduct things which reduce wellbeing. Table 11.7 shows the composition of the original ISEW.

DEFINITION

Index of Sustainable Economic Welfare (ISEW): an index, first constructed in 1989 by two economists, Herman E. Daly and John B. Cobb, that adds to national expenditure things that raise the quality of life (or well-being) and deducts things that reduce well-being. Daly and Cobb have added to and refined the measure to produce a 'Genuine Progress Indicator' (GPI)

The logic of the ISEW, if not its actual calculation, is straightforward to follow:

● *total personal consumption* measures the value which consumers place on the goods and services which they consume – this is assumed to measure the welfare that comes from current production

● *defensive expenditures by the private sector* include spending that takes place to restore or maintain well-being – examples include the costs of commuting, noise pollution and car accidents

● *losses arising from income inequality* are included because it is assumed that an equal increase in income is of greater benefit to the poor than it is to the rich – when income inequality rises, the ISEW falls, and when inequality falls, the ISEW rises

● *the costs of environmental degradation* include the monetary costs of air and water pollution and the long-term damage created by global warming

● *depreciation of natural capital* includes the loss of biological resources such as wetlands and farmlands and the depletion of non-renewable energy sources

● *increases in the stock of man-made capital* refers to spending on machinery and capital goods that allow future generations to produce output

● *the value of domestic labour* includes work done in households to reflect the importance of, for example, childcare, care for elderly relatives, home repairs and housework – these are valued at the market rates that would be charged for such work

● *non-defensive expenditure by the public sector* refers to that part of state spending that does not exist simply to restore or maintain well-being – the main examples are health and education.

The end result of all these calculations is a figure for GDP adjusted for a range of costs and benefits of production and consumption not included in GDP. It is argued that this provides a better guide for policy makers in judging whether sustainable development has taken place or for assessing the possible impact of policy choices.

Composite indicators of sustainability, such as the ISEW, have not made their way into the mainstream of economic policy making, however. There are a number of limitations with composite indicators, such as the ISEW, which partly explains why they have not caught on. These include:

● lack of agreement on the choice of adjustments to be made to GDP – some measures of sustainable development go further than the ISEW (for example, the Measure of Domestic Progress produced by the New Economics Foundation, see Table 11.8) and include crime rates, the costs of family breakdown and the costs of commuting

● the fact that the 'weighting' to give each adjustment cannot be determined objectively, resulting in value judgements having to be made

● the difficulties of placing monetary values on some of the components, such as the costs of environmental damage and the depreciation of natural capital.

These difficulties and differences in the way that composite indicators of sustainability are constructed can mean that differences in assumptions, indicators and valuations can produce large differences in the end result. However, while there may be disagreement on the methods to use to construct an alternative measure of economic progress and the quality of life, there is a consensus that GDP cannot be used for these purposes. After all, GDP simply measures production and consumption and not the benefit this gives to people.

Type	Indicator	Influence on MDP
Economic indicators	Consumer expenditure	+ve
	Value of services from domestic labour	+ve
	Public (non-defensive) expenditures on health and education	+ve
	Difference between expenditures on and service flow from consumer durables	-ve
	Net capital growth	mainly +ve
	Net international position	mainly -ve
Social costs	Effects of inequality in the distribution of incomes	-ve
	Defensive private expenditures on health and education	-ve
	Costs of commuting	-ve
	Costs of car accidents	-ve
	Costs of noise nuisance	-ve
	Costs of crime	-ve
	Costs of family breakdown	-ve
Environmental costs	Costs of personal pollution control	-ve
	Costs of air pollution	-ve
	Costs of water pollution	-ve
	Estimated costs of climate change	-ve
	Costs of ozone depletion	-ve
Prudent use of natural resources	Loss of natural habitats	-ve
	Loss of farmlands	-ve
	Depletion of finite natural resources	-ve

Table 11.8 The Measure of Domestic Progress (MDP), an alternative adjusted indicator of sustainability
Source: *Chasing Progress: Beyond Measuring Economic Growth*, New Economics Foundation, 2004

ACTIVITY

Every society clings to a myth by which it lives; ours is the myth of economic progress. That's why the year-on-year performance of the Gross Domestic Product (GDP) continues to dominate national policy and fascinate the media. New indicators designed to factor in the environmental and social costs of growth highlight how far off-track we might be in our relentless pursuit of GDP.

Source: *Chasing Progress: Beyond Measuring Economic Growth, New Economics Foundation,* 2004 (adapted)

a) Explain the possible environmental and social impacts of economic growth.

b) How might these impacts reduce the benefits of economic growth?

c) Explain one alternative indicator of sustainable development.

STRETCH AND CHALLENGE

d) Evaluate the usefulness of indicators of sustainable economic development in judging economic progress.

National and regional policies and international agreements to promote sustainability.

'By promoting economic growth strategies … which are environmentally responsible and socially acceptable we are bringing a sustainable future closer to today's reality.'

– Katherine Sierra, Vice President for Sustainable Development, World Bank

National policies to promote sustainability include policies to internalise the negative externalities from production and consumption and policies designed to widen the benefits of economic growth. Negative externalities, such as environmental pollution, can be tackled using the price mechanism (for example, through environmental taxation), government regulation (for example, through setting limits on emissions through legislation) or by a mixture of the two approaches (for example, by capping emissions and creating a market in pollution permits).

Each of these approaches has its advantages and disadvantages, which you learnt about in Chapter 3 of *OCR AS Economics*. Widening the benefits of economic growth can be promoted through the greater provision of merit goods such as education and health services and through policies designed to influence the distribution of income and wealth (such as minimum wage legislation).

One of the problems with national policies relates to the increasing globalisation of economic activity, which is dealt with in more detail in the next chapter. The measures referred to above inevitably raise the price of goods, services and the factors of production in order to raise private costs towards the true social costs. In isolation, national policies to promote sustainability are likely to affect adversely a nation's international competitiveness and its attractiveness in terms of foreign multinational investment. Faced with a choice of locating production in a country with strict environmental standards and taxation and high minimum wages and one without, international capital is likely to migrate to the country, or countries, with low environmental and social intervention. This impacts on the incentives of countries to implement national policies to promote sustainability. For as long as GDP and GDP per capita continue to dominate the minds of policy makers, these disincentive effects can be strong.

Regional policies to promote sustainability take very much the same form as the ones outlined above. Their usefulness depends on the degree of regional economic integration. It is very much easier for the European Union to implement environmental policies, such as the Emissions Trading Scheme, for the economies of the EU because it has progressed beyond the free trade and customs union stages of economic integration. Common policies, be they environmental or social, are a central part of the development of economic integration in the EU. They would be much more difficult to implement in NAFTA or ASEAN because of the looser economic integration and the greater national sovereignty that members of these regional blocs have over such policy areas. Even in the EU, however, there have been tensions about social policy, with the UK, for example, for a long time opting out of the EU's Social Charter.

ACTIVITY ····⋗

The EU Emissions Trading System (EU ETS) is based on a recognition that creating a price for carbon through the establishment of a market for emission allowances offers the most cost-effective way for countries to:

● move towards the low-carbon economy of the future

● achieve the deep reductions in global greenhouse gas emissions that are needed to prevent climate change from reaching dangerous levels.

The system should allow the EU to achieve its emission reduction targets under the Kyoto Protocol at a cost of less than 0.1 per cent of GDP, significantly reducing the short-term costs of meeting the targets.

Source: European Commission

a) Go to www.heinemann.co.uk/hotlinks, insert the express code 2230P, and click on 'EU ETS' to find out more about the EU's Emissions Trading System.

b) Describe how the ETS works.

c) Explain the benefits to companies and the environment of the EU ETS.

d) Identify and explain two problems of carbon emissions trading schemes such as the EU's ETS.

International agreements to promote sustainability can be useful ways of providing a spur to national action. International commitments can make it easier for national governments and organisations such as the EU to implement policies that will tackle environmental damage, for example. But their usefulness depends on the extent to which countries are prepared to sign up to agreements.

The United Nations' Framework Convention on Climate Change (UN FCCC), for example, is a long-running series of negotiations dating back to 1990. It took until 1994 to come into force and then only had 50 countries signing up to the agreement. The number of countries signed up has grown since then, with the most important international agreement, the Kyoto Protocol, now signed and ratified by 178 countries. The Kyoto Protocol is an agreement to reduce global emissions of six greenhouse gases to 5.2 per cent below 1990 levels between 2008 and 2012. By capping the emissions of each country (or group of countries such as the EU) and creating allowances that are tradable, it has created markets in emissions trading (see Chapter 3 of *OCR AS Economics*. It is estimated that, globally, these markets traded approximately $60 billion of emissions allowances in 2007.

Critics of the Kyoto Protocol, however, point out that the world's largest emitter of carbon dioxide, the USA, has signed up to the Protocol but not ratified it. What this means is that US governments are not bound by the agreement to take any action to meet the commitments they have made! Critics also point to the inevitable compromises that are necessary to get international agreements. Under the Kyoto Protocol, developing countries refused to sign the agreement

unless they were given exemptions from its major commitments. So 137 developing countries, having signed and ratified the Protocol, are not expected to do anything more than measure and report their emissions. Recently there have been negotiations in Bali to reach an international agreement to replace the Kyoto Protocol, which expires in 2012. As the *Economist* magazine said of the compromises and lack of progress: 'Politics has a habit of undermining economics'.

This is perhaps a useful reminder that what might promote sustainability in theory may be subject to government failures in the hands of nation states and politicians. The wisdom of the economist suffers at the hands of those ultimately responsible for implementing policies.

12 The economics of globalisation

On completion of this chapter, you should be able to:

- understand the different characteristics of globalisation
- explain the factors promoting globalisation
- evaluate the impact of multinational firms
- analyse the influences on the different flows of international finance
- evaluate the impact of globalisation
- explain the roles of
  - the World Trade Organization (WTO)
  - the International Monetary Fund (IMF)
  - the World Bank
- comment upon the issues surrounding current international trade negotiations and trade disputes.

Characteristics of globalisation

Over the past fifty years or so, the world's economies have progressively developed ever closer economic links. If evidence of this was needed, then one need look no further than the middle of 2008, when the world price of oil reached $130 a barrel and was expected to increase even more, raw material prices were escalating, there were substantial price increases and shortages of food and serious worries about the low value of the US dollar in world currency markets. The point was that each of these concerns was having a major bearing on the world's economies, poor as well as rich. Their impact was indicative of **globalisation**.

DEFINITION

Globalisation: the processes that have resulted in ever-closer links between the world's economies

So what is globalisation? In a simple sense, it is the processes by which the world's economies have developed closer links through trade, investment and production. In more recent years, the scope of globalisation has been extended to also include the migration of people and the transfer of technology. The pace and spread of globalisation have accelerated in recent years, to embrace more industries and countries in the world economy. The result has been a 'flattening of the globe' – almost any product or any service can be produced almost anywhere in the world with resources that originate almost anywhere.

Globalisation is manifest in different ways, two of which are global brands and global sourcing.

Global brands are a visible characteristic of globalisation. Not only is the same brand available in most national markets, the product is also standardised. Perhaps the best consumer goods examples are Coca-Cola and McDonald's. A can of

Coke and a Big Mac can be bought in Birmingham (UK), Berlin (Germany), Budapest (Hungary), Buenos Aires (Argentina), Brisbane (Australia) and Beijing (China) as well as in almost any other large town or city that starts with the letter 'B'! Moreover, the quality of the product will be virtually identical, even though the price that you have to pay varies widely.

Table 12.1 shows the results of the 2007 annual Millward Brown global brands survey. As this shows, US brands dominate, accounting for eight out of the top ten places. Vodafone was the best ranked UK brand, with a global brand value of $36.9bn. Although not shown in this table, global brands are also to be found extensively in food processing, finance and in the hotel sector. Companies such as General Foods, Nestlé, Kelloggs, HSBC, Bank of America, Hilton, Marriot and Holiday Inn are typical. All have huge global interests.

Name	Estimated value ($ bn)
Google	86
General Electric	71.4
Microsoft	70.9
Coca-Cola	58.2
China Mobile	57.2
IBM	55.3
Apple	55.2
McDonald's	49.5
Nokia	43.9
Marlboro	37.3

Table 12.1 Rank order of global brands

Globalisation is also very prevalent in grocery retailing and the home furnishings/home improvements markets. Typical are the ways in which European retailers have developed new markets in emerging economies. Tesco, for example, the UK's largest grocery retailer, embarked on an international development strategy in the mid-1990s. This started with acquisitions in central and eastern Europe (particularly Hungary). More recently, the company has expanded into China, Malaysia, Thailand, South Korea and Japan. Its most recent venture is into the convenience food market on the West Coast of the USA.

The most successful global non-food retailer is probably IKEA. As well as having retail outlets in twenty-four European countries, it has stores and franchised stores throughout the Asia Pacific region and the Middle East, as well as in the USA and Canada.

Global sourcing is less obvious. The term refers to the ways in which global companies now source their operations through worldwide production. In many cases, 'local' domestic production has been replaced by manufacturing capacity on a global scale. Often, this capacity has replaced the domestic productive capacity of a company, a clear consequence of de-industrialisation.

Some of the best examples of this characteristic of globalisation can be found in clothing and sportswear, electronics and vehicle manufacturing. In the first two industries, production has moved from domestic sources in the USA, western Europe and Japan to lower-cost countries in South and South East Asia (China especially) and North Africa. In the case of vehicles, European manufacturers have tended to move production to lower-cost production countries still in the EU; the world's largest vehicle manufacturer, Toyota, in contrast, has set up manufacturing and assembly plants worldwide. These plants assemble vehicles from local as well as globally sourced parts.

Figure 12.1 shows in a simple way how globalisation has affected the US car industry. In 1955, the Big Three US manufacturers (General Motors, Ford and Chrysler) had a 100 per cent share of their domestic car market. Since then, their market share has been undermined, initially by European (VW–Audi especially) and then Japanese producers (Toyota especially). This erosion of market share has been particularly severe since 1985. In recent years, General Motors and Ford have been forced into closing manufacturing plants and cutting thousands of jobs.

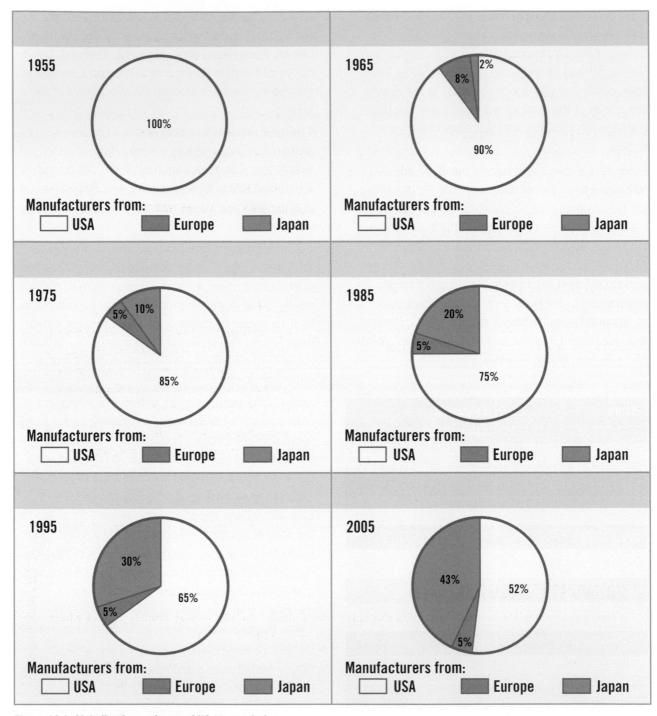

Figure 12.1 Globalisation — shares of US car market

Factors promoting globalisation

The following have contributed to the process of promoting globalisation:

● *A reduction in protection in the world economy.* As referred to below, the World Trade Organization (WTO) has sought to reduce the overall degree of protection in world trade. Tariffs, quotas and other trade-curbing factors in the form of non-tariff barriers are inconsistent with globalisation. Although by no means a situation of multilateral free trade, the global economy is now characterised by a number of 'regional' trading blocs such as the EU, NAFTA, CARICOM (Caribbean Community) and ASEAN, many of which have established mutually beneficial links between one another.

● *A reduction in international capital movement restrictions.* This has been essential for business capital to flow freely within the global economy. Exchange control has been gradually dismantled, allowing **foreign direct investment (FDI)** to flow between developed economies and from developed economies to those that are emerging and developing (see below).

● *Developments in IT and falling communication costs.* The pace of technological change over the past generation or so has been incredible. The way in which businesses are able to communicate, via the Internet and in handling data, has promoted global economic relations. Global supply chains, whereby businesses assemble, produce and sell their products, can now be managed in a very effective way.

● *A fall in real transport costs.* Unit transport costs, particularly for sea transport, have been falling, making it increasingly viable for businesses to source on a global basis. The bulk distribution of products in containers by sea, and to a much lesser extent by air, has increased year on year. Economies of scale can be gained as vessels and aircraft have increased

in size and in terms of energy efficiency. In response, specialist US- and European-owned global logistics carriers have played their part in facilitating the supply of goods between producers and customers worldwide.

● *Liberalisation of domestic markets.* In line with a reduction in protection, many of the world's emerging economies (China especially), have been much more positive and receptive to FDI from developed economies and in forming business partnerships with **multinational companies (MNCs)**. These partnerships

DEFINITIONS

Foreign direct investment (FDI): the establishment of branches and productive processes abroad, or the purchase of foreign firms; investment made by a multinational corporation in a country other than where its operations originate

Multinational companies (MNCs): firms that produce goods and services in more than one country

ECONOMICS IN CONTEXT

INDIA'S IT REVOLUTION

There was a time when economists thought that only visible goods and invisible services involving flows of financial funds could be traded across international borders. This has now changed with the Internet. The fastest-growing item in world trade is that of international business services such as accounting, IT support and payrolls. Many multinational and smaller companies have found that it is cheaper to outsource such services through the Internet to overseas locations where costs are lower.

The global leader in the provision of such services is India. In 2006, business services contributed around US$25 billion to India's exports; a rise to $60 billion is expected by 2010.

Why India? There are four main reasons. These are:

● a highly educated, young workforce, all of whom speak English

● wages for professional workers that are 10 to 25 per cent of those in Europe and the USA

● good Internet access in all major cities

● a deregulated market that has allowed firms like Dell, Hewlett-Packard and IBM to set up operations.

India is now more than just a location for data entry businesses and call centres. High-tech companies located there can see the broader advantages of having research centres in India. A high-profile example is Microsoft, which has a global research centre in Bangalore, a city that is now the base for over 500 international IT companies.

have taken various forms, including joint ventures, licensing, franchising and supplier agreements. It has also been easier for MNCs to directly purchase businesses in other parts of the world.

Effects of globalisation

The main consequence of globalisation is that the world economy is now more integrated through the growth of trade and increasing dependency. Export trade as a percentage of world trade has grown steadily; in 2007 it was estimated to be around 25 per cent of global GDP.

For developing economies such as those in Southern and South East Asia, globalisation has produced certain benefits. These include:

● higher living standards for more people

● enjoyment of global brands

● spreading best practice and technology transfer

● improved medical supplies that could increase life expectancy

Notwithstanding, globalisation has its critics. It is very clear that virtually all economies in the world are heavily dependent upon each other. This has been evident particularly following the Asian financial crisis of 1997/98, the 9/11 terrorist attack on New York and political conflict in the Middle East. These events served to show how the world's economies, rich and poor, were inextricably linked, particularly

Globalisation has its critics

to external shocks affecting the USA. The impact on some developing economies has been relatively more severe than on developed economies, due to the latter's more robust structure that allows them to 'weather the storm' in a more effective way.

ACTIVITY ···⫶

Globalisation has been accused of driving down the wages of unskilled workers and reducing the tax revenue that governments can raise.

The average pay of US workers, for instance, grew less than half as fast as productivity between 2001 and 2008. The increasingly footloose nature of MNCs has also driven down corporate tax rates, with governments competing to attract and keep the MNCs.

On the other hand, a number of benefits have been claimed for globalisation. These include some obvious benefits, such as providing cheap imports and keeping both inflation and interest rates low. There are also less obvious benefits. A

University of California study recently found that when an iPod is sold from China to the USA for $299, only $4 stays in China with the firm that assembles the device. $160 goes to the US firms that design, transport and retail the iPod.

a) What is a possible disadvantage of corporate tax rates being driven down to a low level?

b) Explain how globalisation may keep both inflation and interest rates low.

STRETCH AND CHALLENGE

c) Discuss whether globalisation reduces unemployment.

Further criticisms are more local. It is argued by anti-globalisation groups that globalisation is a new form of imperialism led by the USA, that it accentuates the gap between rich and poor and leads to the exploitation of workers in developing countries. A good example of the latter is how some unscrupulous clothing manufacturers pay below the living wage for workers employed producing garments for retailers based in much more affluent countries.

> **learning tip**
> The use of an AD/AS diagram can help you analyse the macroeconomic effects of globalisation, such as supply-side shocks and increased FDI.

Multinational corporations and foreign direct investment

A multinational corporation (MNC) or transnational corporation (TNC) is defined as a firm that operates in more than one country. In other words, it is a business with a parent company based in one country but with production or service operations in at least one other country. The largest MNCs, such as the Coca-Cola Corporation, Ford, Nestlé, McDonald's, Hilton Hotels and so on, are worldwide operations, with manufacturing and retail outlets in many countries of the world.

Through their activities, MNCs provide foreign direct investment (FDI) to the economies in which they operate. This is investment that is necessary to produce or sell a good or service in a foreign country. FDI, therefore, involves capital flows between countries. It should not be confused with portfolio investment, which is the purchase of shares by foreign investors in businesses that are located in another country.

> **learning tip**
> Take care in considering the impact that MNCs from developed economies have on the material living standards in developing economies. It is important to compare, for example, the wage rates a US MNC pays to its Ethiopian workers, not with wage rates it pays its US workers, but with the wage rates paid by other employers in Ethiopia.

The activities of MNCs and the effects of foreign direct investment on the economies of recipient countries have been the subject of much debate and discussion by economists and politicians.

> ## ACTIVITY ····▸
>
> In the past, MNCs largely set up firms in other countries to carry out the whole productive process – in effect they were smaller versions of the parent company. Now more and more MNCs are acting transnationally. They shape strategy, management and operations as a single global business. They place people and jobs anywhere in the world, based on the right cost, the right skills and the right business environment. They are not bound by geographical boundaries. For instance, IBM employs 330,000 staff in 170 countries. Its call centres are mainly based in India, its financing back office is in Rio de Janeiro and its main procurement office is in Shenzhen in China.
>
> **a)** Explain two factors that have made it easier for firms to act transnationally.
>
> **b)** Analyse the implications of firms acting transnationally for national governments.

BENEFITS AND COSTS OF FDI

Although much depends on the scale and nature of the FDI in an economy, there are in principle many benefits to the receiving economy of investment by foreign-owned businesses. These include:

● *An injection into the circular flow of income.* This leads to multiplier effects for the economy, in particular creating an addition to total expenditure and important employment creation. These jobs are initially an immediate result of the FDI, but there are subsequent multiplier effects that create further employment throughout the economy. This effect should not be understated in economies that are emerging and where the opportunity for domestically funded investment is limited. Longer term, the injection of FDI increases the economy's potential output level.

● *Effects on the balance of payments.* FDI represents a credit item in the financial account of the balance of payments. This could be just a one-off short-term inflow, although it might be sustained once a business is established. In turn, further benefits could be created, for example, if the FDI establishes a manufacturing operation that subsequently exports some of its products. (This has been an important credit to the UK's current account as non-UK vehicle manufacturers have set up plants that produce for the wider EU market.) For example, in the case of multinational hotel companies, their investment in Caribbean islands generates further income through increased flows of tourists and payments received by local carriers.

● *An increase in tax revenue for the government.* This comes about in two ways. First, those employed by the MNC contribute income tax receipts and, when spending their incomes, expenditure taxes on their purchases of goods and services. Second, the MNCs provide additional tax revenue through their purchase of local services and the corporation or profits taxes that they pay. For poor economies with a limited tax base, both provide an important additional source of government revenue.

● *Improved productivity.* This can come about as a result of pressure from an MNC on local suppliers to improve their efficiency.

● *Technology transfer* and the acquisition of specialist equipment. Developing economies receive the benefit of up-to-date technology and products that have been developed by MNCs in their home market.

At the same time it should also be recognised that there are various disadvantages and risks associated from FDI inflows. These include:

● *The employment created may be only short term* and could be less than expected. The reason for this is that MNCs invariably have little affinity to the overseas economies in which they have invested.

Companies may pull out of a country, transferring production to another location. It could also be that MNCs employ workers from their own country in the top management jobs, with the result that employees from the host country are only recruited to fill lower-paid positions. US and Japanese companies, in particular, are well known for this approach.

● *MNCs may invest in labour-saving technology.* This may not seem appropriate in a recipient country with high unemployment and a large amount of surplus labour.

● *Net effects on the balance of payments being less than anticipated.* This could come about as profits earned in a host economy are repatriated and count as a debit item in the invisible section of the current account of that country. Over time, the outflow of such profits may well exceed the initial capital injection.

● *Taxes received by the government may be less than expected*, as a result of fewer than expected new jobs. Account should also be taken of any government subsidies that might have been given to MNCs in order to encourage them to set up in business in the first instance.

● *Productivity gains and the technology transfer effects* could be very limited depending on the type of FDI.

● *Environmental costs* associated with certain types of FDI, especially mineral extraction and natural gas production.

ACTIVITY ····⁝

Unilever, the Anglo-Dutch conglomerate, produces food, household goods and personal care products. It operates in most countries in the world. Unilever's branches in South Africa employ 20,000 people and work with 3,000 suppliers. It has been estimated that, directly and indirectly, Unilever accounts for 0.8 per cent of South Africa's employment and 0.9 per cent of its output.

a) Explain two benefits Unilever may gain from operating in South Africa.

b) Using an AD/AS diagram, analyse the impact on the South African economy if Unilever pulled out of South Africa.

The net effect of an injection of FDI into an economy can therefore in some respects be a mixed blessing. This is why not all governments welcome MNCs with open arms.

ECONOMICS IN CONTEXT

The traditional view of an MNC was that it originated in the USA, Europe or Japan. More recently, however, there has been a significant increase in MNCs from emerging economics buying or setting up companies in the USA, Europe and Japan. By 2006, FDI from developing countries had reached 14 per cent of global FDI, in comparison to only 5 per cent in 1990.

Chinese firms are rapidly spreading throughout the world. Chery Automobile, the country's leading car exporter, is expanding into eastern Europe, the Middle East and South America, both by building new plants and by buying out foreign firms. Haier, the leading producer of white goods in China, has become the fourth largest white goods firm in the world.

Indian firms started to operate abroad on a large scale in 2000 and by 2006 the outflow of FDI from the country exceeded the inflow for the first time. The UK has been a particular target for Indian MNCs. The Tata group, India's largest conglomerate, bought out the British tea firm, Tetley Tea in 2000. Four years later, it took over Corus, the Anglo-Dutch steelmaker, and in 2008 it purchased Jaguar and Land Rover, two British car brands, from Ford.

OTHER FINANCIAL FLOWS

As well as financing FDI, capital finance flows across national borders for several other reasons. 'Hot money' flows around the world to take advantage of changes and expected changes in interest rates and exchange rates. These movements can be disruptive, as the money may only stay in a country for a short period of time before it is moved out should a more profitable opportunity occur elsewhere.

Portfolio investment tends to be longer term. There are a number of factors that attract people to purchase the shares and government bonds of another country. These include relative interest rates and anticipated profit levels. These, in turn, are influenced by government policies and changes in the level of economic activity.

Other investment includes loans made to residents in other countries at commercial rates. The firms in a country may seek loans from abroad if the interest rate charged and conditions of the loan are more favourable than can be obtained at home or if there is a shortage of funds at home.

Some developing countries receive foreign aid in the form of loans at favourable rates. In a number of cases, however, foreign aid has led to a net outflow of funds. More is paid in servicing and repaying past debt than is received in aid.

For some developing countries, more money is now coming from remittances, the pay sent home by people working abroad, than from foreign aid, FDI or even from the sale of exports. Although there are more barriers to labour moving than capital and enterprise, an increasing number of people are working overseas and sending money home. For instance, 9 per cent of the Philippine population is working abroad in various jobs, including domestic helpers and nurses. Table 12.2 shows the significance of remittances in nine countries.

Remittances tend to be the least volatile source of foreign currency for developing countries. Table 12.2

	$ bn	% of GDP
India	27.0	26
China	25.7	22
Mexico	25.0	24
Philippines	17.0	15
France	12.5	12
Spain	8.9	8
Belgium	7.2	7
UK	7.0	7
Germany	7.0	6

Table 12.2 The significance of remittances for selected countries, 2007

shows that remittances are also significant in some developed economies.

WORLD TRADE ORGANIZATION

The **World Trade Organization (WTO)**, with headquarters in Geneva, Switzerland, currently has 150 members. Vietnam was the latest country to be admitted, in 2006. Significantly, after fifteen years of tense negotiations, the People's Republic of China became a member in 2001.

The WTO's mission is a simple one. In its own words, it 'helps trade flow smoothly, freely, fairly and predictably'. In practice, this should produce a trading system with the following characteristics:

● *Non-discrimination.* Two key principles are involved here. The first is known as the *most-favoured-nation treatment.* Under WTO agreements, countries cannot grant a special favour (for example a lower rate of duty or duty free access) to one WTO member over another. In other words, all countries should be treated on an equal basis. The second principle is called *national treatment.* This involves treating foreigners and locals equally. Under this agreement, imported and locally produced goods should be treated equally after goods have reached the domestic market. This does not prohibit a country imposing tariffs on imported goods, but it does mean that the goods then compete on the same basis thereafter. The principle also applies to services, so that foreign firms, for example, trying

to set up in business elsewhere should be treated in exactly the same way as domestic firms wishing to expand their operations.

● *Free trade.* The most obvious way in which this can be done is by lowering trade barriers, tariff and non-tariff barriers. This will enable goods and services to flow more openly and fairly between members, providing the benefits of the gains from trade that were described in Chapter 10.

● *Predictability.* The purpose of this objective is to 'bind' WTO members once they have agreed to open their markets. The rationale behind this is to provide a stable business environment whereby firms will feel secure that trade barriers will not be raised at some future date. This should create a business environment where investment is encouraged, jobs are created and consumers can enjoy the benefits of lower prices and more choice. It has particular relevance for businesses moving into emerging and developing economies, where inevitably there are likely to be concerns over future political stability and economic prospects.

● *Promoting fair competition.* The WTO system allows tariffs and, in some circumstances, other forms of protection. Having said this, once a restriction has been imposed by a member, WTO agreements mean that thereafter there should be free and fair competition in the market. This must not be distorted by further constraints on foreign-produced goods and foreign-owned services.

● *Special provision for developing countries.* From the outset, the WTO has sought to assist the development of developing countries. This has not been easy, given the stances taken by the USA and EU, for example, with respect to trade in certain agricultural products. Nevertheless, the WTO has sought to give such countries time and flexibility to implement various agreements. The agreements build upon the principles of providing special assistance and trade concessions for developing countries.

> ### DEFINITION
>
> **World Trade Organization (WTO):** a global organisation that regulates world trade

ACTIVITY ⋯⟩

At the end of 2007, the WTO instructed the USA to eliminate billions of dollars' worth of illegal subsidies to its cotton farmers. Cotton subsidies are claimed to unfairly boost US exports and depress prices on world markets and so harm cotton farmers in a number of countries, including Brazil. It was Brazil that brought a complaint over the US subsidies to the WTO in 2005. When a member country does not respond to an instruction from the WTO, the organisation allows the complainant to impose retaliatory tariffs on the guilty party.

a) Explain how US cotton subsidies may depress the world price of cotton.

STRETCH AND CHALLENGE

b) Discuss whether the actions of the WTO always lead to freer international trade.

WTO Agreements

WTO agreements cover goods, services and intellectual property. They are often called the WTO's trade rules, since the WTO is a rules-based system of agreements that have been negotiated by governments. The so-called Uruguay Round agreements are the basis of the current WTO system.

The Uruguay Round covered three main areas. These were:

● *Tariff cuts.* Developed country members of WTO agreed a 40 per cent cut in their tariffs on industrial products, to be phased in over a five-year period from 1995. This agreement reduced the average tariff from 6.3 to 3.8 percent. They also agreed that fewer imported products should be charged at higher duty rates. This was of particular benefit to developing countries, which saw the proportion of their exports faced with tariffs of 15 per cent and above in industrialised countries fall from 9 to 5 per cent of total products.

● *More binding tariffs.* This is the term used to denote a commitment by a member to not increase tariffs above the listed rate. Developed countries increased the number of 'bound' product lines to 99 per cent; developing countries increased their pledges to 73 per cent. The purpose behind these agreements is to provide rather more security for traders and other investors.

● *Agriculture.* Substantial progress was made to remove almost all import restrictions of a non-tariff form on agriculture products in world trade. Most of these physical restrictions were converted to tariffs, a process known as tariffication. At the same time, tariffs applying to products from developing countries have been progressively reduced and commitments have been received from developed countries to reduce domestic support and export subsidies for agricultural products. The Uruguay Round represents the first time that such agreement has been reached in principle.

The Doha Round

The current round of negotiations started in November 2001 at the Fourth Ministerial Conference in Doha, Qatar. These have been extremely contentious and agreement on many issues has not yet been reached.

Central to the Doha Round has been the determination of members to put the needs of developing countries at the heart of the WTO's work programme. In particular, there has been some commitment to assist the least developed countries through seeking to provide them with an increasing share of world trade as a means of assisting their economic development.

Some agreement has been forthcoming. Countries have agreed to phase out all export subsidies by the end of 2013; cotton subsidies were terminated by the end of 2006. Other concessions to developing countries are known as the 'Everything But Arms' initiative – an agreement to introduce tariff-free access for goods from least developed countries for 97 per cent of all products that are traded.

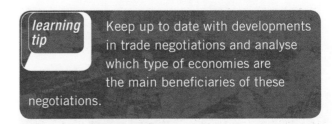

learning tip Keep up to date with developments in trade negotiations and analyse which type of economies are the main beneficiaries of these negotiations.

INTERNATIONAL MONETARY FUND

The **International Monetary Fund (IMF)** was set up in 1945 at the Bretton Woods Conference to help promote the health of the world economy following the catastrophic damage caused by the Second World War. With headquarters in Washington DC, it currently has 184 members. Notable non-members are Cuba and North Korea.

Over the past sixty years of its operation, the IMF's purposes have remained unchanged, although its activities have evolved and developed in line with the emerging global economy. The IMF's purposes and responsibilities are:

● to promote international monetary co-operation

● to facilitate the expansion and balanced growth of international trade

● to provide exchange stability

● to assist in setting up a multilateral system of payments

● to make resources available to members experiencing balance of payments difficulties, provided adequate safeguards are provided.

These activities have been central to the development of global trade, since a stable system of international payments and exchange rates is necessary for trade to take place between two countries. In carrying out its responsibilities, the IMF has three main functions, known as surveillance, technical assistance and lending. The first two are in line with its mission of promoting global growth and economic stability by encouraging countries to adopt sound economic policies. The third function is used where member countries experience difficulties in financing their balance of payments.

The IMF was set up in 1945

The surveillance function takes the form of IMF officers carrying out an annual in-depth appraisal of the economic situation in each member's country. Following relevant statistical analysis and forecasts, there is a detailed discussion with a country's representatives on the policies that are seen by the IMF to be most conducive to achieving stable foreign exchange rates and economic growth. Most assessments are published. The IMF also combines information from individual country consultations to form assessments of regional and global prospects.

Technical assistance and training are offered by the IMF to help member countries design and implement effective economic policies. This assistance provides advice on fiscal, monetary and exchange rate policies especially. It has been widely taken up by emerging **transition economies** in central and eastern Europe and by some developing economies.

DEFINITION

Transition economy: one that is changing from a centrally planned to a free market economy

Many IMF members have experienced severe balance of payments problems. In the twenty-first century, it is mainly developing economies that face fundamental imbalances on their current accounts. In these circumstances, the IMF lends money to such countries to ease their immediate positions – it is, though, a necessary condition for such help that recipients work closely with the IMF to avoid similar, probably more serious, problems in the future.

Not all aspects of the IMF's policy agenda receive universal acclaim. Anti-globalisation supporters, for example, condemn the IMF for favouring military dictatorships that are friendly towards US and EU multinational companies. They are also concerned about the IMF's attitude towards supporting economies where human rights and labour rights mean little. Other criticism comes from economists who are concerned at the IMF's pro-Keynesian approach for dealing with balance of payments disequilibria. They believe that supply-side policies rather than devaluation are the best way for alleviating structural imbalance.

There have also been situations where the IMF has been blamed for causing serious economic problems. In 2001 in Argentina, for example, it is generally believed that IMF-induced budget restrictions and the privatisation of important national resources were responsible for the catastrophic economic crises that ensued. As a consequence, the IMF is not well received in this part of the world and it has to be concluded that its record of success is rather limited. (See discussion of structural adjustment programmes in Chapter 11, pages 295–296.)

> **DEFINITION**
>
> **The International Monetary Fund (IMF):** a global organisation that aims to promote international monetary co-operation and international trade

ACTIVITY ⋯⟫

A number of Asian and Latin American countries borrowed from the IMF in the past when they got into balance of payments and other financial difficulties. Most of these countries have now repaid their debts and a number have now built up large foreign exchange reserves. They have also improved their economic management. These changes have reduced the IMF's lending, which has been its main source of income.

a) Explain what is meant by:

  i) balance of payments difficulties

  ii) improved economic management.

b) Describe one function of the IMF, other than lending.

WORLD BANK

Like the IMF, the **World Bank** arose out of the Bretton Woods agreements; unlike the IMF, though, the World Bank's function is to provide financial support for internal investment projects such as building new roads, improving port infrastructure or constructing new health facilities.

It is best described as the World Bank Group, through the activities of its five constituent agencies. These are the:

- International Bank for Reconstruction and Development (IBRD)

- International Finance Corporation (IFC)

- International Development Association (IDA)

- Multilateral Investment Guarantee Agency (MIGA)

- International Centre for Settlement of Investment Disputes (ICSID).

The IBRD and IDA provide low- or no-interest loans and grants to countries that do not have favourable access to international credit markets. Therefore, the focus of activities is very much on developing economies, including the emerging economies of central and eastern Europe and South East Asia. Grants are only provided to the world's poorest countries. Loans cover areas such as:

- health and education – to enhance human development in a country – for improving sanitation and combating AIDS

- agriculture and rural development – for irrigation programmes and water-supply projects

- environmental protection – for reducing pollution and for ensuring that there is compliance with pollution regulations

- infrastructure – roads, railways, electricity

- governance – for anti-corruption reasons.

Like the IMF's, World Bank loans tend to be linked to conditions that involve wider-reaching changes being made to the economic policies of the recipient countries.

The World Bank has its critics. It has been accused of being a US-/western European-dominated agency for supporting their own economic and political interests. Through its strong advocacy of free market reforms, its policies have been criticised as being harmful to the interests of some countries, particularly where the 'shock therapy' of reform has been introduced too quickly. Notwithstanding these and other criticisms, the World Bank has had a considerable impact in assisting the world's poorest economies.

> **DEFINITION**
>
> **World Bank:** a global organisation that provides development funding

ExamCafé
Relax, refresh, result!

Relax and prepare

Anya

For me economics has really come alive in this last unit of the A2 course. There are so many links between what we studied at AS and what we have done in this unit. I'm glad I didn't bin my notes from last year! When it came to revision, I found the Key Concept Sheets our teacher gave us really useful. Summarising topics on to one sheet of A4 with all the key definitions and diagrams gave me confidence in answering exam style questions.

Joseph

The stimulus material the exam board uses for this unit really focused my revision. Reading it in lessons and talking it through in small groups helped me to spot the concepts we would need in the exam. It was fun to 'be the examiner' and think of questions which could be asked. This helped me to realise what the exam was testing – I learnt so much about assessment objectives and different directive words that I have a much better idea of what a question is asking. I think I now write better answers as a result. Well I hope I do …

Gordon

One of the things that really helped me get to grips with this unit was our weekly 'in the news' lesson. I thought this was going to be difficult, but using the Internet really worked for me – signing up to blogs and email alerts is a great way of getting news. Once I'd read an article, I would copy and paste the key bits and write a short summary of how it illustrated something we had been studying. Some things I read I didn't understand straight away, so I jotted down questions. Talking through something we had found on our own (even if it was just what we didn't understand) was a new way of learning for me – but it worked!

Refresh your memory

Quick-fire quiz

1. Name four stages of the economic cycle.
2. What is the difference between short-run and long-run economic growth?
3. How do a free trade area and a single market differ?
4. What are the benefits of economic integration?
5. Name the components of the Human Development Index.
6. How does the structure of an economy change as it develops?
7. State two benefits and two costs of globalisation.
8. What does the World Trade Organization do?

STIMULUS MATERIAL

The Global Economy examination is based on stimulus material issued 6–8 weeks before the examination. The material below is typical of the type of stimulus material issued by OCR, although it is much shorter than that which you are likely to see before your exam.

EXTRACT 1

Firm holds talks over job losses

Textiles company Ulster Weavers has said it is in talks with union leaders over proposals to cut jobs.

The firm said it plans to close its Dungannon factory, which would lead to the loss of up to 72 jobs as a result of competition from China.

Staff have said they are angry the redundancies are coming at a time when the company is involved in research and development in China.

Adapted from: http://news.bbc.co.uk/1/hi/northern_ireland/4533522.stm, 16 December 2005

EXTRACT 2

Shanghai surprise for Northern Ireland investors

China's rapid economic development has been fuelled by an increasing openness to global trade and low labour costs.

Those are ingredients which, in Northern Ireland, have helped accelerate the decline of the textiles industry.

Several Northern Ireland companies have been taking part in a recent trade mission to China. They have found themselves able to take advantage of the same cost advantages that have put some firms from Northern Ireland out of business – arguing that sourcing components and raw materials in China helps protect jobs at home.

The growing economic muscle of China has created business opportunities that could not have been envisaged a few years ago.

Adapted from: http://news.bbc.co.uk/1/hi/northern_ireland/4526580.stm, 14 December 2005

EXTRACT 3

China 'to be largest energy user'

China's rapid economic development has created an increasing demand for natural resources, raising the world price of commodities and energy.

China is set to become the world's largest consumer of energy by about 2010, according to a study by the International Energy Agency (IEA). Demand for energy in China is expected to have doubled within 20 years, according to the report.

Adapted from: http://news.bbc.co.uk/1/hi/world/asia-pacific/7082475.stm, 7 November 2007

Discuss the extent to which China's rapid economic development will impact on the global economy. (20)

Helen's answer

Comments

Helen has made a good start by identifying the increased competition in global markets. She has analysed the reasons for the impact on jobs in developed economies, picking up on the material in Extract 1.

Helen has gone on to develop the point about the impact on jobs by explaining the costs of unemployment. One concern an examiner might have at this point is that what Helen writes is all about the impact on one industry in Europe – the global perspective is not being developed.

This is a short section, but it contains some useful analysis of the impact of China's economic development. The introduction of AD/AS analysis shows that Helen is relating what is in Extract 1 to her knowledge and understanding of economic theory.

Overall, Helen's response is narrow and one-sided. It only looks at one industry, in one part of the global economy, and argues that the impact is negative. There is no balance to what Helen says. She has not spotted the directive word in the question – to discuss the impact.

If Helen had gone on to analyse some positive impacts of China's economic development, she could have shown that she was able to start to evaluate the impact. Perhaps, she didn't grasp the point in Chapter 10 about the winners and losers from international trade.

China's rapid economic development has increased competition in global markets, such as the textile market. This has brought both threats and opportunities to firms in the global economy. The result has been that some textile companies such as Ulster Weavers have had to make staff redundant and close their production facilities. This is because the price of textiles has fallen and firms in Europe have found it difficult to remain competitive, at a time when their costs are rising. The loss in jobs will cause unemployment in Europe to rise. This could cause family problems and stress and an increase in crime. The government will have to spend more money on unemployment benefits, leading to a budget deficit. Workers are angry at the loss of jobs, which will cause a loss of motivation and production in firms hit by this increased competition. These things will have a negative impact on the economies of many countries, as the diagram below shows. As the rest of the world imports more from China there will be a reduction in aggregate demand in their economies. The AD curve shifts left and there is a reduction of output to Y_1. With lower GDP there will be more people unemployed and a reduction in the standard of living.

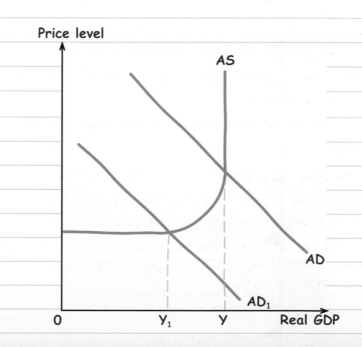

China's rapid economic development will have a significant impact on the global economy. China can be categorised as a large under-developed economy with vast reserves of cheap labour and a government committed to the pursuit of rapid economic growth. It has become a major player in international markets since it joined the World Trade Organization (WTO).

From the perspective of the global economy, China's rapid economic development represents a supply-side shock. The effect of China's rapid development and its integration into the global economy will be that the world's aggregate supply curve will shift to the right to AS_1. The result is that world output will rise (to Y_1) and there will be a fall in

the average or general price level in the global economy (to P_1). China's rapid economic development will be, therefore, a significant boost to the global economy – it will stimulate economic growth and put downward pressure on inflation.

This can best be seen in the way in which economies throughout the world, but particularly in the developed world, have benefited from cheaper imports from China. The influx of Chinese goods onto world markets represents an increase in global competition. This is likely to force existing firms to become more productively efficient, which will lead to improvements in the global allocation of resources.

Again from a global point of view, China's rapid economic development will lead to an increase in the gains from trade. Comparative advantage theory shows that specialisation and trade raises world output and allows countries to consume outside their production possibility frontier (PPF). Since China's rapid economic development has been outward looking, these benefits have been shared globally, although the distribution of these benefits may be unequal, with some countries benefiting more than others. This is especially true for countries that share a similar comparative advantage to China, as they might lose out from China's rapid economic development and huge export drive. The benefits arise from China's comparative advantage in labour-intensive production, which it enjoys because of its endowment of large amounts of cheap labour. The extent of these benefits, though, is difficult to determine as they will depend on the terms of trade – the ratio of export prices to import prices.

This positive view of the impact of China's rapid economic development on the global economy can be challenged. The reason for China's growth is not wholly down to its comparative advantage and factor endowment. The USA has complained that China has deliberately under-valued its exchange rate in order to promote its price competitiveness in the global economy. The argument is that China's rapid economic development has been possible because of the large current account deficits on the balance of payments in the USA. From this point of view, China's rapid economic development has created big trade imbalances in the global economy. This could threaten global economic stability, as countries try to correct current account deficits by raising interest rates or dampening down on economic activity.

It is also true that the increased global competition, which has come hand-in-hand with China's rapid economic development, has caused a decline in manufacturing output and employment in the developed world. These negative impacts could be significant if the unemployment created turns out to be structural rather than frictional. This is more likely to be a problem if the global economy enters a slowdown or recession as alternative employment will be limited. So long as the global economy continues to grow, employment opportunities in other sectors of developed economies will materialise. The extent of any problem of structural unemployment depends on the geographical and occupational mobility, both of which can be improved by appropriate supply-side policies. Economic change requires economies and labour markets to be dynamic and flexible to minimise the costs of change. The location of industry has been affected too, as companies in the developed world have relocated production to China in order to regain international competitiveness. In addition, the rapid growth in China has increased the demand for energy and put upward pressure on oil prices, raising production costs throughout the world. While some countries in the global economy are disadvantaged by rising commodity prices, for others this will be an opportunity to gain higher export revenue and increase their own economic development. For other developing economies, China's rapid economic development represents an increase in export opportunities.

In conclusion, it can be seen that China's rapid economic development is likely to have both a beneficial and a negative impact on the global economy. The benefits of lower prices for consumers come at the cost of jobs, particularly in manufacturing industry in the developed world. Overall, the extent of the impact is likely to be positive. Many of the negative effects reflect changes in the distribution of world output rather than an overall decline. Economic theory would tend to support an increase in competition whether it be at the market or global level.

● The exam on this unit is unique. Stimulus material is issued some 6–8 weeks before the exam which will help to guide your revision.

● There will be three main questions set, the first two of which will be broken down into three parts assessing knowledge and understanding (AO1), application of knowledge (AO2), analysis (AO3) and evaluation (AO4). Get used to what examiners are testing in each of the questions in a typical exam on this unit. Look at mark schemes and be familiar with the different levels examiners will use to mark your responses.

● Use the stimulus material wisely. Don't try to predict questions – there are too many variations possible. The best strategy is to identify sections of the specification that underpin each extract. Revise the terms, concepts and theories in each of these sections. Ask yourself the question 'what light do these shed on the extracts?'

● Practice how to evaluate – there are lots of marks in this exam for evaluation. Think of phrases that you can use to signpost to the examiner that you are evaluating. Think about what determines the impact or consequence of some economic outcome. Be prepared to make judgements on what you analyse. Not everything in economics is clear cut. Remember there is often more than one perspective.

● The best evaluation is supported by reasons and explicit economic analysis. There should be a conclusion to the questions commanding larger marks, particularly the last question in the exam, not just a summary of what you have said before. Practice writing conclusions – they won't come naturally unless you do.

● Avoid the temptation to simply paraphrase what is in the extract material – this won't get you high marks. Always interpret what is in the extract material using economic terms, concepts and theories. This way you are showing the examiner that you can analyse economic issues. Using diagrams also helps to show analysis – but you must integrate them into your answer, don't just plonk them down with the words 'as can be seen in the diagram below'. Examiners can't see unless you tell them what to see. Explaining diagrams is easy – just SWYS (say what you see).

● Never just state something without giving a reason for what you have said. This is assertion and doesn't gain high marks. Stop at the end of each sentence you write and ask yourself the question 'so what?' If there is an answer to your 'so what?' question, write it down – this way you will build up explanation and analysis.

● Start by defining key terms in the question – it gives you confidence and also shows the examiner that you know your stuff.

● Try to spend some time planning out your response, especially to the higher mark questions. A good structure helps you to focus on the question. Knowing what paragraphs are for and using them helps too!

● Always refer back to the question at the end of each paragraph to show that what you have written is relevant to the question asked.

● Remember that for the very highest marks, examiners want to see you making judgements. A good economist will always tell you 'on the one hand …' , 'but on the other hand …', 'so overall, it depends on …., because …' . Always support any judgement you make with a reason.

Exam practice paper

Remember that the exam paper you face will be based on five or six extracts that will be much longer than the ones shown below. The idea of this practice paper is to help you become familiar with the typical structure of the questions in The Global Economy unit.

Start by covering up the questions! You will be tempted to look at them, but don't. Spend some time reading the extracts below and see how they relate to the terms, concepts and theories you have studied in this part of the textbook. This is what you will be doing six or eight weeks before the exam.

Once you have identified and revised the terms, concepts and theories that underpin the extracts, try to tackle the questions in no more than two hours. Good luck!

Stimulus material

EXTRACT 1

The World Bank forecasts that global economic growth will slow down in 2008. The Bank warns that if the economic slowdown in the USA is greater than expected, middle-income countries such as Brazil would be most affected, both by a reduction in their trade and a fall in foreign investment. It also warns of inflationary pressures caused by continued rapid economic growth in China and India.

In the past few years, oil prices have risen fourfold, while the price of grains and other internationally traded foodstuffs has doubled. The Bank points out that the commodity boom has had both positive and negative consequences for developing countries.

Adapted from: China boom 'cushions world slump', Steve Schifferes, 9 January 2008, http://news.bbc.co.uk/1/hi/business/7177397.stm

EXTRACT 2

A few months ago, economic life was so simple. The US and UK housing markets were collapsing, consumer confidence and retail sales were falling and recession was in the air. For central banks, then, the answer was really rather easy. Cut interest rates and hope that recession would be avoided.

Now, though, central bankers seem in an altogether different mood. Their earlier enthusiasm for monetary expansion has disappeared as inflationary pressures have made an unwelcome return. Earlier last week, Ben Bernanke, the chairman of the Federal Reserve, hinted that America's central bank was no longer happy with the dollar's persistent weakness. This is an indication that the Fed might not be cutting interest rates any further.

Adapted from: The mounting dangers of central banks' high-wire act, Stephen King, *Independent*, 9 June 2008, http://www.independent.co.uk/news/business/comment/stephen-king/stephen-king-the-mounting-dangers-of-central-banks-highwire-act-842844.html

EXTRACT 3

In June 2008, politicians from the world's leading developed nations, the G8, met in Japan on the day that oil prices hit $139 per barrel.

US Energy Secretary Samuel Bodman blamed fuel subsidies in the developing world for raising the world demand for oil and pushing up its price. India and China made it clear that they would not end fuel subsidies because of the impact this would have on the poorest members of their societies.

EXTRACT 4

Recent high rates of economic growth in India and other parts of the developing world, while reducing poverty and raising global economic growth, have put considerable stress on the environment even as it is already saddled with high emissions from the developed world. During a lecture at the Australian National University Dr Rajendra K. Pachauri, former chairman of the Intergovernmental Panel on Climate Change, explored whether such growth patterns can be sustained into the future and what options are available for ensuring that the adverse impact of economic growth on the environment is manageable.

Adapted from: Australian National University, August 2007, http://billboard.anu.edu.au/event_view.asp?id–16515

Questions

1 a) Explain what is meant by an economic slowdown. (4)

   b) Using an aggregate demand and supply diagram, analyse how an economy such as Brazil would be affected by an economic slowdown in the USA. (6)

   c) Comment on the problems faced by central banks in setting interest rates to promote economic stability. (10)

2 a) Explain the role of the World Bank. (4)

   b) Analyse one difference between developed and developing countries. (6)

   c) Comment on the extent to which changes in commodity prices affect developing countries. (10)

3 Discuss the extent to which rapid economic growth is consistent with sustainable economic development. (20)

Further reading

An extensive range of material is now available for the effective delivery of OCR's A2 Economics. The list below gives a selection of accessible textbooks, statistical publications and websites for each unit (for the websites listed, go to www.heinemann.co.uk/hotlinks and insert the express code P2216).

Given the synoptic nature of the A2 assessment, students will find it very useful to refer back in places to the OCR-endorsed Heinemann textbook:

Bamford, C.G. and Grant, S. J., *OCR AS Economics*, 2008.

It is strongly recommended that students read a good newspaper on a regular basis. The BBC News website is a particularly valuable source of up-to-date articles and blogs on many of the topics covered in the A2 specification.

Other general resources and websites include:

Economics Today – a magazine containing a range of articles written for A Level students, some written by OCR examiners.

econoMAX – a subscription website produced by tutor2u; has a selection of short classified articles covering the A2 subjects.

The *Economist* magazine and website
The Biz/ed website
The Institute of Economic Affairs website
The Adam Smith Institute website

The resources below are for each Part of the book. Books with an asterisk are reference books for teachers – these are also appropriate for potential A* candidates who wish to learn more about the subjects.

Economics of work and leisure
Books

Cramp, P., *The Economics of Work and Leisure*, Anforme, 2006

Hale, G., *Labour Markets*, Heinemann, 2001

Richards, J. et al., *Ten Top Topics in Labour Economics*, Anforme, 2005

*Smith, S.W., *Labour Economics*, Routledge, 2003

*Tribe, G., *The Economics of Recreation, Leisure and Tourism*, Elsevier, 2005

Wilson, I., *The Economics of Leisure*, Heinemann, 2003.

Other publications

Economic and Labour Market Review (monthly), Office for National Statistics (ONS)

Social Trends (annual), ONS

Transport economics
Books

Bamford, C.G., *Transport Economics*, Heinemann, 2006

Cole, S., *Applied Transport Economics*, Kogan Page, 2005

*Glaister, S. et al., *Transport Policy in Britain*, Palgrave Macmillan, 2006

*Hibbs, J., *Transport Economics and Policy*, Kogan Page, 2003

*Mallard, G. and Glaister, S., *Transport Economics: Theory, Application and Policy*, Palgrave Macmillan, 2008

Other publications

The Department of Transport produces some excellent material (see its website for details).

Recent publications include:

The Eddington Transport Study, 2006
Towards a Sustainable Transport System, 2007
Transport Statistics, Great Britain (annual)
Transport Trends (annual)

Other useful publications are available from:

The Commission for Integrated Transport website
The Independent Transport Commission website

The global economy

Books

Black, I., *The UK Economy*, 1997–2007, Anforme, 2008

Cramp, P., *Economic Development*, Anforme, 2006

Grant, S.J. and Bamford, C.G., *The European Union*, Heinemann, 2006

*Sachs, J., *The End of Poverty*, Penguin, 2005

Smith, C. *International Trade and Globalisation*, Anforme, 2007

*Stiglitz, J. *Making Globalisation Work*, Penguin, 2007

*Stiglitz, J., *Fair Trade for All*, Penguin, 2007

The following websites contain relevant statistics and up-to-date commentary on the UK economy:

HM Treasury
The Bank of England

The following websites contain relevant statistics and up-to-date commentary on the EU economy and global economic issues:

Europa
European Central Bank
World Bank
United Nations Development Programme

Glossary

Absolute advantage: where one country is able to produce more of a good or service with the same amount of resources, such that the unit cost of production is lower

Absolute poverty: the inability to purchase the basic necessities of life

Accelerator: the theory of investment that states that the level of investment depends on the rate of change of national income

Allocative efficiency: where price is equal to marginal cost

Asymmetric inflation target: when deviations below the inflation target are seen to be less important than deviations above the target

Automatic stabilisers: changes in government expenditure and taxation receipts that take place automatically in response to the economic cycle. For example, expenditure on unemployment benefits rises during the recession phase of the business cycle

Average cost: total cost divided by output; also called unit cost of production or unit cost

Average fixed cost: total fixed cost divided by output

Average revenue: total revenue ÷ output sold

Average variable cost: total variable cost divided by output

Backward-sloping labour supply curve: a labour supply curve showing the substitution effect dominating at low wages and the income effect dominating at high wages

Balance of payments: records money flows into and out of a country over a period of time

Barrier to entry: obstacle to new firms entering a market

Barriers to exit: obstacles to firms leaving a market

Bilateral exchange rate: the exchange of one currency against another

Bilateral monopoly: a market with a single buyer and seller

Cabotage: the collection and delivery of goods or the transport of people by a truck, plane or other means of transport within a country other than that where that means of transport is registered

Capital account of the balance of payments: the section of the balance of payments that records long-term flow of capital into and out of an economy. It records purchases and sales of assets and is split into two sections, long-term capital flows and short-term capital flows

Capital-intensive production: where the production of a good or service requires a large amount of capital relative to other factors of production

Capital output ratio: the amount of capital needed to generate each unit of output

Cartel: a group of firms that produce separately but sell at one agreed price

Classical economists: economists who believe that markets will 'clear', that prices and quantities adjust to changes in the forces of supply and demand so that the economy produces its potential output in the long run

Collusion: where firms tacitly or otherwise agree to not compete on prices, service provision and other matters that might adversely affect mutual well-being

Comparative advantage: where one country produces a good or service at a lower relative opportunity cost than others

Concentration ratio: the proportion of the total market shared between the nth largest firms

Congestion charging: a direct charge for access to a designated urban charging zone where the main purpose of the charge is to reduce congestion

Constant returns to scale: long-run average cost remaining unchanged when the scale of production increases

Contestability: the extent to which barriers to entry and exit in a market are free and costless

Contestable market: a market in which there are no barriers to entry and exit and the costs facing incumbent and new firms are equal

Cost-benefit analysis: a technique for assessing the viability of a project, taking into account all of the effects over time

Costs: the value of inputs

Credibility (principle of fiscal policy): a credible fiscal policy framework is one where the government's commitment to economic stability is trusted by the public, business and financial markets

Cross-subsidisation: a business practice where revenue from profitable activities is used to support loss-making ones

Crowding out: when government borrowing reduces the funds available for private sector investment or raises the cost of investment by raising market interest rates

Current account (in balance of payments): includes money flows due to trade (the trade balance – broken down to trade in goods and trade in services), transfers of interest, profit and dividends (the investment income balance) and transfers of money by governments and international organisations (the transfers balance)

Customs union: an agreement between two or more countries to abolish tariffs on trade between them and to place a common external tariff on trade with non-members

Cyclical deficit: a budget deficit that arises because of the operation of automatic stabilisers

Deadweight loss: loss to society of the firm producing where price exceeds marginal cost

Dependency ratio: proportion of the population who are too young, too old or too sick to work and so who are reliant on the output of those who are working

Deregulation: removal of regulations

Derived demand: demand that depends upon the final output that is produced, or on the demand for another item

Developed economies: countries with a high income per capita and diversified industrial and tertiary sectors of the economy. Examples of developed economies would include the USA, the UK, Japan and South Korea

Developing economies: countries with relatively low income per capita, an economy in which the industrial sector is small or undeveloped and where primary sector production is a relatively large part of total GDP

Diseconomy of scale: an increase in long-run average costs caused by an increase in the scale of production

Disequilibrium unemployment: unemployment caused by the aggregate supply of labour exceeding the aggregate demand for labour

Dominant monopoly: a market where a firm has a 40 per cent or more share

Dynamic efficiency: efficiency in terms of developing and introducing new production techniques and new products, whereby unit costs are lowered over time

Earnings: wages plus overtime pay, bonuses and commission

Economic convergence: the process by which economic conditions in different countries become similar. Economists distinguish between monetary convergence (for example, similarities in inflation and interest rates) and real convergence (for example, similarities in the structure of economies)

Economic cycle: fluctuations in the level of economic activity as measured by GDP. Typically, there are four stages in the cycle: recession, recovery, boom and slowdown

Economic development: the process of improving people's economic well-being and quality of life

Economic integration: refers to the process of blurring the boundaries that separate economic activity in one nation state from that in another

Economic rent: a surplus paid to a factor of production above what is needed to keep it in its current occupation

Economic stability: the avoidance of volatility in economic growth rates, inflation, employment and unemployment and exchange rates, in order to reduce uncertainty and promote business and consumer confidence and investment

Economic union: deepens integration in a single market, centralising economic policy at the macroeconomic level

Economically inactive: working age people who are neither in employment, nor unemployed, and so are not part of the labour force

Economy of scale: a reduction in long-run average costs resulting from an increase in the scale of production

Effective exchange rate: the exchange rate of one currency against a basket of currencies of other countries, often weighted according to the amount of trade done with each country

Elasticity of supply of labour: the responsiveness of the supply of labour to a change in the wage rate

Employment rate: the proportion of working-age people who are in work

Equilibrium unemployment: unemployment that exists when the labour market is in equilibrium

Euro area, eurozone: term to describe the combined economies of the countries using the euro

Excess capacity: a consequence of firms producing at above the minimum point on the average cost curve

Expenditure-reducing policies: policies that reduce the overall level of national income in order to reduce the demand for imports and correct a current account deficit on the balance of payments

Expenditure-switching policies: policies that increase the price of imports and/or reduce the price of exports in order to reduce the demand for imports and raise the demand for exports to correct a current account deficit on the balance of payments

External diseconomies of scale: diseconomies of scale resulting from the growth of the industry, affecting firms within the industry

External economic shocks: unexpected events coming from outside the economy that cause unpredicted changes in AS or AD. Examples might include rapid rises in oil prices or a global slowdown

External economies of scale: economies of scale that result from the growth of an industry and benefit firms within the industry

Factor endowments: the mix of land, labour and capital that a country possesses. Factor endowments can be determined by, among other things, geography, historical legacy, and economic and social development

Factor intensities: the balance between land, labour and capital required in the production of a good or service

Financial economies: the cost savings that large firms may receive when borrowing money

Fiscal transfers: occur where taxation raised in one country is used to fund government expenditures in another country

Fixed costs: costs that do not change in the short run with changes in output, that are independent of output produced

Fixed exchange rate: an exchange rate system in which the value of one currency has a fixed value against other countries. This fixed rate is often set by the government

Flexibility (principle of fiscal policy): a flexible fiscal policy framework is one that has the flexibility to deal with macroeconomic shocks, such as sudden and unexpected changes in AD and/or AS

Flexible labour market: a labour market that adjusts quickly and smoothly to changes in the demand for and supply of labour

Forecast: a future estimate usually based on past information

Foreign currency reserves: foreign currencies held by central banks in order to enable intervention in the FOREX markets to affect the country's exchange rate

Foreign direct investment (FDI): investment made by a multinational corporation in a country other than where its operations originate; the establishment of branches and productive processes abroad, or the purchase of foreign firms; investment by multinational companies in physical capital abroad

Foreign exchange (FOREX) market: a term used to describe the coming together of buyers and sellers of currencies

Franchise: the outcome of a competitive system to bid for the provision of services

Free trade area: an agreement between two or more countries to abolish tariffs on trade between them

(Freely) floating exchange rate: a system whereby the price of one currency expressed in terms of another is determined by the forces of demand and supply. See *Semi-fixed/semi-floating exchange rate*

Futures markets: markets where people and businesses can buy and sell contracts to buy commodities or currencies at a fixed price at a fixed date in the future

G8: the group of major economies consisting of Canada, France, Germany, Italy, Japan, Russia, the UK and USA

Game theory: a theory of how decision makers are influenced by the actions and reactions of others

Geographical immobility of labour: barriers to the movement of workers between different areas

Gini coefficient: used to make international comparisons of income inequality. It is found by using a Lorenz curve

Globalisation: the processes that have resulted in ever-closer links between the world's economies

Golden rule: a commitment by the UK government that, over the economic cycle, it will borrow only to invest and not for current expenditure

Growth maximisation: the objective of increasing the size of the firm as much as possible

Harmonisation: establishing a common set of rules and regulations to be followed

Heckscher–Ohlin theory of international trade: a theory that a country will export products produced using factors of production that are abundant and import products whose production requires the use of scarce factors

Hedging: business strategy that limits the risk that losses are made from changes in the price of currencies or commodities

High human development: where the Human Development Index (HDI) is 0.8 and above

High-income countries: countries with a GDP per capita of $11,116 or more

Hit-and-run competition/entry: firms quickly entering a market when there are supernormal profits and leaving it when the profits disappear

Homeworking: working either at home or in different places away from the central office, production or distribution facilities, using the home as a base

Human capital: the knowledge and skills of the labour force

Human Development Index (HDI): a measure that, recognising limitations of GDP per capita as a measure, combines outcomes that might be valued in the development process: life expectancy at birth; adult literacy rate and percentage of the relevant population enrolled in primary, secondary and tertiary education; and GDP per capita in US$ at PPP

Hypothecation: a situation where revenue from a tax is directly allocated to some other purpose

Income effect of a wage change: the effect on the supply of labour caused by the change in the ability to buy leisure

Incumbent firms: firms already in the market

Index of Sustainable Economic Welfare (ISEW): an index, first constructed in 1989 by two economists, Herman E. Daly and John B. Cobb, that adds to national expenditure things that raise the quality of life (or well-being) and deducts things that reduce well-being. Daly and Cobb have added to and refined the measure to produce a 'Genuine Progress Indicator' (GPI)

Infant industries: industries in an economy that are relatively new and lack the economies of scale that would allow them to compete in international markets against more established competitors in other countries

Inflation: the sustained increase in the general level of prices, measured in the UK by changes in the cost of a basket of goods and services bought by a typical household (Consumer Price Index or CPI), weighted according to the expenditure on each item in the basket

Infrastructure: anything that provides for the operation of transport

Integrated transport policy: one that encompasses all modes of passenger and freight transport

Interdependent: where the actions of one firm provoke counter-action by others

Inter-industry trade: trade involving the exchange of goods and services produced by different industries

Internal diseconomies of scale: diseconomies of scale experienced by a firm caused by its growth

Internal economies of scale: economies of scale that occur within the firm as a result of its growth

International competitiveness: the ability of an economy's firms to compete in international markets and, thereby, sustain increases in national output and income

International Monetary Fund (IMF): a global organisation that aims to promote international monetary co-operation and international trade

Intra-industry trade: trade involving the exchange of goods and services produced by the same industry

Intra-regional trade: trade between countries in the same geographical area, for example trade between the UK and Germany or the USA and Canada

J-curve effect: shows the trend in a country's balance of trade following a depreciation of the exchange rate. A fall in the exchange rate causes an initial worsening of the balance of trade, as higher import prices raise the value of imports and lower export prices reduce the value of exports due to short-run price inelasticity of the demand for imports and exports. Eventually the trade balance improves. An appreciation of the currency causes an inverted J-curve effect

Keynesian economists: economists who believe that market failures will result in price and quantity rigidities such that the economy's equilibrium output in the long run may be less than its potential output

Kinked demand curve: a demand curve made up of two parts; it suggests oligopolists follow each others' price reductions, but not price rises

Knowledge and technology transfer: the process by which knowledge and technology developed in one country is transferred to another, often through licensing and franchising

Labour force: all those people of working age who are in employment or actively seeking work

Labour force participation rate: the proportion of working age people who are economically active (in employment or who are actively seeking work)

Labour-intensive production: any production process that involves a large amount of labour relative to other factors of production

Legal monopoly: a market where a firm has a share of 25 per cent or more

Legitimacy (principle of fiscal policy): a legitimate fiscal policy framework is one that has widespread support and about which there is general agreement among the public, business and politicians

Liberalisation: same as *deregulation*; reductions in the barriers to international trade, in order to allow foreign firms to gain access to the market for goods and services that are traded internationally

Licensing arrangements: an agreement that ideas and technology 'owned' by one company can be used by another, often for a charge

Limit pricing: setting a price low to discourage the entry of new firms into the market

Long run: period of time when it is possible to alter all factors of production

Long-run aggregate supply (LRAS) curve: the relationship between total supply and the price level in the long run. The LRAS curve represents the maximum possible output for the whole economy – its potential output

Long-run economic growth: the rate at which the economy's potential output *could* grow as a result of changes in the economy's *capacity* to produce goods and services, sometimes referred to as *potential economic growth*

Long-term capital flows: flows of money used for investment in assets (for example direct investment by a company in setting up production facilities or portfolio investment through buying shares in companies)

Long-term capital transactions: flows of money related to buying and selling of assets such as land, or property, or production facilities (direct investment), or shares in companies (portfolio investment)

Lorenz curve: a diagram commonly used to illustrate income or wealth distribution, named after the American statistician, Max Otto Lorenz

Low human development: where the Human Development Index (HDI) is less than 0.5

Low-income countries: countries with a GDP per capita of $905 or less

Lower middle-income countries: countries with a GDP per capita of $906–$3,595

Managerial economies: savings in long-run average costs due to the specialisation of management

Marginal cost: the change in total cost resulting from changing output by one unit

Marginal product of labour (MPL): the change in output that results from employing one more worker

Marginal propensity to import (MPM): the proportion of additional national income that is spent on imports $= \Delta m / \Delta Y$, where m is imports

Marginal propensity to save (MPS): the proportion of additional national income that is saved $= \Delta s / \Delta Y$, where s is savings, Y is national income and Δ is the change in s or Y

Marginal propensity to tax (MPT): the proportion of additional national income that is taxed $= \Delta t / \Delta Y$, where t is taxation

Marginal revenue: the change in total revenue resulting from the sale of one more unit

Marginal revenue product (MRP): the change in a firm's revenue resulting from employing one more worker

Market concentration ratio: the percentage share of the market of a given number of firms

Market structure: the characteristics of a market

Marshall–Lerner condition: states that for a depreciation of the currency to improve the balance of trade the sum of the price elasticities of demand

(PEDs) for imports and exports must be greater than 1

Medium human development: where the Human Development Index (HDI) is between 0.5 and 0.8

Minimum efficient scale: the lowest level of output at which full advantage can be taken of economies of scale, where long-run average cost (LRAC) is minimised

Mode of transport: means of transport, basically road, rail, air and sea transport

Monetary policy sovereignty: the ability of a country to pursue an independent monetary policy

Monetary transmission mechanism: the way in which monetary policy affects the inflation rate through the impact it has on other macroeconomic variables

Monetary union: the deepest form of integration in which countries share the same currency and have a common monetary policy as a result

Monopolistic competition: a market structure in which there is a large number of small firms selling a similar product and where there are few barriers to entry and exit

Monopoly: a single firm in a market

Monopsonist: a single buyer

Multinational corporation (MNC): a firm that operates in more than one country

Natural monopoly: where a monopolist has overwhelming cost advantage; a market where long-run average costs are lowest when output is produced by one firm

Non-accelerating inflation rate of unemployment (NAIRU): the level of unemployment that exists when the labour market is in equilibrium; also called equilibrium unemployment

Non-price competition: competition between firms on the basis of, for example, branding, customer service, location, range of products, advertising

Non-tariff barriers (NTBs): things that restrict trade other than tariffs

Normal profit: the level of profit needed to keep a firm in the market in the long run

Occupational immobility of labour: barriers to workers changing occupations

Occupational segregation: the dominance of an occupation by one gender

Offshoring: transferring part of the process to another country. The production may be outsourced or may be undertaken by the firm but in another country

Oligopoly: a market structure dominated by a few large firms

Oligopsonist: one of a few dominant buyers

Operational independence: when a central bank is given responsibility for the conduct of monetary policy independent of political interference. The target for inflation, however, is normally set by governments

Optimal currency area: refers to conditions that need to be met to avoid the costs of monetary union. These conditions include: a high degree of labour market flexibility, mechanisms for fiscal transfers, and the absence of external shocks that impact differently on different economies (asymmetric shocks)

Output gap: the difference between the actual and potential output of an economy. It is common practice to refer to a situation where actual output is below potential output as a *negative output gap*. A *positive output gap* occurs when, in the short term, actual output exceeds the economy's potential output

Outsourcing: subcontracting part of the production process to another firm

Part-time workers: people working less than 30 hours a week

Perfect competition: a market structure with many buyers and sellers, free entry and exit and an identical product

Poverty: when income is below the level that would allow someone to enjoy some agreed minimum standard of living. The World Bank defines 'extreme poverty' as living on less that US$1 per day (at PPP) and 'moderate poverty' as living on less than US$2 per day (at PPP)

Prebisch–Singer hypothesis: the argument that countries exporting primary commodities will face declining terms of trade in the long run, which will trap them in a low level of development as more and

more exports will need to be sold to 'pay for' the same volume of imports of secondary sector or capital goods

Predatory pricing: setting price low with the aim of forcing rivals out of the market

Price discrimination: where a monopolist charges different prices for the same product in different markets

Price maker: a firm that influences price when it changes its output

Price stability: when the general price level does not change or if it does change the rate of change is low enough not to significantly affect the decisions of firms and households

Price taker: a firm in a competitive market that has to accept the market price/that has no influence on price

Price transparency: the ability to compare prices of goods and services in different countries

Primary commodities: goods produced in the primary sector of the economy, such as coffee and tin

Primary sector: the first stage of production, including industries such as agriculture, fishing, forestry and mining, involved in the extraction and collection of raw materials

Privatisation: sale of state-owned business to the private sector

Product differentiation: where there are minor variations in the types of products on offer

Productive efficiency: using the least possible amount of scarce resources to produce the maximum output

Profit: the difference between revenue and costs

Profit margin: the difference between a firm's revenue and costs expressed as a percentage of revenue

Profit maximisation: achieving the highest possible profit where marginal cost equals marginal revenue

Profit satisficing: where a firm makes a reasonable level of profit that satisfies its stakeholders without maximising profit

Public Private Partnership (PPP): a contractual arrangement between the public and private sectors in order to fund large-scale projects

Public sector net cash requirement (PSNCR): the difference between the spending of general government (central and local government) and their revenue

Purchasing economies: reduced unit costs due to bulk buying of inputs into a business

Purchasing power of money: what a unit of currency will buy in terms of goods and services

Purchasing power parity (PPP): the exchange rate that equalises the price of a basket of identical traded goods and services in two different countries. PPP is an attempt to measure the true value of a currency in terms of the goods and services it will buy

Real GDP growth: a measure of the total output, expenditure or income of an economy after adjusting for changes in the price level. The growth of real GDP is the percentage change in output during a particular time period, often measured over a year

Reciprocal absolute advantage: where, in a theoretical world of two countries and two products, each country has an absolute advantage in one of the two products

Regional trading bloc: countries in a region that have formed an 'economic club' based on abolishing tariffs and non-tariff barriers to trade, e.g. the European Union (EU), the North American Free Trade Area (NAFTA) and the Association of South East Asian Nations (ASEAN)

Relative opportunity cost: the cost of production of one good or service in terms of the sacrificed output of another good or service in one country relative to another

Relative poverty: a situation of being poor relative to others

Relative unit labour costs: the cost of labour per unit of output of one country relative to its major trading partners

Revenue: receipts from sales

Road pricing: a direct charge for the use of road space

Road user charging: a form of road pricing where a flat-rate charge is made for the use of a stretch of road or access into a designated charging zone

Sales maximisation: an objective that involves the maximisation of the volume of sales

Sales revenue maximisation: the objective of achieving as high a total revenue as possible

Secondary sector: the second stage of production, which involves the processing of raw materials into semi-finished and finished goods. It includes manufacturing and construction

Semi-fixed/semi-floating exchange rate: an exchange rate system that allows a currency's value to fluctuate within a permitted band of fluctuation

Shadow price: a relative price that is proportional to the opportunity cost for the economy

Short run: the time period when at least one factor of production, usually capital, is in fixed supply

Short-run aggregate supply: shows the level of production for the economy at a given price level, assuming labour costs and other factor input costs are unchanged

Short-run economic growth: the actual annual percentage increase in an economy's output, sometimes referred to as *actual economic growth*

Short-term capital flows: flows of money that occur to take advantage of differences in countries' interest rates and changes in exchange rates; sometimes referred to as 'hot money'; highly volatile and exist to take advantage of changes in relative interest rates

Signalling function: changes in demand and supply of goods and services are signalled to producers and consumers through changes in absolute and relative price levels

Single currency: a currency that is shared by more than one country. The euro is shared by 15 countries in the European Union (EU)

Single European Market (SEM): a process adopted in the EU that promoted the free movement of goods, services and capital by harmonising product standards and removing remaining non-tariff barriers to trade

Single market: deepens economic integration from a customs union by eliminating non-tariff barriers to trade, promoting the free movement of labour and capital and agreeing common policies in a number of areas

Spare capacity: exists when firms in the economy are capable of producing more output than they are actually producing

Stability and Growth Pact (SGP): an agreement by members of the EU about the way in which fiscal policy should be conducted to support Europe's single currency. It requires those countries adopting Europe's single currency (the eurozone states) to abide by the following rules: a) budget deficit of 3 per cent of GDP or less, and b) government debt of 60 per cent of GDP or less

Stakeholders: people affected by the activities of a firm

Standard of living: a measure of the material well-being of a nation and its people

Stocks: the amount of finished goods that firms hold in order to be able to satisfy increases in demand

Substitution effect of a wage rise: the effect on the supply of labour caused by a change in the opportunity cost of leisure

Sunk costs: costs incurred by a firm that it cannot recover should it leave the market

Superior good: a good with positive income elasticity of demand greater than one

Supernormal profit: profit earned where average revenue exceeds average cost

Symmetric inflation target: when deviations above and below the target are given equal weight in the inflation target

Tax wedge: the gap between what employers pay for labour and what workers receive in disposable income

Technical economies: increased capacity or a technological development that results in lower long-run average costs

Teleworking: working using a telephone and a computer at home, in an Internet café, or a train or plane

Temporary work: casual work, seasonal work, working for employment agencies, fixed period contract work

Terms of trade: the price of a country's exports relative to the price of its imports. The terms of trade can be measured using the formula:

$$\text{Terms of trade} = \frac{\text{Index of average export prices}}{\text{Index of average import prices}} \times 100$$

Tertiary sector: the third stage of production, which covers industries producing services including education, financial services, health care and tourism

Total cost: the total cost of production or provision of a service

Total revenue: quantity × price

Tourism income multiplier: the extent to which a change in income from tourism causes GDP to change

Trade creation: where economic integration results in high-cost domestic production being replaced by imports from a more efficient source within the economically integrated area

Trade deflection: where one country in a free trade area imposes high tariffs on another to reduce imports but the imports come in from elsewhere in the free trade area

Trade diversion: where economic integration results in trade switching from a low-cost supplier outside the economically integrated area to a less efficient source within the area

Trading possibility curve (TPC): a representation of all the combinations of two products that a country can consume if it engages in international trade. The TPC lies outside the production possibility curve (PPC), showing the gains in consumption possible from international trade

Transaction costs: the costs of trading, which include costs of changing currencies

Transfer earnings: the amount a factor of production could earn in its best alternative occupation; the minimum amount that has to be paid to ensure that a worker stays in her/his present job: if her/his wage falls below this level, s/he will transfer to the alternative employment

Transition economy: one that is changing from a centrally planned to a free market economy

Transnational corporation (TNC): see *Multinational corporation*

Transport: the movement of people and goods for personal and business reasons

Trend rate of growth: the average rate of economic growth measured over a period of time, normally over the course of the economic cycle (from peak to peak or trough to trough)

Unemployment: arises when someone is out of work and actively seeking employment. A measure of the total number of people unemployed (the level of unemployment) or as a percentage of the workforce (the rate of unemployment). Comparisons of unemployment internationally use a standardised measure of unemployment found from a survey of the labour force. Measuring unemployment in the UK by the number of people claiming Job Seekers' Allowance (JSA) tends to underestimate the true level of unemployment

Unit elasticity of demand: when a given percentage change in price causes an equal percentage change in demand, leaving total revenue unchanged

Unit labour costs: the cost of labour per unit of output (including the social costs of employing labour as well as the wage costs)

Upper middle-income countries: countries with a GDP per capita of $3,596–$11,115

Utility maximisation: the aim of trying to achieve as much satisfaction as possible

Variable costs: costs that are directly related to the level of output produced

World Bank: a global organisation that provides development funding

World Trade Organization (WTO): an international body responsible for negotiating trade agreements and 'policing' the rules of trade to which its members sign up. Trade disputes between members are settled by the WTO

X inefficiency: the difference between actual costs and attainable costs

Index

Note: Page numbers in bold indicate location of definitions of key terms